IFIP Advances in Information and Communication Technology

563

Editor-in-Chief

Kai Rannenberg, Goethe University Frankfurt, Germany

Editorial Board Members

TC 1 – Foundations of Computer Science
 Luís Soares Barbosa, University of Minho, Braga, Portugal

TC 2 – Software: Theory and Practice
 Michael Goedicke, University of Duisburg-Essen, Germany

TC 3 – Education
 Arthur Tatnall, Victoria University, Melbourne, Australia

TC 5 – Information Technology Applications
 Erich J. Neuhold, University of Vienna, Austria

TC 6 – Communication Systems
 Burkhard Stiller, University of Zurich, Zürich, Switzerland

TC 7 – System Modeling and Optimization
 Fredi Tröltzsch, TU Berlin, Germany

TC 8 – Information Systems
 Jan Pries-Heje, Roskilde University, Denmark

TC 9 – ICT and Society
 David Kreps, University of Salford, Greater Manchester, UK

TC 10 – Computer Systems Technology
 Ricardo Reis, Federal University of Rio Grande do Sul, Porto Alegre, Brazil

TC 11 – Security and Privacy Protection in Information Processing Systems
 Steven Furnell, Plymouth University, UK

TC 12 – Artificial Intelligence
 Eunika Mercier-Laurent, University of Reims Champagne-Ardenne, Reims, France

TC 13 – Human-Computer Interaction
 Marco Winckler, University of Nice Sophia Antipolis, France

TC 14 – Entertainment Computing
 Rainer Malaka, University of Bremen, Germany

IFIP – The International Federation for Information Processing

IFIP was founded in 1960 under the auspices of UNESCO, following the first World Computer Congress held in Paris the previous year. A federation for societies working in information processing, IFIP's aim is two-fold: to support information processing in the countries of its members and to encourage technology transfer to developing nations. As its mission statement clearly states:

> IFIP is the global non-profit federation of societies of ICT professionals that aims at achieving a worldwide professional and socially responsible development and application of information and communication technologies.

IFIP is a non-profit-making organization, run almost solely by 2500 volunteers. It operates through a number of technical committees and working groups, which organize events and publications. IFIP's events range from large international open conferences to working conferences and local seminars.

The flagship event is the IFIP World Computer Congress, at which both invited and contributed papers are presented. Contributed papers are rigorously refereed and the rejection rate is high.

As with the Congress, participation in the open conferences is open to all and papers may be invited or submitted. Again, submitted papers are stringently refereed.

The working conferences are structured differently. They are usually run by a working group and attendance is generally smaller and occasionally by invitation only. Their purpose is to create an atmosphere conducive to innovation and development. Refereeing is also rigorous and papers are subjected to extensive group discussion.

Publications arising from IFIP events vary. The papers presented at the IFIP World Computer Congress and at open conferences are published as conference proceedings, while the results of the working conferences are often published as collections of selected and edited papers.

IFIP distinguishes three types of institutional membership: Country Representative Members, Members at Large, and Associate Members. The type of organization that can apply for membership is a wide variety and includes national or international societies of individual computer scientists/ICT professionals, associations or federations of such societies, government institutions/government related organizations, national or international research institutes or consortia, universities, academies of sciences, companies, national or international associations or federations of companies.

More information about this series at http://www.springer.com/series/6102

Weizhi Meng · Piotr Cofta ·
Christian Damsgaard Jensen ·
Tyrone Grandison (Eds.)

Trust Management XIII

13th IFIP WG 11.11 International Conference, IFIPTM 2019
Copenhagen, Denmark, July 17–19, 2019
Proceedings

 Springer

Editors
Weizhi Meng (i)
Technical University of Denmark
Lyngby, Denmark

Piotr Cofta
UTP University of Science and Technology
Bydgoszcz, Poland

Christian Damsgaard Jensen
Technical University of Denmark
Lyngby, Denmark

Tyrone Grandison
The Data-Driven Institute
Seattle, WA, USA

ISSN 1868-4238   ISSN 1868-422X   (electronic)
IFIP Advances in Information and Communication Technology
ISBN 978-3-030-33715-5   ISBN 978-3-030-33716-2   (eBook)
https://doi.org/10.1007/978-3-030-33716-2

This Springer imprint is published by the registered company Springer Nature Switzerland AG
The registered company address is: Gewerbestrasse 11, 6330 Cham, Switzerland

Preface

The 13th edition of IFIPTM, the IFIP WG 11.11 International Conference on Trust Management (IFIPTM 2019) was held at the Technical University of Denmark (DTU) in Copenhagen, Denmark, during July 17–19, 2019. The mission of the IFIPTM 2019 conference was to share research solutions to problems of trust and trust management, including related security and privacy issues, and to identify new issues and directions for future research and development work.

IFIPTM 2019 invited submissions in the form of both full and short papers, presenting novel research on all topics related to trust, security, and privacy, especially the following:

- Trust in Information Technology
- Trust and Identity Management
- Socio-Technical and Sociological Trust
- Emerging Technology for Trust

Different from the previous editions, IFIPTM 2019 also welcomed work-in-progress (WIP) papers that presented a promising but not completed idea. This year, we received 32 submissions from 20 different countries/regions, and each submission was reviewed by two or three Program Committee (PC) members. Finally, we accepted seven full papers and three short papers, in addition to six WIP papers. The selected papers represent the broad topical areas of the call for papers.

The program of IFIPTM 2019 included five sessions, a panel discussion, an IFIP Working Group 11.11 meeting, and two keynote speakers: Carmen Fernandez-Gago from University of Malaga, Spain, and Ramin Vatanparast, Chief Product Officer from Trustpilot. The keynote by Carmen also received the William Wins-borough Commemorative Address and Award, which aims to publicly recognize an individual who has significantly contributed to the development of computational trust or trust management, especially achievements with an international perspective.

We would like to express our thanks to everyone who contributed to the organization of IFIPTM 2019. We are grateful to our general chairs: Christian D. Jensen (Technical University of Denmark, Denmark) and Tyrone Grandison, (U.Group, USA) for their great support in organizing the conference. We also thank all the PC members for their great efforts in selecting the papers, and all the external reviewers for assisting the reviewing process. Last but not least, we are grateful to all authors who contributed to our conference.

July 2019

Weizhi Meng
Piotr Cofta

Organization

General Chairs

Christian D. Jensen   Technical University of Denmark, Denmark
Tyrone Grandison   The Data-Driven Institute, USA

Program Committee Chairs

Weizhi Meng   Technical University of Denmark, Denmark
Piotr Cofta   UTP University of Science and Technology, Poland

Program Committee

Isaac Agudo	University of Malaga, Spain
Anirban Basu	Hitachi R&D, Japan
David Chadwick	University of Kent, UK
Kim-Kwang Raymond Choo	The University of Texas at San Antonio, USA
Natasha Dwyer	Victoria University, Australia
Theo Dimitrakos	European Security Competence Center, Huawei Technologies, Germany
Rino Falcone	Institute of Cognitive Sciences and Technologies, CNR, Italy
Carmen Fernandez-Gago	University of Malaga, Spain
Nurit Gal-Oz	Sapir Academic College, Israel
Lenzini Gabriele	University of Luxembourg, Luxembourg
Athanasios Giannetsos	Technical University of Denmark, Denmark
Dieter Gollmann	Hamburg University of Technology, Germany
Ehud Gudes	Ben-Gurion University, Israel
Stefanos Gritzalis	University of the Aegean, Greece
Peter Herrmann	Norwegian University of Science and Technology, Norway
Roslan Ismail	Tenaga National University, Malaysia
Audun Josang	University of Oslo, Norway
James Joshi	University of Pittsburgh, USA
Kwok Yan Lam	Nanyang Technological University, Singapore
Shujun Li	University of Kent, UK
Wenjuan Li	City University of Hong Kong, Hong Kong, China
Peter Lewis	Aston University, UK
Felix Gomez Marmol	University of Murcia, Germany
Sheikh Mahbub Habib	Continental AG, Germany
Stephen Marsh	University of Ontario Institute of Technology, Canada

Sjouke Mauw	University of Luxembourg, Luxembourg
Chris Mitchell	Royal Holloway, University of London, UK
Tim Muller	University of Oxford, UK
Max Muhlhauser	TU Darmstadt, Germany
Yuko Murayama	Tsuda College, Japan
Masakatsu Nishigaki	Shizuoka University, Japan
Mehrdad Nojoumian	Florida Atlantic University, USA
Gunther Pernul	Universitat Regensburg, Germany
Pierangela Samarati	University of Milan, Italy
Masaki Shimaoka	SECOM, Japan
Anna Squicciarini	The Pennsylvania State University, USA
Jan-Philipp Steghofer	Chalmers University of Gothenburg, Sweden
Ketil Stoelen	SINTEF, Norway
Tim Storer	University of Glasgow, UK
Shouhuai Xu	University of Texas at San Antonio, USA
Zheng Yan	Xidian University, China, and Aalto University, Finland
Zonghua Zhang	Institut Mines-Telecom (IMT) Lille Douai, France

Additional Reviewers

Fabian Bohm
Emilio Cartoni
Asbjorn Folstad
Enrique Garcia-Ceja
Manolis Maragoudakis
Alessandro Sapienza
Manfred Vielberth
Nadav Volloch

Contents

GDPR Modelling for Log-Based Compliance Checking

Colombe de Montety[1,3], Thibaud Antignac[1(✉)] ⓘ,
and Christophe Slim[2]

[1] CEA List, Software Safety and Security Laboratory,
PC174, 91191 Gif-sur-Yvette, France
{colombe.de-montety,thibaud.antignac}@cea.fr
[2] CEA, Agreements and Intellectual Prop. Service,
PC144, 91191 Gif-sur-Yvette, France
christophe.slim@cea.fr
[3] DANTE, UVSQ, 3 rue de la division Leclerc, 78280 Guyancourt, France

Abstract. Since the entry into force of the General Data Protection Regulation (GDPR), public and private organizations face unprecedented challenges to ensure compliance with new data protection rules. To help its implementation, academics and technologists proposed innovative solutions leading to what is known today as privacy engineering. Among the main goals of these solutions are to enable compliant data processing by controllers and to increase trust in compliance by data subjects. While data protection by design (Article 25 of GDPR) constitutes a keystone of the regulation, many legacy systems are not designed and implemented with this concept in mind, but still process large quantities of personal data. Consequently, there is a need for "after design" ways to check compliance and remediate to data protection issues. In this paper, we propose to monitor and check the compliance of legacy systems through their logs. In order to make it possible, we modelled a core subset of the GDPR in the Prolog language. The approach we followed produced an operational model of the GDPR which eases the interactions with standard operational models of Information Technology (IT) systems. Different dimensions required to properly address data protection obligations have been covered, and in particular time-related properties such as retention time. The logic-based GDPR model has also been kept as close as possible to the legal wording to allow a Data Protection Officer to explore the model in case of need. Finally, even if we don't have a completed tool yet, we created a proof-of-concept framework to use the GDPR model to detect data protection compliance violations by monitoring the IT system logs.

Keywords: Privacy · Logic · Model · Accountability · Compliance

1 Introduction

Formal methods are a feasible solution to ensure compliance with data protection rules with a high level of trust. In his paper [1], Daniel Le Métayer calls for the use of these techniques to bridge the gap between legal and technical means in reducing privacy

© IFIP International Federation for Information Processing 2019
Published by Springer Nature Switzerland AG 2019
W. Meng et al. (Eds.): IFIPTM 2019, IFIP AICT 563, pp. 1–18, 2019.
https://doi.org/10.1007/978-3-030-33716-2_1

risks related to persons whose data are processed. His work provides a formal framework of legal concepts which can serve as a basis for modelling entities' rights and duties. However, he points out the subtlety of real-life situations, that cannot be replicated in programs, because they often go beyond mere dual and static situations. The recently entry into force of the GDPR aims at protecting data subjects at a high level, creating many obligations for data controllers and rights for data subjects regarding any processing of personal data. We believe a translation of core GDPR rules into a logic programming language can be performed to help and support legal practitioners in their work and help addressing the inherent complexity of the law – though this might not completely bridge the gap between legal and technical domains. Indeed, data protection is known for a long time to be difficult to handle in requirements engineering processes [2].

Our work provides a way for the data controller to comply with its accountability through the demonstration of its compliance (Article 24 of GDPR [3]) while carrying any current or future data processing. To that end, we propose a methodology for building a compliance checker that will point out the issues, for any given processing of personal data, that should be remedied. Thus, this checker is aimed at assisting the Data Protection Officer, whose role is notably is to ensure that its organization processes the personal data in compliance with the applicable rules and will facilitate the compliance verification, which is the starting point for data controllers' accountability. As it will not be possible to give a definitive compliancy diagnosis in each and every case, we adopted a conservative approach by enabling the compliance checker to raise alerts when in doubt. Consequently, a raised alert does not mean there is a non-compliance, but all non-compliances raise alerts. This approach, though increasing the number of false alerts, ensures a high level of trust in the diagnosis.

Many previous works have shown that legal rules can be interpreted sometimes according to very different paradigms than logic rules (see [4] for a data flow diagram-based description for instance). Our work is nevertheless very different from previous developments because of the large concepts and ambiguous writing of some articles of the GDPR. This is why we chose, as a first step, to narrow the scope of our work by focusing on two key articles: Article 5 (principles on processing of personal data) and Article 6 (lawfulness of processing), which cover the main obligations to be considered as compliant for any given personal data processing. Moreover, as they constitute general principles, this creates a core which can be further extended to cover other aspects of the GDPR in the future. Our main contributions are:

1. A model of the core of the GDPR as a Prolog-based logic model which can be further extended to cover more data protection principles;
2. A coverage of timing properties to cover obligations such as retention time;
3. A set-up of a compliance checking architecture that detects violations based on logs of actions having occurred in an IT system.

In Sect. 2, we will describe the method and tools used to carry out this work. The way the IT system and the GDPR are modeled are developed in Sect. 3 while we detail how this comes together to form the basis of a compliance checker along with a small example in Sect. 4. Finally, we refer to related works in Sect. 5 and conclude by stating our plans for further developments in Sect. 6.

2 Method and Tools

Systems can be modelled in many different ways and the choices made depend on the objectives targeted. We will discuss the modelling choices made and their motivations in Sect. 2.1 and briefly present the most prominent features of Prolog in Sect. 2.2.

2.1 Modelling Choices and Rationales

Working on the GDPR entails dealing with a large quantity of material. For this reason, we choose to strictly translate the words from the GDPR, so that we can keep track of the provisions in the program. Also, we can make sure we don't go beyond the legal obligations and principles stated in the regulation.

In such circumstance, the first step is to choose and narrow the scope of the regulation. For instance, we choose not to deal with the situation where a data processor is actually processing the personal data; we only focus on the data controller, who is liable for the processing of personal data. Indeed, the GDPR gives a key role to the controller, who determines the means and purposes of the processing. Thus, the data processor is subject to obligations that are deeply linked with the data controller's ones. As a result, provisions regarding the data processor may be added up to the rules already translated, when such a data processor is involved. This is a situation where a false alert can be raised.

Another benefit of a close translation of the GDPR is to allow the involvement of a person, such as a DPO, whose role is to ensure compliance with data protection issues. Our work aims at being a tool to aid for compliance checking, rather than providing all right answers in order to achieve compliance. In case of inconsistency between the log and the regulation, a data protection practitioner is required to interpret any answer given by the program, and to implement the knowledge base of the program.

Our methodology is driven by Maxwell and Antón's methodology, which implies rights, obligations and permissions as a systematic step, when translating legal rules [5]. However, our approach differs from theirs as it considers the appropriate rules by identifying the involved elements (processings, personal data, data subjects, or other persons, for instance) as well as their relationships to one another. This step implies identifying the conditions for an obligation to be applicable to the data controller as well as any disjunctions. Then, we implement the initial translations of the legal rules into actions and states, to make them closer to how an abstract machine works. For this reason, we adopted a concrete vision of every obligation and constrained compliance to some specific actions or states of the data processing. We also included some deontic propositions to express obligations for the controller. In addition, a pattern is dedicated to verify the conditions of success of a request from the data subject about one of his or her rights.

2.2 Logic Modelling in Prolog

To express legal rules, we use the Prolog language, that deals with implication and instantiation of variables through concrete elements. This language is declarative, meaning we need to declare a knowledge base and define a set of rules in order for the program to resolve a given query. Through a solving strategy called backtracking, which is automatically handled by Prolog, the program will reply using instantiation of the variables used in the rules. For instance, two rules can be defined as depicted in Fig. 1 below.

```
A ← B, C.
A ← ¬D.
```

Fig. 1. Example of Prolog rules.

In the first proposition, we declare that in order to verify A, we have to check whether B <u>and</u> C can be proved. The arrow means the implication relation between A on one hand, and B and C on the other hand: if B and C are proved (considered as true by Prolog), then A is true. The comma means a conjunction between B and C: if B is proved but C is not, then A is not true. The period means the end of the proposition. In these two rules, A is the "head" of the two rules; but the two "bodies" differ. As a consequence, there is two ways to prove A: the period at the end of the propositions implies a disjunction. A can be proved if both B and C are proved, but also if the negation of D is proved. The negation is marked "¬" (or "\+" in Prolog), meaning that in the second proposition, A is proved if the program cannot prove D.

To prove the rules, the program uses the knowledge base we defined. A, B, C and D are variables that the program will try to instantiate to constants that are stated in the knowledge base, i.e. replace the variables by constants. The unification is the operation of instantiating the constants where the variables are declared. Finally, backtracking allows the program to go back to higher rules when an answer is given as "false", in order to try every solution to reach a "true". In the end, the result replied by the program is an affirmation or refutation of the original query [6].

We consider Prolog as an effective programming language that is suitable to translate legal rules in a formal language. Its operation requires to declare a knowledge base, and a set of rules; which is appropriate to achieve legal modelling. Indeed, to check for legal compliance, the controller needs some inputs (a knowledge base) and some obligations to fulfil with (a set of rules). However, Prolog has its own limits, that we need to avoid. As an example, a legal provision doesn't describe all the notions and elements involved, whereas Prolog would need a reference to every element concerned in this provision to translate the legal rule. Consequently, in our work, the constraints due to Prolog syntax impacted the way we translated the legal rules.

As a first step, the modelling of the IT system and of the GDPR allowed us to build the elements we need as inputs to check compliance of an IT system based on its logs.

3 IT System and GDPR Modelling

In Fig. 2, we present the elements on which our work is based. First, the environment is composed of devices and networks on one hand, and the GDPR's provisions and other sources on the other hand. These elements help us create two models, the IT system model and GDPR model.

Firstly, the IT system represents any information system that is processing data, under the responsibility of a data controller. Then, we provide a model of this system that describes the evolution of the data processing, through actions and states.

On the other hand, the GDPR provides broad provisions and obligations that data controllers need to comply with, when processing personal data. Our approach focuses on Articles 5 and 6, and other articles that relate to these ones. However, the GDPR itself is not sufficient to understand the concepts stated (in the provisions) and their scopes; to this end, we need to read other sources, such as opinions of the Article 29 Data Protection Working Party, or the French supervisory authority opinions' (CNIL) or take into consideration the recitals of the GDPR.

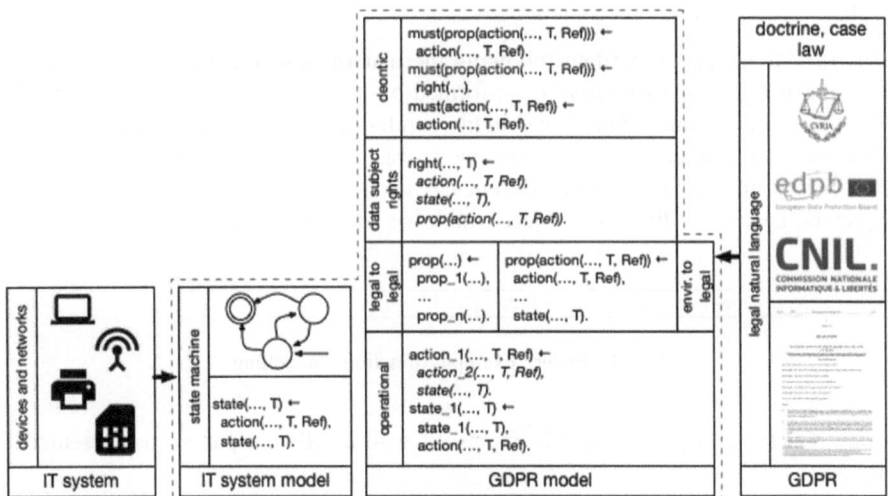

Fig. 2. IT system and GDPR models.

Section 3.1 describes the model and syntax used in the IT system, providing some examples; and Sect. 3.2 focuses on the model and syntax of the GDPR's rules.

3.1 IT System Modelling

We consider any information system that is processing data. We assume that the data is personal data (Article 4(1)). This system is modelled so that actions and states express the evolution of the system, i.e. the evolution of every action happening about the data processing. One of the main contributions of this work is the use of the "time" indicator, in the IT system model and in the GDPR model. A first section will present the state machine, and two following sections will describe how we consider actions and states in this system model.

State Machine. The state machine describes the evolution of the machine, through the states of that machine. In order to change of state, an action must happen. For instance, if an action in the processing happens, a state may be reached. But, to reach a state, another state may be required. This idea is expressed in Fig. 3.

```
<state>(…, T) ←
    action(…, T, Ref),
    …
    <state>(…, T).
```

Fig. 3. Pattern for state machines modelling.

We use the "<" and ">" quotation marks to indicate that the word will be substituted in the language. The next two sections explain how we define actions and states in our work.

Actions. All actions are written following the pattern shown in Fig. 4: an action (action) consisting in an Operation, is performed by someone, identified as a Doer. This action happens at time (Time) and holds a reference (Reference) to allow a direct reference later. For instance, the reference consists in a document the data controller must record in order to prove a consent has been given. This reference can then be expressed later when the data subject withdraws his or her consent.

```
action(Doer, Operation, Time, Reference).
```

Fig. 4. Pattern example of actions modelling.

States. On the contrary, a state is expressed with a different pattern as presented in Fig. 5.

```
<state>(PersonConcerned, Object, PersonalData, Time).
```

Fig. 5. Pattern example of states modelling.

The state (state) concerns a person (PersonConcerned), who is directly involved in the situation which is described; for example, the data controller or the data subject. This state relates to an element (Object), for instance, a request; and is linked to personal data (PersonalData). In addition, the state is reached at a time (Time). Even though actions are written with the word "action", here the word "state" doesn't appear in this syntax: it is always replaced by an expression describing the state, including a present perfect verb. For instance, "isProvided" or "isMinimised" are expressed as states, and replace the word "state". This choice of a present perfect verb is made in order to faithfully express a state of the system.

Therefore, the model of the IT system expresses that if an action and/or a state is proved by the program, then a state is reached in the system. Figure 6 illustrates the conditions for a state to be reached; here, for a consent to be considered as withdrawn. If the two actions are completed, then the state is considered as reached:

```
isWithdrawn(DataSubject, document(ProofConsent), PersonalData, Time_Withdrawal) ←
    action(DataSubject, withdrawsConsent(DataSubject, Purpose, PersonalData),
        Time_Withdrawal, ReferenceProcessing),
    action(DataController, recordsDocument(document(ProofConsent, DataSubject),
        Time_Withdrawal, _).
```

Fig. 6. Rule for withdrawn consent.

To verify this state, two actions must happen: the data subject withdraws his or her consent, and the data controller records a document related to the consent and its withdrawal.

Actions and states are also used in the GDPR model, at an operational level. Indeed, this modelling of the GDPR provisions is structured into several levels to articulate the rules.

3.2   GDPR Modelling

The GDPR provides rules to ensure data protection for subjects whose personal data are processed. As stated before, we face difficulties reading the GDPR's rules; the scope and the wording of the text bring us to adopt an approach that remains close to the terms. We choose not to provide too much details in our model, leaving a supervisory authority or a competent person the power to decide on the meaning behind a given word (for instance, what "a task carried out in the public interest" in Article 6(1)(e) may refer to).

The other difficulty for us is to derive logic rules from the European regulation: the syntax we use has to reflect the rules in their extent, without translating beyond or above the legal text. To achieve this goal, we are driven by previous works on legal modelling, that focus on expression of rights, permissions, obligations, but also on implied rights, permissions and obligations drawn from the provisions [7].

Furthermore, these logic rules need to be articulated in order for a logic organization to be designed between them. For instance, we need to know what obligation relates on another one. The GDPR does not systematically provide such logic articulation between the provisions, but introduces some cross-references. Thus, modelling the GDPR leads us to separate the rules into several levels, following a hierarchy that is deduced from the text. We then propose an architecture that is drawn from the GDPR's rules.

However, as stated before, the GDPR model must be expressed using the syntax used for the state machine, i.e. the syntax expressing actions and states. As a consequence, an operational level in the GDPR model is expressed through actions and states. These actions and states will then be linked to the GDPR's provisions.

In the following, we will detail each level from the GDPR model from Fig. 2.

Deontic Level. This level in our model aims at expressing obligations for the controller, when an action occurs in the system. Figure 7 provides an example of the use of deontic concepts about the GDPR's rules.

```
must(<prop>(action(..., T, Ref))) ←
    action(..., T, Ref),
    \+ <prop>(action(..., T, Ref)).
```

Fig. 7. Pattern for obligations modelling.

This pattern expresses a deontic obligation for a doer, when an action occurs in the system, and the obligation on this action is not fulfilled yet. If the two conditions can be proved by the program, then the controller needs to comply with this top-obligation. First, we explain the use of "must" in these propositions.

Must. Deontic obligations are implied in the GDPR, but we formulate them in order to detect the obligations that the data controller has to comply with, when an action happens. This deontic idea is expressed through the word "must", meaning the data controller must comply with a legal obligation, if the relevant action happens, as shown in Fig. 8. Thus the deontic level uses the actions recorded in the system to infer obligations for the controller.

```
must(processesCompliant(action(DataController, processes(DataSubject, Purpose,
        PersonalData), Time_Process, Reference))) ←
    action(DataController, processes(DataSubject, Purpose, PersonalData),
        Time_Process, Reference).
```

Fig. 8. Rule for compliant processing obligation.

Data Subjects Rights Level. Another part of the program deals with requests from data subjects concerning their rights. The idea is that the controller must accept the request concerning a right if the conditions are proved by the program. To this aim, an action may be required, or a state, to verify that the conditions are checked.

Property. A property pertaining to an action is denoted by "prop". For instance, an action representing a data processing might be "processesCompliant" or not, which is a property. If an action is not verified (i.e. is not compliant), then the data controller may have an obligation to accept a request from a data subject as shown in Fig. 9.

```
<isToSucceedRequest>(…) ←
    action(…, T, Ref),
    <state>(…, T),
    \+ <prop>(action(…)),
    \+ action(…, T, Ref).
```

Fig. 9. Pattern for success for data subject request conditions modelling.

For example, we express the conditions for a request about the right to object to be successful in Fig. 10.

```
isToSucceedObjectionRequest(DataSubject, objection(Reference), PersonalData, _) ←
    action(DataController, processes(DataSubject, Purpose, PersonalData),
        Time_Process, Reference),
    action(DataSubject, asksForRight(objectsProcessing(DataController, Purpose),
        Time_Request, Reference)),
    Time_Process =< Time_Request,
    action(DataSubject, motivatesRequest(DataSubject, Purpose, PersonalData),
        Time_Request, Reference),
    \+ action(DataController,
assertsLegitimateGroundsForProcessingOverrideRightsFreedoms(DataSubject,
        Purpose, PersonalData), Time_2, Reference),
    Time_Request =< Time_2.
```

Fig. 10. Rule for success of the right to object requests.

Three actions have to be recorded in the log, and one has to not be proved by the program. Precisely, the first action is a processing of personal data, the second one is a request from the data subject about the right to objection ("asksForRight"); the third one expresses the data subject motivating its request ("motivatesRequest"). Then, the last proposition refers to an action from the controller who asserts that he finds legitimate grounds for the processing which override the rights and freedoms of the data subject. Indeed, if this action is not proved, then the controller can't refuse the objection to the processing, he must accept the request.

Translating these conditions for the right to objection to succeed, enables us to state later in the model that the controller must stop the processing when this property is proved.

"Legal to Legal" Level. This part in our model aims at expressing how the legal rules are articulated between each other. In that way, several sub-obligations are needed to verify if a higher obligation is considered as fulfilled (see Fig. 11 below).

```
<prop>(action(…, T, Ref)) ←
    <prop_1>(action(…, T, Ref)),
    <state>(…, T),
    action(…, T, Ref),
    <declaration>(…),
    …
    <prop_n>(action(…, T, Ref)).
```

Fig. 11. Pattern for legal to legal rules modelling.

Again, we use "prop" to express a property upon an action. This property is proved if other properties upon the same action are proved. The obligation ("prop") and sub-obligations ("prop_1", "prop_n") are always linked to the same action performed by a doer (Doer). But a state or an action may also be required to verify the top property.

Finally, we need to add some declarations ("declaration") that bring values we need to resolve the query.

For instance, Fig. 12 illustrates the conditions for a transparent processing to be proved by the program. Here, the sub-obligation to be fulfilled is "providesTransparentInformation", and an action and a state ("isDemonstrableCompliance") are also required.

```
processesTransparent(action(DataController, processes(DataSubject, Purpose,
        PersonalData), Time_Process, Reference)) ←
    action(DataController, processes(DataSubject, Purpose, PersonalData),
        Time_Process, Reference),
    providesTransparentInformation(action(DataController, processes(DataSubject,
        Purpose, PersonalData), Time_X, Reference)),
    Time_X =< Time_Process,
    isDemonstrableCompliance(demonstratesTransparency(document(ProofProcess)),
        DataController, Reference, PersonalData, Time_Compliance).
```

Fig. 12. Rule for transparent processings.

In addition, we introduce the use of time indicators. We state in Fig. 12. that the time of the process ("Time_Process") has to be greater (the symbol "=<") than the time for the controller to deliver the information ("Time_X"). If not proved, this time constraint would terminate the query resolution with a false reply.

"Environment to Legal" Level. This level in the architecture deals with the actions and states that will prove an obligation is fulfilled. In Fig. 13, we show the pattern: to verify a property is fulfilled, an action or a state is required, and some declarations are added to provide more details about the elements involved in the rule.

```
<prop>(action(…, T, Ref)) ←
    action(…, Time_n, Ref),
    <declaration>(…),
    …
    <state>(…, Time_n).
```

Fig. 13. Pattern for environment to legal rules modelling.

For instance, the example below in Fig. 14 illustrates the obligation for the controller to process personal data fairly ("processesFair").

```
processesFair(action(DataController, processes(DataSubject, Purpose,
        PersonalData), Time_Process, Reference)) ←
    action(DataController, assertsFairInformation(DataSubject, Purpose,
        PersonalData), Time_X, Reference),
    action(DataController, assertsFairProcessingTowardsDataSubject(DataSubject,
        Purpose, PersonalData), Time_Process, Reference),
    Time_X =< Time_Process,
    isDemonstrableCompliance(demonstratesFairness(document(ProofProcess)),
        DataController, Reference, PersonalData, Time_Compliance).
```

Fig. 14. Rule for fair processings.

For this obligation to be verified, two actions performed by the controller must happen, and a state has to be reached. The first action is an assertion from the controller who confirms that the information provided to the data subject is fair ("assertsFair-Information"). This action is linked to the transparency principle of processings, but we choose not to bind transparency and fairness together here. The second action refers to a fair processing towards the data subject ("assertsFairProcessingTowardsDataSubject") and does not concern transparency.

Indeed, the translation of the fairness principle led us to some difficulties. The fairness principle appears to have a key role among data protection rules, according to its repetition in the GDPR. However, the regulation doesn't give any detail nor condition to consider a fair processing. In order to translate "fairness" into the two actions described earlier, we read other sources, such as the Guidelines of the Data Protection Working Party on transparency under the GDPR [8]. We understand that fairness is not an autonomous principle. In the Guidelines, fairness is deeply linked to transparency of the information delivered to the data subject[1]. However, Recital 39 in the GDPR states that "natural persons should be made aware of risks, rules, safeguards and rights in relation to the processing of personal data" to fulfil the fairness principle. Yet, we chose not to link fairness to transparency, and remain close to the Recital 39, because the two principles are clearly divided in Article 5.

Consequently, we express two actions by the controller; the first one reflects the relation between fairness and transparency of the information; the second one refers to the substance of the information. In doing so, we assume that the controller or the DPO will perform a positive action to assert that fairness of the processing and fairness of the information are satisfied. The last proposition in the rule refers to the accountability obligation: the state "isDemonstrableCompliance" would be reached if the controller can demonstrate he is compliant about fairness.

Operational Level. The last level in this architecture is an operational one, that links actions and states. The pattern shown in Fig. 15 allows us to define how a state may be reached in the system: when actions and states are proved by the program.

```
<state>(…, T) ←
    action(…, T, Ref),
    <state_1>(…, T),
    <declaration>(…).
```

Fig. 15. Pattern for operational rules modelling.

As an operational level example, Fig. 16 provides the definition of a processing necessary for the performance of a task carried out in the public interest.

---

[1] "Transparency is intrinsically linked to fairness and the new principle of accountability under the GDPR", p.5.

```
isNecessaryProcessingForPerformanceTaskPublicInterest(DataController,
        TaskPublicInterest, PersonalData, Time_X) ←
    action(DataController, processes(DataSubject, Purpose, PersonalData),
        Time_Process, Reference),
    taskPublicInterestByDataController(TaskPublicInterest, DataController),
    action(DataController,
        assertsProcessingNecessaryForPerformanceTaskPublicInterest(DataSubject,
        Purpose, PersonalData), Time_X, Reference),
    Time_X =< Time_Process.
```

Fig. 16. Rule for public interest processings.

Two actions are required in order to reach this state. The first action concerns the processing of personal data undertaken by the controller; the second action relates to the controller asserting the processing is necessary for the task he is carrying out in the public interest ("assertsProcessingNecessaryForPerformanceTaskPublicInterest"). Through a declaration, we are able to express which task is carried out by this data controller in the public interest ("taskPublicInterestByDataController"). Finally, the program will compare two "time" indicators: the assertion of the controller must happen before the beginning of the processing.

Consequently, we have two models, the IT system model that must reflect exactly the state of the IT system, and the GDPR model, that must reflect exactly the data protection rules from the regulation. Then, the compliance checker we propose will compare a log from the IT system (the list of actions that happened in the system), with the two models. This dynamic approach is carried out to check for compliance about a processing of personal data.

4 Log-Based Compliance Checking

When checking for potential violations under the GDPR's provisions (Fig. 17), the compliance checker gathers the two models, and takes as input the log of every actions that happened in the system. However, we need additional information, about the context of the processing. This information is provided through a complementary source, and does not depend on the log: the set of declarations. Then, the compliance checker will reply a query about a potential violation of the GDPR's rules translated in the models. Finally, a diagnosis is provided, and determines if the processing undertaken presents any violation.

Section 4.1 will present the context and the log of the system as inputs to the compliance checker; Sect. 4.2 will describe the compliance checker, illustrating a query. Finally, Sect. 4.3 will give a small example to show how violation can be detected.

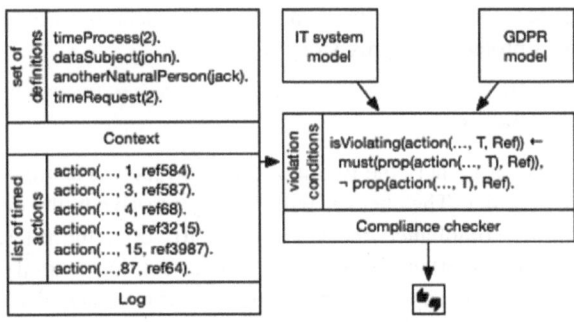

Fig. 17. Compliance checking architecture.

4.1 IT System Logs

As input to the compliance checker, the log of the system is composed of the actions that happen about a certain processing of data. Here, the values of the actions are concrete, i.e. instantiated. Therefore, the log represents the knowledge base of the compliance checker. In addition, the actions are recorded in the log with the time when they happen.

```
action(google, givesInformationRightToWithdrawConsent(jack), id_jack, 5,
privacy_form).
```

Fig. 18. Example of an instantiated action.

Figure 18 illustrates an example of an action recorded in the log; the data controller (Google) provides information about the right to withdraw the data subject's (Jack) consent, at time 5, including a reference to the form used to provide this information ("privacy_form"), and the personal data being processed ("id_jack").

Furthermore, the compliance checker relies on another knowledge base, which describes the concrete context of the processing of personal data. These declarations permit to add some information to the actions from the log. Figure 19 illustrates three declarations.

```
taskPublicInterestByDataController(police, intelligenceService).
taskOfficialAuthorityByDataController(dataProtection, supervisoryAuthority).
legitimateInterestOfDataController(fraudPrevention, anyAuthority).
```

Fig. 19. Example of an instantiated context declaration.

These declarations allow us to know that "police" is designated as a task carried out by the "intelligenceService" which is the data controller here. In the same way, the "supervisoryAuthority" carries out a task that is "dataProtection". The third declaration states that "fraudPrevention" is a legitimate interest defended by the data controller ("anyAuthority").

As a consequence, the log and the context are used as a knowledge base to detect violations with data protection's provisions.

4.2   Compliance Checker

The compliance checker gathers the two models, and receives as input the knowledge base presented in Sect. 4.1. The checker will then try to solve to the query we address. In order to do so, the compliance checker will try to verify the rules, relying on the knowledge base. One important assumption here is the log soundly reflects the IT system behavior: all actions appearing in the log should have actually happened in and all actions actually happening should appear in the log.

Using Prolog's instantiation of the variables, the checker replies if a processing of personal data performed through the system is violating the rules, or not. To this aim, the query is defined as it follows in Fig. 20 below.

```
isViolating(action(…, T, Ref)) ←
    must(<prop>(action(…, T, Ref))),
    \+ <prop>(action(…, Time, Ref)).
```

Fig. 20. Pattern for violation modelling.

The checker can thus be queried about an obligation for the controller to fulfil upon an action ("must"). This part refers to the deontic level we exposed earlier. The second proposition asks if the property upon the same action is not proved ("\+ prop"). If the obligation exists and if the property is not proved (i.e. the conditions cannot be met by the program), then the program will reply "isViolating", meaning that the action is violating the GDPR's provisions.

For instance, in Fig. 21, we express that if the data controller has an obligation to process personal data compliantly ("processesCompliant"), and if this processing is not proved as compliant ("\+ processesCompliant"), then it is violating the relevant data protection rules.

```
isViolating(action(Doer, processes(DataSubject, Purpose, PersonalData),
        Time_Process, Reference)) :-
    must(processesCompliant(action(Doer, processes(DataSubject, Purpose, Personal
        Data), Time_Process, Reference))),
    \+ processesCompliant(action(Doer, processes(DataSubject, Purpose, Personal
        Data), Time_Process, Reference)).
```

Fig. 21. Rule for compliance violation detection.

Therefore, the compliance checker's role is to detect when a processing doesn't fulfil the obligations needed to achieve compliance. The time of actions are taken into consideration, as part of the compliance checking.

We do not claim to substitute entirely the task and experience of a person who is competent for checking compliance with data protection (as a lawyer), so the checker does not provide an answer that is to be taken for granted, our aim is to increase the level of trust in the compliance of the system.

4.3   Example

In this section, we give an example of a rule that is analyzed by the compliance checker. The rule described below in Fig. 22 expresses the three actions needed for an information provided by the controller to be proved as being transparent. (These conditions are the clarity, the conciseness, and the accessibility of this information.)

```
isProvidedTransparentInformation(DataController, Reference, PersonalData, Time_X)
←
    action(DataController, givesClearInformationDataSubject(DataSubject,
        Purpose, PersonalData), Time_X, Reference),
    action(DataController, givesConciseInformationDataSubject(DataSubject,
        Purpose, PersonalData), Time_X, Reference),
    action(DataController, givesAccessibleInformationDataSubject(DataSubject,
        Purpose, PersonalData), Time_X, Reference).
```

Fig. 22. Rule for information transparence.

On the other hand, the logs of the actions in the IT system are recorded as shown in Fig. 23 (with the data controller being a bank).

```
action(bank, givesClearInformationDataSubject(john, archiving, johnBankDetails),
1, archives_X).
action(bank, givesConciseInformationDataSubject(john, archiving, johnBankDetails),
7, archives_X).
action(bank, processes(john, archiving, johnBankDetails), 28, process_john).
```

Fig. 23. Log excerpt.

In this setting, we prompt the query "isViolating" about the processing of John's personal data, with the instantiations from the above as depicted in Fig. 24.

```
?- isViolating(action(bank, processes(john, archiving, johnBankDetails), 28,
process_john)).
```

Fig. 24. Violation query prompt.

The program will then verify whether there is an obligation to process the personal data compliantly, and then check for every condition to achieve compliance. Considering the transparency rule in Fig. 22, the program will try to instantiate the variables of the rule. But as we can see in Fig. 23, only two actions – in top of the processing action itself – are recorded in the log, whereas the rule requires three actions. Indeed, "givesAccessibleInformation" doesn't appear in the log. As a consequence, the program will reply "true" and thus deduced that the processing is not compliant. To be able to capture the condition that is not fulfilled, the "trace" module of Prolog provides instrumented ways to guide the auditor to the missing elements.

5   Related Works

Formal methods, in spite of their weaknesses, are largely accepted as a solution to translate legal rules into a modelling even though they face limitations and should thus be adequately tailored to address well-identified domains. Tschantz and Wing give several examples in which these methods are relevant to check privacy violations [9]. In our approach, we focus on "a posteriori" verification of compliance to data protection rules, when processing of personal data has already happened. However, many works relate to privacy by design [10], for instance to implement data minimization into engineering systems. Also, in this work, we chose to focus on the GDPR only, though a few other documents were also used to help analyze the concepts that are ambiguous in the regulation. Our aim was to get a model as close as possible to the legal wording of the GDPR. Other work proposed approaches relying on many sources, not only legal ones [11], which would require more work to be appropriately handled through formal methods.

The Prolog language appears to be a relevant programming choice for expressing legal rules; we can relate to former works that chose this programming logic to resolve queries about compliance to legislations. Maxwell and Antón [5], for instance, give a methodology for production rule models concerning HIPAA based on Prolog. They have been able to cover rights, obligations, permissions and declarations, and implied rights, obligations, and permissions. They provide a model that checks the requirements, so that inconsistent requirements are flagged and then rechecked with legal domain experts. We adopted the same method that flags potential issues that must be analyzed by a Data Protection Officer (DPO). The main difference between our work and theirs is that they aim at facilitating communication between requirements engineers and legal domain experts. Also, previous work focuses on short parts of legal texts, that is straightforward and documented.

When translating legal rules into a formal language, Breaux, Vail and Antón bring a methodology for automatically implying an obligation upon the counterparty from a right [7]. We took inspiration of this work to help understand all the implications of the GDPR's rules, but have been limited by the expressivity of the GDPR, compared to legal requirement coming from HIPAA. As we aimed at remaining close to the Regulation itself, we decided not to go beyond and neither states new rights nor obligations that are deducible from them.

Furthermore, even if previous works about legal modelling of data protection rules provide interesting methods to translate them, we cannot rely entirely on these methods because the GDPR's rules are highly nested and interconnected. Our approach is different from previous works: the syntax is new, mainly divided into actions and states (leading to a more formal semantics than what is proposed in [12] for instance; and organizing the rules, from the "top" one, reasoning on legal implications, to go "down" to the actions required in order to verify the legal rules. Finally, our approach brings a new element, the variable for the time of the action. Not only this allows us to consider whether an action takes place before or after another one but we can also consider durations and detect violations of time limitations.

Working on logs as a mean to secure compliance and accountability is not new [13]. In this paper, the authors discuss what information must be included in the logs: only essential information, but also contextual ones, as we also used. They also rise two challenges we met in our work: the ambiguity in the logs, when the log is not explicit enough; and the need for human verification in complement to the log analyzer. However, their formalism is further from the GDPR than ours and would require extensions to address the same data protection properties.

6   Conclusion

In conclusion, we built two concurrent models – one for the IT system and the other one for the GDPR – that are used by a compliance checker. This checker is able to provide an answer about which compliance aspects may not be properly covered by the data controller by relying on a log which records all actions having occurred in the IT system. The checker will thus raise flags for points which are to be checked by a DPO. These alerts may be false alerts because of a lack of contextual information, which can then be added by the DPO, or because of actual violations, for which the DPO can proceed to a remedy, helped by the compliance checker showing which requirement is not met (i.e., which action was expected in the log and not found). A prototype of the core principles of these models has been implemented. Future work will consist in evaluating, improving our contribution, and implementing it through a bigger scale proof of concept.

The requirements that we stated above, both legal and technical, brought us to provide an extensible architecture that organizes how the rules from the GDPR model can be operationalized through an interface between technique-oriented levels (modelled as state machines) and legal-oriented levels (modelled as property definitions). These models are then used by a deontic-based compliance checker to reason about possible violations.

Nevertheless, we faced limitations, both legal and technical. The main legal difficulty concerns the elusive notions that the GDPR states inviting us to rely on soft law. Then, the heart of the technical difficulties lies at the articulation of rules and exceptions, that can lead to long sets of rules, especially when some of them might have to be repeated to several places because of cross-references. Better handling of this could have been possible at the cost of more elaborate logic patterns and of more distance from the GDPR structure.

We plan to extend this work by developing more properties taking benefit of the time indication embedded in the actions (for instance by handling obligations concerning notifications in case of a breach). In addition, we also plan to implement a way to prioritize violations in order to help a DPO to take the best action possible. The prioritization strategy should be parametrizable, depending on the wish of the DPO. This could be, for instance, based on a list of principles which have been deemed to be of particular importance at corporate level, for a given sector, or based on the output of a data protection impact analysis.

References

1. Métayer, D.: Formal methods as a link between software code and legal rules. In: Barthe, G., Pardo, A., Schneider, G. (eds.) SEFM 2011. LNCS, vol. 7041, pp. 3–18. Springer, Heidelberg (2011). https://doi.org/10.1007/978-3-642-24690-6_2
2. Guarda, P., Zannone, N.: Towards the development of privacy-aware systems. Inf. Softw. Technol. **51**(2), 337–350 (2009)
3. EU Parliament, Council of the EU: Regulation (EU) 2016/679 of the European Parliament and of the Council of 27 April 2016 on the protection of natural persons with regard to the processing of personal data and on the free movement of such data, and repealing Directive 95/46/EC (General Data Protection Regulation) (Text with EEA relevance). Official Journal of the European Union, L119/1, 4 May 2016
4. Deng, M., Wuyts, K., Scandariato, R., Preneel, B., Joosen, W.: A privacy threat analysis framework: supporting the elicitation and fulfillment of privacy requirements: Requirements. Eng. J. **16**(1), 3–32 (2011)
5. Maxwell, J.C., Antón, A.I.: Developing production rule models to aid in acquiring requirements from legal texts. In: 17th IEEE International Requirements Engineering Conference 2009, pp. 101–110 (2009)
6. Lloyd, J.W.: Foundations of Logic Programming, 1st edn. Springer, Heidelberg (1984). https://doi.org/10.1007/978-3-642-96826-6
7. Breaux, T.D., Vail, M.W., Antón, A.I.: Towards regulatory compliance: extracting rights and obligations to align requirements with regulations. In: 14th IEEE International Requirements Engineering Conference 2006, pp. 46–55 (2016)
8. Article 29 Data Protection Working Party, Guidelines on transparency under Regulation 2016/679, 9 November 2017
9. Tschantz, M.C., Wing, J.M.: Formal methods for privacy. In: Cavalcanti, A., Dams, D.R. (eds.) FM 2009. LNCS, vol. 5850, pp. 1–15. Springer, Heidelberg (2009). https://doi.org/10.1007/978-3-642-05089-3_1
10. Gürges, S., Troncoso, C., Diaz, C.: Engineering privacy by design (2011)
11. Visser, P., Bench-Capon, T., van den Herik, J.: A method for conceptualising legal domains: an example from the Dutch unemployment benefits act. Artif. Intell. Law **5**, 207–242 (1997)
12. Palmirano, M., Martoni, M., Rossi, A., Bartolini, C. Robaldo, L.: PrOnto privacy ontology for legal compliance. In: Proceedings of 18th European Conference on Digital Government (2018)
13. Butin, D., Chicote, M., Le Métayer, D.: Log design for accountability. In: 2013 IEEE Security and Privacy Workshops (2013)

A Role and Trust Access Control Model for Preserving Privacy and Image Anonymization in Social Networks

Nadav Voloch[1(✉)], Priel Nissim[1], Mor Elmakies[1], and Ehud Gudes[1,2]

[1] Ben-Gurion University of the Negev, P.O.B. 653, 8410501 Beer-Sheva, Israel
voloch@post.bgu.ac.il
[2] Achva Academic College, Shikmim Mobile Post 79800, Arugot, Israel

Abstract. Over the last decade Online Social Networks (OSN) privacy has been thoroughly studied in many aspects. Some of these privacy related aspects are trust and credibility involving the OSN user-data conveyed by different relationships in the network. One of OSN major problems is that users expose their information in a manner thought to be relatively private, or even partially public, to unknown and possibly unwanted entities, such as adversaries, social bots, fake users, spammers or data-harvesters. Preventing this information leakage is the target of many OSN privacy models, such as Access Control, Relationship based models, Trust based models and many others. In this paper we suggest a new Role and Trust based Access Control model, denoted here as RTBAC, in which roles, that manifest different permissions, are assigned to the users connected to the Ego-node (the user sharing the information), and in addition, every user is evaluated trust wise by several criteria, such as total number of friends, age of user account, and friendship duration. An interesting extension of the model of image anonymization is also given, where a user that has a certain role with a proper permission can access a partial instance of the data, if a sufficient trust level is not achieved. These role and trust assessments provide more precise and viable information sharing decisions and enable better privacy control in the social network.

Keywords: Social networks privacy · Access control · Trust-based privacy models

1 Introduction

Online Social Networks (OSN) privacy models have been a source of many researches over the past couple of years. Some of which focus on handling the OSN information sharing instances as an Access Control system, in which there is a selective restriction of access to the network's resources. The permission to access a resource is the main concern of the different models. The decision of giving a certain user authorization to such a resource is usually made by several criteria, based on many different factors.

Access Control models have different variations, some are more widely used than others. [1] presents a new model for privacy control based on sharing habits on which,

W. Meng et al. (Eds.): IFIPTM 2019, IFIP AICT 563, pp. 19–27, 2019.
https://doi.org/10.1007/978-3-030-33716-2_2

we have preliminary based our research. This model controls the information flow by a graph algorithm that prevents potential data leakage.

This paper presents a new privacy model for access control in an OSN, in which the decisions of permission granting combines both pre-defined roles and trust-based factors derived from user-attributes, such as total number of friends, age of user account, and resemblance attributes between the two users. Similar attributes have appeared in a previous work [2], which deals with information-flow control, and creates a model for adversary detection. However, in this paper we present specific parametric values for these attributes, which are experimentally based. The model's extension of a partial data visibility is used here in an implementation of image anonymization, in which a certain role that inherently has a permission of seeing images, can see a partial (relatively blurry) image if he does not gain the necessary minimal Trust value for getting the full permission.

The rest of this paper is structured as follows: Sect. 2 discusses the background for our work, with explanations on the related papers it relies on, Sect. 3 describes and defines our model thoroughly with several examples of its operation and presents its preliminary evaluation. Section 4 is the model's extension of partial data visibility for image anonymization in the OSN. Section 5 discusses the model and concludes it.

2   Background and Related Work

Access Control models, and specifically ones describing OSN privacy, have been studied extensively over the past decade. A major problem, existing especially in OSN, is an information flow to unwanted entities, violating the privacy of individuals. The main Access Control model used in OSN is Role-Based Access Control (RBAC) that has many versions, as presented in [3], and limits access by creating user-role assignments. The user must have a role that has permission to access that resource.

The most prominent advantage of this method is that permissions are not assigned directly to users but to roles, making it much easier to manage the access control of a single user, since it only must be assigned the right role.

To this model an addition of the Trust factor is done in [4], and it is based on the network users' interaction history, which could be problematic in assessing relatively unknown new connections. In this paper we circumvent this problem by adding independent user attributes to this estimation. An example of using RBAC specifically in Facebook is done in [5], that describes the use of roles in it and the possible breaches that can occur due to the flexible privacy settings of the network. [6] present a model named IMPROVE-Identifying Minimal Profile Vectors for similarity-based access control. It elaborates on this specific subject, and gives a 30-item list of attributes, some direct and some derived, that define the user information in an OSN. We have based our Role and Trust Based Access Control (RTBAC) model on the above works, and it is presented in the following section. The novelty of our model is that the relationships and their strengths do not determine Access Control directly, but are used along with other characteristics to compute the trust of an OSN user in accordance with a specific Ego-user.

3   OSN Role and Trust Based Access Control (RTBAC)

3.1   The RTBAC Model

The basic idea of the model is that besides the general roles given to different users, each user will be given a certain level of trust, and permissions to different data instances will be authorized only if the trust level passes a certain threshold. In this manner, the generalization disadvantage of RBAC can be solved, and better data distribution can be achieved. We should first emphasize the way, relative to a specific Ego-user, RBAC is generally used in an OSN. A user may belong to multiple hierarchic roles, but all of them are on a single path (as seen in [7]). Therefore, when a user, and an Access chosen for it, is the lowest in the hierarchy it has the maximal set of permissions per role. We denote this role as R (U, Ego), but we will use just R as a short notation. The main contribution of RTBAC is the way Trust is computed.

Trust is computed by assigning values of credibility and connection strength to the different users, based on the criteria presented below. A minimum trust value threshold is the core condition of accessing a specific permission. The purpose of combining trust is to provide an additional stage of screening besides the RBAC roles. Another advantage of the model is that the combination of trust elements allows dynamic assignments of permissions to users over time, meaning their trust level can be dropped, and vice versa. The formal definition of the RTBAC model instance is as follows:

An RTBAC instance is a tuple $<u\_id, R, P(R), UTV, MTV, P(U)>$ where:

- u_id – the identification of a user connected to the Ego-node.
- R – the assigned user role of u_id, same as in RBAC
- P – An access permission to an OSN data instance
- B (P, R) - the preliminary access Permission P of the assigned role R
- UTV-, the User Trust Value for u_id, that will be explained in the following part, values range between 0 and 1
- MTV (P, R) - the Minimal Trust Value of role R for permission P, that will be explained in the following part, values range between 0 and 1
- B (U, P) - the final access decision for u_id U for permission P

In Fig. 1 we can see an example for the model's structure – The Ego-user is the user sharing the information. There are 7 other users in the system in this example, that obtain different roles. In this example, we give a minimal trust value (MTV) of 0.745 for a family member role to access the permission of "Tagging". This value can be altered per role and per permission in other cases. An Example of the trust decision making can be clearly seen in User 6. Users 6 and 7 have a "Family" role, but only User 7 achieves a trust value > 0.745 and gets the "Tagging" permission that User 6 does not obtain.

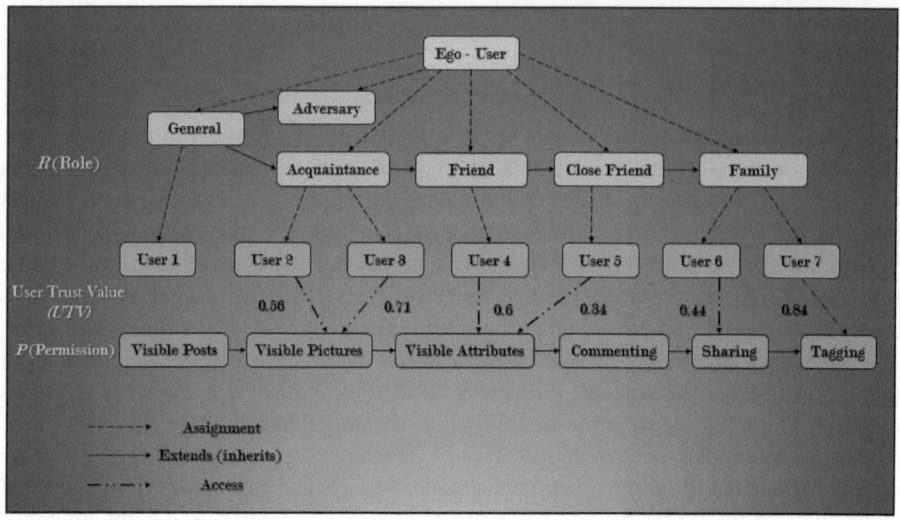

Fig. 1. RTBAC model example of 7 users. Users 6 and 7 have a "Family" role, but only User 7 achieves a trust value > 0.745 and gets the "Tagging" permission.

3.2 Criteria Choice for Trust Estimation

The choice of the attributes, for determining the level of trust for the model, is based on the criteria mentioned in the above sections, and the two main categories of criteria for our model are:

- **Connection strength (c):** the connection strength of users is determined by characteristics that indicate their level of closeness such as Friendship Duration (FD), Mutual Friends (MF), Outflow/Inflow Ratio (OIR) and Resemblance Attributes (RA). The notation given to these factors is c. For example, c_{MF} is the value for the Mutual Friends attribute.
- **User credibility (u):** the user credibly criterion assesses the user attributes that convey his OSN reputation and trustworthiness. These are Total number of Friends (TF) and Age of User Account (AUA) calculated from the time the user joined the OSN, and Followers/Followees Ratio (FFR). The notation given to these factors is u. For example, u_{AUA} is the value for the Age of User Account attribute.

3.3 Calculating Trust Parameters' Values

Setting the values for the Trust variables is done in this model in a scale of 0 to 1, since the decision of sharing information with a certain user is defined as a probability variable, 0 being no sharing willingness at all, 1 being definite sharing willingness.

All the parameters' values presented in this section are based on an experimental evaluation we have performed and is discussed in more detail in Sect. 3.5 of this paper.

Table 1. Threshold values for trust attributes

TF	AUA (months)	FD (months)	MF
245	24	18	37

The threshold values for TF, AUA, FD and MF are presented in Table 1, FFR is defined as a ratio by default, as well as OIR, while if one of these values is larger than 1, it is calculated as 1 for the model.

For the c_{RA} value we take into consideration 10 of the users' attributes, based on the researches presented above (e.g. IMPROVE [6]), that resemble the Ego-user's attributes that are gender, age (range), current educational institute, past educational institute, current workplace, past workplace, current town, home-town, current country, home-country.

Let us denote the following factors:

- TA_{ego} is the total number of non-null attributes (from the 10 attributes mentioned above) of the Ego-user. The values of these attributes must be defined by non-null values.
- $TRA_{ego,\ other}$ is the total number of non-null resembling attributes (from the 10 attributes mentioned above) of the Ego-user and the other user. The values of these attributes must be defined by non-null values.

Now we can define c_{RA}:

$$c_{RA} = \frac{TRAego, other}{TAego} \tag{1}$$

This value cannot be larger than 1, since the maximal number of common attributes could be the total number of Ego-user's attributes at most. Now we can assess the access permission decisions by defining the total values of user credibility and connection strength in a manner of averaging the different factors noted above.

$$u = \langle WiUi \rangle = \frac{\sum_{i=1}^{|u|} WiUi}{\langle W \rangle |u|} = \frac{WuTF + WuAUA + WuFFR}{5.24 \cdot 3}$$
$$= \frac{5.37uTF + 5.2uAUA + 5.16uFFR}{15.72} \tag{2}$$

$$c = \langle WiCi \rangle = \frac{\sum_{i=1}^{|c|} WiCi}{\langle W \rangle |c|} = \frac{WcMF + WcFD + WcOIR + WcRA}{5.52 \cdot 4}$$
$$= \frac{5.93cMF + 5.1cFD + 5.7cOIR + 5.34cRA}{22.8} \tag{3}$$

These weights (W_i) were the survey results for the significance (weight) of every attribute-factor (U_i or C_i) in u and c. They could theoretically be altered by other user-preferences or future results.

We can now conclude the definition of the model's User Trust Value (*UTV*), taking into consideration that there are 7 attributes: 4 connection attributes and 3 user attributes (marked as |*c*| and |*u*|):

$$UTV = \frac{c \cdot |c| + u \cdot |u|}{|c + u|} = \frac{4 \cdot c + 3 \cdot u}{7} \tag{4}$$

The Minimal Trust Value (*MTV*) set in this model is based on the Trust-based dynamic RBAC model presented above and is altered per role and per permission by the user-preferences if such exist, or by an OSN administration policy, if such exists for these specific cases. It is important to state here that the users were not asked directly about the parameter values, but those were derived from the experimental evaluation that will be described in the following part of this paper. A certain user can set its own trust threshold dependent on his privacy preferences.

The values presented here are validated by the experimental evaluation but are subject to flexible changes by necessity.

In Table 2 we can see an example, portrayed in Fig. 1, where there is a difference between two users that have the same role, but not the same *UTV*, thus not getting the same permission. The *MTV* set for this specific role and permission (Family - Tagging) is 0.745, and User 6 achieves a *UTV* value of 0.44 and does not get the permission, whilst User 7 achieves a *UTV* of 0.84, thus gets the permission.

In the following parts we will see the model's algorithm, and the experimental evaluation done for determining its different parameters.

Table 2. Difference in *UTV* between same-role users

User	*WuTF*	*WuAUA*	*WuFFR*	*WcRA*	*WcFD*	*WcOIR*	*WcMF*	*u*	*c*	*UTV*	*MTV*
6	0.44	0.33	0.89	0.4	0.67	0.13	0.22	**0.55**	**0.36**	**0.44**	**0.745**
7	0.78	0.59	0.91	0.8	0.86	0.96	1	**0.76**	**0.91**	**0.84**	**0.745**

3.4 The Model's Algorithm

The decision algorithm is depicted in Algorithm 1:

Algorithm 1. PermissionDecisionOfRTSBAC (User *U*, Role *R*, Permission *P*)

Input: Minimal Trust value: *MTV(P(R))*
Output: The decision of granting or denying access.
      if *P(R(U))* = 1   *// permission belongs to role*
          if *UTV (U)* ≥ *MTV(P(R))* *// UTV: pre-calculated, set as attribute*
              Grant Access
        else
              Deny Access
     else
         Deny Access

3.5 Experimental Assessment and Real OSN Data Estimation of Trust

As mentioned above, the experimental evaluation of the model's trust parameters consisted of two parts:

A. A validation of the parameters by a survey of 282 OSN users that were asked for the importance of various attributes in their decisions to grant various permissions to their private data. The survey included the quantifiable attributes of user credibility and connection strength. For all these attributes, the request was for the needed threshold value of Trust of a certain user. For example, an average of 245 total friends (TF) and above was considered as a trustworthy user, to which we can share information. The results of the most important ones are presented in Table 1. Two more aspects were examined in the survey: the importance (weight) of every one of the Resembling Attributes (RA) on a scale of 1 to 10, and the importance of every one of the model's Trust attributes.

B. In the second experimental evaluation we attempt to validate the trust computation in a real OSN dataset that included 162 user nodes and their attributes, all were friends of a single ego user. This dataset of user nodes was checked for the model parameters' Trust quantifiable attribute values mentioned in the previous parts. The nodes' UTV was calculated by the formulas presented above, and the average UTV achieved by the 162 users was 0.745. When we set the MTV threshold to 0.5, we get that only 3 users were denied access. The ego user confirmed that these three users should not have been in his friends' role.

4 The Model's Extension – Partial Access for Data Anonymization

Our model's algorithm enables the complete access of information to highly trusted users or blocks it completely to undesirable ones. In this section we suggest an extension of the model such that the information access is generalized or anonymized based on the user's trust level and distance from the Ego-user. We demonstrate this idea using image anonymization, but it can also be applied to text, profile attributes and other information instances, similarly. The main idea of the model's extension of partial access is that a certain instance of data is not fully seen or unseen but can be partially scaled in its appearance. This option gives a wider information access, with the benefit of secure data anonymity. In image anonymization this feature helps reducing data leakage from facial recognition algorithms, vastly used in OSN and other Web applications. In Fig. 2 we can see the manifestation of such a partial access, where the Ego-user's profile picture is anonymized in the access granting seen in Fig. 1. For the given scenario we assume the value of 0.7 as the MTV, and the permission handled is the "visible pictures" that User 2 and User 3 obtain. User 1 does not see the image at all (left part of Fig. 2) since it does not have a fitting Role (he is "General" and the relevant Role is "acquaintance"). User 2 has a fitting Role but has a UTV of 0.56, hence he gets a blurrier image (middle part of Fig. 2) then User 3 obtains. User 3 has the fitting Role and the needed Trust value ($UTV = 0.71$), thus he gets the full image (right part of

Fig. 2). It is important to state here that this extension of the model is relevant only to these permissions that logically enable partial access. Permissions of "sharing" or "tagging" are binary by nature, hence cannot allow a partial access model.

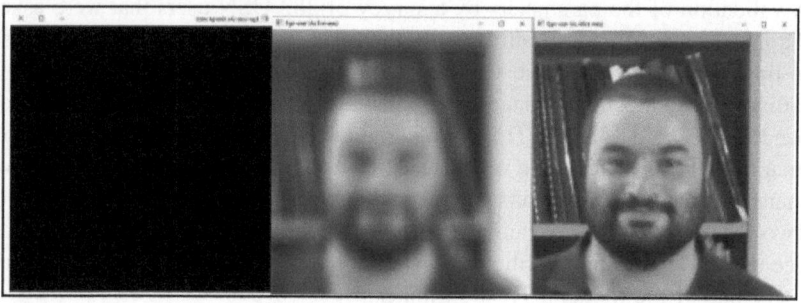

Fig. 2. Visibility of profile picture as seen by the users of Fig. 1, with a threshold *MTV* of 0.7 Left: User 1, Middle: User 2, Right: User 3.

5 Discussion and Conclusions

In this paper we have presented an Access-Control model for privacy in OSN. The novelty of our RTBAC model is its combination of User-Trust attributes, based on real OSN characteristics, in an RBAC, that usually grants permissions solely to roles, and by that improving the privacy features of the network. In this manner, it is better than current Role-based models, in which members of the same role (e.g. family or close friend) have the same set of permissions, disregarding their relationship with the Ego-user and other users, and not taking into consideration their dynamic behavior. Our model makes this permission's decision dynamic in time, since these attributes can change during time: The user gains or loses friends, its age of user account grows over time, etc. In addition, the model's extension of data anonymization is an important feature, that helps reducing the data leakage for OSN users, giving the OSN a better privacy infrastructure.

Acknowledgments. The authors would like to thank Eyal Pickholz for his assistance in the part of the model's extension of image anonymization and its software implementation. We also thank the BGU cyber center for supporting this project.

References

1. Levy, S., Gudes, E., Gal-Oz, N.: Sharing-habits based privacy control in social networks. In: Ranise, S., Swarup, V. (eds.) DBSec 2016. LNCS, vol. 9766, pp. 217–232. Springer, Cham (2016). https://doi.org/10.1007/978-3-319-41483-6_16
2. Gudes, E., Voloch, N.: An information-flow control model for online social networks based on user-attribute credibility and connection-strength factors. In: Dinur, I., Dolev, S., Lodha, S. (eds.) CSCML 2018. LNCS, vol. 10879, pp. 55–67. Springer, Cham (2018). https://doi.org/10.1007/978-3-319-94147-9_5

3. Sandhu, R.S., Coyne, E.J., Feinstein, H.L., Youman, C.E.: Role-based access control models. Computer **29**(2), 38–47 (1996)
4. Lavi, T., Gudes, E.: Trust-based dynamic RBAC. In: Proceedings of the 2nd International Conference on Information Systems Security and Privacy (ICISSP), pp. 317–324 (2016)
5. Patil, V.T., Shyamasundar, R.K.: Undoing of privacy policies on Facebook. In: Livraga, G., Zhu, S. (eds.) DBSec 2017. LNCS, vol. 10359, pp. 239–255. Springer, Cham (2017). https://doi.org/10.1007/978-3-319-61176-1_13
6. Misra, G., Such, J.M., Balogun, H.: IMPROVE-identifying minimal PROfile VEctors for similarity-based access control. In: Trustcom/BigDataSE/ISPA 2016, pp. 868–875. IEEE (2016)
7. Facebook help: roles. https://www.facebook.com/help/323502271070625/

Why We Trust Dynamic Consent to Deliver on Privacy

Arianna Schuler Scott[1]([⊠]) [iD], Michael Goldsmith[1], Harriet Teare[2], Helena Webb[1], and Sadie Creese[1]

[1] Department of Computer Science, University of Oxford, Oxford, UK
arianna.schulerscott@cs.ox.ac.uk
[2] Centre for Health, Law and Emerging Technologies,
University of Oxford, Oxford, UK

Abstract. Dynamic consent has been discussed in theory as a way to show user preferences being taken into account when data is accessed and shared for research purposes. The mechanism is grounded in principles of revocation and engagement – participants may withdraw or edit their permissions at any time, and they receive feedback on the project they are contributing to if they have chosen to do so. The level of granular control offered by dynamic consent means that individuals have informational control over what they are sharing with the study, and to what extent that data can be used further. Rather than attempt to redefine privacy, this paper takes the position that data controllers have certain obligations to protect a data subject's information and must show trustworthy behaviour to encourage research participation. Our model of privacy is grounded in normative, transaction-based requirements. We argue that dynamic consent is a mechanism that offers data controllers a way to evidence compliance with individual privacy preferences, and data subjects with control as and when they require it. The key difference between dynamic consent and a "rich" database consisting of a dataset with the ability for a subject to revoke access is human engagement, or relations of trust. We must re-think how consent is implemented from the top-down (policy-based) and bottom up (technical architecture) to develop useful privacy controls.

Keywords: Dynamic consent · Privacy · Trustworthiness · Engagement · Revocation

1 Introduction

Giving consent for a research study to make use of personal information is widely considered to be a personal and individual choice. Historically, consent procedures were meant to prevent physical harm to participants caused by unethical medical research [1]. The degree to which the choice to participate is a free one, given societal obligations and personal motivation varies depending on the study and context in which it is being done [2] but it is generally accepted that researchers are trusted to have ethical oversight of their work and are required to be able to prove that human participants elected to take part. Societal expectations around research such as to

W. Meng et al. (Eds.): IFIPTM 2019, IFIP AICT 563, pp. 28–38, 2019.
https://doi.org/10.1007/978-3-030-33716-2_3

advance thinking in expert areas, provide solutions and contribute to the betterment of society, create individual expectations which contribute to an individual's motivation to take part. They generally wish to contribute and choose what their information is used for, opting to delegate implementation to those with relevant expertise – namely, researchers [3]. There has been work done to explore the concept of "trustworthiness" where experts must demonstrate behaviour/s that justify this inherent trust in research to invite and encourage participation.

This shift towards two-way, transactional knowledge development draws parallels with some of the conceptual development around privacy, especially in medical research. In "Rethinking Informed Consent in Bioethics" [4] the authors discuss privacy as normative, grounded in how information is communicated rather than what is communicated. General privacy rules fall short, they argue, because these rules are too vague. Trying to define "data acquisition" in general as a privacy violation is too broad as there are legitimate reasons for wanting to gather data. Instead, the authors focus on narrower definitions where the means of acquisition are problematic rather than the kind of data being collected - acquiring information through intrusive or impermissible action results in violation. Technology increases the amount of information that can be put together about an individual, and be used for good or ill. Rather than simply trying to increase general trust levels, O'Neill argues that it is the placement of trust (or mistrust) that is key [5]. For individuals to place trust, institutions must show trustworthiness, or consent decisions will be made based on the lack of it. Being specific about what an individual consents to, allows controllers to be more specific as to what constitutes a violation.

This paper makes the claim that a dynamic form of consent goes some way to meeting the requirements put forward by a normative, transactional privacy model. We do not make the claim that informed consent can be used as a way for an individual to control information as this dives into a conversation that we will later address, on contemporary positions as to why current implementations of consent cannot be used to protect data (for an excellent discussion on this, see [6]). Data holds value and we discuss data protection obligations held by those who collect, store, control, use and share personal data in a research context. The term "personal information" includes: data gathered directly from someone such as name and medical history, the meaning drawn from these attributes, and inferences that can be made as part of the wider research process. Such an overwhelming amount of information can be difficult to access, to parse and to make informed decisions about and while accounts differ as to whether individuals want that level of control, institutions ultimately have legal obligations and business interests (such as not being fined) to consider.

2 Literature

Consent is a mechanism for protecting an individual's rights within research [7] and consent decisions must have the potential to change over time, simply because people are prone to changing their minds. A dynamic choice is more representative. There are areas of concern regarding informed consent: people's choices can be coerced, especially where there is a power imbalance, (online for example, where they may be forced to agree to data-sharing in order to access a service) and they often do now know the options available to them (due to obscure privacy policies and an overwhelming amount of information being presented). Even if these problems did not exist then the issue remains as to how much control data subjects actually exercise. This can be unclear due to differences between business and user requirements that often cannot be bridged [8]. Solutions exist - promoting informed consent has been shown to reduce decisional conflict and increase perceived knowledge and understanding [9], and focusing on "genuine" (rather than wholly informed consent) where individual control over permissible actions for a data controller to take, and the amount of information received from that controller [10] are the priority.

There are two significant cases where trust collapsed due to poor consent management and engagement with the public in a medical context: the scandal at Alder Hey Children's Hospital and the case of NHS England's Care.data project. Alder Hey Children's hospital did not ask parents of deceased children whether their child's organs could be used for research purposes before collecting tissue. Interestingly, it was not that the organs were used that constituted a violation, it was that parents were not asked beforehand. While medical professionals may have been guided throughout their training and careers to protect patients from hard news or difficult decisions, this case signals a shift from paternalism to more inclusive practice. While post-mortems may be carried out without parents' consent, hundreds of organs were kept for years after death which meant unfettered access to samples that were unethically procured. On the recommendations of an independent enquiry, The Human Tissue Act was established in 2004 to mandate how organs were to be used for research purposes, and an oversight committee was established: the Human Tissue Authority [11].

Care.data was not so retrospective, the project simply broke down. England's National Health Service (NHS England) wanted to implement a national database for medical records that crossed primary and secondary care. Despite the obvious benefits centralizing this kind of information might result in, the overall rollout strategy did not prioritise communication with the Great British Public. The scheme was opt-out by default which made people feel as if the decision had already been made for them, and there were no doctors or public-facing experts who could field questions or convince the public that the initiative was in any way trustworthy. Public trust in NHS England plummeted and a project that could have provided valuable services to many people was dropped. The national data guardian produced a report after the fact where she suggested that a more thought-out communication strategy and dynamic consent/opt-out procedure may have resulted in a more receptive response [12, 13].

2.1 Dynamic Consent

The "dynamics" of dynamic consent consist of: enabling individuals to give and revoke consent to the use of their samples, centralizing all transactions and interactions, allowing individuals to be approached for different projects or their feedback on emergent ethical considerations, and letting consent preferences be modified over time [18].

Dynamic consent, built on the principles of revocation and engagement, was created to address problems with one-time, broad consent. The most significant issue with broad consent is that it is not informed, due to only asking the participant once for their consent and delegating future decisions to an unseen "expert". Developed to build trust and improve participant recruitment and participation over time [14], dynamic consent builds on work done by the Ensuring Consent and Revocation (EnCoRe) project that aimed "to make giving consent as reliable and easy as turning on a tap, and revoking that consent as reliable and easy as turning it off again" [15].

Allowing people to revoke consent for data-use is one of the two underlying concepts of this model. Engaging in communication around data-use is the other. Arguments against dynamic consent decry the expense generated having to design revocation and engagement into research practice at an early stage. Granted, it may be the case that new procedures may need to be adopted, or the relationship between researcher and participant reconsidered [16] but dynamic consent improves trust in how electronic records are used because control is passed to the participant. If information has been shared without authorisation or sold then trust is lost, and when this happens then data is less likely to be shared [17] and research relies on data.

2.2 Trustworthiness

People can show trust in an institution despite a lack of trustworthy behaviour (such as transparency [18]) that they claim should be the norm. We make this point because it is pertinent that people do not have the option to behave in the way they would like to due to a lack of institutional support. Further discussion on institutional expectation lies outside the scope of this paper.

We make the distinction here between trustworthiness (shown by a data controller) and trust (given by a data subject). The fact that people are willing to entrust their data to researchers in the absence of trustworthy practice, as shown in the Alder Hey example, is significant because it strengthens the idea of a social contract between science and society. Data is derived from the public, so it must benefit them [19]. This social contract means that scientific improvement must meet the needs of the public [20], needs which can be collected and formalised using dynamic consent [21].

Privacy gives people the opportunity to negotiate how others access or use their information, and the attitude towards these "others" is influenced by the level of trust in them. There is a level of trust in research institutions that is strong enough for individuals to feel comfortable delegating decisions about unknown, broad uses of their personal data. As long as data is handled correctly, consent is revocable and studies are ethically approved [22] then broad consent is acceptable. Trust is fundamental for broad consent to be an option. Researchers are assumed to be trustworthy or have trustworthy infrastructure in place such as ethics review boards, so research participants can trust them with their consent decisions.

2.3 Privacy

Privacy is often associated with notions of self-identity [23] and individuals have been shown to want control over personal information and the decisions they make pertaining to that data [24]. There has been interesting discussion framing privacy as the freedom of an individual to make decisions that let them shape who they are [25]. In this case, the author's criticism of many privacy discussions is that while information controls are often discussed, more attention needs to be given to underlying philosophical and ethical foundations, as well as the information itself that's being controlled. In terms of research data-use, asking "which data are being used, and for what purposes" might begin to address this.

While discussing information under control, a significant area of research to mention is the development of contextual integrity, where information flows provide privacy (my doctor sends medical information to another consultant) and their breakdown constitutes a violation (my doctor sends medical information to a non-medical party) [26]. This normative stance on privacy has directly influenced the approach this paper has taken towards data-use.

3   Results

In this section we present a privacy model that compares acceptable and unacceptable scenarios given normative privacy modelling around data-sharing for research use, and an initial specification for dynamic consent as it might be implemented as part of a research project. This is novel in that we do not have any way to measure whether or not an implementation of dynamic consent is achieving what the literature positions it to do. What we find is that the unacceptable scenarios could be mitigated by incorporating dynamic consent into the research process at the design stage.

For example, just knowing what individual preferences are in terms of who data can be shared with could be used as a filter when exporting data or creating reports that are to be shared, as the EnCoRe project was able to demonstrate. We suggest that the following serve as indicators of conceptual evidence for the use of dynamic consent by data controllers as a privacy mechanism.

3.1   Privacy Model

The key sources used to build the comparisons in Table 1 were the General Data Protection Regulation (GDPR) [27] and Onora O'Neill's "Rethinking Informed Consent in Bioethics" [4]. The former provides obligations that data controllers must meet, while the latter provided a normative approach to what privacy violations could look like and how those might be avoided through developing a consent process that asks an individual for their preferences when they are recruited and allows them to change their mind.

In the case where an individual is asked about sharing their data with a third party for example, these preferences must have some level of granularity as this overarching question can be broken down further. Options may include sharing data with a third party for research use, sharing data with a third party for any purpose, and "ask me before you share my data with a third party for any reason".

In Table 1, while the placement of most statements will appear obvious, the fourth row may appear untenable to some readers. "Data is shared with explicit consent to do so" is placed under "Unacceptable" because the point of this system is not to overload the data subject with every single request for their data.

Table 1. Normative privacy in the context of research.

Acceptable	Unacceptable
Data is processed for the purposes stated with consent (of any kind) to share data for stated purposes	Data is processed for the purposes stated without consent (of any kind) to share data for stated purposes
Data is processed for unstated research purposes, with consent to only share for research purposes	Data is processed for unstated research purposes, without consent to share for other research purposes
Data is processed for commercial purposes, with consent to share for commercial purposes	Data is processed for commercial purposes, without consent to share for commercial purposes
Data is shared without explicit consent	Data is shared with explicit consent to do so
Second-order enforcement of consent means that secondary use is possible because this was indicated at the time of consent	Second-order enforcement of consent is not carried out as data is used and consent was not originally given
Second-order enforcement of consent means that secondary use is possible because this was indicated after the original consent	Second-order enforcement of consent is not carried out as data is used and consent was not given at any point

3.2   Dynamic Consent Specification

The following (Table 2) has been constructed from existing literature on dynamic consent (basic principles [16, 21], trust-building [17], interface design [29], biobank consent methods [3, 28]) and inclusive approaches to engagement (reciprocity [30, 31], awareness [32, 33] and trust [34]). This specification is currently a list of design and implementation prompts aimed at encouraging thought around data-use at the start of a research project that will make use of personal data.

Table 2. Prompts for incorporating dynamic consent and building trustworthiness into the research process.

Included	Design prompt	Implementation
☐	Will dynamic consent impact participant recruitment?	☐ Standardised recruitment ☐ No geographical limitations ☐ Process entirely/partly online ☐ Other
☐	Will dynamic consent impact how informed consent is collected?	☐ Various info. formats ☐ Record is viewable online ☐ Process can be entirely/partly online ☐ Communication options set ☐ Other
☐	Will dynamic consent impact consent management?	☐ Electronic authorisation ☐ Standardised access to preferences ☐ Secure storage/access ☐ Revocation options available ☐ Other

(*continued*)

Table 2. (*continued*)

Included	Design prompt	Implementation
☐	Will dynamic consent impact participant retention?	☐ Online forums ☐ Feedback is delivered online ☐ Data can be collected online ☐ Other
☐	Is dynamic consent going to save resources?	☐ Money ☐ Time ☐ Other
☐	What does the researcher/participant relationship look like?	☐ Is this a culture change? ☐ Participants feed into process ☐ Other
☐	Who do you have buy-in from (who gains from/supports the project)?	☐ Researchers ☐ Clinicians ☐ Public services ☐ Other
☐	How will you feed back to participants?	☐ Regularly/occasionally/when prompted ☐ Using a method they have specified ☐ Other
☐	What will you feed back to participants?	☐ Information about the research process ☐ Where their data is used ☐ Who their data has been used by ☐ Parties data is shared with ☐ Other

4 Discussion

Dynamic consent is a model resting on participant engagement and the facilitation of data, participation and consent revocation if necessary. Rather than protecting privacy as an abstract concept, this protects tangible privacy interests. Individuals need to be given the option to say no and this option needs to be communicated. There need to be options that allow data-sharing as well as options to share sharing privileges. Data subjects may want a flexible level of participation and it is the controller's responsibility to check-in (and keep checking in, especially in the case of longitudinal studies) to gauge understanding of the study, which could also indicate whether understandings are shared between controller and subject. One concern with recent data protection legislation is the level of ambiguity around implementation. Establishing transparent and relevant policy is important, but to be able to communicate and measure those rules institutionally would be invaluable when providing an audit trail, for example.

Consent provides assurance about what data is used for and why, but it has not been helpful as an information control. This is largely due to it being considered n obstacle, particularly in research where ethical oversight can delay or otherwise impact research. Rather than talk about controlling data, proponents of contextual integrity aspire to control flows of data, the contexts in which those flows act, and what happens when data crosses contexts it is not meant to. This "socialised" construct can direct technical implementation - dynamic consent could support the flow of new knowledge between the laboratory and the clinic, central to translational research and personalised medicine [21]. Consent was not designed to work as an assurance in every possible case. It can be unclear at the point of initial consent as to what exactly data might be used for and individual preferences should be direct future action. This thinking is in a similar vein as EnCoRe's development of consent preferences as filters for automated data-use [15].

Informed consent was established to prevent harm, specifically research consequences which are identifiable as they are physical or otherwise obvious. In terms of data-use, it is much harder to know what information could be used for and the impact, or impacts, this might have. Bad consent practice is demonstrated online through cookies that coerce data-donation, privacy policy obfuscation, and designs that actively draw attention away from options that inhibit data-sharing. Research involving human beings makes heavy use of consent and this is especially the case in medical research. Consent can be used as a basis for data-processing as enshrined in recent data-protection legislation like GDPR, but so can contracts, legal obligation, vital interests, public contribution or "legitimate interests". Cases in which consent might not be required might mean that anonymised datasets can be used, but individuals still express a preference for ultimate control even when publicly accessible data about them is used.

This paper models privacy as the "how" rather than the "what", focusing on safeguarding interests rather than specific pieces of information. Dynamic consent originated in the context of bio-banking where those who donate tissue may wish to delegate consent to an oversight panel or retain ultimate control over who uses what and when. In a similar vein, individuals must also make their own risk calculations when sharing personal data. As different people have different risk levels, the way in which these preferences are going to be collected must take these differences into account. This does not exclude automation – preferences should be able to be translated as rules that are checked before data is transmitted or put to use. Privacy is a moral and social issue, as is consent. A key driver behind why people should have a say is because organisations are obliged to give them one. As society tends towards inclusivity and away from paternalism in research, there is still considerable trust in experts to make decisions in the best interests of data subjects. These subjects want a say but also want to leave the details to those who know better.

5   Conclusion

Rather than trying to re-word consent forms or privacy policies the position of this paper is that an overhaul is needed. By claiming that dynamic consent can be used as a privacy control, we mean that it can be used by data subjects to manage how they share information and the extent to which those details can be shared further, and by data controllers to provide evidence that they are complying with individual consent preferences. This, by extension, provides evidence of compliance with data-protection regulations like the GDPR and the Data Protection Act.

While there are persuasive arguments as to why consent in its current form has no place in conversations around privacy, these arguments are largely grounded in two assumptions: that privacy is a social construct and that there is an ideal version of informed consent that current implementations will eventually become through various modifications. We address these concerns through two things. The first, by modelling privacy as the "how" rather than the "what", rather than focusing on which data are shared (or not) we explore how privacy interests can be safeguarded. The second is that our approach to consent is that there is no single solution, it must be flexible and allow the participant to indicate their preference or preferences for the data controller to act on accordingly.

To conclude, there are few cases in which user preferences are not sought at all regarding data-use. They may be coerced, obfuscated or hidden but they are there. Consent is a central tenet of research and needs developing as technology improves and the way we think about data changes. Dynamic consent provides an updated model for privacy control and rather than exclaim "Death to Consent!", it is our intention to demonstrate that given the very real concerns around data ownership in the digital age we find ourselves in, current practices are unfit for purpose and the need to re-think consent as a privacy control is very much alive.

6 Future Work

This is part of a work in progress, there is a clear need for empirical work that looks at whether projects that are actually implementing dynamic consent match up to the academic claims made by the literature.

References

1. Rickham, P.: Human experimentation. Code of ethics of the world medical association. Declaration of Helsinki. Br. Med. J. **2**, 177 (1964)
2. Barreteau, O., Bots, P., Daniell, K.: A framework for clarifying participation in participatory research to prevent its rejection for the wrong reasons. Ecol. Soc. **15**(2), 1–22 (2010)
3. Whitley, E., Kanellopoulou, N., Kaye, J.: Consent and research governance in biobanks: evidence from focus groups with medical researchers. Public Health Genomics **15**(5), 232–242 (2012)
4. Manson, N., O'Neill, O.: Rethinking Informed Consent in Bioethics. Cambridge University Press, Cambridge (2007)
5. O'Neill, O., Bardrick, J.: Trust, Trustworthiness and Transparency. European Foundation Centre, Brussels (2015)
6. Nissenbaum, H.: (Interview) Stop Thinking About Consent: It Isn't Possible And It Isn't Right. https://hbr.org/2018/09/stop-thinking-about-consent-it-isnt-possible-and-it-isnt-right. Accessed 25 Sept 2018
7. Boulton, M., Parker, M.: Informed consent in a changing environment. Soc. Sci. Med. **65**(11), 2187–2198 (2007)
8. Whitley, E., Kanellopoulou, N.: Privacy and informed consent in online interactions: evidence from expert focus groups. In: International Conference on Information Systems, Missouri (2010)
9. Kinnersley, P., et al.: Interventions to promote informed consent for patients undergoing surgical and other invasive healthcare procedures. Cochrane Database Syst. Rev. **7** (2013)
10. O'Neill, O.: Some limits of informed consent. J. Med. Ethics **29**, 4–7 (2003)

11. Hall, D.: Reflecting on Redfern: what can we learn from the Alder Hey story? Arch. Dis. Child. **84**(6), 455–456 (2001)
12. Limb, M.: Controversial database of medical records is scrapped over security concerns. Br. Med. J. Online **354** (2016)
13. Godlee, F.: (Editor's Choice) What can we salvage from care.data? Br. Med. J. (2016)
14. Schuler Scott, A., Goldsmith, M., Teare, H.: Wider research applications of dynamic consent. In: Kosta, E., Pierson, J., Slamanig, D., Fischer-Hübner, S., Krenn, S. (eds.) Privacy and Identity 2018. IAICT, vol. 547, pp. 114–120. Springer, Cham (2019). https://doi.org/10.1007/978-3-030-16744-8_8
15. EnCoRe: EnCoRe - Ensuring Consent and Revocation (2008). http://www.hpl.hp.com/breweb/encoreproject/index.html. Accessed 03 July 2018
16. Budin-Ljøsne, I., et al.: Dynamic consent: a potential solution to some of the challenges of modern biomedical research. BMC Med. Ethics **18**(1), 4–14 (2017)
17. Williams, H., et al.: Dynamic consent: a possible solution to improve patient confidence and trust in how electronic patient records are used in medical research. JMIR Med. Inform. **3**(1) (2015)
18. Aitken, M., Cunningham-Burley, S., Pagliari, C.: Moving from trust to trustworthiness: experiences of public engagement in the Scottish Health Informatics Programme. Sci. Public Policy **43**(5), 713–723 (2016)
19. Goodman, J. R.: A data dividend tax would help the NHS monetise health data. Br. Med. J. Opin. (2019)
20. Meslin, E.M., Cho, M.K.: Research ethics in the era of personalized medicine: updating science's contract with society. Public Health Genomics **13**(6), 378–384 (2010)
21. Kaye, J., Whitley, E., Lund, D., Morrison, M., Teare, H., Melham, K.: Dynamic consent: a patient interface for twenty-first century research networks. Eur. J. Hum. Genet. **23**, 141–146 (2015)
22. Hansson, M.G., Dillner, J., Bartram, C.R., Carlson, J.A., Helgesson, G.: Should donors be allowed to give broad consent to future biobank research? Lancet Oncol. **7**(3), 266–269 (2006)
23. Whitley, E.: Informational privacy, consent and the 'control' of personal data. Inf. Secur. Tech. Rep. **14**(3), 154–159 (2009)
24. Hammami, M.M., et al.: Patients' perceived purpose of clinical informed consent: Mill's individual autonomy model is preferred. BMC Med. Ethics **15**(1), 2 (2014)
25. Kanellopoulou, N.: Legal philosophical dimensions of privacy. EnCoRe Project Briefing Paper (2009)
26. Nissenbaum, H.: Privacy in Context: Technology, Policy, and the Integrity of Social Life. Stanford University Press, Stanford (2009)
27. European Parliament, Regulation (EU) 2016 of the European Parliament and of the Council, on the protection of natural persons with regard to the processing of personal data and on the free movement of such data, and repealing Directive 95/46/EC (General Data Protection Regulation), vol. 2012/0011 (COD) (2016)
28. Teare, H., Morrison, M., Whitley, E., Kaye, J.: Towards 'Engagement 2.0': insights from a study of dynamic consent with biobank participants. Digit. Health **1**, 1–13 (2015)
29. Sanders, C., Van Staa, T., Spencer, K., Hassan, L., Williams, H., Dixon, W.: Dynamic Consent Workshop Report: exploring new ways for patients to consent for research and use of health data (2014)
30. Gottweis, H., Gaskell, G., Starkbaum, J.: Connecting the public with biobank research: reciprocity matters. Nat. Rev. Genet. **12**(11), 738 (2011)

31. Hobbs, A., Starkbaum, J., Gottweis, U., Wichmann, H., Gottweis, H.: The privacy-reciprocity connection in biobanking: comparing German with UK strategies. Public Health Genomics **15**(5), 272–284 (2012)
32. Riordan, F., Papoutsi, C., Reed, J.E., Marston, C., Bell, D., Majeed, A.: Patient and public attitudes towards informed consent models and levels of awareness of Electronic Health Records in the UK. Int. J. Med. Inform. **84**(4), 237–247 (2015)
33. Ludman, E.J., et al.: Glad you asked: participants' opinions of re-consent for dbGaP data submission. J. Empir. Res. Hum. Res. Ethics **5**(3), 9–16 (2010)
34. Lipworth, W., Morrell, B., Irvine, R., Kerridge, I.: An empirical reappraisal of public trust in biobanking research: rethinking restrictive consent requirements. J. Law Med. **17**, 119–132 (2009)

The Reputation Lag Attack

Sean Sirur[1]([⊠]) and Tim Muller[2]

[1] University of Oxford, Oxford, UK
sean.sirur@stx.ox.ac.uk
[2] University of Nottingham, Nottingham, UK
tim.muller@nottingham.ac.uk

Abstract. Reputation systems and distributed networks are increasingly common. Examples are electronic marketplaces, IoT and ad-hoc networks. The propagation of information through such networks may suffer delays due to, e.g., network connectivity, slow reporting and rating-update delays. It is known that these delays enable an attack called the reputation lag attack. There is evidence of impact of reputation lag attacks on existing trust system proposals. There has not been in-depth formal analysis of the reputation lag attack. Here, we present a formal model capturing the core properties of the attack: firstly, the reputation of an actor failing to reflect their behaviour due to lag and, secondly, a malicious actor exploiting this for their personal gain. This model is then used to prove three key properties of the system and the attacker: if there is no decay of reputation, then the worst-case attacker behaviour is to cooperate initially, then wait, then behave badly; increasing communication between users was found to always be of benefit to the users; performing a specified number of negative interactions given any instance of the system is an NP-hard problem.

Keywords: Reputation lag · Reputation · Trust system · Attack · Malicious peer

1 Introduction

Ratings can be found as a basis for trust in various networks including e-commerce and social media. Typically, actors will rate their interactions with one another. These individual ratings are propagated through the system, and considered by others when judging who is trustworthy. Timely and effective propagation is necessary for actors to accurately judge each other. Non-ideal networks introduce lag due to network connectivity, people providing ratings late, or other reasons. An attacker can exploit this lag by engaging actors who, due to lag, have not received news of the attacker's prior negative behaviour and still consider them trustworthy. Broadly, we define a reputation lag attack as any instance where an attacker exploits a lag in the propagation of their negative reputation to allow them to perform negative actions they otherwise couldn't have.

© IFIP International Federation for Information Processing 2019
Published by Springer Nature Switzerland AG 2019
W. Meng et al. (Eds.): IFIPTM 2019, IFIP AICT 563, pp. 39–56, 2019.
https://doi.org/10.1007/978-3-030-33716-2_4

No substantial research or well-reported instances of the reputation lag attack exist (not much work has followed up [7], which introduced the notion). We do not know the scale, prevalence and effect on vulnerable networks remains unknown. Nonetheless, existing research [8] shows that the attack is viable on proposed trust systems. Attacks on trust systems often combine different types, and, e.g., fake ratings, Sybil accounts or camouflaging tactics are more obvious, so combined attacks may have been classified as these.

There is general theoretical model of reputation lag attacks. A formal model provides insight into the attacks, even without data. This paper takes a first step towards defining a general formal model of reputation lag attacks. The model successfully captures the core mechanism of the reputation lag attack: some user(s) must trust an attacker who they would not have trusted had no lag been present in the system. Three primary insights were gained from the model. Firstly, if users judge all actions equally regardless of when they occurred, there exists an ordering to the attacker's actions which is always superior to any other ordering: the attacker first behaves positively; waits for that reputation to spread through the system; and then attempts to behave negatively as much as possible before being rejected by the users. This drastically reduces the search space of possible optimal sequences of actions for the attacker. Secondly, increasing the rate of communication between users relative to the attacker is always detrimental to the attacker in the average case. Finally, how to successfully performing a specified number of negative actions for a given instance of the system is an NP-hard decidability problem for the attacker.

2   Related Work

Distributed systems can use ratings or recommendations between actors as a basis for trust, where an actor's reputation is defined through these ratings [19]. In such systems, reputation is imperative to actors' decision-making processes, for example in marketplace environments [5,18]. The delay present in the propagation of these ratings was first identified as a vulnerability by Kerr and Cohen [7] as the "reputation lag attack". The vulnerability is not present in previous surveys on reputation systems [4,13]. Hoffman, Zage and Nita-Rotaru [4] is an example of how the attack often went unrecognised. The authors decompose reputation systems into their constituent parts and discuss the vulnerabilities present in each. They are prudent in making rating propagation explicit within the *dissemination* stage. However, no notion of lag is considered here so the authors miss a likely environment for exploitation (focusing primarily on transmission integrity).

Even once discovered, the reputation lag attack remained largely unnoticed by the trust community, appearing in some subsequent surveys (e.g. [6,15]) but not others (e.g. [10]). The first analysis is performed by Kerr and Cohen [8], when investigating the success of dishonest sellers against various proposed trust systems in a simulated marketplace. They conclude that the reputation lag attack, though somewhat successful, was largely less so than other attacks, acquiring less profit and beating fewer trust systems. This finding comes with two major caveats, however: Firstly, the authors' intuitive but informal definition of reputation lag attacks assumes the attacker must at some point behave honestly. We find that no such restriction is necessary when defining the attack. The second caveat is the implementation of the lag. Every sale suffers from a constant lag before the buyer learns whether they have been cheated. There is no lag in the propagation of this information, however. This makes it difficult to separate how reputation lag effects buyers' decision given that every sale is subject to the same reputation lag effect. An implication of the above two caveats is that according to their analysis the "re-entry attack" was more successful. We argue that, due to limitations in analysis, the attack was functionally identical to the "reputation lag attack", except the attacker never needed to behave honestly (with even the author's noting this). An issue is that, beyond the initial intuition, it is not always clear what a reputation lag attack entails. We feel the issues faced in existing research motivate an abstract formal model to avoid conflating the idiosyncrasies of an attack's implementation with its analysis.

The reputation lag attack is not restricted to traditional reputation systems with many distributed networks being vulnerable to it. Commonly, strong security guarantees exist through the use of trusted authorities or shared secrets. In some networks, however, it is necessary to establish trust between nodes on a more ad-hoc basis [17]. Any delay in the communication of trust establishing information (and perhaps other "hopping" protocols) would be vulnerable to reputation lag attacks. For example, while research on reputation lag attacks in these contexts are not widespread, many instances of such networks encounter malicious peers and it is possible that the mechanisms against these attackers (e.g. distributed warning systems) are vulnerable to reputation lag attacks. Examples include peer-to-peer networks used for file-sharing (Gnutella, BitTorrent) [11,20]; ad-hoc networks (mesh networks, vehicle-to-vehicle communication) [2,14]; hardware networks (BGP/routing, IoT) [12]; and overlay networks (Tor, I2P) [1].

3 Preliminaries

In this section, some mathematical tools are defined for use later in the paper.

Sequences of events are an important notion through the paper as they are used to describe the sequential behaviour in time of the model presented herein. First, we define sequences recursively:

Definition 1 (Sequence). *A sequence $\sigma \in \Sigma$ over an alphabet $\mathcal{C}$ is recursively defined:*

$$\sigma := \begin{cases} \emptyset \\ \sigma :: c \in \mathcal{C}. \end{cases}$$

We may write $\sigma :: \sigma'$ as a shorthand, where $\sigma :: \emptyset = \sigma$ and $\sigma :: (\sigma' :: c) = (\sigma :: \sigma') :: c$. It is useful to reason about the length of a sequence, $|\overline{\sigma}|$, by letting $|\emptyset| = 0$ and $|\overline{\sigma} :: c| = |\overline{\sigma}| + 1$. This provides a mechanism for both differentiating the number of elements in sequences and assigning positions to elements of the sequence. To refer to elements or subsequences of a sequence by their position, we introduce indexing as follows:

$$\sigma_t = \begin{cases} \sigma'_t & t < |\sigma| \wedge \sigma = \sigma' :: c \\ c & t = |\sigma| \wedge \sigma = \sigma' :: c \end{cases} \tag{1}$$

$$\sigma_{x \sim y} = \begin{cases} \sigma_{x \sim y - 1} :: \sigma_y & x < y \\ \sigma_x & x = y \end{cases} \tag{2}$$

It is useful to discuss the number of occurrences of a particular subset of elements in a sequence as well as the order in which that particular subset occurs irrespective of the other elements e.g. when analysing the behaviour of that particular subset alone. This is done by extracting the subsequence of a particular element from within a sequence. The function $\sqsubset : 2^{\mathcal{C}} \times \Sigma \to \Sigma$ returns the subsequence of $\bar{\sigma}$ consisting only of the members $c \in C$ of the set of elements $C \subseteq \mathcal{C}$:

$$C \sqsubset \sigma = \begin{cases} (C \sqsubset \sigma') :: c & \text{if } \sigma = \sigma' :: c \text{ where } c \in C \\ (C \sqsubset \sigma') & \text{if } \sigma = \sigma' :: c' \text{ where } c' \notin C \\ \emptyset & \text{if } \sigma = \emptyset \end{cases} \tag{3}$$

It is useful to be able to compare two sequences, where one sequence is essentially the same as another sequence, except it has certain additional actions sprinkled in. Intuitively $\sigma \prec_C \sigma'$ means that we can transform σ' into σ, by removing certain elements $c \in C$ from σ'. So, for $c, c' \in C \subseteq \mathcal{C}$ s.t. $c \neq c'$, we define $\prec_C : 2^{\mathcal{C}} \times \Sigma \to \Sigma$:

$$\sigma \prec_C \sigma' = \begin{cases} True & \text{if } |C \sqsubset \sigma| < |C \sqsubset \sigma'| \\ & \wedge ((\mathcal{C} \backslash C) \sqsubset \sigma) = ((\mathcal{C} \backslash C) \sqsubset \sigma') \\ False & \text{otherwise} \end{cases} \tag{4}$$

Probability theory plays a significant part in the paper as the system is defined on continuous-time stochastic processes. If X is a (continuous) random variable, then $X(\omega)$ represents the outcome of X, $p(X = x)$ represents the probability density at x, $\Pr(X < x)$ represents the probability that the outcome of X is below x; so $\Pr(X < x) = \int_{-\infty}^{x} p(X = x) dx$.

The relevant stochastic processes can be modelled using continuous-time Markov chains [16]. Intuitively, a CTMC is a series of random variables indexed with a time t, representing the state at time t. More recent states are not influenced by older states, as the process must be memoryless [16].

Definition 2. *A* continuous-time Markov chain *[16] is a continuous series of random variables* $(S)_t$ *for* $t \in \mathbb{R}$, *such that for* $x > y > z$, $\Pr(S_x = s | S_y = t) = \Pr(S_x = s | S_y = t, S_z = u)$ (Fig. 1).

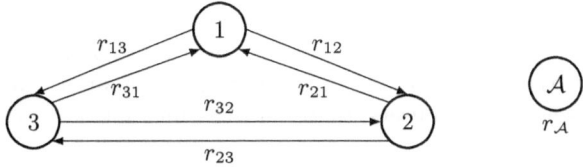

Fig. 1. A graph of users $\mathcal{U} = \{1, 2, 3\}$ and the independent attacker $\mathcal{A}$ with rate $r_{\mathcal{A}}$.

4   Model

Our aim is to model the reputation lag attack. Honest users may communicate information to each other, but when and how often depends on external factors, such as internet connectivity, configuration settings or preference. We assume that honest users do not communicate strategically, and thus model them as stochastic processes. The attacker behaves strategically and tries to act in a way to maximise how often he can cheat others, relative to cooperating with others. However, the attacker is still bound to physical limitations, and cannot act at infinite speeds. The first step is to construct a model that defines how often certain users tend to communicate, as well as how often the attacker may be able to act. We refer to this model as the *abstract model*. The *concrete model* (Sect. 4.3) is an instantiation of the abstract model, and tells us the exact communication between users.

4.1   Abstract Model

The abstract model does not tell us what is being communicated, or what actions have occurred. In order to be able to reason about the concrete communications and actions (and thus the attacker's strategy), we need to instantiate the attacker's actions appropriately. The concrete model is defined in Sect. 4.3 to facilitate this. The final step will be to define and reason about the behaviour of the attacker.

The abstract model defines when two users communicate but not what they communicate. Attacker behaviour is not explicit in the abstract model, only when the attacker has an opportunity to act. We introduce the notion of abstract traces, which specify how and when users and the attacker communicate, but not what they communicate. Users may communicate at different rates. The attacker's independent communication rate describes the rate at which they receive the opportunity to act.

Definition 3. *An abstract system $\overline{\psi} \in \overline{\Psi}$ consists of a tuple $\overline{\psi} = (\mathcal{U}, R, r_A)$: a set of users $\mathcal{U} = \{i \in \{1, ..., n\} \mid n \in \mathbb{N}_{>0}\}$; an $n \times n$ matrix R describing the communication rates between users, with $r_{ij} \in \mathbb{R}_{\geq 0}$ and $r_{ii} = 0$; and the rate $r_A \in \mathbb{R}_{\geq 0}$ with which the attacker acts.*

An abstract trace is a sequence of abstract interactions between users and the attacker. It describes in what order interactions occurred for some particular instance of the stochastic system described in Subsect. 5. It is comprised of either the empty trace; an interaction between two users; an abstract attacker action; or the concatenation of two other traces. The trace semantics takes the form of sets of messages assigned to users, representing which messages those users have received:

Definition 4 (Abstract Trace). *An abstract trace* $\overline{\sigma} \in \overline{\Sigma}$ *is a sequence over the alphabet* $\overline{C} = \{c_{ij} \mid i, j \in \mathcal{U}\} \cup \{c_{\mathcal{A}}\}$.

As a shorthand, we may write r_c to mean r_{ij} or r_A if $c = c_{ij}$ or $c = c_{\mathcal{A}}$, respectively.

The abstract model defines a stochastic system (or *probabilistic run*) describing who interacts when. In this system, the actors communicate at intervals. The time between each communication is independent of the time between the preceding communications. Formally, every action in the abstract alphabet can be modelled as a series of random variables representing the time between occurrences of that action.

Definition 5. *A* probabilistic run *of the abstract system* $\overline{\psi}$ *consists of collection of series of random variables satisfying the Markov property. For each* $c \in \overline{C}$, *the probability density functions of the corresponding series* $(m \geq 0)$ *of random variables are:*

$$p(\tau_c^m = t) = r_c e^{-r_c t}$$

We let λ_c^k be a random variable representing the time in which the kth c-action occurred: $\lambda_c^k(\omega) = \sum_{0 \leq i \leq k} \tau_c^i(\omega)$.

The probabilistic run can be viewed as a distribution over possible traces. In particular, we can say that the probabilistic run defines a (continuous-time) Markov chain, where the state consists of the current trace. First, we define the

Definition 6. *The* abstract system execution *is a continuous series of random variables* $(S)_t$ *for* $t \geq 0$, *such that* $S_0(\omega) = \emptyset$, *and for every* t, *there exists* $t' < t$ *such that either* $S_t(\omega) = S_{t'}(\omega)$ *or* $S_t(\omega) = S_{t'}(\omega) :: c$. *The latter case occurs if and only if* $t' \leq \lambda_c^k(\omega) \leq t$.

The random variable S_{10} would give you the distribution of all abstract traces of the abstract system running for 10 time units. Intuitively, the state only changes at times where the probabilistic run determines an action occurs. The definition implicitly assumes that no two actions happen at exactly the same time (and the probability of this occurring is indeed 0).

First we prove a lemma showing that the occurrence of an interaction within a particular time range is independent from any events occurring before that time range.

Lemma 1. $\Pr(t < \lambda_c^{k+1} < t' \mid \lambda_c^{k+1} > t) = \Pr(\tau_c^{k+1} \leq t' - t)$.

Proof. $\Pr(t < \lambda_c^{k+1} < t' \mid \lambda_c^{k+1} > t) = \Pr(t < \lambda_c^k + \tau_c^{k+1} < t' \mid \lambda_c^k + \tau_c^{k+1} > t) =$
$\Pr(t - \lambda_c^k < \tau_c^{k+1} < t' - \lambda_c^k \mid \tau_c^{k+1} > t - \lambda_c^k) = \frac{\Pr((t - \lambda_c^k < \tau_c^{k+1} < t' - \lambda_c^k) \wedge (\tau_c^{k+1} > t - \lambda_c^k))}{\Pr(\tau_c^{k+1} > t - \lambda_c^k)}$

$= \frac{\int_{t - \lambda_c^k}^{t' - \lambda_c^k} r_c e^{-r_c t_c} dt_c}{\int_{t - \lambda_c^k}^{\infty} r_c e^{-r_c t_c} dt_c} = \frac{e^{-r_c(t - \lambda_c^k)} - e^{-r_c(t' - \lambda_c^k)}}{e^{-r_c(t - \lambda_c^k)}} = 1 - e^{-r_c(t' - t)} = \Pr(\tau_c^{k+1} \leq t' - t)$ □

The abstract system execution is a continuous-time Markov chain:

Proposition 1. *The abstract system execution satisfies, for $x > y > z$, that $\Pr(S_x = \overline{\sigma}_x | S_y = \overline{\sigma}_y) = \Pr(S_x = \overline{\sigma}_x | S_y = \overline{\sigma}_y, S_z = \overline{\sigma}_z)$.*

Proof. Recall that user communications are exponentially distributed. The definition of an abstract system execution trivially implies that $\overline{\sigma}_{1 \sim x} = \overline{\sigma}_{1 \sim y} :: \overline{\sigma}'$, for some $\overline{\sigma}'$. If $\overline{\sigma}_{1 \sim x} = \overline{\sigma}_{1 \sim y}$, then $\Pr(S_x = \overline{\sigma}_x | S_y = \overline{\sigma}_y) = \Pr(\forall_{c,m} \lambda_c^m \notin [y, x]) = \Pr(S_x = \overline{\sigma}_x | S_y = \overline{\sigma}_y, S_z = \overline{\sigma}_z)$. If $\overline{\sigma}_x = \overline{\sigma}_y :: c$, then $\Pr(S_x = \overline{\sigma}_x | S_y = \overline{\sigma}_y) = \Pr(\forall_{c' \neq c, m} \lambda_{c'}^m \notin [y, x] \wedge \exists_m^1 \lambda_c^m \in [y, x]) = \Pr(S_x = \overline{\sigma}_x | S_y = \overline{\sigma}_y, S_z = \overline{\sigma}_z)$, again, by the memorylessness of the exponential distribution. If $\overline{\sigma}'$ isn't $\emptyset$ or in $\overline{C}$, then we can take $x > y' > y$ and recursively apply the argument.   □

In the abstract trace, the probability distribution for the "next" interaction to occur is independent of all previous occurrences. Specifically, the probability is dependent only on the relative interaction rates.

Proposition 2. *For all times t and t' s.t. $t' > t$ and for all abstract alphabets $\overline{C}$, $\Pr(S_{t'} = \overline{\sigma} :: c | S_t = \overline{\sigma})$ increases with r_c relative to $r_{c'} \in R$.*

Proof. W.l.o.g. for each set of occurrences of some interaction c we define a single natural number k_c such that $\forall_{c \in \overline{C}} \exists_{k_c}^1 \lambda_c^{k_c} \leq t < \lambda_c^{k_c + 1}$. Again, w.l.o.g. we define $t' = \min \{\lambda_c^{k_c + 1} \mid c \in \overline{C}\}$.

By applying Lemma 1, we note that the probability that some interaction c occurs within an interval $[t, t']$ is $\Pr(\lambda_c^{k+1} \in [t, t'] \mid \lambda_c^{k+1} > t) = \Pr(\tau_c^{k+1} \leq t' - t)$ which is a result of the memorylessness of the exponential distribution.

From this we may conclude that for two interactions c and c' with distributions $\tau_c = r_c e^{-r_c t_c}$ and $\tau_{c'} = r_{c'} e^{-r_{c'} t_{c'}}$ respectively: $\Pr(t < \lambda_c^{k_c + 1} < \lambda_{c'}^{k_{c'} + 1} \mid \lambda_c^{k_c + 1}, \lambda_{c'}^{k_{c'} + 1} > t) = \Pr(\tau_c^{k_c + 1} < \tau_{c'}^{k_{c'} + 1}) = \int_0^\infty r_{c'} e^{-r_{c'} t_{c'}} \int_0^{t_{c'}} r_c e^{-r_c t_c} dt_c dt_{c'} = \int_0^\infty r_{c'} e^{-r_{c'} t_{c'}} (1 - e^{-r_c t_{c'}}) dt_{c'} = r_c / (r_c + r_{c'})$. This monotonically increase with r_c and decreases with $r_{c'}$.

Thus, $\Pr(S_{t'} = \overline{\sigma} :: c \mid S_t = \overline{\sigma}) = \Pr(\lambda_c^{k_c + 1} = \min \{\lambda_{c'}^{k_{c'} + 1} \mid c' \in \overline{C}\}) = \bigwedge_{c' \in \overline{C}, c' \neq c} \Pr(t < \lambda_c^{k_c + 1} < \lambda_{c'}^{k_{c'} + 1} \mid \lambda_c^{k_c + 1}, \lambda_{c'}^{k_{c'} + 1} > t) = \prod_{c' \in \overline{C}, c' \neq c} r_c / (r_c + r_{c'})$ which monotonically increase with r_c and decreases with each $r_{c'}$. The last step follows from the fact that each interaction is independently distributed. Thus the theorem holds.   □

4.2 Reputation

Before defining the concrete model, it is important that we capture the notion of reputation. We do this through the judgement function δ. We define a judgement function as any function that defines a metric over ratings (messages) that establishes the reputation of the attacker. Users will not accept interactions with a disreputable attacker. Despite this generalised definition of δ, there are some properties which we consider key to the definition of a rational judgement function:

1. Only information known by a user can be made when judging an incoming interaction on behalf of that user.
2. Positive actions must be rewarded and negative actions punished.
3. The judgement function must accept interactions from an attacker with no known prior behaviour to ensure they can enter the system.

There are many additional properties a judgement function could satisfy. Furthermore, it would be simple to extend the model to allow different users to utilise different judgement functions thus representing the various tolerances different users may have to the attacker's behaviour. However, for the purposes of an initial analysis, the simple δ defined for all users in this paper considers only the number of $\top$ and $\bot$ interactions known to user i as arguments. This means, for instance, it is independent of the order in which messages were received and the time at which interactions occurred.

Definition 7. *The function $\delta : \mathbb{N}_0 \times \mathbb{N}_0 \to \mathbb{R}$ is an arbitrary function with the following properties:*

$$\delta(m', n) > \delta(m, n) \text{ when } m' > m \tag{5}$$
$$\delta(m, n') < \delta(m, n) \text{ when } n' > n \tag{6}$$
$$\delta(0, 0) \geq 0 \tag{7}$$

4.3   The Concrete Model

In the concrete model, the attacker instantiates their abstract actions with concrete actions consisting of an action applied to a user. Actions can have a positive impact or a negative impact, increasing or decreasing the actor's reputation respectively. Positive actions are denoted $\top$ and negative ones $\bot$. When the attacker interacts with a user through one of the above actions, a message, held by that user, is generated. This message contains information regarding what action the attacker performed. It is then propagated through the graph of users, who then use this information to judge the trustworthiness of the attacker. This captures the notion of reputation. A user receiving messages from different users reporting e.g. a positive action, must be able to distinguish which particular action is being reported. We assume users can distinguish different actions and model this using a unique index for each action.

Definition 8. *The concrete system $\psi \in \Psi$ is composed of a tuple $\psi = (\mathcal{U}, R, r_A, M, \Theta, \delta, \mathcal{A}, \varrho, \Gamma)$: set of users $\mathcal{U} = \{1, \ldots, n\}$; an $n \times n$ matrix R describing the communication rates between users, with $r_{ij} \in \mathbb{R}_{\geq 0}$ and $r_{ii} = 0$; the rate $r_A \in \mathbb{R}_{\geq 0}$ with which the attacker acts; a set of concrete messages $M = \{(\theta, i, x) \mid \theta \in \Theta, i \in \mathcal{U}, x \in \mathbb{N}\}$; two possible results $\Theta = \{\top, \bot\}$; a judgement function δ; an attacker function $\mathcal{A}$; an attacker profit function ϱ; and an instantiation function Γ.*

Every abstract trace $\overline{\sigma}$ has a set of corresponding concrete traces. A concrete trace σ is an abstract trace $\overline{\sigma}$ that has had every abstract attacker action c_A substituted with a concrete attacker action. Concrete actions consist of interacting positively or negatively with a user i ($c_i^{\top}$ or $c_i^{\bot}$) or skipping a turn ($c^{\leftharpoondown}$).

Definition 9 (Concrete Trace). *An concrete trace σ is a sequence over the alphabet $\mathcal{C} = \{c_{ij}|i,j \in \mathcal{U}\} \cup \{c_i^\theta | \theta \in \Theta, i \in \mathcal{U}\} \cup \{c^\neg\}$.*

The family of functions defining the set messages known by users in the concrete system is defined:

Definition 10. *The function $\mu_{i>0}^{O \subseteq \Theta} : \Sigma \to 2^M$ returns the set of messages held by user i concerning actions of a type in T given that the trace σ occurred:*

$$\mu_i^O(\sigma) = \begin{cases} \mu_i^O(\sigma') \cup \mu_j^O(\sigma') & \sigma = \sigma' :: c_{ji} \\ (\theta, i, |\sigma|) \cup \mu_i^O(\sigma') & (\sigma = \sigma' :: c_i^\theta) \wedge (\theta \in O) \\ \mu_i^O(\sigma') & \sigma = \sigma' :: c, \text{ for other } c \\ \emptyset & \sigma = \emptyset \end{cases} \tag{8}$$

We introduce the shorthand:

$$\mu^O(\sigma) = \bigcup_{i=1}^{\mathcal{U}} \mu_i^O(\sigma) \tag{9}$$

$$\delta_i(\sigma) = \delta(|\mu_i^\top(\sigma)|, |\mu_i^\perp(\sigma)|) \tag{10}$$

$$\delta(\sigma) = \delta(|\mu^\top(\sigma)|, |\mu^\perp(\sigma)|) \tag{11}$$

5   Reputation Lag Attack

Above we have defined the environment in which the reputation lag attack can occur. Now, we define the attacker model and the attack itself.

5.1   The Attacker Model

In this model, the attacker $\mathcal{A}$ is captured as a function which outputs a trace of concrete attacker actions which, when substituted into an abstract trace, instantiates a set of abstract attacker action. The attacker function can instantiate each abstract action with one of three actions $c_i^\top$, $c_i^\perp$ or $c^\neg$. The attacker aims to maximise their profit.

Informally, profit is (rationally) defined as any function which monotonically increases with the attacker's negative interactions and decreases with their positive interactions i.e. the profit depends on the number of negative interactions the attacker has committed relative to the number of positive interactions they have invested into the system. As such, an "optimal attacker" is defined as an attacker which, for all abstract traces $\overline{\sigma}$, can commit the maximum number of negative interactions when restricted to a particular number of positive interactions and/or given an abstract trace of finite length i.e. maximise their profit given finite resources and/or finite time.

Definition 11. *The attacker's profit function $\varrho : \Sigma \to \mathbb{R}$ is subject to the following constraints:*

$$\varrho(\sigma) < \varrho(\sigma') \text{ when } \mu^\top(\sigma) > \mu^\top(\sigma') \text{ if } \mu^\perp(\sigma) = \mu^\perp(\sigma') \tag{12}$$

$$\varrho(\sigma) > \varrho(\sigma') \text{ when } \mu^\perp(\sigma) > \mu^\perp(\sigma') \text{ if } \mu^\top(\sigma) = \mu^\top(\sigma') \tag{13}$$

In this model, different types of attacker can be delineated by how much information they have of the system when making decisions i.e. what subset of the system is considered by the attacker $\mathcal{A}(s \subseteq \psi)$. For example, it is important to consider how much of the abstract trace $\overline{\sigma}$ and attacker is aware of when making decisions. Note, for the purposes of a security analysis, assuming an apparently overestimated attacker is useful for testing the constraints of the system and providing strong guarantees of the system's resilience against attack. We will consider this when choosing $\mathcal{A}$:

1. *Attacker Model 1* in which the attacker is omniscient to the past and future i.e. the attacker can view the full abstract trace $\overline{\sigma}$ at will. This attacker's power is somewhat unrealistic as it grants the attacker the ability to see the future when making decisions but, as stated, for the purposes of a security analysis this is not unreasonable. For instance, an eavesdropping attacker that monitors a system long enough to notice a pattern in the system behaviour could be captured somewhat realistically by this model. Thus, this is the model considered in this paper.
2. *Attacker Model 2* in which the attacker is an eavesdropper to the entire system but is only aware of the past when making decisions i.e. for each abstract attacker action $\overline{\sigma}_x = c_{\mathcal{A}}$, the attacker can view $\overline{\sigma}_{1 \sim x-1}$.
3. *Attacker Model 3* in which the attacker is blinded to every interaction in $\overline{\sigma}$ which is not an attacker action i.e. the attacker only sees $c_{\mathcal{A}} \sqsubseteq \overline{\sigma}$.

Similarly, the attacker's knowledge of other aspects of the system such as the user rates R or the judgement function δ can also be allowed or restricted to different extents. However, given the fact that the attacker is solely concerned with instantiating an abstract trace such that their profit is maximised, for the most powerful attacker it is sufficient to only consider the abstract trace $\overline{\sigma}$ and the and judgement function δ.

Using this information the attacker generates a trace of concrete attacker actions $\dot{\sigma}$ such that $|\dot{\sigma}| = |c_{\mathcal{A}} \sqsubseteq \overline{\sigma}|$. This attack trace is then substituted into the full abstract trace to make a concrete trace σ:

Definition 12 (Attack Trace). *An attack trace $\dot{\sigma} \in \dot{\Sigma}$ is a sequence over the alphabet $\dot{\mathcal{C}} = \{c_i^\theta | \theta \in \Theta, i \in \mathcal{U}\} \cup \{c^\lnot\}$.*

Definition 13. *Attack traces are constructed by the attacker function $\mathcal{A} : \overline{\Sigma} \times (\mathbb{N}_0 \times \mathbb{N}_0 \to \mathbb{R}) \to \dot{\Sigma}$ defined thus:*

$$\mathcal{A}(\overline{\sigma}, \delta) = \begin{cases} \emptyset \\ \dot{\sigma} :: c_i^\theta & \text{where } (i > 0) \wedge (\theta \in \Theta) \\ \dot{\sigma} :: c^\lnot \end{cases} \tag{14}$$

We give no explicit definition of the function itself and instead explore its properties in Sect. 6. The attack trace $\dot{\sigma}$ is then substituted into the abstract trace $\overline{\sigma}$ to construct the concrete trace σ. This is performed by an instantiation function. To model the fact that users will not accept interactions with a disreputable attack, the instantiation function will substitute any rejected attacker actions with a $c^{\hookleftarrow}$ action. User i judges the attacker at each attacker action $c_i^{\theta \in \Theta}$ via δ with only the information known to them:

Definition 14. *The instantiation function $\Gamma : \overline{\Sigma} \times \dot{\Sigma} \to \Sigma$ is defined:*

$$\Gamma_\delta(\overline{\sigma}, \dot{\sigma}) = \begin{cases} \emptyset & if \ \overline{\sigma} = \dot{\sigma} = \emptyset \\ c_{ij} :: \Gamma_\delta(\overline{\sigma}', \dot{\sigma},) & if \ \overline{\sigma} = c_{ij} :: \overline{\sigma}' \\ c :: \Gamma_\delta(\overline{\sigma}', \dot{\sigma}') & if \ (\overline{\sigma} = c_{\mathcal{A}} :: \overline{\sigma}') \wedge (\dot{\sigma} = c :: \dot{\sigma}') \wedge (\delta_i(\sigma') \geq 0) \\ c^{\hookleftarrow} :: \Gamma_\delta(\overline{\sigma}', \dot{\sigma}') & if \ (\overline{\sigma} = c_{\mathcal{A}} :: \overline{\sigma}') \wedge (\dot{\sigma} = c :: \dot{\sigma}') \wedge (\delta_i(\sigma') < 0) \end{cases}$$

$$(15)$$

If none of the attacker's actions are denied by a user, we deem that attack trace *complete* for $\overline{\sigma}$. Otherwise, we deem it *incomplete* for $\overline{\sigma}$.

5.2 The Reputation Lag Attack

Here the reputation lag itself is defined in terms of the model presented thus far. Informally, a reputation lag attack occurs when the attacker is allowed to perform a (presumably malicious) interaction with a user who would have rejected the interaction had they had perfect information of the attacker's prior actions. By construction, any example of imperfect user knowledge within this model stems directly from a failure of the system to propagate the messages in a timely manner. While this definition is very high-level, it successfully captures every instance which could be considered a reputation lag attack.

If an attacker interaction with user i is accepted by that user using only the information (messages) known to them but is rejected when using all the information present in the system, then a reputation lag attack has occurred.

First, we define an omniscient instantiation function in which users judge the attacker with all the information available in the system:

Definition 15. *The omniscient instantiation function $\Gamma^* : \overline{\Sigma} \times \dot{\Sigma} \to \Sigma$ is defined:*

$$\Gamma_\delta^*(\overline{\sigma}, \dot{\sigma}) = \begin{cases} \emptyset & if \ \overline{\sigma} = \dot{\sigma} = \emptyset \\ c_{ij} :: \Gamma_\delta^*(\overline{\sigma}', \dot{\sigma}) & if \ \overline{\sigma} = c_{ij} :: \overline{\sigma}' \\ c :: \Gamma_\delta^*(\overline{\sigma}', \dot{\sigma}') & if \ (\overline{\sigma} = c_{\mathcal{A}} :: \overline{\sigma}') \wedge (\dot{\sigma} = c :: \dot{\sigma}') \wedge (\delta(\sigma') \geq 0) \\ c^{\hookleftarrow} :: \Gamma_\delta^*(\overline{\sigma}', \dot{\sigma}') & if \ (\overline{\sigma} = c_{\mathcal{A}} :: \overline{\sigma}') \wedge (\dot{\sigma} = c :: \dot{\sigma}') \wedge (\delta(\sigma') < 0) \end{cases}$$

$$(16)$$

Here we define the reputation lag attack indicator. If the attacker has an increased profit when instantiated normally compared to when instantiated by the omniscient function (i.e. if the attacker has successfully exploited the lag for their own gain), a reputation lag attack has occurred.

Definition 16. *The reputation lag attack indicator is defined:*

$$\mathrm{RLA}_\delta^\varrho(\overline{\sigma}, \dot{\sigma}) = \begin{cases} 1 & \varrho(\Gamma_\delta(\overline{\sigma}, \dot{\sigma})) > \varrho(\Gamma_\delta^*(\overline{\sigma}, \dot{\sigma})) \\ 0 & \varrho(\Gamma_\delta(\overline{\sigma}, \dot{\sigma})) = \varrho(\Gamma_\delta^*(\overline{\sigma}, \dot{\sigma})) \end{cases} \tag{17}$$

6   Results

The primary motivation for the above formalism is to provide insight into the reputation lag attack. Here we elicit the three following key properties of the attack: the definition of δ defined herein is shown to be vulnerable to a superior ordering of attacker actions; increasing the rate of user communication is shown to never be detrimental to the users and could be detrimental to the attacker in the average case; the decidability problem of whether the attacker can perform a specified number of negative actions is shown to be have an NP-hard computational complexity.

6.1   Attack Ordering

The order in which the attacker executes their actions has an impact on their success. In a structured attack trace, the attacker goes through three phases: a $\top$ phase, a $\llcorner$ phase and a $\bot$ phase. In a given phase, the attacker only executes actions of that type. We show that structured attack traces, under the particular δ defined in the above model, are always superior to unstructured strategies. Intuitively, this results from the fact that positive actions occurring earlier in the trace gives them more chance to be propagated whilst negative occurring later in the trace have less time to be propagated.

Definition 17. *Define the reflexive partial order $<_\mathcal{A}$ on attacker actions, s.t. $c_i^\top <_\mathcal{A} c^\llcorner <_\mathcal{A} c_j^\bot$, for all i,j. We define the partial order $<_\mathcal{A}$ on traces as $\dot{\sigma} :: c :: c' :: \dot{\sigma}' <_\mathcal{A} \dot{\sigma} :: c' :: c :: \dot{\sigma}'$ iff $c <_\mathcal{A} c'$.*

Proposition 3. *For every $\dot{\sigma}$, there is a minimal element $\dot{\sigma}' <_\mathcal{A} \dot{\sigma}$, and this minimal element has the property that it is a structured attack trace.*

Proof. If $\dot{\sigma}'$ is structured, then there is no $\dot{\sigma}' = \dot{\sigma}_1 :: c :: c' :: \dot{\sigma}_2$ where $c' <_\mathcal{A} c$, so $\dot{\sigma}'$ is a minimal element. Vice versa, any minimal element may not be of the shape $\dot{\sigma}' = \dot{\sigma}_1 :: c :: c' :: \dot{\sigma}_2$ either, so it must structured.

Theorem 1. *For all abstract traces $\overline{\sigma}$; attack traces $\dot{\sigma}$ and $\dot{\sigma}' <_\mathcal{A} \dot{\sigma}$ (where $\dot{\sigma}$ is complete for $\overline{\sigma}$); users i; and locations $x \leq |\overline{\sigma}|$: $\delta_i(\Gamma_\delta(\overline{\sigma}, \dot{\sigma}')) \geq \delta_i(\Gamma_\delta(\overline{\sigma}, \dot{\sigma}))$*

Proof. Consider two adjacent attacker actions $\dot{\sigma}_a$ and $\dot{\sigma}_{a+1}$. We denote their corresponding positions in the abstract (or concrete) traces as $\overline{\sigma}_y$ and $\overline{\sigma}_z$ respectively. Two cases follow from this: $\dot{\sigma}_a <_\mathcal{A} \dot{\sigma}_{a+1}$ and $\dot{\sigma}_{a+1} <_\mathcal{A} \dot{\sigma}_a$.

Case 1 ($\dot{\sigma}_a <_\mathcal{A} \dot{\sigma}_{a+1}$): This implies $\dot{\sigma}'\dot{\sigma}$. In this, it follows trivially that $\delta_i(\Gamma_\delta(\overline{\sigma}, \dot{\sigma}')) \geq \delta_i(\Gamma_\delta(\overline{\sigma}, \dot{\sigma}))$

Case 2 ($\dot{\sigma}_{a+1} <_{\mathcal{A}} \dot{\sigma}_a$): We construct $\dot{\sigma}'$ by swapping the two elements in question: $\dot{\sigma}' = \dot{\sigma}_{1\sim a-1} :: \dot{\sigma}_{a+1} :: \dot{\sigma}_a :: \dot{\sigma}_{a+2\sim|\dot{\sigma}|}$. This implies that $\sigma_{1\sim x-1} = \sigma'_{1\sim x-1}$ and $\sigma_{y+1\sim|\sigma|} = \sigma'_{y+1\sim|\sigma'|}$. We consider the case where $\dot{\sigma}_{a+1} = \dot{\sigma}'_a = c_i^\top$. We notice two things: firstly, user i is still aware of the $c_i^\top$ action at the time of σ'_z and so has lost no information in comparison to σ.

Secondly, we notice that the earlier introduction of $c_i^\top$ creates the opportunity for it to be propagated between σ'_y and σ'_z and thus possibly even further. Essentially, more users $u \neq i$ may be aware of the $c_i^\top$ in σ' than in σ from point y onward: for all users u and locations $x \geq y$, $\mu_u^\top(\Gamma_\delta(\overline{\sigma}, \dot{\sigma})_{1\sim x}) \subseteq \mu_u^\top(\Gamma_\delta(\overline{\sigma}, \dot{\sigma}')_{1\sim x}) \implies |\mu_u^\top(\Gamma_\delta(\overline{\sigma}, \dot{\sigma}')_{1\sim x})| \geq |\mu_u^\top(\Gamma_\delta(\overline{\sigma}, \dot{\sigma}')_{1\sim x})|$.

A symmetrical argument in the case that $\dot{\sigma}_a = \dot{\sigma}'_{a+1} = c_i^\perp$ leads us to conclude that the each user is aware of less or equal negative actions after the swap: for all users u and locations $x \geq |\sigma|$, $|\mu_u^\perp(\Gamma_\delta(\overline{\sigma}, \dot{\sigma}')_{1\sim x})| \leq |\mu_u^\perp(\Gamma_\delta(\overline{\sigma}, \dot{\sigma})_{1\sim x})|$. We also see from both arguments that the case in which one of the swapped attacker actions are $c^\hookleftarrow$, that particular action has no effect on the knowledge of the users i.e. the inequality holds trivially. By the definition of $<_{\mathcal{A}}$, it is not possible for two actions to be swapped where both actions are of the same type (e.g. where both are positive).

The increased awareness of positive interactions and the decreased awareness of negative ones coupled with the monotonicity of δ implies that, for all users i and locations $x \leq |\sigma|$, $(|\mu_u^\top(\Gamma_\delta(\overline{\sigma}, \dot{\sigma}')_{1\sim x})| \geq |\mu_u^\top(\Gamma_\delta(\overline{\sigma}, \dot{\sigma})_{1\sim x})|) \wedge (|\mu_u^\top(\Gamma_\delta(\overline{\sigma}, \dot{\sigma}')_{1\sim x})| \leq |\mu_u^\top(\Gamma_\delta(\overline{\sigma}, \dot{\sigma})_{1\sim x})|) \implies \delta_i(\Gamma_\delta(\overline{\sigma}, \dot{\sigma}')_{1\sim x}) \geq \delta_i(\Gamma_\delta(\overline{\sigma}, \dot{\sigma})_{1\sim x})$.

By transitivity of $<_{\mathcal{A}}$, the proof for pairs holds for all traces. Proposition 3 shows that the optimal ordering is structured. $\qquad\square$

Thus, for all complete attack traces, structured traces are superior. We restrict our theorem to complete attack traces as incomplete traces contain counterexamples and any optimal attack trace will be complete. Structuring may not affect profit but it reduces the search space of attack traces as the optimal strategy must be structured. However, structuring is dependent on the judgement function. A judgement function in which reputation decays with time would be sensitive to abrupt changes in behaviour such as in a structured attack trace, thus making time-dependent judgement a simple but effective mitigation.

6.2   Effect of Communication Rates on the Attacker Strategy

Considering a structured attack trace $\dot{\sigma}$ with optimal dealing (i.e. the users are aware of every $\top$ in the system when the attacker is in their $\perp$ phase), we show that increasing the communication rates is detrimental to the attacker. For the purposes of this analysis we focus on effectively cheating users, hence the assumption that we are in a state where the knowledge of the deals has spread to all users, and the attacker is in the $\perp$ stage of their structured attack.

We formulate our theorem as follows:

Theorem 2. *Let $\overline{\psi}, \overline{\psi}'$ be a pair of abstract systems differing only in their respective matrices R, R', such that $\exists_{i,j}(r_{ij} < r'_{ij}) \wedge (\forall_{p \neq i, q \neq j} r_{pq} = r'_{pq})$.*

For any time $t > 0$; any attack trace $\acute{\sigma} <_A \dot{\sigma}$; any concrete trace $\sigma = \sigma^\top$ :: $\sigma^\smile$ :: $\sigma^\perp$ s.t. $\forall_{i \in \mathcal{U}} c_i^\perp \sqsubseteq (\sigma^\top :: \sigma^\smile) = \emptyset$ and $\forall_{i \in \mathcal{U}} \mu_i^\top (\sigma^\top :: \sigma^\smile) = \mu^\top (\sigma^\top :: \sigma^\smile)$; and any pair of system executions S_t and S'_t corresponding to abstract systems $\overline{\psi}$ and $\overline{\psi}'$ then:

$$\Pr(\text{RLA}_\delta^\varrho(S'_t(\omega), \dot{\sigma}) = 1) < \Pr(\text{RLA}_\delta^\varrho(S_t(\omega), \dot{\sigma}) = 1)$$

Proof. For notational convenience, we define $C_{\mathcal{U}} = \{c_{ij} \mid r'_{ij} = r_{ij}\}$ and $C'_{\mathcal{U}} = \{c_{ij} \mid r'_{ij} > r_{ij}\}$

We prove that if $\sigma \prec_{C'_{\mathcal{U}}} \sigma'$, then the attacker's reputation during their misbehaving phase (i.e. during $\sigma^\perp$) can only decrease in σ' compared to their reputation in σ. If $\sigma = \sigma_1 :: \sigma_2$ and $\sigma' = \sigma_1 :: c_{ij} :: \sigma_2$ for some $c_{ij} \in C'_{\mathcal{U}}$, then for every user h, either $\mu_h(\sigma') = \mu_h(\sigma)$ or $\mu_h(\sigma') = \mu_h(\sigma) \cup \mu_j(\sigma_1)$. The latter means that the messages j told i after σ_1 have reached h, the former means that they have not, implying $\mu_h(\sigma) \subseteq \mu_h(\sigma')$. For any two traces with $\sigma \prec_{\{c_{ij}\}} \sigma'$ we can iteratively apply this argument for the additional messages. Due to the well-disseminated good messages $\forall_{i \in \mathcal{U}} \mu_i^\top (\sigma^\top :: \sigma^\smile) = \mu^\top (\sigma^\top :: \sigma^\smile)$ and the fact that no new good interactions occur in $\sigma^\perp$, it is not possible for the users to learn any good messages during $\sigma^\perp$. This, combined with the monotonicity of δ, implies that the users may only know additional negative messages during the attacker's $\perp$ phase. Thus the reputation can only decrease along with the possibility of a reputation lag attack occurring. For notational convenience (and brevity), if we define w.l.o.g. $\{k_1, \ldots, k_n\}$ as the set of indices of the attacker's $\perp$ actions in trace σ and $\{k'_1, \ldots, k'_n\}$ as the corresponding indices in σ': $\forall_{i \in \mathcal{U}} \forall_{x \in [1,n]} (\mu_i^\top (\sigma_{1 \sim k_x}) = \mu_i^\top (\sigma'_{1 \sim k'_x})) \wedge (\mu_i^\perp (\sigma_{1 \sim k_x}) \subseteq \mu_i^\perp (\sigma'_{1 \sim k'_x})) \implies \delta_i(\sigma'_{1 \sim k'_x}) \leq \delta_i(\sigma_{1 \sim k_x}) \implies \text{RLA}_\delta^\varrho(\overline{\sigma}', \dot{\sigma}) \leq \text{RLA}_\delta^\varrho(\overline{\sigma}, \dot{\sigma})$. Thus, σ' is more robust to the reputation lag attack than σ. This is our first finding.

Now we show that $\overline{\psi}'$ has a higher probability of outputting traces with more communication (and which are thus more likely to be robust) than $\overline{\psi}$. By definition, the probability of n occurrences of c_{pq} before some time t is described by a homogeneous Poisson process [9]: $\Pr(N(t)_{pq} = n) = \frac{(r_{pq}t)^n}{n!} e^{-r_{pq}t}$. When t is the time of the last event in an abstract trace, this shows us that the expected number of occurrences of c_{pq} within a trace increases with the rate r_{pq} independently of any other rate or interaction $c_{ij} \neq c_{pq}$.

Similarly to Lemma 1, it can also be shown that the probability of n occurrences of c_{pq} happening between times t_1 and t_2 is dependent only on the time range $[t_1, t_2]$ and independent of the events preceding t_1. Thus, $\forall_{t_2 > t_1} \Pr(N(t_1 < t < t_2)_{pq} = n \mid t > t_1)) = \Pr(N(t_2 - t_1)_{pq} = n)$. From this we see that the expected number of c_{pq} occurrences within a given time range increases with only its own rate r_{pq} independently of events prior to that time range or any other rate. For example, the number of c_{pq} occurrences between two other actions $\overline{\sigma}_1, \overline{\sigma}_2 \neq c_{pq}$ is dependent only on r_{pq} and the time between the actions.

From the above two findings alongside the premise, we may infer that the system execution S'_t is as likely to output a particular number and ordering of $C_{\mathcal{U}}$ interactions as S_t but is more likely to output $C'_{\mathcal{U}}$ interactions between any two $C_{\mathcal{U}}$ interactions. Hence, the traces output by S'_t are more communicative and, by our first finding in this proof, more likely to be robust than those of S_t:

$$\left(\frac{\Pr(|C'_{\mathcal{U}} \sqsubset S'_t(\omega)| > |C'_{\mathcal{U}} \sqsubset S_t(\omega)|)}{\Pr(|C'_{\mathcal{U}} \sqsubset S'_t(\omega)| < |C'_{\mathcal{U}} \sqsubset S_t(\omega)|)} > 1\right) \wedge \left(\frac{\Pr(|C_{\mathcal{U}} \sqsubset S'_t(\omega)| > |C_{\mathcal{U}} \sqsubset S_t(\omega)|)}{\Pr(|C_{\mathcal{U}} \sqsubset S'_t(\omega)| < |C_{\mathcal{U}} \sqsubset S_t(\omega)|)} = 1\right)$$

$$\implies \frac{\Pr(S_t\omega \prec_{C'_{\mathcal{U}}} S'_t\omega)}{\Pr(S'_t\omega \prec_{C'_{\mathcal{U}}} S_t\omega)} > 1 \implies \Pr(\mathrm{RLA}^\varrho_\delta(S'_t(\omega), \acute\sigma) = 1) < \Pr(\mathrm{RLA}^\varrho_\delta(S_t(\omega), \acute\sigma) = 1).$$

Thus the theorem holds. □

6.3 NP-Hardness

While strategies may exist to improve the attacker's profit in different scenarios, it is important to consider the feasibility of the optimal attacker. A polynomial optimal strategy for a given judgement function would be the ideal goal for any attacker. However, we show below that, for any judgement function, the computation complexity of constructing a strategy which can perform a specified number of negative interactions is NP-hard.

Theorem 3. *For any judgement function δ, the decidability problem of whether it is possible to perform m cheats without performing deals is NP hard.*

Proof. We provide a reduction to the 3-SAT problem, which is NP-complete [3]. In this proof outline, we provide the reduction itself, but omit the full proof that it is indeed a reduction. The full proof is a tedious exercise in bookkeeping, whereas the reduction provides insight in why it is NP-hard.

Let $X = x_1 \ldots x_k$ be the set of variables in the 3-sat problem. Let ℓ_{ij} be the jth literal in the ith clause. Assume there are n clauses.

For each variable take a user for its positive and negative atom, take a user for each literal in the formula, and we add an additional pair of users for every variable: $\mathcal{U} = \{u_{x_i}, u_{\neg x_i} | x_i \in X\} \cup \{v_{ij} | \ell_{ij}\} \cup \{v_{x_i}, v_{\neg x_i} | x_i \in X\}$. A pseudo clause is formed by each pair of users in the last set – they represent the clause $x \vee \neg x$. There are a total of $n + k$ (pseudo) clauses. The set $U^{\geq h} = \{v_{ij} | i \geq h, \ell_{ij}\} \cup \{v_{x_i}, v_{\neg x_i} | i + n \geq h, x_i \in X\}$. As a short-hand, we say a set of users performs a kill-communication, if they communicate their messages to all other users $(O(n^2))$.

Consider an abstract trace $\bar\sigma$ with the following shape:

- The trace starts with k attacker actions.
- Then, for $h \in [1, \ldots k + n]$ do:
  - Users $U^{\geq h}$ perform a kill-communication.
  - The users u_x, u_y, u_z, corresponding to the inverse of literals $\ell_{h1}, \ell_{h2}, \ell_{h3}$ send a single communication to the respective literals.
  - The attacker gets 1 action.
  - All users u_x and $u_{\neg x}$ communicate to $\ell_{h1}, \ell_{h2}, \ell_{h3}$.

– After performing these $k + n$ steps, the attacker gets k more actions.

The decidability question for k variables and n clauses is whether the attacker can perform $n + 3k$ actions. The size of the trace $\overline{\sigma}$ is $O(n^3)$, which is polynomial. $\square$

7   Conclusion

The formalism captured the two core properties of the attack: firstly, users inaccurately judging the reputation of the attacker due to incomplete knowledge caused by reputation lag and, secondly, a malicious actor exploiting this for their personal gain. The primary aim of the paper was to gain insight regarding the attacker's strategies to help with both mitigation and detection of the attack. There were three key outcomes: Theorem 1 shows how to re-order the attacker's actions, to increase the power of the attack: the attacker behaves positively; waits for this reputation to spread to as many users as possible; then begins behaving as negatively as possible before the users reject them. The fact that our judgement function, which models reputation, does not have a decay factor is a crucial ingredient for this theorem. Trust/reputation with decay factors may be somewhat more resistant against these attacks. Theorem 2 showed that, when dealing with an optimally dealing attacker, increasing user communication rates cannot be detrimental to users and may be detrimental to the attacker. Intuitively, this follows directly from the definition of the reputation lag attack which relies on poor user communication. However, as also evidenced by Theorem 3, the issue of determining the effectiveness of attacks is difficult, so it is important to have a proof of our intuitions. Finally, Theorem 3 showed that performing a specified number of negative interactions given any instance of the system $\overline{\sigma}$ is an NP-hard problem, implying the optimal attacker is computationally unfeasible.

Our definitions were chosen to be sufficiently abstract to cover a variety of systems and are readily extendable to more than one particular reputation system. The class of systems we consider are those systems where users communicate certain information about how other users have acted in the past, where good behaviour offsets bad behaviour, and too much bad behaviour leads to refusing to interact. We argue that many systems that consist of a distributed set of entities communicating knowledge about one another could be defined through the presented model with some modification.

Here we discuss further study. There is much to learn about the system and its effect on the attacker e.g. the effects of different judgement functions or how profit functions affect them. Investigating the combination of the reputation lag attack with other attacks may be of use for learning in which environments the attack is likely to be. Identifying real-world examples of the attack would also offer insight into the effectiveness of the model. Further investigation into the attacker's strategy is a vital next step as understanding identifying likely attack patterns is imperative not only to mitigating but also to detecting reputation lag attacks in the wild.

This paper provided a formal model of the reputation lag attack. The formalism captured the core properties of reputation lag attacks. The formalism allowed us to prove three interesting properties of the reputation lag attack: deals before cheats, communication benefits users but not the attacker, and finding optimal attacks is NP-hard. However, the analysis presented here is still in early stages. We hope to apply some of our techniques in practice, as well as continue to strengthen the formalism. The attacker's strategies and their relationship with the system as a whole warrants further study.

References

1. Egger, C., Schlumberger, J., Kruegel, C., Vigna, G.: Practical attacks against the I2P network. In: Stolfo, S.J., Stavrou, A., Wright, C.V. (eds.) RAID 2013. LNCS, vol. 8145, pp. 432–451. Springer, Heidelberg (2013). https://doi.org/10.1007/978-3-642-41284-4_22

2. Fogue, M., et al.: Securing warning message dissemination in VANETs using cooperative neighbor position verification. IEEE Trans. Veh. Technol. **64**(6), 2538–2550 (2015). https://doi.org/10.1109/TVT.2014.2344633

3. Garey, M., Johnson, D.: Continuous-time Markov chains I, pp. 259–260. W. H. Freeman & Co. (1990)

4. Hoffman, K., Zage, D., Nita-Rotaru, C.: A survey of attack and defense techniques for reputation systems. ACM Comput. Surv. **42**, 1–31 (2009). https://doi.org/10.1145/1592451.1592452

5. Jolivet, G., Jullien, B., Postel-Vinay, F.: Reputation and prices on the e-market: evidence from a major French platform. Int. J. Ind. Organ. **45**, 59–75 (2016). https://doi.org/10.1016/j.ijindorg.2016.01.003. http://www.sciencedirect.com/science/article/pii/S0167718716000059

6. Jøsang, A., Golbeck, J.: Challenges for robust trust and reputation systems. In: Proceedings of the 5th International Workshop on Security and Trust Management (STM 2009) (2009)

7. Kerr, R., Cohen, R.: Modeling trust using transactional, numerical units, pp. 21:1–21:11 (2006). https://doi.org/10.1145/1501434.1501460

8. Kerr, R., Cohen, R.: Smart cheaters do prosper. In: AAMAS 2009 Proceedings of The 8th International Conference on Autonomous Agents and Multiagent Systems, vol. 2, pp. 993–1000 (2009)

9. Kingman, J.: Poisson Processes. Clarendon Press, Oxford (1990)

10. Koutrouli, E., Tsalgatidou, A.: Taxonomy of attacks and defense mechanisms in P2P reputation systems - lessons for reputation system designers. Comput. Sci. Rev. **6**(2), 47–70 (2012). https://doi.org/10.1016/j.cosrev.2012.01.002. i/S1574013712000093

11. Lee, S., Zhu, S., Kim, Y., Chang, J.: Analysis on malicious peer's behavior of the P2P trust resource chain model. In: Lee, R. (ed.) Software Engineering, Artificial Intelligence, Networking and Parallel/Distributed Computing. SCI, vol. 149, pp. 89–102. Springer, Heidelberg (2008). https://doi.org/10.1007/978-3-540-70560-4_8

12. Liu X., Abdelhakim, M., Krishnamurthy, P., Tipper, D.: Identifying malicious nodes in multihop IoT networks using diversity and unsupervised learning, pp. 1–6 (2018). https://doi.org/10.1109/ICC.2018.8422484

13. Marti, S., Garcia-Molina, H.: Taxonomy of trust: categorizing P2P reputation systems. Comput. Netw. **50**(4), 472–484 (2006). https://doi.org/10.1016/j.comnet.2005.07.011

14. Meng, Y., Li, W., Kwok, L.: Evaluation of detecting malicious nodes using Bayesian model in wireless intrusion detection. In: Lopez, J., Huang, X., Sandhu, R. (eds.) NSS 2013. LNCS, vol. 7873, pp. 40–53. Springer, Heidelberg (2013). https://doi. org/10.1007/978-3-642-38631-2_4

15. Muller, T., Liu, Y., Mauw, S., Zhang, J.: On robustness of trust systems. In: Zhou, J., Gal-Oz, N., Zhang, J., Gudes, E. (eds.) IFIPTM 2014. IFIPAICT, vol. 430, pp. 44–60. Springer, Heidelberg (2014). https://doi.org/10.1007/978-3-662-43813-8_4

16. Norris, J.: Continuous-time Markov chains I, pp. 59–111. Cambridge University Press (1997). https://doi.org/10.1017/CBO9780511810633

17. Pirzada, A., M.C.: Establishing trust in pure ad-hoc networks. In: Proceedings of the 27th Australasian Conference on Computer Science, vol. 26, pp. 47–54. Australian Computer Society, Inc. (2004)

18. Przepiorka, W.: Buyers pay for and sellers invest in a good reputation: more evidence from eBay. J. Socio-Econ. **42**, 31–42 (2013). https://doi.org/10.1016/j. socec.2012.11.004. http://www.sciencedirect.com/science/article/pii/S105353571 2001163

19. Yahalom, R., Klein, B., Beth, T.,: Trust relationships in secure systems-a distributed authentication perspective. In: Proceedings of 1993 IEEE Computer Society Symposium on Research in Security and Privacy, pp. 150–164 (1993). https:// doi.org/10.1109/RISP.1993.287635

20. Zeinalipour-Yazti, D.: Exploiting the security weaknesses of the Gnutella protocol (2002)

An Unforeseen Equivalence Between Uncertainty and Entropy

Tim Muller[(✉)]

University of Nottingham, Nottingham, UK
tim.muller@nottingham.ac.uk

Abstract. Uncertainty and entropy are related concepts, so we would expect there to be some overlap, but the equality that is shown in this paper is unexpected. In Beta models, interactions between agents are evidence used to construct Beta distributions. In models based on the Beta Model, such as Subjective Logic, uncertainty is defined to be inversely proportional to evidence. Entropy measures measure how much information is lacking in a distribution. Uncertainty was neither intended nor expected to be an entropy measure. We discover that a specific entropy measure we call *EDRB* coincides with uncertainty whenever uncertainty is defined. EDRB is the expected Kullback-Leibler divergence between two Bernouilli trials with parameters randomly selected from the distribution. EDRB allows us to apply the notion of uncertainty to other distributions that may occur in the context of Beta models.

Keywords: Uncertainty · Entropy · Information theory · Beta model · Subjective logic

1 Introduction

The Beta model paradigm is a powerful formal approach to studying trust. Bayesian logic is at the core of the Beta model: "agents with high integrity behave honestly" becomes "honest behaviour evidences high integrity". Its simplest incarnation is to apply Beta distributions naively, and this approach has limited success. However, more powerful and sophisticated approaches are widespread (e.g. [3,13,17]). A commonality among many approaches, is that more evidence (in the form of observing instances of behaviour) yields more certainty of an opinion. Uncertainty is inversely proportional to the amount of evidence.

Evidence is often used in machine learning. It is no surprise that there is a close link between trust models and machine learning, since the goal is to automatically create a model, based on observed data. The Beta model is based a simple Bayesian technique found in machine learning. More involved techniques may introduce hidden variables [13] or hidden Markov models [3,18]. Uncertainty as the inverse of (or lack of) evidence makes sense in this context.

© IFIP International Federation for Information Processing 2019
Published by Springer Nature Switzerland AG 2019
W. Meng et al. (Eds.): IFIPTM 2019, IFIP AICT 563, pp. 57–72, 2019.
https://doi.org/10.1007/978-3-030-33716-2_5

We have obtained successful results applying information theory to analyse trust ratings [15,16]. Informative ratings are more useful than uninformative ones. Others have applied information theory to trust modelling in different ways, e.g. [1,2]. However, these approaches contrast the evidence-based approaches – they were not considered to be equivalent approaches. In fact, we have studied the possibility of combining uncertainty and entropy, to understand their interplay, in [12] – and we had not expected that they would turn out to coincide.

The purpose of this paper is to demonstrate a surprising equivalence. The uncertainty used in this paper is fundamentally different from entropy in information theory. There are various entropy measures that one can define, but the standard measures do not yield an equivalence to uncertainty. However, we formulate a specific entropy measure – that we call expected Kullback-Leibler divergence of random-parameter Bernoulli trials (EDRB) – which does equate to uncertainty. The proof is based on a specific properties of functions related to Beta distributions, and does not seem provide insight in why the two are equivalent.

The main motivation for this paper, is to present this surprising result. However, there are possible practical applications too. First, EDRB allows us to compute uncertainty of a given Beta distribution with unknown parameters. Secondly, EDRB can provide the uncertainty of other distributions than the Beta distribution, generalising uncertainty. Thirdly, using EDRB, we can apply techniques from information theory on uncertainty (e.g. apply MAXENT on uncertainty).

The paper is organised as follows: In Sect. 2, we introduce and shortly discuss existing definitions and properties. In Sect. 3, we discuss the general relation between uncertainty and entropy in the setting of the Beta model. In Sect. 4, we present our main result, Theorem 1. Finally, in Sect. 5, we look at the application of Theorem 1 on more general opinions.

2   Preliminaries

In this section, we introduce the existing definitions and formalisms that are relevant to our work. The definitions can be grouped into two types, definitions surrounding the Beta model and related models (Sect. 2.1), and information-theoretic definitions (Sect. 2.2).

2.1   Beta Models

The Beta models are a paradigm, and whether a specific model is a Beta model is up to debate. The core idea behind Beta models is a specific Bayesian approach to evidence [4]. Interactions with agents form evidence, and they are used to construct an opinion. The interactions correspond to Bernoulli trials [5]:

Definition 1. *A Bernoulli trial is has two outcomes, "success" and "failure", and the probability of success is the same every time the trial is performed. A Bernoulli distribution is a discrete distribution with two outcomes, 0 and 1.*

Its probability mass function $f_B(p)$ has $f_B(0; p) = 1-p$ and $f_B(1; p) = p$. A random variable B_i from a Bernoulli trial is distributed according to the Bernoulli distributions, so $P(B_i=1) = p$ and $P(B_i=0) = 1 - p$.

There are agents $A \in \mathcal{A}$. Each agent A has an unknown parameter x_A, called its *integrity*. An agent may betray another agent, or the agent may cooperate. Which choice an agent makes is assumed to be a Bernoulli trial, where the probability of cooperating is equal to its integrity. A series of interactions, therefore, is a series of Bernoulli trials. Let $B_{A,i}$ be the random variable corresponding to the ith interaction with agent A, then $P(B_{A,i} = 1) = x_A$. We refer to outcome 1 as *success* and 0 as *failure*. However, x_A is not a known quantity, so we apply the Bayesian idea of introducing a random variable X_A for the integrity of agent A. An *opinion* about an agent can be denoted as the probability density function $p_{X_A}(x_A|B_{A,1}, B_{A,2}, \dots)$.

We assume that the opinion without evidence is the uniform distribution – so $p_{X_A}(x_A) = 1$. One reason to select this prior distribution, is the principle of maximum entropy, which essentially dictates that we should pick the distribution with the highest entropy, if we want to model that we do not have any evidence – and this distribution is the uniform distribution. Another reason to select this prior distribution, is that it simplifies the notion of combining opinions. Most importantly, the prior can be changed to any arbitrary probability density function f, simply by multiplying $f(x_A) \cdot p_{X_A}(x_A|B_{A,1}, B_{A,2}, \dots) \cdot NF$.

The reason for the name "Beta model" comes from a special relationship to Beta distributions. The Beta distribution is defined as:[5,8]

Definition 2. *The Beta distribution is a continuous distribution with support in the range $[0,1]$, with a probability density function $f_\beta(x; \alpha, \beta) = \frac{x^{\alpha-1}(1-x)^{\beta-1}}{B(\alpha,\beta)}$, where B is the* Beta function, $B(\alpha, \beta) = \int_0^1 x^{\alpha-1}(1-x)^{\beta-1}\, dx$, *which acts as a normalisation factor. Its cumulative distribution function is $\frac{\int_0^x t^{\alpha-1}(1-t)^{\beta-1}\, dt}{B(\alpha,\beta)}$, which is also known as the regularised incomplete Beta function $I_x(\alpha, \beta)$.*

We are using important properties of the Beta function and the regularised incomplete Beta function (see [8]):

Proposition 1. *The following two equalities hold:*

$$\frac{B(\alpha+1, \beta)}{B(\alpha, \beta)} = \frac{\alpha}{\alpha+\beta} \quad and \quad I_x(\alpha+1, \beta) = I_x(\alpha, \beta) - \frac{x^\alpha(1-x)^\beta}{\alpha B(\alpha, \beta)}$$

Given the relations between the random variables, we find that any opinion $p_{X_A}(x_A|B_{A,1}, B_{A,2}, \dots)$ is a Beta distribution. In fact, if the outcomes of the Bernoulli trials $B_{A,1}, \dots, B_{A,n})$ contain n_s success and $n - n_s = n_f$ failures, then the opinion $p_{X_A}(x_A|B_{A,1}, \dots, B_{A,n}) = f_\beta(x_A; n_s + 1, n_f + 1)$ [10].

Proposition 2. *Let $b_{A,1}, \dots, b_{A,n}$ be a list with all elements 0 or 1, $\sum_{1 \le i \le n} b_{A,i} = n_s$ and $n_f = n - n_s$. $p_{X_A}(x_A|B_{A,1}=b_{A,1}, \dots, B_{A,n}=b_{A,n}) = f_\beta(x_A; n_s + 1, n_f + 1)$*

We can define a fusion operator $\oplus$, as $p_1(x) \oplus p_2(x) = \frac{p_1(x)p_2(x)}{\int_0^1 p_1(y)p_2(y)\,dy}$. The fusion operator simply merges the evidence [5]:

Proposition 3. *For any series of outcomes of Bernoulli trials* $b_{A,1}, \ldots, b_{A,n}$ *and* $b'_{A,1}, \ldots, b'_{A,n'}$, $p_{X_A}(x_A | B_{A,1} = b_{A,1}, \ldots, B_{A,n} = b_{A,n}, B'_{A,1} = b'_{A,1}, \ldots, B'_{A,n'} = b'_{A,n'}) \propto p_{X_A}(x_A | B_{A,1} = b_{A,1}, \ldots, B_{A,n} = b_{A,n}) \cdot p_{X_A}(x_A | B'_{A,1} = b'_{A,1}, \ldots, B'_{A,n'} = b'_{A,n'})$.

In particular $f_\beta(x; \alpha, \beta) \oplus f_\beta(x; \alpha', \beta') = f_\beta(x; \alpha + \alpha' - 1, \beta + \beta' - 1)$.

Using a distribution to denote an opinion is a feasible approach, based on Bayesian logic, but the results are not intuitively obvious to people that may use the opinions. Subjective Logic is a formalism within the Beta model paradigm, which is developed with the purpose of being understandable to non-experts [7][1]. A Subjective Logic opinion is defined [6]:

Definition 3. *An opinion is a triple of components* (b, d, u), *for positive real* b, d, u *with* $b + d + u = 1$. *The first component is belief, the second is disbelief, and the third is uncertainty.*

Subjective logic also has a fusion operator, denoted $(b, d, u) \oplus (b', d', u')$. The purpose of fusion in Subjective Logic is the same as fusion of distributions, namely to merge evidence. See [6].

Definition 4.

$$(b, d, u) \oplus (b', d', u') = \left(\frac{bu' + b'u}{u + u' - uu'}, \frac{du' + d'u}{u + u' - uu'}, \frac{uu'}{u + u' - uu'} \right).$$

That there is an isomorphism between fusion of Beta distributions and Subjective Logic fusion, is a known result [7]. In fact, this isomorphism is the primary argument in favour of the shape of Definition 4. It turns out that there is a family of isomorphisms between the two:

Proposition 4. *Let* $\mathbb{B}, \mathbb{S}$ *be the groups of Beta distributions with fusion, and of SL opinions with SL fusion. Let* f_r *be a function* $f_r : \mathbb{B} \to \mathbb{S}$ *with* $f_r(\alpha, \beta) = \left(\frac{\alpha - 1}{\alpha + \beta - 2 + r}, \frac{\beta - 1}{\alpha + \beta - 2 + r}, \frac{r}{\alpha + \beta - 2 + r} \right)$. *For* $r > 0$, f_r *is an isomorphism between* $\mathbb{B}$ *and* $\mathbb{S}$.

Proof. Keep in mind Proposition 3, so fusion simply adds α's and β's. The inverse of f_r is $f_r^{-1} = \left(\frac{br}{u} + 1, \frac{dr}{u} + 1 \right)$, since (w.l.o.g. for α):

$$f_r^{-1}(f_r(\alpha, \beta)) = \frac{\alpha - 1}{\alpha + \beta - 2 + r} \frac{\alpha + \beta - 2 + r}{r} + 1, \cdots = r\frac{\alpha - 1}{r} + 1, \cdots = \alpha, \beta.$$

---

[1] For the purpose of this paper, we restrict ourselves to so-called *binary* Subjective Logic opinions, which corresponds to the notion that the integrity parameter determines a Bernoulli trial.

Remains to prove that f_r and f_r^{-1} are homomorphisms between $\mathbb{B}$ and $\mathbb{S}$:

$$f_r^{-1}\left(\frac{bu'+b'u}{u+u'-uu'}, \frac{du'+d'u}{u+u'-uu'}, \frac{uu'}{u+u'-uu'}\right)$$

$$=\left(r\frac{bu'+b'u}{uu'}+1, r\frac{du'+d'u}{uu'}+1\right)$$

$$=\left(r\frac{b}{u}+r\frac{b'}{u'}+1, r\frac{d}{u}+r\frac{d'}{u'}+1\right)$$

$$=\left(r\frac{b}{u}+1, r\frac{d}{u}+1\right) \oplus \left(r\frac{b'}{u'}+1, r\frac{d'}{u'}+1\right)$$

$$=f_r^{-1}(b,d,u) \oplus f_r(b',d',u')$$

Let $D = \alpha + \beta - 2 + r$ and $D' = \alpha' + \beta' - 2 + r$. Then:

$$f_r(\alpha + \alpha' - 1, \beta + \beta' - 1)$$

$$=\left(\frac{\alpha+\alpha'-2}{\alpha+\alpha'+\beta+\beta'-4+r}, \frac{\beta+\beta'-2}{\alpha+\alpha'+\beta+\beta'-4+r}, \frac{r}{\alpha+\alpha'+\beta+\beta'-4+r}\right)$$

$$=\left(\frac{\alpha+\alpha'-2}{D+D'-r}, \frac{\beta+\beta'-2}{D+D'-r}, \frac{r}{D+D'-r}\right)$$

$$=\left(\frac{\frac{\alpha-1}{D}\frac{r}{D'}+\frac{\alpha'-1}{D'}\frac{r}{D}}{\frac{r}{D}+\frac{r}{D'}-\frac{r^2}{DD'}}, \frac{\frac{\beta-1}{D}\frac{r}{D'}+\frac{\beta'-1}{D'}\frac{r}{D}}{\frac{r}{D}+\frac{r}{D'}-\frac{r^2}{DD'}}, \frac{\frac{r^2}{DD'}}{\frac{r}{D}+\frac{r}{D'}-\frac{r^2}{DD'}}\right)$$

$$=\left(\frac{\alpha-1}{D}, \frac{\beta-1}{D}, \frac{r}{D}\right) \oplus \left(\frac{\alpha'-1}{D'}, \frac{\beta'-1}{D'}, \frac{r}{D'}\right)$$

$$= f_r(\alpha, \beta) \oplus f_r(\alpha', \beta')$$

Since Beta distributions and Subjective Logic are isomorphic w.r.t. fusion, we can apply notions of Subjective Logic directly to Beta distributions. So we can say that the uncertainty of $f_\beta(x; \alpha, \beta)$ is $\mathrm{unc}_r(f_\beta(x; \alpha, \beta)) = \frac{r}{\alpha+\beta-2+r}$). Unless we explicitly state which isomorphism f_r we use, we assume that f_1 was used – so $\mathrm{unc} = \mathrm{unc}_1$. Observe that a Beta distribution based on $n = n_s + n_f$ pieces of evidence has uncertainty $\mathrm{unc}(f_\beta(x; n_s+1, n_f+1)) = \frac{1}{n_s+n_f+1}$), so the inverse of uncertainty is equal to the amount of evidence (plus 1, to avoid divide-by-zero).

2.2   Information Theory

A core notion in information theory, is the notion of *surprisal*, also known as self-information or information content. The symbol I_X is often used, but it is also used for the regularised incomplete Beta function, so we denote the surprisal of X with J_X instead. The surprisal is defined: $J_X(x) = -\log(P(X = x))$ or $J_X(x) = -\log(p_X(x))$ for discrete and continuous random variable X, respectively.

Shannon entropy is used to measure the expected amount of information carried in a random variable, which is determined by the uncertainty of the random variable [9]:

Definition 5. *The Shannon entropy of a discrete random variable X is given:*

$$H(X) = \mathrm{E}_x(J_X(x)) = -\sum\nolimits_{x_i \in X} P(X{=}x_i) \cdot \log(P(X{=}x_i))$$

The Shannon entropy is maximal when all possible outcomes are equiprobable. It means that our expected surprisal is maximal, which is a common way to express we know nothing about the random variable.

Shannon entropy can be generalised for continuous random variables, to differential entropy. Differential entropy does not provide absolute values – values can go below 0 – but is useful for measuring the difference in information present in distributions.

Definition 6. *The differential entropy of a continuous random variable X is given:*

$$H(X) = \mathrm{E}_x(J_X(x)) = -\int_X p_X(x) \cdot \log(p_X(x)) \, \mathrm{d}x$$

Kullback-Leibler divergence, also known as relative entropy, measures the distance from one distribution to another.

Definition 7. *For discrete random variables X, Y, the Kullback-Leibler divergence from X to Y is:*

$$D_{\mathrm{KL}}(X\|Y) = \mathrm{E}_x(J_X(x) - J_Y(x)) = \sum\nolimits_{x_i \in X} P(X{=}x_i) \cdot \log\left(\frac{P(X{=}x_i)}{P(Y{=}x_i}\right)$$

For continuous random variables X, Y, it is:

$$D_{\mathrm{KL}}(X\|Y) = \mathrm{E}_x(J_X(x) - J_Y(x)) = \int_X p_X(x) \cdot \log\left(\frac{p_X(x)}{p_Y(x)}\right) \, \mathrm{d}x$$

Note that in general, $D_{\mathrm{KL}}(X\|Y) \neq D_{\mathrm{KL}}(Y\|X)$. Typically, X is the "true" random variable and Y is a model, in which case $D_{\mathrm{KL}}(X\|Y)$ tells us how far the model is from the truth. A divergence of 0 implies that the two random variables are identically distributed.

3 Beta Models and Entropy

In this section, we discuss different entropy measures that can be applied to a Beta distribution. We formally state each of these measures, we discuss their intuitive meaning, their application, and how they differ from uncertainty. The measure of entropy that does match uncertainty will be introduced in the next section. This section helps appreciate why that measure of entropy is the way it is.

3.1   Integrity Parameter Entropy

The most obvious measure of entropy that can be applied, is the (differential) entropy of the integrity parameter. To be precise, the entropy measure is:

$$H(X) = -\int_0^1 p_X(x) \cdot \log(p_X(x))\, \mathrm{d}x.$$

The standard intuition of differential entropy applies. In the case of differential entropy, values are negative and the absolute quantity tells you how much information is gained relative to the uniform distribution. The information that is gained is about the precise value of the integrity parameter. Differently put, it measures how far away from the uniform distribution, values in the distribution tend to be. Figure 1 provides two examples of graphs, Fig. 1a depicts a distribution with less information about integrity than Fig. 1b.

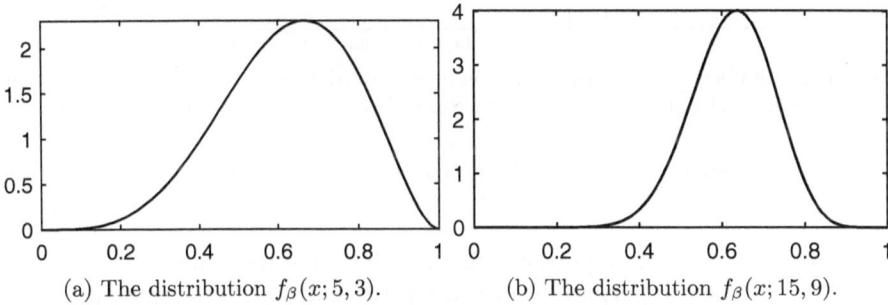

(a) The distribution $f_\beta(x; 5, 3)$.   (b) The distribution $f_\beta(x; 15, 9)$.

Fig. 1. Two Beta distributions equal in expected value, but not uncertainty.

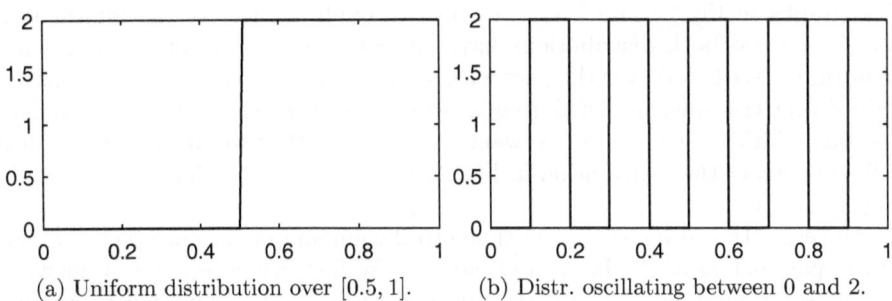

(a) Uniform distribution over $[0.5, 1]$.   (b) Distr. oscillating between 0 and 2.

Fig. 2. Two distributions with uniform support on half the interval.

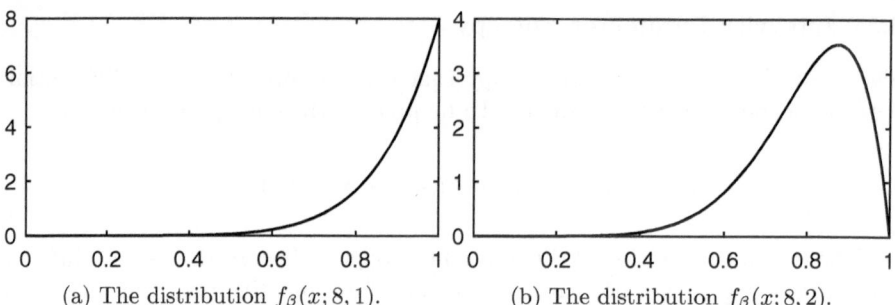

(a) The distribution $f_\beta(x; 8, 1)$.   (b) The distribution $f_\beta(x; 8, 2)$.

Fig. 3. Two Beta distributions with entropy increasing when adding evidence.

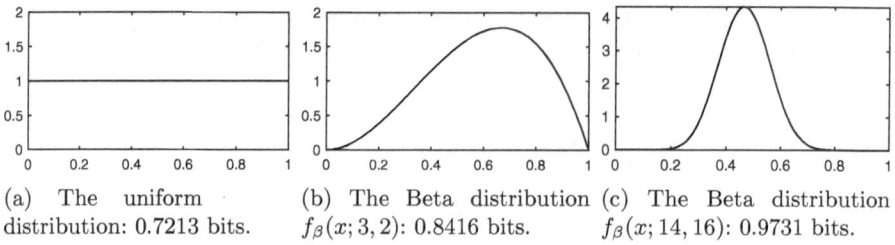

(a) The uniform distribution: 0.7213 bits.   (b) The Beta distribution $f_\beta(x; 3, 2)$: 0.8416 bits.   (c) The Beta distribution $f_\beta(x; 14, 16)$: 0.9731 bits.

Fig. 4. More evidence continues to decrease information.

In reality, it is not important whether the integrity value is exactly 0.7, or say 0.705. For the purpose of measuring the entropy of the integrity value, these two values are considered to be completely different. For graphs such as the ones depicted in Fig. 1, this is not a major issue, since the probabilities of similar integrity values tend to be similar too. However, in more extreme cases, such as in the graph depicted in Fig. 2, it becomes an issue for our intuition. The graphs in Fig. 2a and b are identical through the lens of the information measure, since both distributions have support on half the interval, and are uniformly distributed over the part with support. In both cases, the information gained over the uniform distribution is 1 bit – since we can exclude exactly half the possibilities. However, if we want to know whether we are dealing with a reliable person, the distribution in Fig. 2a is likely to be helpful, but the one in Fig. 2b is not.

Uncertainty is inversely proportional to the amount of evidence (i.e., the sum of the parameters of the Beta distribution). Adding evidence tends to increase the information about the integrity parameter too, as the peak tends to become narrower, as illustrated in Fig. 1. However, it is not necessarily the case that adding evidence decreases the entropy, as illustrated in Fig. 3. The distribution $f_\beta(8, 1)$ has an entropy of 1.7376 bits, whereas the distribution $f_\beta(8, 2)$ has an entropy of 1.1468 bits. Therefore, entropy about the integrity parameter fails to meet the basic criterion of uncertainty, which is being that it is monotonically decreasing as evidence is added.

3.2   Bernoulli Trial Entropy

An ingredient that was missing from integrity parameter entropy, was to take into account the values of integrity parameter, rather than just its probability density. Arguably, we are not necessarily interested in the exact integrity of other agents, but we are interested in knowing whether they will betray us or not. Whether an agent would betray us is determined by a Bernoulli trial based on the integrity parameter. In other words, an agent will not betray us with a probability equal to its integrity parameter. Since the Beta distribution is the estimate of that integrity parameter, the expected entropy of the Bernoulli trial is:

$$H(B) = -\mathrm{E}_x(x\log(x) + (1-x)\log(1-x))$$
$$= -\int_0^1 p_X(x) \cdot (x\log(x) + (1-x)\log(1-x))\,\mathrm{d}x$$

Although we are computing the expectation of the entropy, the standard intuition of entropy applies: how much information about the outcome of the Bernoulli trial do we (expect to) have. The entropy of a Bernoulli trial is between 0 and 1 bits, where values close to 0 bits mean near certainty about whether we will be betrayed or not. The Beta distribution with maximal uncertainty – the uniform distribution – has an entropy of 0.7213 bits in this measure; strictly less than 1.

It can certainly be useful to measure how much you about the Bernoulli trial, but this measure has barely any connection to uncertainty. Consider a user with an integrity parameter of 0.5. A reasonable progression of Beta distributions as more evidence is accumulated is depicted in Fig. 4. What we see in Fig. 4 is that we are increasingly certain that the integrity parameter must be near 0.5. If the integrity parameter is 0.5, then we have 1 bit entropy of the Bernoulli trial, whereas the values near the extremes have near 0 bits entropy. As the evidence accumulates, this measure converges to 1 bit entropy. Again, this breaks the most basic requirement that entropy decreases as uncertainty decreases.

3.3   KL-Divergence from Truth

The problem with Bernoulli trial entropy as a measure for uncertainty, is that as evidence is added, it provides a value that is closer to the true Bernoulli entropy of that agent, rather than a smaller value. Assume that, somehow, we have access to the true integrity parameter of an agent, then we can measure the information-theoretic distance to that value. The standard technique is to use Kullback-Leibler divergence. Given a true integrity parameter of value x, we can apply KL-divergence to the Bernoulli trial entropy as:

$$\mathrm{E}_y(D_{\mathrm{KL}}(f_B(x)\|f_B(y))) = \int_0^1 p_X(y)(x\log(\frac{x}{y}) + (1-x)\log(\frac{1-x}{1-y}))\,\mathrm{d}y$$

As an example, say we measure 6 successes and 1 failure with an agent with parameter 0.85, then we get the KL-divergence from the truth as: $\int_0^1 f_\beta(y; 6, 1)\cdot$

$(0.85 \log(\frac{0.85}{y}) + 0.15 \log(\frac{0.15}{1-y})) \, dy = 0.1247$ bits. However, it is possible that we measure 6 successes and 1 failure with an agent with parameter 0.4, in which case the distance is 1.2460. The measure does not just depend on the distribution itself.

This measure cannot be applied to compute the entropy, given an arbitrary Beta distribution, since the true integrity parameter is an unknown. Notice that the shape of the equation is such that the formula for the expectation of what behaviour will be observed is similar to the equation for the expectation of the integrity parameter given the observed behaviour. By applying Bayes' theorem, we can alter this term to talk about the expected true integrity parameter given the observed behaviour: $E_{x,y}(D_{\text{KL}}(f_B(x)||f_B(y)))$. This formula turns out to be EDRB, as we see in the next section.

4   Entropy-Uncertainty Equivalence

It may not be immediately obvious what it means for entropy measures and uncertainty measures to be equivalent. Both uncertainty and EDRB (expected KL-divergence of random Bernoulli trials) are actually families of measures, rather than a singular measure. Recall that if n_e is the amount of evidence, the general expression for uncertainty is $\frac{r}{n_e+r}$. EDRB provides different outcomes, depending on the choice of the base of the logarithm b, we will prove that it is $\frac{\log(b)}{n_e+2}$. In the case $r = 2, b = e^2$, the two formulas are equal. However, we argue that the equivalence is stronger, since every member of the two families shares the crucial property that its inverse is a linear function of the amount of evidence.

Our goal, therefore, is to prove that $E_{x,y}(D_{\text{KL}}(f_B(x)||f_B(y))) = \frac{\log(b)}{n_e+2}$. Note that if we have s successes and f failures, our Beta distribution is $f_\beta(x; \alpha, \beta)$, with $\alpha = s+1$ and $\beta = f+1$. Therefore, $\alpha + \beta = s+f+2 = n_e + 2$. Therefore, we can state our Theorem as the following equation:

Theorem 1.

$$\int_0^1 \int_0^1 f_\beta(x; \alpha, \beta) f_\beta(y; \alpha, \beta)((x \log_b(\frac{x}{y}) + (1-x) \log_b(\frac{1-x}{1-y})) \, dy \, dx = \frac{\log(b)}{n_e + 2}$$

Proof. We will prove that :

$$\int_0^1 \int_0^1 f_\beta(x; \alpha, \beta) f_\beta(y; \alpha, \beta) x \log_b\left(\frac{x}{y}\right) \, dy \, dx = \frac{\log(b)\beta}{(\alpha + \beta)^2}.$$

Swapping α and β while substituting x for $1 - x$ and y for $1 - y$, it follows:

$$\int_0^1 \int_0^1 f_\beta(x; \alpha, \beta) f_\beta(y; \alpha, \beta)(1-x) \log_b\left(\frac{1-x}{1-y}\right) \, dy \, dx = \frac{\log(b)\alpha}{(\alpha + \beta)^2}.$$

This suffices to prove the theorem, since $\frac{\log(b)\beta}{(\alpha+\beta)^2} + \frac{\log(b)\alpha}{(\alpha+\beta)^2} = \frac{\log(b)}{\alpha+\beta}$.

$$\int_0^1 \int_0^1 f_\beta(x;\alpha,\beta) f_\beta(y;\alpha,\beta) x \log_b\left(\frac{x}{y}\right) \, dy \, dx$$

$= \{\log_b(x/y) = \log_b(x) - \log_b(y)\}$

$$\iint_0^1 f_\beta(x;\alpha,\beta) f_\beta(y;\alpha,\beta) x \log_b(x) \, dy \, dx - \iint_0^1 f_\beta(x;\alpha,\beta) f_\beta(y;\alpha,\beta) x \log_b(y) \, dy \, dx$$

$= \{\text{Erase } y \text{ left. Isolate } x \text{ right, replace with } B(\alpha+1,\beta)/B(\alpha,\beta). \text{ Rename } y \text{ to } x.\}$

$$\int_0^1 x f_\beta(x;\alpha,\beta) \log_b(x) - \frac{B(\alpha+1,\beta)}{B(\alpha,\beta)} f_\beta(x;\alpha,\beta) \log_b(x) \, dx$$

$= \{\text{Integration by parts on both summands. Recall Definition 2.}\}$

$$\left[\log_b(x) \int_0^x \frac{t^\alpha(1-t)^{\beta-1}}{B(\alpha,\beta)} \, dt \right]_0^1 - \int_0^1 \log(b) \frac{1}{x} \left(\int_0^x \frac{t^\alpha(1-t)^{\beta-1}}{B(\alpha,\beta)} \, dt \right) dx$$

$$- \frac{B(\alpha+1,\beta)}{B(\alpha,\beta)} \left(\left[\log_b(x) \int_0^x \frac{t^{\alpha-1}(1-t)^{\beta-1}}{B(\alpha,\beta)} \, dt \right]_0^1 - \int_0^1 \log(b) \frac{1}{x} \left(\int_0^x \frac{t^{\alpha-1}(1-t)^{\beta-1}}{B(\alpha,\beta)} \, dt \right) dx \right)$$

$= \{\text{Simplify to regularised incomplete Beta functions (Definition 2).}\}$

$$\left[\log_b(x) I_x(\alpha+1,\beta) \frac{B(\alpha+1,\beta)}{B(\alpha,\beta)} \right]_0^1 - \int_0^1 \log(b) \frac{1}{x} I_x(\alpha+1,\beta) \frac{B(\alpha+1,\beta)}{B(\alpha,\beta)} \, dx$$

$$- \frac{B(\alpha+1,\beta)}{B(\alpha,\beta)} \left(\left[\log_b(x) I_x(\alpha,\beta) \right]_0^1 - \int_0^1 \log(b) \frac{1}{x} I_x(\alpha,\beta) \, dx \right)$$

$= \{\text{Terms in square brackets evaluate to 0 at 0 and 1. Simplify formula.}\}$

$$\int_0^1 \log(b) \frac{1}{x} \frac{B(\alpha+1,\beta)}{B(\alpha,\beta)} (I_x(\alpha,\beta) - I_x(\alpha+1,\beta+1)) \, dx$$

$= \{\text{Apply Proposition 1.}\}$

$$\int_0^1 \log(b) \frac{1}{x} \frac{B(\alpha+1,\beta)}{B(\alpha,\beta)} \frac{x^\alpha(1-x)^\beta}{\alpha B(\alpha,\beta)} \, dx$$

$= \{\text{Use } 1/x \text{ to subtract 1 from the exponent } \alpha, \text{ apply Proposition 1.}\}$

$$\log(b) \frac{\alpha}{\alpha+\beta} \cdot \frac{\beta}{\alpha(\alpha+\beta)} = \frac{\log(b)\beta}{(\alpha+\beta)^2}$$

There are two ways to interpret the theorem. Firstly, we can use the intuition from Sect. 3.3, and say that $f_\beta(x;\alpha,\beta)$ is the Bayesian estimate of the true integrity parameter that generated the history, and we measure the expected KL-divergence between the Bernoulli trial with the true integrity parameter and a new randomly selected parameter (y). Simply put, we reuse the measure from Sect. 3.3, but substituting the true integrity for the expected integrity. KL-divergence is an oft-used way to measure the quality of a model distribution, compared to the real one. EDRB measures the expectation of the distance between the KL-divergence of the Bernoulli trail based on an estimated true one and an estimated model. Of course, taking the expectation of the true integrity used for the Bernoulli trial is intuitively dubious.

The alternative intuition does not involve true integrities for this reason. EDRB can be interpreted to say, given two agents with the same history, how much do we learn about one agent, if we observe a new interaction with the other. As more evidence accumulates, the possible choices for the parameter for the Bernoulli trial becomes more centered around a specific value. If the probability that two Bernoulli trials use similar parameters increases, then the KL-divergence between the two decreases. This intuition is a more direct reading of the actual formula, as we are taking the expectation of a pair of integrity parameters, distributed along the same Beta distribution. The weakness of this intuition is that KL-divergence is an asymmetric measure, where one distribution represents the true distribution and the other one the model distribution, whereas this intuition is measuring the distance between two model distributions.

While both intuitions are imperfect, they do offer an explanation why we might expect uncertainty and EDRB to be related. The fact that they are indeed equivalent is non-obvious, however. The proof does not provide us with an insight as to why they are indeed equivalent – other than the fact that they are. Based on the fact that the intuitions are imperfect, and the proof does not provide any intuition either, we consider the equivalence to be surprising.

Uncertainty is a useful concept and a basic tenet of Subjective Logic. To compute the uncertainty, from a Beta distribution $f_\beta(x; \alpha, \beta)$, simply take $u = \frac{1}{\alpha+\beta-1}$. However, this definition uses the parameters of the distribution, rather than the probability density function. Given a probability density function f, that happens to represent a Beta distribution, there is no elegant way to compute the uncertainty. For example if $f = 6(x(1-x)^5 + (1-x)^6)$, then how to determine its uncertainty – given it may not be trivial to realise $f = f_\beta(6, 1)$. Alternatively, we can compute $E_{X,Y}(D_{KL}(f_BX \| f_BY))$ for $X, Y \sim f$, and obtain $\frac{1}{\alpha+\beta}$ without knowing α and β.

The fact that we can use our new measure as an alternative way to compute the uncertainty of a Beta distribution without explicitly using the parameters, is interesting in itself. More interesting, however, is the fact that the input probability density function need not be a Beta distribution at all, for it to work. As we more rigorously argue in the next section, there are cases where it does not make sense to use a Beta distribution as opinions. These cases have been recognised implicitly in the literature (e.g. [14]), but are not typically explicitly addressed. We can now reason about the uncertainty present in more esoteric distributions that may pop up. In the next section, we present some of the implications to these generalised distributions.

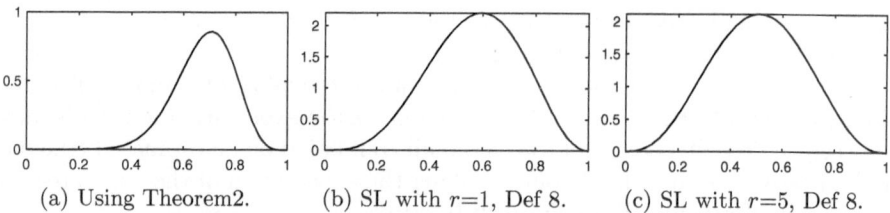

(a) Using Theorem2.   (b) SL with $r=1$, Def 8.   (c) SL with $r=5$, Def 8.

Fig. 5. Three differently computed conjunctions of $f_\beta(x; 8, 4)$ and $f_\beta(x; 9, 2)$.

5   Generalised Opinions

That models of information fusion found in Subjective Logic are isomorphic to Beta distributions is not surprising. After all, these models are created with this purpose in mind. Subjective Logic further incorporates logical operations, and transitive trust operations. As shown in [10] and [11] respectively, the resulting distribution of these operations is not a Beta distribution (using the assumptions of the Beta model). In other words, the isomorphism does not hold if we add the new operations. In this section, we show examples of distributions resulting from logical or transitive operations, discuss why they are not Beta distributions, and extend the result from the previous section to these distributions.

5.1 Opinion Logic

Consider performing logic on the opinions. For example, we have a distribution for A and for A', but in order to obtain a success, we need both A and A' to succeed. In the case that A and B are independent agents, the probability that $A \wedge A'$ succeeds is a Bernoulli trial with parameter $x_A \times x_{A'}$ [10]. According to [10], if we want to obtain our opinion on $A \wedge A'$, based on our opinions on A and A', then we need to take their product distribution:

Theorem 2. *If $B_{A,k}$ and $B'_{A',k'}$ are independent Bernoulli trials, then let C be 1 iff $B_{A,k} = 1$ and $B'_{A',k'} = 1$. Let $p(C = 1|X_C = x_C) = x_C$ then the distribution*

$$p_{X_C}(x_C|B_{A,1} \ldots B_{A,k-1}, B'_{A',1} \ldots B'_{A',k'-1}) = \int_{x_C}^1 \frac{1}{y} p_{X_C}(\frac{x_A}{y}|B_{A,1} \ldots B_{A,k-1}) \cdot p_{X_{A'}}(y|B_{A',1} \ldots B_{A',k'-1}) \, dy;$$ *the product distribution of the opinions on A, A'.*

Proof. Theorem 4 in [10]. $\square$

In Subjective Logic, conjunction is defined as:

Definition 8. *Conjunction*
$(b, d, u) \wedge (b', d', u') = (bb', d + d' - dd', bu' + b'u + uu')$.

In Fig. 5, we see the conjunction of $f_\beta(x; 8, 4)$ and $f_\beta(x; 9, 2)$ as derived from the product distribution, as well as the results computed using the Subjective Logic conjunction definition under f_1 and f_5. We can see that neither f_1 nor f_5 are isomorphisms w.r.t. conjunction, since the graphs differ. In fact, for no choice of r, or even for any other Subjective Logic definition for conjunction, will f_r be an isomorphism. The reason is that all opinions in Subjective Logic are isomorphic to a Beta distribution, but the result of the product distribution is not generally (in fact, almost never) a Beta distribution. Therefore, no isomorphism can exist.

Although the resulting opinion is not a Beta distribution, we can compute the uncertainty via its equivalence to EDRB. The uncertainty of $f_\beta(x; 8, 4)$ and $f_\beta(x; 9, 2)$ is, therefore, equal to 0.0775.

5.2 Transitive Trust

Transitive trust is a fiercely debated topic. Using the assumptions of the Beta model, an issue arises. The formula contains a term χ, which is the attacker's strategy. In other words: how to use the advice of another agent, depends on how the agent would act, if he were malicious. See [11] for more details. The attacker strategy is not a topic for this paper, so we will assume the simplest attack strategy: random behaviour.

If an advisor A is honest with probability x_A, and the advisor gives us the opinion p_{X_c}, then our resulting opinion is simply $x_A \cdot p_{X_c}(x_c) + (1 - x_A)$. This can be derived from Theorem 2 in [11]. However, the intuition behind it is also clear, namely that if the advisor speaks the truth, we should listen, and if he lies, we know nothing. We do not typically know x_A, but we can use our opinion p_{X_A} to estimate this value.

The result of obtaining an opinion from advice, therefore, is not a Beta distribution, but a weighted sum of Beta distributions[2]. However, like in Sect. 5.1, Subjective Logic must return a Beta distribution as the result of transitive trust. In fact, Subjective Logic defines transitive trust:

Definition 9. *Propagation* $(b, d, u) \cdot (b', d', u') = (bb', bd', bu' + d + u)$.

In Fig. 6, we see the propagation of $f_\beta(x; 8, 4)$ and $f_\beta(x; 9, 2)$ as derived from the summing Beta distributions, as well as the results computed using the Subjective Logic propagation definition under f_1 and f_5. Compared to conjunction, we see that the difference between the two approaches is even larger. In particular, we notice that Fig. 6a has raised flat tails. These raised flat tails are a consequence of the fact that, no matter what malicious agents say, if they are lying, then extremely high/low integrity values remain probable.

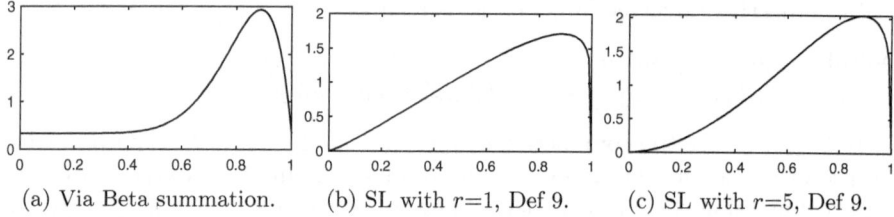

(a) Via Beta summation.   (b) SL with $r=1$, Def 9.   (c) SL with $r=5$, Def 9.

Fig. 6. When an agent with $f_\beta(x; 8, 4)$ claims to have opinion $f_\beta(x; 9, 2)$.

Although the resulting opinion is not a Beta distribution, we can compute the uncertainty via its equivalence to EDRB. The uncertainty of the opinion resulting from hearing $f_\beta(x; 9, 2)$ from an agent that we have the opinion $f_\beta(x; 8, 4)$ about, is equal to 0.5354. In this case, the uncertainty is (significantly) larger than the uncertainty of $f_\beta(x; 9, 2)$ (which is 0.1000). However, it need not be the case that summing Beta distributions changes the uncertainty in a meaningful way. In particular, the uncertainty of $1/3(f_\beta(x; 3, 1) + f_\beta(x; 2, 2) + f_\beta(x; 1, 3))$ is the maximum: 1, even though the individual distributions have far smaller uncertainty. There may be a more subtle pattern in the EDRB entropy of a sum of Beta distributions, but this is future work.

---

[2] This is true also when the attack strategy is not trivial.

A reasonable approach to selecting a strategy for the attacker, is to select the strategy that is the least informative. Typically, that means the strategy that gives the highest entropy. No closed formula has been found that maximises either the integrity entropy or the Bernoulli trial entropy. An open question is whether this approach can be more fruitful when using EDRB as the measure of entropy.

6   Conclusion

Theorem 1 is our main result. It states that uncertainty (the inverse of amount of evidence) is equal to a specific measure of entropy that we introduce: expected Kullback-Leibler divergence of random-parameter Bernoulli trials (EDRB). The intuition behind EDRB is that it measures the expected distance between two Bernoulli trials selected from a distribution – a more narrow distribution will have less distance between the Bernoulli trials.

While both entropy and uncertainty can be used to describe lack of knowledge. Any entropy measure is based on surprisal, whereas uncertainty is based on Bayesian evidence. Hence is surprising that they should coincide.

We discuss alternative measures of entropy in Sect. 3. Measures such as integrity entropy and Bernoulli trial entropy certainly have use-cases. Uncertainty simply measures something else than these two measures.

Finally, we study the implications of having EDRB on generalised opinions. These are distributions other than the Beta distributions. In Sect. 5, we show how these distributions arise, and why they are of interest. We plan to further study of the implications of generalised opinions under EDRB. In particular we want to explore the notion of malicious advisors maximising EDRB entropy.

References

1. Burt, D.R.: Bandwidth and echo: trust, information, and gossip in social networks (2001)
2. Che, S., Feng, R., Liang, X., Wang, X.: A lightweight trust management based on bayesian and entropy for wireless sensor networks. Secur. Commun. Netw. **8**(2), 168–175 (2015)
3. ElSalamouny, E., Sassone, V., Nielsen, M.: HMM-based trust model. In: Degano, P., Guttman, J.D. (eds.) FAST 2009. LNCS, vol. 5983, pp. 21–35. Springer, Heidelberg (2010). https://doi.org/10.1007/978-3-642-12459-4_3
4. Ismail, R., Jøsang, A.: The beta reputation system. In: BLED 2002 Proceedings, p. 41 (2002)
5. Jaynes, E.T.: Probability Theory: The Logic of Science. Cambridge University Press, Cambridge (2003)
6. Jøsang, A.: Artificial reasoning with subjective logic. In: Proceedings of the Second Australian Workshop on Commonsense Reasoning. vol. 48, p. 34. Citeseer (1997)
7. Jøsang, A.: Subjective Logic. Springer, Switzerland (2016). https://doi.org/10.1007/978-3-319-42337-1

8. Kotz, S., Balakrishnan, N., Johnson, N.L.: Continuous Multivariate Distributions, vol. 1. John Wiley & Sons, Hoboken (2004)

9. McEliece, R.J.: Theory of Information and Coding, 2nd edn. Cambridge University Press, New York (2001)

10. Muller, T., Schweitzer, P.: A formal derivation of composite trust. In: Garcia-Alfaro, J., Cuppens, F., Cuppens-Boulahia, N., Miri, A., Tawbi, N. (eds.) FPS 2012. LNCS, vol. 7743, pp. 132–148. Springer, Heidelberg (2013). https://doi.org/10.1007/978-3-642-37119-6_9

11. Muller, T., Schweitzer, P.: On beta models with trust chains. In: Fernández-Gago, C., Martinelli, F., Pearson, S., Agudo, I. (eds.) IFIPTM 2013. IAICT, vol. 401, pp. 49–65. Springer, Heidelberg (2013). https://doi.org/10.1007/978-3-642-38323-6_4

12. Muller, T., Wang, D., Jøsang, A.: Information theory for subjective logic. In: Torra, V., Narukawa, Y. (eds.) MDAI 2015. LNCS (LNAI), vol. 9321, pp. 230–242. Springer, Cham (2015). https://doi.org/10.1007/978-3-319-23240-9_19

13. Teacy, W.L., Luck, M., Rogers, A., Jennings, N.R.: An efficient and versatile approach to trust and reputation using hierarchical bayesian modelling. Artif. Intell. **193**, 149–185 (2012)

14. Teacy, W.L., Patel, J., Jennings, N.R., Luck, M.: Travos: trust and reputation in the context of inaccurate information sources. Auton. Agent. Multi-Agent Syst. **12**(2), 183–198 (2006)

15. Wang, D., Muller, T., Irissappane, A.A., Zhang, J., Liu, Y.: Using information theory to improve the robustness of trust systems. In: Proceedings of the 2015 International Conference on Autonomous Agents and Multiagent Systems, pp. 791–799. International Foundation for Autonomous Agents and Multiagent Systems (2015)

16. Wang, D., Muller, T., Zhang, J., Liu, Y.: Is it harmful when advisors only pretend to be honest? In: Thirtieth AAAI Conference on Artificial Intelligence (2016)

17. Wu, X., Huang, J., Ling, J., Shu, L.: BLTM: beta and LQI based trust model for wireless sensor networks. IEEE Access **7**, 43679–43690 (2019)

18. Xiao, S., Dong, M.: Hidden semi-markov model-based reputation management system for online to offline (o2o) e-commerce markets. Decis. Support Syst. **77**, 87–99 (2015)

User Recognition Based on Daily Actigraphy Patterns

Enrique Garcia-Ceja$^{(\boxtimes)}$ and Brice Morin

SINTEF Digital, Oslo, Norway
{enrique.garcia-ceja,brice.morin}@sintef.no

Abstract. The use of inertial sensors such as accelerometers and gyroscopes, which are now often embedded in many wearable devices, has gained attention for their applicability in user authentication applications as an alternative to PINs, passwords, biometric signatures, etc. Previous works have shown that it is possible to authenticate users based on fine-grained kinematic behavior profiles like gait, hand gestures and physical activities. In this work we explore the use of actigraphy data for user recognition based on daily patterns as opposed to fine-grained motion. One of the advantages of the former, is that it does not require to perform specific movements, thus, easing the training and calibration stages. In this work we extracted daily patterns from an actigraphy device and used a random forest classifier and a majority voting approach to perform the user classification. We used a public available dataset collected by 55 participants and we achived a true positive rate of 0.64, a true negative rate of 0.99 and a balanced accuracy of 0.81.

Keywords: User recognition · Accelerometer · Authentication · Machine learning

1 Introduction

The use of inertial sensors (accelerometers, gyroscopes) for continuous monitoring has become very common due to their ubiquity. Such sensors are increasingly embedded in many wearable devices such as smartphones, smart-watches, fitness bracelets, actigraphy devices and so on. These sensors have been used to monitor physical activities [14], sport activities [16], mental health [10], social interactions [8], to name a few. Recently, the use of inertial units has been explored for user identification and user authentication applications [1,15]. As pointed out by Yang et al. [21], current authentication schemes for wearable devices are often impractical. For example, given the small screen of a smart-watch, the use of a PIN is cumbersome. Furthermore, remembering PINs and passwords for different programs is difficult. An appealing alternative is the use of kinetic patterns based on user movement data. Previous works have demonstrated the use of wrist worn devices for user authentication [1,21]. The majority of those works

© IFIP International Federation for Information Processing 2019
Published by Springer Nature Switzerland AG 2019
W. Meng et al. (Eds.): IFIPTM 2019, IFIP AICT 563, pp. 73–80, 2019.
https://doi.org/10.1007/978-3-030-33716-2_6

build a biometric profile based on fine grained motion patterns. For example, Kwapisz et al. [15] performed biometric user identification and authentication based on physical activity patterns captured with a smartphone. The type of activities they used were walking, jogging and climbing stairs.

One of the limitations of those approaches is that they require high sampling rates in order to capture detailed movement patterns. This translates into higher computational and storage demands, thus, reducing battery lifetime. Furthermore, in order to build biometric profiles, the users need to perform specific movements or activities to train and use the system. The process of collecting this calibration data is generally tedious and time consuming, which hinders the applicability of the systems. In this work we perform user recognition using motion data collected with actigraphy devices based on daily activity patterns. The advantage of this approach is that it can be used with reduced sampling rates since it is based on higher level patterns as opposed to previous works that use fine grained patterns. Furthermore, this approach is more flexible since it does not require its users to follow detailed instructions such as performing specific movements or activities. Users just need to wear the device and perform their daily activities as usual. To test our approach, we used a dataset collected by 55 participants, which is one of the biggest ones used for user recognition based on wearable sensors. Our results for user recognition showed that there is potential to use daily patterns for user identification.

The rest of this paper is organized as follows: Sect. 2 presents the background and related works. Section 3 describes the details of the used dataset. Section 4 explains the preprocessing, feature extraction and user recognition approach. In Sect. 5 we present the experiments and results. Finally, in Sect. 6 we draw conclusions and propose possible future directions.

2   Background

Advances in sensor miniaturization enabled new capabilities for wearable devices. Specifically, inertial sensors have become very popular and are now embedded in many devices. Inertial sensors capture acceleration forces and orientation measurements. Within the context of smartphones, these sensors were initially intended for some specific purposes such as finding the phone's orientation so the screen can be rotated accordingly, and as a means of interaction for games and applications. Later, these sensors started to be used to infer contextual information about the device and user. For example, it is now common to have pedometer smartphone applications that are capable of counting the number of steps [11]. Inertial sensors in a smartphone can also be used for indoor localization using odometry techniques [20]. Inertial sensors have even been used for mood recognition in combination with physiological sensors [22].

Recently, it has been shown that the data produced by inertial sensors can also be used to generate behavior profiles for user authentication applications [1]. For example, Buriro et al. [4] used the accelerometer and gyroscope from a smart-watch to perform user authentication based on finger-snapping.

They evaluated three approaches: a Bayesian network, a multilayer perceptron and a random forest classifier. Their best results were obtained with the multilayer perceptron with a true acceptance rate of 66.14%. In another work, the same authors used a similar smartwatch setting but instead of recording finger-snapping, the users were asked to write their names in the air [3]. They achieved a true acceptance rate of 69.55% with a one-class multilayer perceptron trained with 10 samples. Some previous works have also used touchscreen interactions to capture behavior. For example, Jain and Kanhangad [12] proposed a method for user verification based on touchscreen interactions using common gestures such as scroll, swipe, zoom, tap, etc. Their method achieved an equal error rate of 0.31% on a relatively large dataset of 104 users. Another recent trend is the use of gait analysis using smartphones for user authentication [18]. Mufandaidza et al. [17] used a combination of dynamic time warping and a feed forward neural network to analyze walking patterns and achieved a true positive rate of 0.73, i.e., the system correctly identifies the authorized user 73% of the time.

Another potential source of information that could be used for user authentication is *actigraphy data*. Actigraphy is a method to monitor user activity levels using inertial sensors. Actigraphy devices are commonly worn on the wrist and they have less computational power compared to a smartphone or smartwatch but their battery lasts for longer periods of time which makes them suitable for long period studies, specially, in the medical field. These devices record activity levels based on acceleration and can be used to monitor sleep patterns [19], bipolar disorder patients [13], differentiate between bipolar disorder and attention-deficit/hyperactivity disorder [5], to name a few. In this work we explore the potential use of actigraphy data for user authentication. Instead of looking at fine grained movements, we analyze daily activity patterns in order to recognize users.

3   Dataset

For our experiments, we used the *DEPRESJON dataset* which is publicly available [9]. This dataset was collected by 55 participants wearing an actigraphy watch (Actiwatch, Cambridge Neurotechnology Ltd, England, model AW4) on their right wrist. On average, the participants wore the device for 20 continuous days. The device captures activity levels using a piezoelectric accelerometer that captures the amount and duration of movement in all directions. The sampling frequency is 32 Hz and movements over 0.05 g are recorded. A corresponding voltage is produced and is stored as an activity count in the memory unit of the device. The number of counts is proportional to the intensity of the movement. The accumulated activity counts are continuously recorded in one minute intervals. 23 of the participants were depressed patients and 32 were non-depressed controls. In this study, we did not take into account the participants' condition (depressed/non-depressed) since the main objective is to recognize the user and not the condition. Figure 1 shows an example of a portion of the collected data by one of the participants. The first column is the time of the day, the second column is the date and the third column contains the activity count.

Fig. 1. Example data from one of the participants.

4 Feature Extraction and User Recognition

From the raw activity counts, 51 features were extracted in a per day basis. The first set of features are the mean activity counts for each hour of the day (f1–f24). We also computed the standard deviation for each hour of the day (f25–f48). Finally, we computed 3 more features. The overall activity *mean, median* and *standard deviation* across all hours of the day. After that, the features were normalized between 0 and 1. Missing values were set to −1 and the first day from each user was excluded since it usually began at midday, thus, having a lot of missing values before that. After feature extraction, the total number of instances (feature vectors) were 1089, each, representing a single day of data.

For the recognition part, we trained a random forest classifier [2] since they have been shown to produce good overall results on many tasks [6]. The target label was the user id. A subset of the data from each user was used for training and an independent subset was used for testing (more details in Sect. 5). To get the final prediction, a majority vote approach was used. That is, for each user, predict the label for each of her/his testing days and output the most common label (user id).

5 Experiments and Results

For our experiments, we selected at random 50% of the users' days for training and the remaining for testing and we repeated this procedure 50 times to account for variability. The number of trees for the random forest was set to 500. Table 1 shows the resulting performance metrics. The overall obtained accuracy was 0.64 whereas the balanced accuracy was 0.82. The later is the average of the True Positive Rate (TPR) and the True Negative Rate (TNR). Figure 2 shows the resulting confusion matrix for the 55 users' classification. The antidiagonal shows the TPR. The white color represents a low value (0.0) whereas more solid colors represent higher values with a maximum of 1.0. Here, it can be seen that several users have high TPRs. Six users have a TPR of 1.0. On the other hand, some users have very low TPRs. Two of them have a TPR of 0.02. Although these results are far from perfect, they look promising given that we have data just for

1 min epochs compared to previous works where they have several samples per second. All in all, these results show potential for further improvement and the possibility to use daily activity patterns as means to perform user authentication.

Table 1. User recognition results

Metric	Value
Accuracy	0.64
True Positive Rate (TPR)	0.64
True Negative Rate (TNR)	0.99
Balanced accuracy	0.81

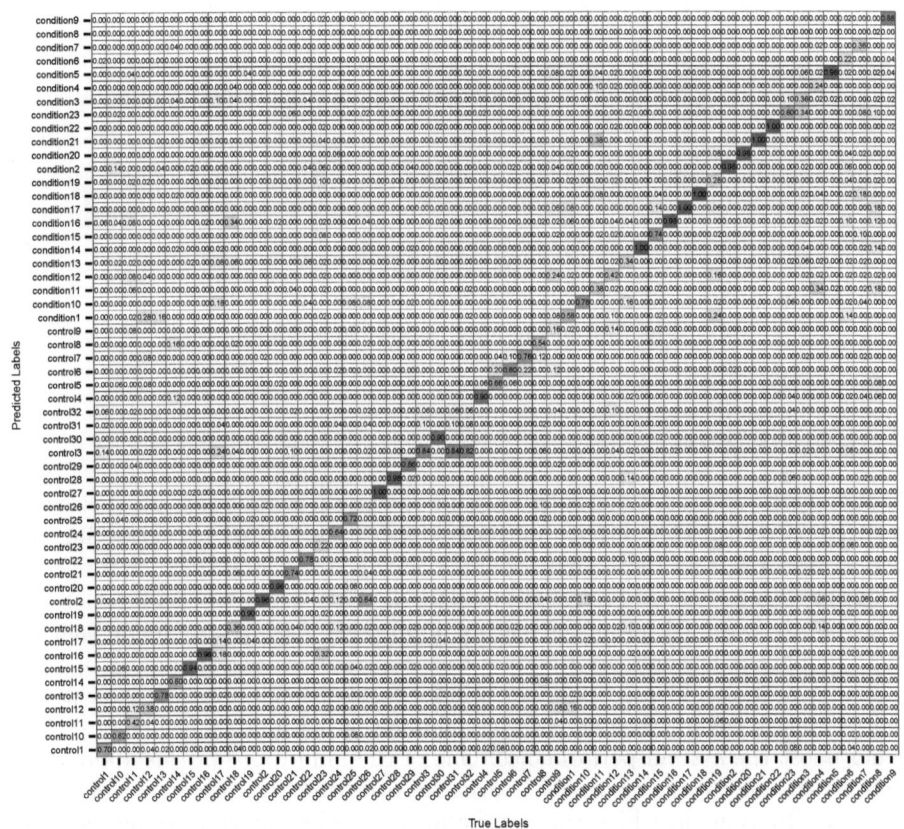

Fig. 2. Confusion matrix. The antidiagonal shows the true positive rates

Figure 3 shows the feature importance as obtained by the random forest classifier using the out-of-bag data based on mean decrease accuracy for the top

20 features. It can be seen that the two most important variables are the standard deviation (sd) and the mean. These two features capture patterns across all hours of the day. The next top important feature is *f7* which represents the mean activity counts between 6:00 and 7:00 a.m. Based on this, the most important features are based on the captured patterns across all hours of the day and the mean activity counts for each individual hour of the day. Within the top 20 features, three of them (f31, f33 and f40) are based on the standard deviation of the individual hours of the day.

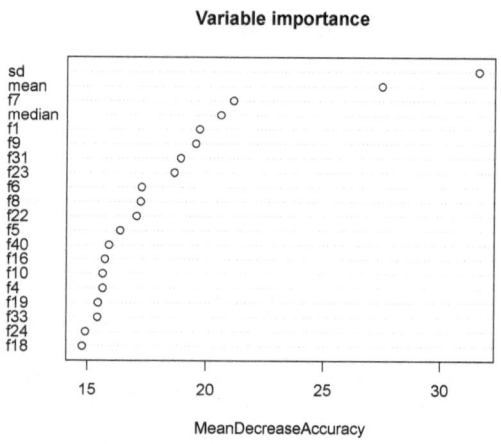

Fig. 3. Random forest feature importance.

6   Conclusions

In this work we used actigraphy data to recognize users based on their daily activity patterns. The activity patterns were characterized by extracting statistical features from the activity counts. Finally, a random forest classifier and majority voting were used to get the final predictions. The user classification true positive rate was 0.64. From the feature importance analysis, we found that the most significant features are the ones that capture overall patterns as opposed to hourly patterns. These results are still far from optimal but they show potential for improvement or to be used in combination with other techniques which could boost the system performance. One of the limitations of this approach is that it can suffer from within-user variances over time, i.e., users' patterns may change. Situations in which this can happen are when moving to another city, starting a new job, etc. This is known as concept drift [7] and we will explore possible solutions for future work. Another future direction is the extraction of more meaningful features, e.g., differentiating between morning, evening, and night patterns. Furthermore, the use of deep learning methods to find features automatically from the raw data is another possible future direction.

Acknowledgements. Research leading to these results has received funding from the EU ECSEL Joint Undertaking under grant agreement no 737459 (project Productive4.0) and from the Research Council of Norway.

References

1. Al-Naffakh, N., Clarke, N., Li, F.: Continuous user authentication using smartwatch motion sensor data. In: Gal-Oz, N., Lewis, P.R. (eds.) IFIPTM 2018. IAICT, vol. 528, pp. 15–28. Springer, Cham (2018). https://doi.org/10.1007/978-3-319-95276-5_2
2. Breiman, L.: Random forests. Mach. Learn. **45**(1), 5–32 (2001)
3. Buriro, A., Acker, R.V., Crispo, B., Mahboob, A.: AirSign: a gesture-based smartwatch user authentication. In: 2018 International Carnahan Conference on Security Technology (ICCST), pp. 1–5, October 2018. https://doi.org/10.1109/CCST.2018.8585571
4. Buriro, A., et al.: SNAPAUTH: a gesture-based unobtrusive smartwatch user authentication scheme. In: Saracino, A., Mori, P. (eds.) ETAA 2018. LNCS, vol. 11263, pp. 30–37. Springer, Cham (2018). https://doi.org/10.1007/978-3-030-04372-8_3
5. Faedda, G.L., et al.: Actigraph measures discriminate pediatric bipolar disorder from attention-deficit/hyperactivity disorder and typically developing controls. J. Child Psychol. Psychiatry **57**(6), 706–716 (2016)
6. Fernández-Delgado, M., Cernadas, E., Barro, S., Amorim, D.: Do we need hundreds of classifiers to solve real world classification problems? J. Mach. Learn. Res. **15**(1), 3133–3181 (2014)
7. Gama, J., Žliobaitė, I., Bifet, A., Pechenizkiy, M., Bouchachia, A.: A survey on concept drift adaptation. ACM Comput. Surv. **46**(4), 44 (2014)
8. Garcia-Ceja, E., Osmani, V., Maxhuni, A., Mayora, O.: Detecting walking in synchrony through smartphone accelerometer and Wi-Fi traces. In: Aarts, E., et al. (eds.) Ambient Intelligence, pp. 33–46. Springer, Cham (2014)
9. Garcia-Ceja, E., et al.: Depresjon: a motor activity database of depression episodes in unipolar and bipolar patients. In: Proceedings of the 9th ACM on Multimedia Systems Conference, MMSys 2018, pp. 472–477. ACM, New York (2018). https://doi.org/10.1145/3204949.3208125. http://doi.acm.org/10.1145/3204949.3208125
10. Garcia-Ceja, E., et al.: Mental health monitoring with multimodal sensing and machinelearning: a survey. Pervasive Mob. Comput. **51**, 1–26 (2018). https://doi.org/10.1016/j.pmcj.2018.09.003. http://www.sciencedirect.com/science/article/pii/S1574119217305692
11. Gowda, A.K.S.N., Babu, S.R., Sekaran, D.C.: UMOISP: usage mode and orientation invariant smartphone pedometer. IEEE Sens. J. **17**(3), 869–881 (2017). https://doi.org/10.1109/JSEN.2016.2635691
12. Jain, A., Kanhangad, V.: Exploring orientation and accelerometer sensor data for personal authentication in smartphones using touchscreen gestures. Pattern Recogn. Lett. **68**, 351–360 (2015). Special Issue on "Soft Biometrics"
13. Jones, S.H., Hare, D.J., Evershed, K.: Actigraphic assessment of circadian activity and sleep patterns in bipolar disorder. Bipolar Disord. **7**(2), 176–186 (2005)
14. Kwapisz, J.R., Weiss, G.M., Moore, S.A.: Activity recognition using cell phoneaccelerometers. SIGKDD Explor. Newsl. **12**(2), 74–82 (2011). https://doi.org/10.1145/1964897.1964918. http://doi.acm.org/10.1145/1964897.1964918

15. Kwapisz, J., Weiss, G., Moore, S.: Cell phone-based biometric identification. In: 2010 4th IEEE International Conference on Biometrics: Theory Applications and Systems (BTAS), pp. 1–7, September 2010. https://doi.org/10.1109/BTAS.2010.5634532

16. Mitchell, E., Monaghan, D., O'Connor, N.E.: Classification of sporting activities using smartphone accelerometers. Sensors 13(4), 5317–5337 (2013)

17. Mufandaidza, M.P., Ramotsoela, T.D., Hancke, G.P.: Continuous user authentication in smartphones using gait analysis. In: 44th Annual Conference of the IEEE Industrial Electronics Society, IECON 2018, pp. 4656–4661, October 2018. https://doi.org/10.1109/IECON.2018.8591193

18. Patel, V.M., Chellappa, R., Chandra, D., Barbello, B.: Continuous user authentication on mobile devices: recent progress and remaining challenges. IEEE Signal Process. Mag. 33(4), 49–61 (2016). https://doi.org/10.1109/MSP.2016.2555335

19. Sadeh, A., Acebo, C.: The role of actigraphy in sleep medicine. Sleep Med. Rev. 6(2), 113–124 (2002)

20. Solin, A., Cortes, S., Rahtu, E., Kannala, J.: Inertial odometry on handheld smartphones. In: 2018 21st International Conference on Information Fusion (FUSION), pp. 1–5, July 2018. https://doi.org/10.23919/ICIF.2018.8455482

21. Yang, J., Li, Y., Xie, M.: MotionAuth: motion-based authentication for wrist worn smart devices. In: 2015 IEEE International Conference on Pervasive Computing and Communication Workshops (PerCom Workshops), pp. 550–555, March 2015. https://doi.org/10.1109/PERCOMW.2015.7134097

22. Zenonos, A., et al.: HealthyOffice: mood recognition at work using smartphones and wearable sensors. In: 2016 IEEE International Conference on Pervasive Computing and Communication Workshops (PerCom Workshops), pp. 1–6, March 2016. https://doi.org/10.1109/PERCOMW.2016.7457166

Value-Based Core Areas of Trustworthiness in Online Services

Danny S. Guamán[1,2(✉)] ⓘ, Jose M. del Alamo[1] ⓘ,
Hristina Veljanova[3], Stefan Reichmann[4], and Anna Haselbacher[3]

[1] Universidad Politécnica de Madrid, 28040 Madrid, Spain
ds.guaman@dit.upm.es, jm.delalamo@upm.es
[2] Escuela Politécnica Nacional, Quito 170525, Ecuador
[3] University of Graz, 8010 Graz, Austria
{hristina.veljanova, anna.haselbacher}@uni-graz.at
[4] Graz University of Technology, 8010 Graz, Austria
stefan.reichmann@tugraz.at

Abstract. In the digital domain, users can be expected to place their trust in online services if they have a reason to believe that, in addition to the functional and quality of service aspects, their rights will be protected and their shared values respected. However, recent studies and surveys suggest that users do not actually trust in online services, one of the reasons being that technology unable to meet their values and address their concerns. To bridge this gap, this work-in-progress paper presents a set of core areas of trustworthiness for online services that have emerged from an interdisciplinary discussion involving a social, ethical, legal and technological perspective while paying due attention to the protection of European fundamental rights and values. It then analyses the manner in which each of these core areas of trustworthiness maps to well-known system properties and (post-compliance) operational requirements.

Keywords: Trustworthiness · Trust · Privacy · Data protection ·
Requirements · Ethical · Sociological · Legal · Label · Assurance

1 Introduction

Online services are an inherent component of most organisation processes and individuals' daily activities. Still, besides the numerous benefits they provide, there are several concerns regarding some of their features that can undermine their trustworthiness and this, in turn, users' trust. As indicated by a Eurobarometer survey, the general public's trust in digital applications and services remains quite low. For instance, 63% of the respondents do not trust online businesses [1]. On the one hand, the extensive literature on trust offers multiple perspectives, although most of them define interpersonal trust in terms of a relationship between a trustor (i.e. the subject that places trust in a target entity), and the trustee (i.e. the entity that is trusted) [2]. Accordingly, trust forms the basis for allowing a trustee to perform a particular action important to the trustor, regardless of the ability to monitor or control the trustee. Moving to the digital realm, wherein often there is no personal trustee, trust requires an

© IFIP International Federation for Information Processing 2019
Published by Springer Nature Switzerland AG 2019
W. Meng et al. (Eds.): IFIPTM 2019, IFIP AICT 563, pp. 81–97, 2019.
https://doi.org/10.1007/978-3-030-33716-2_7

objective assessment of the system trustworthiness in order to assure that it will perform as expected by the trustor [3].

On the other hand, the literature conceives trustworthiness as a multidimensional construct, as users can expect an online service to perform a diverse set of actions [4–6]. These actions have been approached primarily through mature system properties, such as security and dependability [4], focusing on those aspects that protect online services from (malicious) users, but not on those aspects that protect users from (malicious) online services [7]. Trends in users' attitudes suggest that trustworthy services need also to carry out actions to safeguard fundamental rights, such as privacy and autonomy, and to avoid a growing lack of user trust. As suggested by a Eurobarometer survey, the general public's trust in digital applications and online services remains quite low as 72% of Internet users are worried about being asked for a lot of personal data online [1]. Therefore, users can be expected to place their trust in those services if they have a reason to believe that their rights will be protected, and their shared values will be respected.

A sufficient understanding of the concepts of trust and trustworthiness thus needs to be interdisciplinary and include inputs from ethics, law and sociology, addressing concerns regarding users' fundamental rights and values by defining a set of core areas of trustworthiness. Subsequently, these core areas can be (partially) translated into operational requirements to be considered by online services that, in addition to supporting the reliability and dependability of online services, also contribute to engendering trust. The user's trust is not based solely on concrete technical practices for trustworthiness [7] as the core areas of trustworthiness, stemmed from Social Sciences and Humanities (SSH) realm, cannot be simplified and fully achieved only by technical systems, as they themselves are only subsystems of more complex socio-technical systems. This is why novel core areas of trustworthiness emerging from an interdisciplinary perspective can complement and extend the understanding of building, assessing, and providing trustworthy online services.

Towards this end, this paper presents some results of the H2020 TRUESSEC.eu project (https://truessec.eu). Taking into account that to this point labels have generally focused either on security or privacy, TRUESSEC.eu envisions a lightweight trustworthiness labelling scheme which overcomes the limitations of current labels by providing a label that not only contains security and privacy aspects but also goes beyond them. By having a strong focus on European values and fundamental rights, the TRUESSEC.eu label stipulates a set of requirements that make an ICT product and service trustworthy thus directly addressing the issue of how to enhance users' trust in ICT. In this direction, this work-in-progress paper presents a multidisciplinary discussion on identifying a set of core areas of trustworthiness and further analysing how this set could be translated into ICT system properties and detailed operational requirements.

The remainder of this paper is structured as follows. Section 2 introduces the core areas of trustworthiness and how they are approached from the perspective of three SSH disciplines, namely, sociology, law and ethics. Subsequently, Sect. 3 presents the approach followed to translate the core areas of trustworthiness into operational requirements. In Sect. 4, we outline the related works that is relevant for our proposal. Finally, Sect. 5 provides the conclusion of this paper and outlines future work.

2 Core Areas of Trustworthiness

This section starts by approaching the concept of trust and trustworthiness in the digital realm from a sociological (Sect. 2.1), ethical (Sect. 2.2) and legal (Sect. 2.3) perspective. Subsequently, based on the European values and fundamental rights and interdisciplinary work six common core areas of trustworthiness are defined, namely transparency, privacy, anti-discrimination, autonomy, respect, and protection. These core areas reflect the values that should be considered when developing and evaluating ICT products and services which ought to be trustworthy. Table 1 as well as the following subsections summarize our findings and showcase (a) how each of the three disciplines approach trust and trustworthiness against the background of European values and fundamental rights and (b) the disciplinary understanding of the six core areas. The sociological perspective provides a brief overview over the concept of trust. Additionally, based on survey data collection, the sociological input in Table 1 analyses the core areas from a macro level. The section on ethics presents those aspects that are relevant for trustworthy ICT products and services from a normative point of view. The focus of the legal perspective lies mainly on the European values (Art 2 Treaty on European Union) and the European fundamental rights as stated in the Charter of Fundamental Rights of the European Union as well as the European Convention on Human Rights. For a more detailed description of the core areas interested readers can refer to [8] and [9, 10] for details of the support studies.

2.1 Trust, Trustworthiness, and Social Interaction

Trust is irreducibly social. In many situations, users display "default trust" [11], i.e. trust based on individual assumptions regarding societal expectations pertinent to a given situation. In this way, trust acts as a proxy for cooperation, thereby reducing complexity [12]. Reduction of complexity becomes especially poignant in the wake of industrialization. Industrial and post-industrial division of labour entails, among other things, that users are increasingly forced to rely on expert knowledge which they do not understand. This has to do with a shift in worldview; pre-modern (traditional) societies believe in a universal order that foregrounds individual action. In such a worldview, there is no place for risk. On the other hand, moderns believe in individual autonomy; intentional actions have unintended consequences, which entails individual and collective risks. Trust thus gains traction in modernity: *"The uncertainties and risks modernity entails necessitate a belief in the good intentions of strangers"* [13]; however, "risk" should not, for this reason, be part of a definition of trust, as trust is a fundamental aspect of social interaction, whereas risk is part and parcel of a specifically modern ontology. The widespread use of digital products and services can be conceived in terms of reliance on experts (developers, companies, and lawmakers). Trust in experts can, therefore, be conceived as a proxy for relying on the technologies themselves.

A lack of trust is the main reason for consumers not to use digital products and services [14]. Contrary to recent theories of e-trust [15], which are overtly behaviourist/cognitive, social theorists stress the fundamentally social nature of trust. Conceptions of e-trust suffer from a cognitive/rationalistic bias that stems from the inability of accounts that ground trust in motivations or morality to apply to artefacts (which have no motivation and hence, no morality). Some authors acknowledge that trust is predicated upon contingency [16]; "trust begins where prediction ends" [11]. Contingency implies expectations. Without expectations, action would be impossible. Social action is directed towards the actions of others. Sociologically, trust is therefore conceived as "a reciprocal orientation and interpretative assumption that is shared, has the social relationship itself as the object, and is symbolized through intentional action" [17]. Georg Simmel observed that there can be love unrequited, but no unrequited trust [18]. "Faithfulness", as Simmel put it, is the only emotion sociological in form; it stems from interacting with others and it is epistemically situated between (complete) knowledge and (complete) ignorance of the other. In any case, it is insufficient to conceive of trust in digital products and services as merely psychological or merely behavioural, because trust necessarily refers to principles of morality, of mutual interests, and to social norms that oblige users to trust and be trustworthy.

2.2   Ethics, Trustworthiness, and ICT

Like any other technology, ICT has introduced numerous benefits to the individual and society, but at the same time, it has also created new ethical concerns and challenges. These concerns and challenges mainly stem from the pervasive and ubiquitous character of ICT. Moreover, ICT is also considered to have a tendency to demote particular values [19]. In that sense, taking values as a starting point for conducting an ethical analysis helps at arriving at a better understanding of the ethical issues related to ICT and paves the way for identifying the central requirements for trustworthy ICT products and services from a normative perspective.

The primary "currency" of today's ICT society is data. This has made *privacy* one of the most pressing issues. Privacy has a normative dimension and can be understood as an individual's claim to exercise control over one's data. Ethical concerns often arise when users lack answers as to activities with their personal data.

Privacy is closely related to the concept of *autonomy* because the former creates the conditions for the exercise of the latter. One way to reinforce autonomy is through informed consent which stands for the possibility of being informed about data processing activities and having the freedom to act upon one's decisions regarding data. Cases, where informed consent lacks, are ethically problematic as they directly undermine the very essence of autonomy.

The most significant concern in the domain of *justice* arises around practices of data-based discrimination and biased-decision making. The concerns pertain to cases where decisions are made based on individual's data that may lead to unjust treatment, bias or exclusion of some users or groups from certain opportunities.

The issues of *responsibility and accountability* play an essential role as well, in particular, due to the possible consequences of ICT. Responsibility and accountability can be observed in a two-fold manner: (a) forward-looking, where responsibility is understood as a duty concerning who should do what, and (b) retrospectively, where the morality of someone's actions is inspected [20].

Security is also one of the leading concepts as it is directly related to privacy, for instance. One way to analyse security issues in an ICT context is as the security of data and systems where data are stored. However, security can also be understood in a much broader sense as freedom from harm and protection of rights and liberties.

Transparency can be considered as the key concept in the ICT discourse as it serves as a means to realising, for instance, privacy, justice, responsibility. Transparency is also even more important due to the extensive informational asymmetry between users and providers of ICT products and services, that is, the lack of clear answers to the question *who* does *what, how,* and *why* with individual's personal data.

2.3   Legal Perspective of Trustworthiness in ICT

When two parties decide to establish a legal relationship, its fundament ideally must be mutual trust. We have therefore mapped out the European Union's legal framework regarding ICT, also taking into account the European fundamental rights and values.

Transparency constitutes one main core area of trustworthiness, which is legally assured by information duties. The GDPR's (*General Data Protection Regulation*) severe monetary fines particularly fuel its enforcement. Just like another requirement, transparency does not constitute a stand-alone area but is rather interconnected with others, such as autonomy or anti-discrimination.

While aiming to strengthen user's trust, *privacy* plays an essential role, which is emphasized by the fact that the Right to protection of personal data (Article 8 of the EU Charter of Fundamental Rights - CFR) and respect for private and family life (Art 7 CFR) are the two most referenced CFR in secondary EU legislation regarding ICT.

Legally considered, the core area regarding *justice* means that besides ensuring rights and freedoms to individuals; one must also be provided with effective remedies to effectively enforce the rights (TITLE VI CFR: JUSTICE). From a broader legal understanding justice includes equal treatment of individuals and thus non-discrimination (TITLE III CFR: EQUALITY). Within the ICT context, *anti-discrimination* is the key term to consider, meaning humans must not implement any discriminative features or processes in the online service.

Autonomy constitutes another core area of trustworthiness, legally referring to the individual's guaranteed fundamental freedoms (TITLE II CFR: FREEDOMS; including respect for private and family life and protection of personal data as well as the freedom to conduct business). As it is likely that conflicts will arise between the preserved Freedoms and other guaranteed fundamental rights, the aim is to find a balance between them. Considering ICT, autonomy results in the user's freedom to freely make decisions, thus being respected by the online service provider.

Legally speaking, the requirement of *respect* is referred to as lawfulness and must especially consider consumers. The fact that inside the ICT EU legal framework a usually high number of secondary legal acts can be observed within the area of consumer protection, namely a considerable number of fourteen, supports this view.

From a legal perspective, *security* means protecting individuals from harm, with the utmost fundamental Right to human dignity and life (TITLE I CFR: DIGNITY). In the ICT context, this implies actively providing *protection* to users, by preventing them from harm through fulfilling safety and cybersecurity standards

Table 1. Core areas of trustworthiness (*) The statistical data stem from the Eurobarometer Reports and Summaries and were collected between 2011 and 2017. Details in [10]

Sociological perspective (*)	Legal perspective	Ethical perspective	Core areas of trustworthiness
–Only a minority reads privacy statements (less than a fifth) in general while about 4 out of 10 internet users read the terms and conditions of the online platform –Over 90% want to be informed if their data ever was lost or stolen –Users who feel well-informed are more likely to adapt their security behaviour (e.g. changing passwords)	Transparency as in information duties laid down in the GDPR, the Directive on consumer rights or the e-commerce Directive	Transparency relates to two aspects: (i) providing clear and sufficient information about the products and services, and (ii) providing information to users regarding activities with their personal data	**Transparency:** The ICT product or service is provided in line with information duties regarding personal data processing and the product/service itself
–72% are concerned about the data collected about them on the Internet –More than half of internet users are uncomfortable with the use of their personal data for targeted advertising –General concern about misuse of personal data by corporate entities and public authorities (CMPD)	Privacy as preserving Respect for private life (Art 7 CFR) and the Protection of personal data (Art 8 CFR) in the context of ICT. This includes the GDPR and Directive 2002/58/EC	Privacy stands for the individual's claim to control the access to and the use of one's personal information. The idea behind it is that people have the claim to determine who knows what about them thus preventing unjustified interferences by others	**Privacy:** The ICT product or service allows the user to control access to and use of their personal information and it respects the protection of personal data
–7 out of 10 are concerned about their personal information being used for other purposes that it was collected for –Citizens state a negative impact of state surveillance activities on their general trust in ICT	Lawfulness as in lawful conduct and taking preventative care in accordance with the law, especially when dealing with consumers (Art 38 CFR)	Under the concepts of responsibility and accountability fall the following aspects: (i) Attribution of responsibility, (ii) Accepting responsibility, and (iii) Prevention	**Respect:** ICT products or services are to be provided in accordance with the legitimate expectations related to them

Sociological perspective	Legal perspective	Ethical perspective	Core areas of trustworthiness
–20% have changed the default settings of their browser, social network account and so on –A majority of respondents who use online social networks have tried to change their privacy settings from the default mode –Two-thirds are concerned about not having complete control over the information they provide online	Autonomy as preserving freedoms, such as Freedom of thought, conscience and religion (Art 10 CFR), Freedom of expression and information (Art 11 CFR), Freedom to conduct a business (Art 16 CFR) and the Right to (intellectual) property (Art 17 CFR)	Autonomy can be seen as relating to (i) capacity for self-determination, i.e. capacity/ability to lead one's life and make decisions based on one's beliefs, values and motives, and (ii) possibility (freedom) to act upon one's judgment regarding aspects that affect one's life	**Autonomy:** The ICT product or service gives users the opportunity to make decisions and respects those decisions. The ICT product or service also respects other parties'/persons' rights and freedoms
–Concern about targeted advertising and search engine results, which some users expect to be adapted to their needs. However, this is not a majority	Justice as the remedies against the unjustified use of force by the state, such as the Right to a fair trial (Art 47 CFR) and the Presumption of innocence (Art 48 CFR). This meaning further entails Equality before the law (Art 20 CFR) and Anti-discrimination (Art 21 CFR)	Justice relates to aspects such as: (i) anti-bias, (ii) fairness, and (iii) distributive justice	**Anti-discrimination:** The ICT product or service does not include any discriminative practices and biases
–Two thirds to a quarter of EU citizens are concerned about being a victim of cybercrime or that their online personal information is not kept secure by websites or public authorities –In general, European citizens dislike public authorities having access to their Internet usage data (fear of surveillance)	Security as the protection from harm, such as the Right to liberty and security (Art 6 CFR) as well as the Right to the integrity of the person (Art 3 CFR) and the Right to life (Art 2 CFR)	Security is understood as freedom from (physical, psychological, economic etc.) harm and protection of one's rights, liberties	**Protection:** ICT products and services are provided in accordance with safety and cybersecurity standards

3 From Core Areas of Trustworthiness to Operational Requirements

The six core areas (transparency, privacy, anti-discrimination, autonomy, respect, and protection) represent high-level concepts that need to be broken down into a set of requirements in the sense that they relate to more specific, well-known system properties of online services. We acknowledge that the core areas of trustworthiness, stemmed from sociological, legal, and ethical contexts, cannot be simplified and fully achieved only by technical systems, as they themselves are only subsystems of more complex socio-technical systems. However, they, can still contribute to satisfying the aforementioned core areas to certain extents. This section, therefore, presents a translation process consisting of two stages: a mapping of the core areas of trustworthiness to meaningful system properties along with the extent to which these contribute to satisfying the core areas (Sect. 3.1) and an operationalization process of the system properties to operational requirements (Sect. 3.2).

3.1 Mapping of Core Areas of Trustworthiness to System Properties

A system property defines a quality or behavioural characteristic of a system that can be evaluated qualitatively or quantitatively. There are numerous system properties enabling trustworthiness already studied in the technical realm (each with a different maturity level), so the knowledge base around them can be leveraged to elicit the specific operational requirements that need to be met and assessed for trustworthy online services. For instance, the S-Cube model considers nine categories of properties or attributes [21], whereas OPTET refines them into 11 categories and 29 sub-attributes [22]. Moreover, Hansen et al. [23] have further divided the notion of privacy into more concrete system properties, and these, in turn, have been broken down them into more concrete requirements for protecting privacy [24]. Our approach does not criticise individual contributions on system properties, but we propose building on these works to build a bridge between the leading SSH requirements and their corresponding operational requirements.

By following a top-down approach proposed in a previous work [25] and backed by interdisciplinary supporting studies (i.e. sociological [10], ethical [9], legal [26], and technological [27]), the core areas of trustworthiness have been mapped into a subset of the more relevant and concrete system properties of online services. When analysing the system properties, several interrelations were observed. Each system property relates to specific Core Areas; however, each system property does not need to address all Core Areas as long as all of them are addressed by a few of the system properties to a satisfactory degree. Table 2 provides an overview of this mapping along with the extent to which a system property contributes to the core areas. A brief rationale for the mapping is elaborated in the following paragraphs; note also that, although the system properties may contribute to multiple core areas to different extents, they are presented within the core area to which they mostly contribute.

Table 2. Core areas and related system properties enabling trustworthiness (●: covers the core area to a high extent; ◐: covers the core area to a medium extent; ◔: covers the core area to a low extent; ○: does not cover the core area)

System property	Core areas of trustworthiness					
	Transparency	Privacy	Anti-discrimination	Autonomy	Respect	Protection
Transparency (Accessibility)	●	●	◔	●	◔	◔
Transparency (Processing of personal data)	●	●	○	◐	◐	○
Intervenability (Consent)	◐	●	○	●	◔	○
Intervenability (Control)	◐	●	◔	●	◐	◔
Unlinkability	○	●	●	◔	○	◔
Explainability	◔	○	●	◐	◔	○
Traceability/Auditability	●	●	●	○	●	◔
Security	◐	○	○	○	◔	●

Transparency. This core area mainly relates to *transparency* including both *accessibility* and *processing of personal data* dimensions and *auditability*. *Transparency, in terms of accessibility* [28], refers to the form in which information is provided to users. Thus, while information can refer to the system's functionality, usage or quality features, *accessibility* ensures that it has an impact on users' awareness. To this end, an online service must provide information that is easy to find and access as well as easily understandable by users.

Transparency, in terms of the processing of personal data, is one of the three well-known system properties defined in the privacy realm (i.e. transparency, unlinkability, and intervenability [23]). This allows informing users whenever their personal data is processed by providing information on data processing, e.g., the categories of data being collected and used, who access them, the duration for which the data is retained, and the location wherein the data is stored.

Traceability/auditability reflects the capability of a system to generate, collect, and avail the evidence (e.g., records or logs) of a processing instance or any relevant event and, in turn, enable the relative ease of auditing a system. Thus, whereas the target for the above two properties is the user, the target for this property could be a supervisory authority. Increasing transparency requires service providers to clarify how they use and process personal data, and traceability and auditability allow for reconstructing, examining, and using the sequence of events to achieve transparency as well as to demonstrate compliance.

Finally, it can be noted that *transparency,* as a precursor for specific, comprehensive, and understandable information, is a prerequisite for satisfying other core areas. For instance, *autonomy* cannot be ensured if users are unable to understand information for decision-making. *Privacy*, in the sense of control over personal data processing, is ineffective if users do not understand information related to the processing of their personal data. Similarly, *auditability* allows for retrospective accountability (which is essential for the *Respect core area*) by providing evidence to help demonstrate compliance, for example, with. a predetermined privacy policy.

Privacy. This core area mainly relates to *transparency, intervenability (control and consent)* and *unlikability. Intervenability,* in the sense of *control,* allows providing stakeholders (e.g. data subjects and supervisory authorities) with the means "*to interfere with the ongoing or planned data processing*" [23]. To this end, an online service should keep users in the loop by providing them with accessible means to access and review the accuracy and completeness of their data, as well as update and delete their personal data. Accessibility to control options is essential, i.e. users should be able to exercise them with a reasonable effort.

Intervenability (consent) allows users can give and/or withdraw their consent to the processing of their personal data. Therefore, an online service must be able to provide relevant and sufficient information promptly to enable users to make informed decisions about the use of the service and what information is processed about them. It should be noted that *transparency,* particularly in the sense of *accessibility,* is a precondition for consent, as users are free to give their consent to something they know and understand.

Unlinkability allows for greater (implicit) control over the processing of personal data. The rationale behind this mapping is that by preventing one event from being linked to another, an online service limits the potential impact on the users' privacy. Unlinkability could prevent that online services built to use unique identifiers (e.g., IP address, SIM mobile, or a Wi-fi SSID) from being associated to users and ultimately prevent undesirable profiling based on the actions or data generated by them. Unlinkability is related to *data minimization*, which states that the amount of data processed should be limited to the minimum possible while the consented purpose is achieved.

Anti-discrimination. This core area mainly relates to *unlinkability, explainability* and *auditability.* As already mentioned, *unlinkability* aims at preventing online services from linking personal data within and across domains. This is particularly important, as today's online services can use technologies that have the potential to process large amounts of (personal) data, very often from multiple domains, allowing significant levels of customization and decision making based on criteria such as religion, political affiliation, social status, incomes, and further on.

Explainability [29–32] allows decision factors or the decision-making process to be informed to the different stakeholders, allowing them to determine whether online services may have any bias. This property aims at explaining the factors used (or not used) by an online service to make a specific decision rather than a detailed explanation of the system's inner behaviour. For example, if an organization claims that an individual was denied a loan because their income is low, then the online service is expected to consider the individual when his income increases.

Autonomy. This core area mainly relates to *transparency* and *intervenability.* Autonomy is linked to supporting users in delivering informed consent, i.e., the system should provide the means for users to have the possibility to make an informed decision, e.g., on any processing instance regarding their personal data. In this regard, informed consent encompasses two system properties already explained above, i.e. *transparency and intervenability. Transparency* ensures that decision-making is supported by comprehensive, accessible, and precise information, while *intervenability* supports decision-making including the possibility of both granting and withdrawing consent.

Respect. This core area mainly relates to *traceability/auditability*. As *respect* implies accountability and liability, this cannot be covered through purely technical measures but requires organizational measures such as the definition of governance, a statement of legal compliance or an appropriate dispute resolution process. Nevertheless, *traceability/auditability* (already explained) is primarily aimed at supporting this core area by providing the evidence to demonstrate compliance with legal requirements.

Protection. This core area mainly relates to *safety, security* (i.e. properties of *confidentiality, integrity,* and *availability*), and *reliability. Safety* ensures the absence of risks that may cause physical injury or damage to the users' well-being, whether direct or indirect, as a result of the damage to the system or its environment [4].

Security, on the other hand, assures online service protection against malicious unauthorized access (*confidentiality*), modification (*integrity*), or use (*availability*) [4]. From these initial properties, other refined properties can be identified, e.g., *authenticity, non-repudiability,* and *control* [33].

It can be noted that the protection-related properties are relevant to the '*privacy*' core area. Privacy has a great value in the trustworthiness discourse; however, it cannot be guaranteed without the existence of a solid security infrastructure that ensures the security capabilities of online services. It can serve as a shield against any security breaches and cases of identity theft, unauthorized access of third parties, etc.

3.2   From System Properties to Operational Requirements

Once the system attributes have been identified, they can be used as a basis for carrying out an operationalization process and deriving a set of more specific operational requirements. When doing that, a challenge arouse with respect to abstaining from turning it into a compliance checklist, as already there is a law regulating this aspect, which ensures that online services act within the legal framework in this regard. This challenge was addressed by distinguishing between compliance and beyond compliance [12]. In this sense, compliance is an important aspect of building trust among citizens. However, very often, it is not sufficient. A measure that could help in filling in this gap is the adoption of a "post-compliance approach". It implies doing more than what the law requires and addressing those aspects that the law does not address in their entirety or to which it does not offer straightforward guidance. Introducing ethics is one way to do so, as it could provide solutions to questions that the law leaves unanswered. Against this background, the operational requirements elicited stand on this post-compliance level. At the time of writing, a set of 81 operational requirements has been outlined in [34].

Figure 1 depicts the interrelations among the elements of the operationalization process. The operational requirements define the capabilities that an online service should guarantee in order to satisfy one or more of the aforementioned system properties. They can be used as a precursor to the selection of more concrete (standard) measures or countermeasures that are known as *controls*. Finally, controls are realised by one or more specific *techniques*, which are implementable ways to meet a control.

There are subtle differences and interrelations between the guiding elements of the operationalization process. Although both *operational requirements* and *controls* specify system capabilities required (problem domain) and provided (solution domain), respectively, an *operational requirement* recognises that a capability seldom derives from a single *control* (i.e., fulfilling an *operational requirement* may require multiple *controls*). *Controls,* therefore, are more concrete measures than *operational requirements* and often detail a concrete *technique(s)* to be implemented in a particular context. Accordingly, *operational requirements* can be satisfied to different extents by implementing different *controls* and *techniques*, depending on the needs of the context (e.g. a higher risk scenario may require stronger controls). A *trustworthiness profile* represents a particular set of controls and techniques necessary to meet the operational requirements of an online service to be used in a particular context.

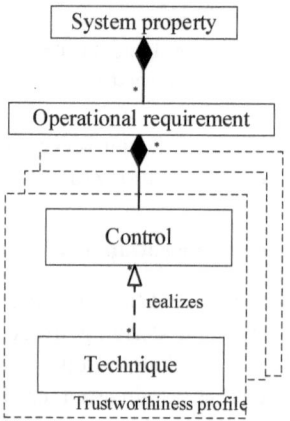

Fig. 1. Guiding elements of the operationalization process [25]

Finally, *does the state of the art support the implementations of the operational requirements related to the core areas of trustworthiness?* Security and privacy task force has provided some inputs regarding some barriers that may prevent existing technologies from satisfying the core areas of trustworthiness (in particular, members of the IoTUK[1], AIOTI WOG03[2], and IoTMark initiatives have been surveyed[3]). The input received has been crossed with European reports and literature, and the following are highlighted:

- While it should be recognised that the state of the art already provides plenty of *controls* contained in standard catalogues and frameworks for other more mature properties (ECSO presents a syllabus with around 290 standards and certification

---

[1] https://iotuk.org.uk.

[2] https://aioti.eu/working-groups.

[3] Appendix B of this document shows the survey carried out in the task force: https://truessec.eu/content/deliverable-52-technical-gap-analysis.

schemes for the cybersecurity realm [35]), *controls* related to anti-discrimination or autonomy are scarce and only recently there are some efforts and initiatives to address them (General).

- Many system properties that enable trustworthiness (e.g. privacy, security, and transparency properties) are fragile with respect to composition, i.e. *"if a system that fulfils a certain property is embedded within or connected to another system, it is hard to assess if that property is preserved"* [36]. The fragility of these properties is becoming even more critical in the current ICT landscape, where an online service is actually a system of systems, being challenging to ensure end-to-end trustworthiness (General).

- The increasing complexity of the supply chain also increases the difficulty of holding an entity accountable for some action, as "obligations" travels across multiple parties. For instance, it is difficult defining a closed set of technical measures that support the enforcement and auditing of the organizational or legal security obligations due to the cascading effect from the interdependent threats (coming from multiple parties) (General).

- Lack of user-centric assurance mechanisms to inform about trustworthiness-related risks. The information on the functional operation and quality attributes of online services is usually conveyed through assurance mechanism (e.g. third-party certification), and they are mainly oriented to the business market instead of the consumer market. For instance, cybersecurity certification of online services can involve the assessment of hundreds of security controls, so it is impossible for users to identify the level of security offered by online services [7]. It is necessary, therefore, to have alternative user-centric mechanisms, such as ratings, labels and sales, so that users are able to appraise and compare capabilities of different products or services without feeling overwhelmed with technical details (General).

- Controls (and techniques) to ensure anti-discrimination are expensive, as explaining everything is expensive. This is not a purely technical barrier, but it is related to creating a system that, besides performing complex tasks, must provide an explanation that is a non-trivial engineering task. Thus, as remarked by Doshi-Velez et al. *"requiring explanation all the time may create a financial burden that disadvantages smaller companies; if the decisions are low enough risk, we may not wish to require explanation"* [37] (Anti-discrimination).

- Conflation about the scope and target audience of transparency mechanisms. Providing transparency about data protection activities has proven to be difficult, with privacy policies being the primary means of informing data subjects. Privacy policies, however, are very complex as users are not familiar with the terminology used by privacy experts, and they do not clearly understand the consequences of accepting the policy because assessing the subsequent risks is not straightforward [28]. Accordingly, only a minority of users read privacy statements (Transparency).

- One of the essential precursors for informed decision making is to understand what we are agreeing with. Therefore, users cannot exercise their right to autonomy without transparency. However, an issue identified in some of today's online services is that non-expert users cannot connect notices about the processing of their personal data with the risks of consenting to it [38] (Autonomy and transparency).

- Users exercise their privacy preferences based on the configuration of permissions or access control rules. For instance, in mobile phones *"[some app] should be able to access [some resource]"*. For these mechanisms to be effective, users must be able to exercise them with reasonable effort. However, current online services (e.g. those accessed through mobile apps) require users to manually set one or two hundred on/off options, requiring an amount of time that could overwhelm them (Privacy).
- Currently, some PETs look like stand-alone solutions that are initiated by users as self-defence measures (e.g. installing web browser add-ons or using anonymity-enhanced browsers), but they are not part of the implementation of the service itself, nor are they considered during the initial design stages. This fact is also observed by ENISA (European Union Agency for Network and Information Security) which claims that *"software development tools for privacy need to be provided to enable the intuitive implementation of privacy properties"* [36] (Privacy).
- Plenty of privacy techniques and technologies have been proposed in the last years [36], however, one of the key challenges to build a privacy-friendly system *"is the difficulty to decide when a PET may be mature enough to implement it in a system"* [39]. It could lead engineers to try to meet an operational privacy requirement using a low-quality PET. This issue can be found in the literature (e.g., [40]), where some supposedly anonymized data sets may be actually linked to the data subjects' identities (Privacy).

4   Related Works

Several works have been developed to address different aspects of trustworthiness of online services. Most of them, however, are only approached from a technological perspective addressing only their technical features [7, 22], thus failing to adopt a multidisciplinary perspective to address concerns regarding values and fundamental rights. Others, which are also in the technological realm, focus on a particular system property, primarily concentrating on security or safety ([4, 33]) and recently even on privacy ([23, 41, 42]), without taking into account other relevant system properties to meet further core areas of trustworthiness. Thus, the work presented in this paper and, in particular, the criteria of trustworthiness represent a novelty owing to several reasons. First, they are the result of a comprehensive interdisciplinary work comprising ethical, legal, societal and technical aspects. Second, substantial emphasis is particularly placed on the ethical input, as the study conducted by Gibello [43] suggests that it misses existing labels very often or is overshadowed by concerns related to the quality of service or by the dominant legal aspects and the focus on compliance. Third, the criteria of trustworthiness focus on cybersecurity and privacy as the most mature domains regarding certification and labelling (e.g., around 290 cybersecurity standards and certifications schemes are available according to ECSO [35]). However, at the same time, these criteria of trustworthiness go beyond these two domains and cover various aspects of more recently established ones such as transparency, autonomy, and anti-discrimination.

Against this background, the notion that underlies the development of these criteria of trustworthiness, in conjunction with its great focus on the ethical aspects, most closely resembles the framework provided by Luciano Floridi [44]. When referring to digital services, Floridi distinguishes between hard and soft ethics. According to him, the former informs and shapes the law, whereas the latter is *"what we usually have in mind when discussing values, rights, duties, and responsibilities – or, more broadly, what is morally right or wrong and what ought or ought not to be done"*. In this sense, soft ethics operates on the post-compliance level and in this way addresses the issues and aspects that the law does not. This distinction between hard and soft ethics can be valuable in addressing the aforementioned gaps, including the extremely limited focus on ethics or too extensive dominance of legal requirements or service-related concerns in the current labels.

5 Conclusions

In this work, we have presented a set of six high-level core areas of trustworthiness (transparency, privacy, anti-discrimination, autonomy, respect, and protection) which is the result of comprehensive interdisciplinary research, comprising ethical, legal, societal and technical aspects. They complement and extend the state of the art for building and assessing trustworthy online services. Subsequently, these core areas have been translated into well-known properties and turned into (post-compliance) requirements that can be realised and assessed. It should be noted, however, that the requirements described in this paper address ICT products and services in general. This implies that once they are applied to a particular context i.e. particular product or service a certain modification or adjustment can be expected. In this respective, businesses need to recognise the added value of implementing such requirements, which may seem costly in the short run, but actually form an outstanding benefit on the market in the long run.

These contributions pave the way to move towards a lightweight and automated labelling solution for the trustworthiness of ICT products and services. In this context, our future work points in two directions: (i) enable machine-to-machine integration based on required trustworthiness levels (defined by users through a policy configuration) and trustworthiness levels offered by the labelling subject matters and (ii) a scalable architecture for the automated assessment of elicited operational requirements applied to the mobile ecosystem.

Acknowledgement. The research leading to these results has received funding from the European Union's Horizon 2020 research and innovation programme under grant agreement No 731711. The first author would like to extend thanks to his sponsor Escuela Politécnica Nacional.

References

1. Keighley, T.C.: Special Eurobarometer 431: Data Protection Report (2015)
2. Grandison, T., Sloman, M.: Trust in internet applications. Communications, 2–16 (2000)

3. Taddeo, M.: Modelling trust in artificial agents, a first step toward the analysis of e-trust. Minds Mach. **20**(2), 243–257 (2010)
4. Avižienis, A., Laprie, J.C., Randell, B., Landwehr, C.: Basic concepts and taxonomy of dependable and secure computing. IEEE Trans. Dependable Secur. Comput. **1**(1), 11–33 (2004)
5. Mohammadi, N.G.: Trustworthiness attributes and metrics for engineering trusted internet-based software systems. Cloud Comput. Serv. Sci. **1**, 165–184 (2012)
6. Hoffman, L.J., Lawson-Jenkins, K., Blum, J.: Trust beyond security. Commun. ACM **49**(7), 94–101 (2006)
7. Osterwalder, D.: Trust through evaluation and certification? Soc. Sci. Comput. Rev. **19**(1), 32–46 (2011)
8. Stelzer, H., et al.: TRUESSEC D4.3: First draft Criteria Catalogue and regulatory recommendations (2018). https://truessec.eu/content/d43-first-draft-criteria-catalogue-and-regulatory-recommendations. Accessed 05 Oct 2018
9. Stelzer, H., Veljanova, H.: TRUESSEC D4.2: Support Study of Ethical Issues (2017)
10. Reichmann, S., Griesbacher, M.: TRUESSEC D3.1: Assurance and certification of privacy and security of ICT products and services as a question of trust, acceptance and perceived risks across Europe (2017)
11. Lewis, J.D., Weigert, A.J.: The social dynamics of trust: theoretical and empirical research, 1985–2012. Soc. Forces **91**(1), 25–31 (2012)
12. Luhmann, N.: Trust and power/two works by Niklas Luhmann; with Introduction by Gianfranco Poggi. Wiley, Chichester (1979)
13. Reichmann, S.: TRUESSEC.eu-European values and the digital single market from a sociological perspective. In: Proceedings of the 21st International Legal Informatics Symposium (2018)
14. Bons, R.W.H., Lee, R.M., Wagenaar, R.W.: Obstacles for the development of open electronic commerce. Erasmus University, Erasmus University Research Institute for Decision and Information Systems (EURIDIS) (1995)
15. Taddeo, M., Floridi, L.: The case for e-trust. Ethics Inf. Technol. **13**(1), 1–3 (2014)
16. Sztompka, P.: Trust: A Sociological Theory. Cambridge University Press, Cambridge (1999)
17. Lewis, J.D., Weigert, A.J.: Social atomism, holism, and trust. Sociol. Q. **26**(4), 455–471 (1985)
18. Möllering, G.: The nature of trust: from Georg Simmel to a theory of expectation, interpretation and suspension. Sociology **35**(2), 403–420 (2001)
19. Brey, P.: Values in Technology and Disclosive Computer Ethics. The Cambridge Handbook of Information and Computer Ethics, pp. 41–58. Cambridge University Press, Cambridge (2010)
20. Williams, G.: Responsibility. Internet Encycl. Philos. (2006)
21. Gehlert, A., Metzger, A.: Quality Reference Model for SBA, vol. 215483 (2013)
22. Mohammadi, N.G., Paulus, S., Bishr, M., Metzger, A., Koennecke, H.: An Analysis of Software Quality Attributes and Their Contribution to Trustworthiness, pp. 542–552 (2015)
23. Hansen, M., Jensen, M., Rost, M.: Protection goals for privacy engineering. In: Proceedings of - 2015 IEEE Security and Privacy Workshop, SPW 2015, pp. 159–166 (2015)
24. Meis, R., Heisel, M.: Computer-aided identification and validation of intervenability requirements. Information **8**(1), 30 (2017)
25. Martín, Y., del Alamo, J.M., Yelmo, J.C.: Engineering privacy requirements: valuable lessons from another realm. In: 2014 IEEE 1st International Workshop on Evolving Security and Privacy Requirements Engineering (ESPRE), pp. 19–24 (2015)
26. Gibello, V.: TRUESSEC D4.1: Legal Analysis (2017). https://truessec.eu/content/deliverable-41-legal-analysis

27. Guamán, D.S., Del Álamo, J., Martin, S., Yelmo, J.C.: TRUESSEC D5.1: technology situation analysis: Current practices and solutions (2017). https://truessec.eu/content/deliverable-51-technology-situation-analysis-current-practices-and-solutions. Accessed 05 Oct 2018

28. Schaub, F., Balebako, R., Cranor, L.F.: Designing effective privacy notices and controls. IEEE Internet Comput. 21(3), 70–77 (2017)

29. Ribeiro, M.T., Singh, S., Guestrin, C.: 'Why Should I Trust You?': Explaining the Predictions of Any Classifier (2016)

30. Adler, P., et al.: Auditing black-box models for indirect influence. Knowl. Inf. Syst. 54(1), 95–122 (2018)

31. Kindermans, P.-J., et al.: Learning how to explain neural networks: PatternNet and PatternAttribution, pp. 1–12 (2017)

32. Goodman, B., Flaxman, S.: European Union regulations on algorithmic decision-making and a 'right to explanation,' pp. 1–47 (2016)

33. Parker, D.: Our excessively simplistic information security model and how to fix it. ISSA J. 8, 12–21 (2010)

34. Medina, M., et al.: Trust- Enhancing Label launching roadmap (2018). https://truessec.eu/sites/default/files/evidence/d7.5_european_trust_enhancing_label_launching_roadmap.pdf

35. ECSO: State-of-the-Art Syllabus Overview of existing cybersecurity standards and certification schemes (2017). https://www.ecs-org.eu/documents/publications/5a31129ea8e97.pdf. Accessed 05 Oct 2018

36. Danezis, G., et al.: Privacy and Data Protection by Design - from policy to engineering, December 2015

37. Doshi-Velez, F., et al.: Accountability of AI Under the Law: The Role of Explanation, pp. 1–15 (2017)

38. Felt, A., Ha, E., Egelman, S., Haney, A.: Android permissions: user attention, comprehension, and behavior. In: Proceedings of SOUPS, pp. 1–14 (2012)

39. Hansen, M., Hoepman, J.-H., Jensen, M.: ENISA REPORT: Readiness Analysis for the Adoption and Evolution of Privacy Enhancing Technologies, December 2015

40. Narayanan, A., Shmatikov, V.: Robust de-anonymization of large sparse datasets. In: Proceedings of the IEEE Symposium on Security and Privacy, pp. 111–125 (2008)

41. Meis, R., Heisel, M.: Understanding the privacy goal intervenability. In: Katsikas, S., Lambrinoudakis, C., Furnell, S. (eds.) TrustBus 2016. LNCS, vol. 9830, pp. 79–94. Springer, Cham (2016). https://doi.org/10.1007/978-3-319-44341-6_6

42. Meis, R., Wirtz, R., Heisel, M.: A taxonomy of requirements for the privacy goal transparency. In: Fischer-Hübner, S., Lambrinoudakis, C., Lopez, J. (eds.) TrustBus 2015. LNCS, vol. 9264, pp. 195–209. Springer, Cham (2015). https://doi.org/10.1007/978-3-319-22906-5_15

43. Gibello, V.: Evaluation of existing trustworthiness seals and labels (2018). https://truessec.eu/content/deliverable-71-evaluation-exiting-trustworthiness-seals-and-labels. Accessed 05 Oct 2018

44. Floridi, L.: Soft ethics: its application to the general data protection regulation and its dual advantage. Philos. Technol. 31(2), 163–167 (2018)

Trusting the IoT: There Is More to Trust Than Trustworthiness

Piotr Cofta$^{(\boxtimes)}$ (iD)

University of Science and Technology (UTP), Bydgoszcz, Poland
piotr.cofta@utp.edu.pl

Abstract. The emergence of the IoT as an everyday fact raises the question how the IoT can be trusted. Considering that the IoT is pervasive to the level of being secretive, practically monopolistic and that human participation is often involuntary, it hardly satisfies the assumptions that associate the often researched types of trust relationships. In order to study trust in the IoT, alternative views on trust may be needed. This paper analyses the IoT as a representation of imperfect systems, i.e. systems that by architectural choices are unable to guarantee predictably repeatable operations. This property may invalidate the metaphor of trusting technology that is constructed out of replicating human-to-human trust. This paper examines alternative views on trust that may better fit the specificity of the IoT and generally imperfect systems, adopted from psychology, sociology or ergonomics. While no definitive approach is indicated, this paper serves as an overview of possible directions in trust research.

Keywords: Internet of Things · IoT · Trust models · Trust metaphor · Imperfect systems

1   Introduction

Internet of Things (IoT) is one of the current defining trends of the Internet, eventually linking billions of devices with cloud and fog computing into an infrastructure that will sense and control our environment. The vision of IoT assumes that it will be pervasive, invisible and monopolistic while our participation will be involuntary [4].

As such, the question of trusting the IoT is of paramount importance. This paper argues that we are currently ill-prepared to answer this question. This is because the problem introduced by the rise of IoT correlates with the paradigm shift in computing, towards imperfect computing. That, in turn, should shift a discussion from assuring the trustworthiness of the system to discussing ways of trusting systems that are currently not considered fully trustworthy, in situations that are devoid of real choices.

While the IoT is a prominent example of imperfect systems, it is not the only one. This paper starts with the introduction to imperfect computing, providing a brief summary of its common characteristics. Subsequently it analyses common assumptions about trust, mostly invalidated by the IoT. Next, it investigates some of the theories that may be applicable to explain situations of trust in the IoT. The paper concludes with some comments regarding suggested directions in research.

© IFIP International Federation for Information Processing 2019
Published by Springer Nature Switzerland AG 2019
W. Meng et al. (Eds.): IFIPTM 2019, IFIP AICT 563, pp. 98–107, 2019.
https://doi.org/10.1007/978-3-030-33716-2_8

2 IoT as Imperfect Computing

Imperfect computing, as the name suggests, happens when computing systems occasionally provide incorrect or incomplete answer, not because of their fault or because they are intentionally made to do so, but because of the inherent architectural properties of those systems. Thus, imperfect computing cannot be made more perfect without significant changes to its architecture.

In a way, computing is experiencing what physics did in the last century: the transition from the Newtonian paradigm of deterministic repeatability and predictability to statistical approach that now permeates all fields of physics. In a similar manner, imperfect computing indicates the transition from the paradigm of deterministic outcome out of deterministic data to the uncertainty of it, which is not always statistical in its nature.

While the notion of imperfect computing covers several techniques, following is a brief overview of select ones.

Eventual consistency is a technical property shared by such diverse technologies as blockchain [27], NoSQL databases [14] and stream processing [16]. The state of the system is by design inconsistent, on assumption that eventually, under some conditions, it will converge to a consistent one. As the body of knowledge available to the system changes in time and is inconsistent between locations of the elements of the system, the response depends on both: time and place.

Learning algorithms are a form of imperfection associated with machine learning classification systems [11]. It is a property of the learning algorithm that its internal state changes as the result of learning, in a way that is not explainable. Thus, the response to the same query may change in time, reflecting the learning process.

Approximate computing [13, 30] is a form of imperfect computing where deterministic algorithm produces imprecise results as precise output is not required while being computationally expensive or energy inefficient. Both hardware and software solutions are available, e.g. from the area of lossy compression where perceptual limitations set the limit to required perfection.

The IoT is more than just an embodiment of some of those techniques. It provides a computational layer on top of the physical phenomena. As such, it faces the duality of imperfection: the one that comes from physics (mostly from the uncertainty of measurements) and the one that comes from the selection of imperfect information technologies [33]. If 'normal' imperfect computing deals with certain data in an uncertain way, the IoT deals with uncertain data in an uncertain way.

It does not invalidate the usefulness of the IoT. After all, an imperfect answer is quite often better than no answer at all. However, for the user conditioned to trust computers unconditionally in expectation for certain perfection, dealing with such dual imperfection may lead to doubt, and distrust.

3   Trustworthiness, Trust and the IoT

The current approach to trust and trustworthiness, as discussed throughout literature (see e.g. [8] for an overview) tends to focus on the relationship between an enlightened trustor (the one who potentially trusts) and a trustee (the one that is hopefully trusted). The current approach can be characterised by the following assumptions, immediately contrasted with the properties of the IoT:

- The trustor can identify the trustee. That is, trustees are somehow distinguishable from the environment, e.g. in a form of persons, corporations or web sites. In contrast, pervasive IoT is almost indistinguishable from the environment while various subsystems and operators are also not distinguishable from each other.
- The trustor can exercise his free will in choosing to trust one of the trustors, or not trusting anyone at all, with no or little discomfort to itself. For the pervasive IoT, the trustor has no choice but to trust or not to be able to proceed.
- The trustor trusts willingly and cannot be coerced into trusting, as he subjects himself to being vulnerable to and dependent on the trustee without the ability to control them. Again, for the IoT the trustor is effectively coerced into trusting under the threat of discontinuation of vital services.
- For each trustee it is possible to satisfactory determine the extent of its internal quality of trustworthiness. Trustworthiness of the IoT, being new, technically complex and not directly observable by users, is hardly a subject of easy determination of its trustworthiness.
- The extent of trust that the rational trustor grants the trustee approximates the level of trustworthiness of this trustee. That, for the IoT, is not relevant, as it is neither distinguishable nor its trustworthiness can be determined.

Being an imperfect system, the IoT has one more hurdle to overcome: algorithm aversion [10]. This phenomenon describes the aversion to the use of algorithms that are known to be imperfect and favouring human decision-making even if algorithms lead to consistently better results.

4   How to Trust the IoT

As the IoT is an imperfect system, it cannot become trustworthy (hence it cannot be started) using a current understanding of this construct, i.e. by applying the current thinking of the human-to-human relationship.

However, the fact that current considerations are not applicable to the IoT does not preclude it from being trusted, and does not absolve the research from studying trust between people and imperfect systems.

It requires, however, an alternative view on what it means to be trustworthy and what it means to trust imperfect systems. To this end, the remainder of this section is devoted to the discussion about alternative approaches that can help explain and facilitate research in trust in the IoT, and in other imperfect systems.

4.1   Trusting Machines

There is a question whether the notion of trust between people can be applied to situations between people and machines, ie. whether the situation between people and the IoT can be discussed in terms of trust at all. In other words, whether humans use the same mechanism of trust for their human trustees as for the machines, specifically considering that humans have intentions while machines are devoid of them.

There is ample evidence that this is indeed the case: people behave as if they trust machines, whether this is considered real trust or a cheap substitute of it. This section highlights only some of many research streams that touched upon this problem.

Dennett [9] introduced a concept of three stances that the user can assume while exploring an artefact. The physical stance requires the artefact to be explorable on the physical level; the design stance require the artefact to be explainable through some simplifying mental models. For more complex systems, the intentional stance applies.

The intentional stance relies on treating the computing system as a human, with all the implications of it. Thus, the user may assume that the system is intentional - has intentions, moods, desires, dislikes etc., and will try to develop the relationship with the system as if the human would have developed the relationship with another human.

The intentional stance makes the perception of an imperfect system bearable for the human, but it makes trusting those systems more human too. Lessons learned from interpersonal trust can be applicable to the relationship between the human and the imperfect system, while lessons learned from studying trust in computers may be less applicable.

Ergonomics approached the problem of trusting machines from a more pragmatic angle: to what extent it is advisable to support the development of such trust in machines, knowing that they are in fact not intentional, as the 'as if intentional' behaviour can be easily traced to clever programming. The notion of an appropriate level of trust has been developed [20] (see also [8] for a similar consideration), where the main objective is not to encourage more trust than is due.

Following these lines of thoughts, trust can be considered as an explanation to some of the human behaviours while dealing with machines [32]. The emergence of animate software agents reinforced this role of trust [7]. Still, the problem of lack of actual intentionality in machines remained. Some authors (e.g. [29]), stated that it is the intentionality of the designer that modern technology exhibits, so that trusting machines is not a metaphor but an actual act of trust towards people and organisations, only conveyed through technical means.

One of the differences that emerged here is the fact that trust between people is supposed to be reciprocated [21, 22]. That is, trust is not a one-way relationship between a trustor and a trustee, but a two-way trust-building exercise in mutual dependency and vulnerability. Currently, machines do not reciprocate, as IoT is not dependent on us while we are increasingly dependent on it. An interesting concept of device comfort [23] may alter this situation so that devices and systems may become partners in two-way trust relationships.

4.2   Disconnect Between Trust and Trustworthiness

There is a trend in research as well as in the industry practices that focuses on trust-worthiness of information systems, in assumption that such trustworthiness warrants trust. For reference, in that context, trustworthiness is usually defined as an objectified, collective statement regarding qualities of a trustee that may lead to trust. Such a statement is maintained by social interactions, e.g. in a form of a reputation.

Trustworthiness of information systems has been the subject of several research projects (see e.g. http://www.optet.eu/, http://www.inter-trust.eu, http://www.trescca.eu). Despite the multiplicity of definitions [2], the key element is relatively simple: a trustworthy system does what it is supposed to do. That is, a trustworthy system delivers predictable and stable functionality.

This definition worked rather well for deterministic systems. Technical procedures such as trusted computing [28] made sure that computers never strayed from the set path, while security and reliability [3] made sure that the functionality of the system is resistant to both malicious and unintentional changes in its environment.

By the same definition, for imperfect systems the user neither knows nor can verify that the system does what it is supposed to do, thus rendering them untrustworthy. Actually, the user cannot even distinguish between an imperfect algorithm and a sinister attack [15].

This calls for the relaxation of a popular assumption of "trust out of trustworthiness" being the only explanation for trusting. Fortunately, the relationship between trust and trustworthiness (often represented by reputation) is not straightforward, as exemplified by those two statements [17] being equally plausible: "I trust you because of your good reputation" and "I trust you despite your bad reputation".

While imperfect systems are not trustworthy in the traditional meaning of this word, the observation that there is no direct implication of trust out of trustworthiness can be beneficial. Indeed, as trust may be extended towards untrustworthy entities as well as towards trustworthy ones, there is more to trust than just attuning to the level of trustworthiness.

4.3   Imperfect Signalling Systems

Trust in imperfect machines (known here as imperfect signalling systems) has been a research subject for some time in ergonomics [6]. The primary interest came from the area of work automation, where the operator should be able to trust their monitoring/advisory systems despite knowing that their advice or monitoring is imperfect.

Current study (see e.g. [18] for an overview) focuses on the impact that two categories of events (false alarms and misses) have on trust. While dealing with imperfections, trust may affect operator's strategies [1]. Experiments conducted in laboratory settings focus on operators' allocation of attention in high-load work environment where operators must split their attention between multiple concurrent tasks (e.g. [5]).

Findings from those experiments vary, and to the author's knowledge, no established model to explain the relationship between trust and the workload or the level of reliability emerged as yet. The theoretical model of trust in human-automation uses three informational bases: performance, process and purpose, where performance refers to what automation is doing, process reflects how automation operates, and purpose describes why automation is developed [19].

For as long as the overall demand for operators' attention is bearable, operators tend to correctly calibrate their trust, i.e. they trust those systems that are more trustworthy (i.e. provide more consistently accurate information) [20]. Once the demand for attention (i.e. the workload) becomes excessive, trust is not calibrated correctly, resulting in the overall lower trust towards imperfect technology.

However, some as yet unpublished works suggest that an increase in workload can actually increase trust, specifically if not trusting is the riskier strategy. This means that operators can exhibit trusting behaviour that does not reflect the reliability of the signalling system, but rather the precarious situation of the operator.

There is an apparent similarity between imperfect signalling systems and imperfect systems in general, and IoT in particular. The ability to fail from time to time, in a way that is not easily explainable to the user is a defining characteristic for all those systems. The main difference lies in the fact that for imperfect signalling systems, the user is able to eventually determine when the system is not operating properly while for the IoT or any imperfect system it is not always attainable.

4.4   Ontological Security and Basic Trust

While the construct of trust is inherited from human-to-human relationships, it is not the only relationship that can be called 'trust'. It may be therefore worth exploring different trusts that are definitely reported by human trustors yet directed towards the non-human trustee. Amongst them, there is a concept of ontological security that leads to basic trust, known also as ontological trust or ontological security [12].

Ontological trust is a stable mental state derived from a sense of continuity of one's experience. It is - in a nutshell - an expectation that the world is predictable. It can be disturbed by the perception of chaos, uncertainty and unpredictability. If supported, ontological security allows for person's basic trust (i.e. disposition to trust) to develop.

The interest in ontological security and basic trust is specific to psychological studies in early childhood (where it contributed to the sense of self-identity and building the disposition to trust in general [34]), learning contexts, but also to studies in international relationships [25], family stability and other areas.

Giddens [12] states that ontological security allows for the attitude where a person accepts what cannot be controlled, within the limits of some variability of its behaviour, on the basis that it is a stable, anticipated behaviour. For example an unexpected summer rain does not undermine ontological security, as it is expected that such a rain may come, even if it is not known when. In contrast, an earthquake in a geologically quiet area shatters not only the buildings but also related basic trust.

As IoT increasingly becomes an indistinguishable part of our environment, it would be worth considering whether IoT systems can be trusted 'as weather' rather than 'as devices'. That is, whether trust in the IoT would be better explained by basic trust out of ontological security than about the human-to-human trust.

To the author's knowledge there is no research in forms of ontological trust in technology. However, several trust models (e.g. [24, 31]) used in this area contain a component that is similar to the basic trust: the propensity (or a disposition) to trust.

4.5   Trust in Abstract Systems

Abstract systems are a concept introduced by Giddens [12]. Abstract systems use visible symbols or tokens (prescription, credit card) to represent the outcome of work of an otherwise opaque system (medicine, financial system). The average person does not know how those opaque systems work, but they know how to deal with those tokens. Hence, the person is in a position where they have to trust expert systems that they do not understand, on the basis of tokens alone. Tokens, are often, in fact, symbols of trust or evidence on which trust is assumed.

Note the precarious position of a user of such systems. Abstract systems are unavoidable and pervasive. They are usually monopolistic or near-monopolistic in nature. They are complex and their operations are hard to grasp. They are not directly controllable and yet they are trusted, with occasional complaints.

The parallel between the IoT and abstract systems is clearly visible, as the average person has no skills to comprehend their operation and is only exposed to some symbols of its operation (e.g. displays, end user devices, information).

Abstract systems do a lot to stabilise our lives and for that reason they are usually trusted. It is not because of their inherent trustworthiness, nor for the choice that the user has, but because of their usefulness. They empower people to do things that could have been otherwise impossible, whether it is a new treatment or a payment in a shop.

One may ask whether it is a genuine trust, but then how can one tell a difference between a person trusting e.g. banks 'genuinely' and trusting banks 'out of convenience or necessity'. The visible outcome of such trust will be approximately the same, while any decision may be post-rationalised by a person.

4.6   Social Systems and Their Theory

One of the key features of the imperfect system is the radical departure from the notion of a single truth (or a single meaning). In it, there is a striking parallel between the way imperfect systems work and the way the social systems theory models the operation of a society. Considering that there is a lot of computational concepts that took inspiration from social behaviours, than this parallel is worth exploring.

Social systems theory ([22], see also [26]) assumes that society is structured into systems that consist of communications. Systems can be very abstract (such as the legal system) or more specific (such as an organisation or even a particular single interaction). Systems continuously grow by acquiring communications and by evolving their meanings.

As a result, meanings that systems hold not only alter over time, but they can also be local to various interactions - i.e. the reaction of a system may differ depending on time and place. For example, a legal system may come to different conclusions now than it did several years ago, and the conclusions may differ between countries.

Positioning imperfect system (specifically the IoT) as a technical analogue to the social system allows to define trust in the IoT in the same way as one social system can trust another one, that is to reduce its complexity.

The challenge every social system face is not to be overwhelmed with the complexity it deals with. One of the possible solutions is to rely on other systems by trusting them. That is, the 'trustor' is exporting some of its complexity to the other system (the 'trustee'), thus making itself dependent on its vagaries. Drawing from this, an analogy would be for people to export some of the decision-making complexity to the IoT and become dependent on imperfections of the technology and its decisions.

Such trust does not require the trustee to have any particular properties of trustworthiness, nor the trustor to have a choice of trustees. The trustor often has to trust someone, picking the best option it has, even if it is the only one.

However, this analogy has limitations. Trust between social systems develops as a mutual one: both systems export some of their complexity to their counterparty and both become vulnerable. This situation does not translate easily into the relationship with the IoT, unless the (already mentioned) concept of device comfort [23] will be taken into consideration.

5   Conclusions

The IoT does not fit easily into the established way of thinking of trust in technology, that essentially mimics relationships between empowered humans. This leaves several questions open. Specifically, around the monopolistic position of the imperfect IoT that asks for revisiting the concept of trust.

The author does not have a definitive solution how to approach human trust in the IoT. However, the author believes that there is more to trust than studying humans trusting humans, and that some of those alternative views better resonate with the position the IoT will take in the society.

Therefore, instead of a solution, the overview of possible approaches is presented, derived from various research domains. This paper discussed the following approaches to trust that are applicable to IoT in particular and to trust in imperfect systems in general.

- Trust by replicating human-human trust (intentionality)
- Trust out of trustworthiness (trustworthy information systems)
- Trust because of reliability (imperfect signalling systems)
- Trust in stability and predictability (ontological security and basic trust)
- Trust out of necessity and usefulness (trust in abstract systems)
- Trust by replicating social trust (between social systems)

There is no single theory that can explain the whole relationship between people and the IoT, but each one will explain some of its elements. Collectively, those approaches provide sufficient substrate to draw from in order to develop a more relevant theory of trust.

After all, there's more to trust than trustworthiness.

References

1. Bailey, N.R., Scerbo, M.W.: Automation-induced complacency for monitoring highly reliable systems: the role of task complexity, system experience, and operator trust. Theor. Issues Ergon. Sci. **8**(4), 321–348 (2007)
2. Becker, S., et al.: Trustworthy software systems: a discussion of basic concepts and terminology. ACM SIGSOFT Softw. Eng. Notes **31**, 1–18 (2006). https://doi.org/10.1145/1218776.1218781
3. Bishop, M.: Introduction to Computer Security. Addison-Wesley, Boston (2005). ISBN 0-321-24744-2
4. Blanter, A., Holman, M.: Internet of Things 2020: A Glimpse into the Future (2017). http://aradinfocenter.com/wp-content/uploads/2017/07/A.T.%20Kearney_Internet%20of%20Things%202020%20Presentation_Online.pdf
5. Bliss, J.P., Dunn, M.C.: Behavioral implications of alarm mistrust as a function of task workload. Ergonomics **43**(90), 1283–1300 (2000)
6. Bliss, J.P., Gilson, R.D., Deaton, J.E.: Human probability matching behaviour in response to alarms of varying reliability. Ergonomics **38**, 2300–3212 (1995)
7. Castelfranchi, C.: Modelling social action for AI agents. Artif. Intell. **103**, 157–182 (1998)
8. Cofta, P.: Trust, Complexity and Control: Confidence in a Convergent World. Wiley, Hoboken (2007). https://doi.org/10.1002/9780470517857. ISBN 9780470061305
9. Dennett, D.C.: Intentional Stance. MIT University Press Group Ltd., Cambridge (1989). ISBN 9780262540537
10. Dietvorst, B.J., Simmons, J.P., Massey, C.: Overcoming algorithm aversion: people will use imperfect algorithms if they can (even slightly) modify them. Manag. Sci. **64**(3), 1155–1170 (2016). https://doi.org/10.1287/mnsc.2016.2643
11. Flasiński, M.: Wstęp do sztucznej inteligencji (in Polish). WN PWN, Wydawca (2011). ISBN 978-83-01-16663-3
12. Giddens, A.: Modernity and Self-Identity. Self and Society in the Late Modern Age. Polity Press, Cambridge (1991)
13. Han, J., Orshansky, M.: Approximate computing: an emerging paradigm for energy-efficient design. In: 2013 18th IEEE European Test Symposium (ETS). IEEE (2013)
14. Hewitt, E.: Cassandra: The Definitive Guide. O'Reilly Media, Newton (2010). ISBN 978-1449390419
15. Huang, L., Joseph, A.D., Nelson, B., Rubinstein, B.I.P., Tygar, J.D.: Adversarial machine learning. In: Proceedings of the 4th ACM Workshop on Security and Artificial Intelligence, Chicago, Illinois, USA (2011). ISBN 978-1-4503-1003-1
16. Jain, A.: Mastering Apache Storm: Real-Time Big Data Streaming Using Kafka, Hbase and Redis. Packt Publishing, Birmingham (2017). ISBN-13 978-1787125636
17. Jøsang, A.: Trust and reputation systems. In: Aldini, A., Gorrieri, R. (eds.) FOSAD 2006-2007. LNCS, vol. 4677, pp. 209–245. Springer, Heidelberg (2007). https://doi.org/10.1007/978-3-540-74810-6_8
18. Karpinsky, N.D., Chancey, E.T., Palmer, D.B., Yamani, Y.: Automation trust and attention allocation in multitasking workspace. Appl. Ergon. **70**, 194–201 (2018). https://doi.org/10.1016/j.apergo.2018.03.008
19. Lee, J.D., Moray, N.: Trust, control strategies and allocation of function in human-machine systems. Ergonomics **35**, 1243–1270 (1992)
20. Lee, J.D., See, K.A.: Trust in automation: designing for appropriate reliance. Hum. Factors **46**(1), 50–80 (2004)

21. Lewicki, R.J., Bunker, B.B.: Developing and maintaining trust in work relationships. In: Kramer, R.M., Tyler, T.R. (eds.) Trust in Organizations: Frontiers of Theory and Research, pp. 114–139. Sage, Thousand Oaks (1996)
22. Luhmann, N.: Social Systems. Stanford University Press, Stanford (1995)
23. Marsh, S., et al.: Defining and investigating device comfort. Inf. Media Technol. **6**(3), 914–935 (2011)
24. Mayer, R.C., Davis, J.H., Schoorman, F.D.: An integrative model of organizational trust. Acad. Manag. Rev. **20**(3), 709–734 (1995). https://doi.org/10.5465/amr.1995.9508080335
25. Mitzen, J.: Ontological security in world politics: state identity and the security dilemma. Eur. J. Int. Relat. **12**(3), 341–370 (2006)
26. Moeller, H.-G.: Luhmann Explained: From Souls to Systems. Open Court, Chicago (2006). ISBN-13 978-0812695984
27. Nakamoto, S.: Bitcoin: a peer-to-peer electronic cash system (2008). https://bitcoin.org/bitcoin.pdf
28. Pearson, S., et al.: Trusted Computing Platforms: TCPA Technology in Context. Prentice-Hall, Upper Saddle River (2002)
29. Rasmussen, J., Pejterson, A.M., Goodstein, L.P.: Cognitive Systems Engineering. Wiley, New York (1994)
30. Ritschel, T., Grosch, T., Kim, M.H., Seidel, H.-P., Dachsbacher, C., Kautz J.: Imperfect shadow maps for efficient computation of indirect illumination. In: Hart, J.C. (ed.) ACM SIGGRAPH Asia 2008 Papers (SIGGRAPH Asia 2008), Article no. 129, 8 p. ACM, New York (2008). https://doi.org/10.1145/1457515.1409082
31. Tan, Y., Thoen, W.: Toward a generic model of trust for electronic commerce. Int. J. Electron. Commer. **5**, 61–74 (2001)
32. Tenney, Y.J., Rogers, W.H., Pew, R.W.: Pilot opinions on cockpit automation issues. Int. J. Aviat. Psychol. **8**, 103–120 (1998)
33. Varga, E., Draškovic, D., Mijic, D.: Scalable Architecture for the Internet of Things (2018). ISBN 9781492024132
34. Winnicott, D.W.: The Maturation Process and the Facilitating Environment. Studies in the Theory of Emotional Development. The International Psycho-Analytical Library, vol. 64, pp. 1–276. The Hogarth Press and the Institute of Psycho-Analysis, London (1965)

A Granular Approach to Source Trustworthiness for Negative Trust Assessment

Davide Ceolin[1]($\boxtimes$) and Giuseppe Primiero[2]

[1] Centrum Wiskunde & Informatica, Amsterdam, The Netherlands
Davide.Ceolin@cwi.nl
[2] Department of Philosophy, University of Milan, Milan, Italy
Giuseppe.Primiero@unimi.it

Abstract. The problem of determining what information to trust is crucial in many contexts that admit uncertainty and polarization. In this paper, we propose a method to systematically reason on the trustworthiness of sources. While not aiming at establishing their veracity, the method allows creating a relative reference system to determine the trustworthiness of information sources by reasoning on their knowledgeability, popularity, and reputation. We further propose a formal rule-based set of strategies to establish possibly negative trust on contradictory contents that use such source evaluation. The strategies answer to criteria of higher trustworthiness score, majority or consensus on the set of sources. We evaluate our model through a real-case scenario.

1 Introduction

Assessing information quality is a challenging task. Assuming a minimal definition of information as 'data + semantics', assessing its quality means to establish fitness for purpose for a given piece of information. Given the huge number of possible purposes and to make its computation feasible, information quality is often broken down into 'dimensions' [13], like accuracy, precision, completeness. Despite its complexity, humans deal with quality on a daily basis using heuristics to approximate ideal values and using them as a proxy for deciding whether to trust information or not. Notwithstanding the possibility of being deceived by our heuristics, a formalization of such strategies is a useful tool for understanding and prediction. We provide here a framework to mimic such strategies and a relative reference system of sources. When an oracle or fact-checking service is available, such a reference system can be turned into an absolute one, i.e., determining which sources are veracious and which not. Otherwise, our result will still provide a relative ranking of the importance of sources. This task relies on providing appropriate understandings of trust and trustworthiness.

Among the large number of its definitions in the literature, for our purpose trust on contents can be minimally identified with the result of a consistency

© IFIP International Federation for Information Processing 2019
Published by Springer Nature Switzerland AG 2019
W. Meng et al. (Eds.): IFIPTM 2019, IFIP AICT 563, pp. 108–121, 2019.
https://doi.org/10.1007/978-3-030-33716-2_9

assessment: a piece of information consistent with the agent's current set of beliefs or knowledge base is trusted when it allows to preserve other information considered truthful. This approach requires a methodology to deal with inconsistent information and it calls upon the problem of assessing source trustworthiness. The logic (un)SecureND [20] provides a mechanism to deal with this aspect through the introduction of separate protocols to deal with failing consistency. An agent A reading a piece of information ϕ from an agent B, where ϕ is inconsistent with A's knowledge base, has two possibilities: (1) *distrust*: to reject ϕ and preserve $\neg\phi$ and its consequences; and (2) *mistrust*: to remove $\neg\phi$ from her profile and to accept ϕ. (un)SecureND does not have a selection mechanism for either form of negated trust. In real case scenarios, the choice between distrust and mistrust will be determined by evaluating the source. While *trust* is the mechanism to establish admissible consistent information, we call *trustworthiness* the assessment quality on sources. We introduce an ordering function and several decision strategies aiming at providing computational mechanisms to mimic the subjective quality assessment process called *trustworthiness*. Through any of these mechanisms, A can decide whether the estimated trustworthiness of B is high enough to trust the new information ϕ. Consider a simplified scenario, with a finite set of sources sharing information on a common topic and referencing each other (to a lesser or greater degree): some of them will be in conflict and some will be consistent with one another. We identify three dimensions:

- *Knowledgeability*: the number of sources to whom a source B refers. This value is used as an indicator of B's knowledge of other views;
- *Popularity*: the number of sources referring to B. This counts the number of inbound links, and it does not involve their polarity. Citing a source, even to attack it, is seen as an indication of the popularity of the latter;
- *Reputation*: the proportion between positive and negative evaluations of B.

These dimensions are used for assessing the trustworthiness of B, to compare contradictory sources by a receiver, and to formulate decision strategies.

The paper continues as follows. Section 2 describes formal preliminaries, Sect. 3 describes the different strategies available to resolve the presence of contradictory contents, Sect. 4 translates these strategies in implementable rule-based protocols, Sects. 5 and 6 present and discuss a use case implementation of the proposed logic. Section 7 surveys related work, and Sect. 8 concludes.

2   Formal Preliminaries

Consider a set of sources $\mathcal{S}$ and a (possibly partial) order relation $\leq_t$ over sources $\mathcal{S} \times \mathcal{S}$ expressing source trustworthiness; once defined, this is used as a proxy to establish trust in contents in the rule-based semantics presented in Sect. 4. We define the trustworthiness order $\leq_t$ as a function over three dimensions: reputation, popularity, and knowledgeability.

Reputation is an order relation $\leq_R$ over sources $\mathcal{S} \times \mathcal{S}$: intuitively, $S \leq_R S'$ means that source $S \in \mathcal{S}$ has at least the same reputation as $S' \in \mathcal{S}$. For simplicity, reputation is evaluated on the following criteria:

- we denote with $w(S)_{S'}$ a fixed weight of S received by S';
- $w = \{1, -1\}$, respectively for a positive and a negative assessment;
- we denote each $w(S)_{S'} = 1$ as *pos* and each $w(S)_{S'} = -1$ as *neg*;
- for any source $S \in \mathcal{S}$, a reputation assessment $r(S)$ by other sources in $\mathcal{S}$ is

$$r(S) = \frac{|pos| + 1}{|pos| + |neg| + 2}$$

We note that instead of computing the simple ratio of positive assessments over the total number of assessments, we add a smoothing factor like in Subjective Logic [15]. This allows us to represent assessment as performed in a 'semi-closed world': we base ourselves on the evidence at our disposal, but our sample is limited. The smaller our sample, the more the resulting reputation will be close to the neutral prior 0.5, since no prior knowledge is available to believe the source is fully trustworthy or untrustworthy. The larger our sample, the more the weight of the sample ratio will count on the reputation estimation. On the basis of the reputation assessment, we establish the corresponding order on $\mathcal{S}$:

Definition 1 (Reputation). *For any $S, S' \in \mathcal{S}, S \leq_R S' \leftrightarrow r(S) \geq r(S')$*

A second-order relation $\leq_P$ over sources $\mathcal{S} \times \mathcal{S}$ is defined: intuitively, $S \leq_P S'$ means source S has at least the same popularity as S', where popularity reflects the number of sources which refer to S. We denote the referenced sources as *outbound_links* and the referencing sources as *inbound_links*; non-referenced or non-referencing sources are denoted as *missing_links*. Note that $\forall S, S'$, if $S \in$ *outbound_links*(S') and $S' \in$ *outbound_links*(S), we can assume both sources have explicit knowledge of each other's information. We assume this fact and express that S' reads from S (or alternatively that S writes to S') as $S' \in$ *outbound_links*(S). Note that in the calculus presented in Fig. 1 these access operations are explicit. By our definition of reputation, we can assume that for every source S referenced by S', $w(S)_{S'} \in r(S)$. Hence, the popularity of S is

$$p(S) = \frac{|inbound\_links| + 1}{|inbound\_links| + |missing\_links| + 2}$$

On its basis, we establish the corresponding order on $\mathcal{S}$:

Definition 2 (Popularity). *For any $S, S' \in \mathcal{S}, S \leq_P S' \leftrightarrow p(S) \geq p(S')$.*

Finally, we define a third order relation $\leq_K$ over sources $\mathcal{S} \times \mathcal{S}$: intuitively, $S \leq_K S'$ means that source S has at least the same knowledgeability as S', where knowledgeability reflects the number of sources to which S refers. For simplicity, given the definition of $p(S)$ based on $r(S)$, knowledgeability $k(S)$ is the inverse of $p(S)$, computed as

$$k(S) = \frac{|outbound\_links| + 1}{|outbound\_links| + |missing\_links| + 2}$$

On its basis, we establish the corresponding order on $\mathcal{S}$:

Definition 3 (Knowledgeability). *For any* $S, S' \in \mathcal{S}, S \leq_K S' \leftrightarrow k(S) \geq k(S')$.

The highest value of knowledgeability corresponds to the totality of the available sources. For simplicity, we include in this count the source itself:

Definition 4 (Source Completeness). *A source S satisfies source completeness if* $|outbound\_links| = |\mathcal{S}|$.

The three dimensions of reputation, popularity, and knowledgeability establish a generic computable metric on the trustworthiness of a source S:

Definition 5 (Source Trustworthiness). *Source trustworthiness is computed*

$$t(S) = \Phi(\phi(r(S)), \psi(p(S)), \xi(k(S)))$$

with Φ *a given function and* ϕ, ψ, ξ *appropriate weights on the parameters.*

The choice of ϕ, ψ, ξ is essentially contextual, as it determines the role that each parameter has in the computed value of $t(s)$, e.g. to stress knowledgeability as more important than popularity, or reputation as more relevant than knowledgeability. Fixing these parameters to 1 provides the basic evaluation with all equipollent values. Φ can be interpreted e.g. as $\sum X$, $\overline{X}$, $max(X)$: again, this choice can be contextually determined.

To distinguish between different semantic strategies for information conflict resolution, we first weight the notion of source trustworthiness with respect to source order and calculate an average value.

Definition 6 (Sources with Higher Trustworthiness). *Let* $\mathcal{S}^{\sim}_{<_t S}$ *denote the set of sources with higher trustworthiness* $<_t$ *than a given source* $S \in \mathcal{S}$.

We now partition this set as follows: we denote with $\mathcal{T}$ the subset of $\mathcal{S}^{\sim}_{<_t S}$ such that $\forall S' \in \mathcal{T}$, S' trusts information ϕ; we denote with $\mathcal{T}_\perp$ the complement of $\mathcal{T}$.

Definition 7 (Weighted Trustworthiness). *Average trustworthiness of* $\mathcal{T}$ *is*

$$t(\mathcal{T}) = \frac{\sum_{\forall S' \in \mathcal{T}}^{|\mathcal{T}|} t(S')}{|\mathcal{T}|}$$

Let $t(\mathcal{T}_\perp)$ *denote the average trustworthiness for the complement partition. If* $t(\mathcal{T}) > t(\mathcal{T}_\perp)$, *then* S *trusts* ϕ, *else* S *trusts* $\neg\phi$.

In the case of weighted trustworthiness there is a possible parity outcome: either the selection of a different strategy (e.g., the simpler majority trustworthiness) or a random assignment is possible. Finally, on the basis of the trustworthiness assessment, we establish the corresponding order on $\mathcal{S}$:

Definition 8 (Trustworthiness). *For any* $S, S' \in \mathcal{S}, S \leq_t S' \leftrightarrow t(S) \geq t(S')$.

Note that the general definition allows for a partial order, as it is possible that the trustworthiness values of two distinct sources be equivalent or incomparable. The following resolution strategies assume that a strict order is being obtained.

3   Trustworthiness Selection Strategies

We define several strategies to implement negative trust based on the Trustworthiness relation defined in Sect. 2. Recall that distrust requires an agent to reject incoming contradictory information in favor of currently held data. In this context, we establish such a choice on the basis of higher trustworthiness.

Definition 9 (Distrust). *Assume $S <_t S'$, $S \in outbound\_links(S')$. If S' trusts ϕ and ϕ is inconsistent with the profile of S, then S distrust ϕ and trusts $\neg\phi$.*

With this protocol in place, a source with a higher trustworthiness will always reject incoming contradictory information from a lower ranked source. It is also fair to assume that where $t(S) = t(S')$, a conservative source S will not change its current information. The process of modifying currently held information to accommodate for newly incoming one (mistrust) starts therefore on the assumption that the source of incoming information has lower trustworthiness degree than the receiver. On this basis, implementing a mistrust strategy has a complex dynamic: the user can be more or less inclined to a belief change and it can require more or less evidence for it to happen. Therefore, different strategies can be designed. One strategy requires that a *majority* of agents with higher trustworthiness agree on the new incoming data. A stronger strategy requires that the *totality* of agents with higher trustworthiness agree. Reaching the desired number of agents to implement a mistrust strategy might be a dynamic process resulting from a temporally extended analysis of the set of sources. We design the different strategies assuming Definition 6 of the subset $S^{\sim}_{<_t S}$ of sources with higher trustworthiness as the sources which the receiver S has to consider.

The weakest strategy is defined by an agent which allows for a mistrust operation based on the presence of *at least one* source with higher reputation that contradicts her current belief state:

Definition 10 (Weak Trustworthiness). *If $\exists S' \in S^{\sim}_{<_t S}$ such that S' trusts information ϕ, then S trusts ϕ.*

To accommodate a contradicting ϕ, the source S has to modify the current set of belief, Γ, to some subset Γ' which can be consistently extended with ϕ, i.e. removing any formula implying $\neg\phi$. A stronger strategy is for the agent to accept the content on which the majority of sources with higher trustworthiness agree:

Definition 11 (Majority Trustworthiness). *Assume $\mathcal{T} \subseteq S^{\sim}_{<_t S}$ such that $\forall S' \in \mathcal{T}$, S' trusts information ϕ. We denote with $\mathcal{T}_\perp$ the complement of $\mathcal{T}$. If $|\mathcal{T}| > |\mathcal{T}_\perp|$, then S trusts ϕ, else S trusts $\neg\phi$.*

In the case of a parity outcome, either the selection of a different strategy or a random assignment are possible. Note that the above strategy does not account for the order *within* the subset $S^{\sim}_{<_t S}$: it only partitions it according to the truth value of a formula and then selects the partition with higher cardinality. A more refined majority strategy will weight each member $S' \in \mathcal{T}$ and $\mathcal{T}_\perp$ on the basis of their trustworthiness value $t(S')$. Then an average value will be assigned to the corresponding partition and the strategy will select the formula held by the partition with a higher value. If the cardinality of the partition has to be considered, the sum of the trustworthiness values of the sources can be assigned to each partition. The strongest strategy requires the agent to change her mind if all other agents with higher trustworthiness agree:

Definition 12 (Complete Trustworthiness). *If $\forall S' \in \mathcal{S}^{\sim}_{<_t S}$, S' trusts information ϕ, then S trusts ϕ.*

The Majority and Complete Trustworthiness strategies above have a strong effect on knowledge diffusion in the presence of full communication. The Consensus rule below holds even if the content from the most trustworthy source is not initially held by the majority of agents.

Proposition 1 (Consensus). *Assume $S' \in outbound\_links(S)$ holds $\forall S < S' \in \mathcal{S}^{\sim}$. Then S converges towards consensus on the information trusted by the most trustworthy source.*

4   Rule-Based Semantics for the Strategies

The natural deduction calculus (un)SecureND [20] defines trust, mistrust and distrust protocols according to the informal semantics described in Sect. 1. It formalizes a derivability relation on formulas from sets of assumptions (contexts) as accessibility on resources issued by sources. In this section, we provide an extension of the calculus with a rule-based implementation of the trustworthiness selection strategies from Sect. 3.

Definition 13 (Syntax of (un)SecureND).

$$\mathcal{S}^{\sim} := \{A <_t B <_t \cdots <_t N\}$$
$$BF^S := a^S \mid \phi^S_1 \rightarrow \phi^S_2 \mid \phi^S_1 \wedge \phi^S_2 \mid \phi^S_1 \vee \phi^S_2 \mid \perp$$
$$mode := Read(BF^S) \mid Write(BF^S) \mid Trust(BF^S)$$
$$RES^S := BF^S \mid mode \mid \neg RES^S$$
$$\Gamma^S := \{\phi^S_1, \ldots, \phi^S_n\}$$

Every $S \in \mathcal{S}$ is a content producer which has a trustworthiness value based on its interactions with any other $S' \in \mathcal{S}$. Any $S \in \mathcal{S}$ is ordered with respect to the others by the trustworthiness order.[1] Formulas in the set BF^S express content produced by source S and they are closed under logical connectives. Functions on contents in the set *mode* refer to reading, writing and trusting formulas. Every source S is identified by the set of contents it produces, denoted by Γ^S called the profile of S. A formula expresses access from a source S to content issued by another source S' (metavariables S, S' are substituted by variables A, B):

---

[1] In other versions of this logic, the order between elements in $\mathcal{S}$ is differently defined, e.g. imposed by access policies, see e.g. [20,22,23].

Definition 14. *An* (un)SecureND*-formula* $\Gamma^A \vdash RES^B$ *says that under the content expressed by source A, some content from source B is validly accessed.*

The rule-based semantics of the calculus is given in Fig. 1. *Atom* establishes derivability of formulas from well-formed contexts and under consistency preserving extensions. We use the judgment $\Gamma : profile$ for a profile consistently construed by induction from the empty set. For brevity, we skip here the introduction and elimination rules for logical connectives, see [20] and focus only on the access rules. Differently from other versions of the same calculus, we drop here negation-completeness: a source without access to a content item from another source, will not assume access to its negation, i.e. uncertainty is admissible. *read* says that from any well-formed source profile A, formulas from a profile B can be read. *trust* says that if a content item is read and it preserves consistency when added to the reading profile, then it can be trusted. *write* says that a readable and trustable content can be written. By *distrust*, source A distrusts content ϕ^B if it induces contradiction when reading from Γ^A and A has higher trustworthiness than B. Its elimination uses $\rightarrow$-introduction to induce *write* from the receiver profile for any content that follows a distrust operation. This allows $Write(\neg\phi^B)$ when $\neg Trust(\phi^B)$ holds. Each of the *mistrust* rules applies one different strategy from Sect. 3 for a content item ϕ^B inducing contradiction when reading from Γ^A and A has lower trustworthiness than B. By *weak mistrust*, A accepts ϕ (and removes from its own profile any conflicting information) by the simple presence of B in the set of sources with a higher reputation of A: this formulation is general enough to accommodate for the substitution of B in this condition by any other source that A considers absolutely essential (appeal to authority). *majority mistrust* requires computing the partitions of the set of sources with higher trustworthiness than A and comparing their cardinality: *any* content ϕ held by the larger partition will be kept by A (even when this reduces to an application of a *distrust* rule). In *weighted majority*, the condition is expressed by the higher average reputation of the partition. By *complete mistrust* the source A requires that every element in the set of sources with higher reputation agrees on ϕ. By the rule *write*, every trusted content can be written.

5   Evaluation

5.1   Use Case Description

In 2015, a measles outbreak took place in Disneyland, California. This event received much attention online, and a quite strongly polarised discussion followed up the news regarding this event. Public authorities and pro-vaccination sources pointed out the importance of vaccination, and some of them blamed the low vaccination rate as the main reason for this outbreak. On the other hand, the anti-vaccination movement accused the government agencies and the pro-vaccination movement of misinforming the public, since the children involved in the outbreak were vaccinated. Two main factions are at work, the pro and the

$$\frac{\Gamma^A : profile \qquad \Gamma^A; \Gamma^B : profile}{\Gamma^A; \Gamma^B \vdash \phi^B} \text{ Atom, for any } \phi \in \Gamma^B$$

$$\frac{}{\Gamma^A \vdash Read(\phi^B)} \text{ read} \qquad \frac{\Gamma^A \vdash Read(\phi^B) \qquad \Gamma^A; \phi_i^B : profile}{\Gamma^A \vdash Trust(\phi_i^B)} \text{ trust}$$

$$\frac{\Gamma^A \vdash Read(\phi^B) \qquad \Gamma^A; \phi^B \vdash \bot \qquad A <_t B}{\Gamma^A \vdash \neg Trust(\phi^B)} \text{ distrust}$$

$$\frac{\Gamma^A \vdash Read(\phi^B) \qquad \Gamma^A; \phi^B \vdash \bot \qquad \Delta^{B <_t A} \vdash \phi}{\Gamma'^A \vdash Trust(\phi^B)} \text{ weak mistrust, for some } \Gamma^A \supset \Gamma'^A; \phi^B \vdash wf$$

$$\frac{\Gamma^A \vdash Read(\phi^B) \qquad \Gamma^A; \phi^B \vdash \bot \qquad \Delta^{\mathcal{T}} \vdash \phi}{\Gamma'^A \vdash Trust(\phi^B)} \text{ majority mistrust, for some } \Gamma^A \supset \Gamma'^A; \phi^B \vdash wf$$

with $\mathcal{T} \subset \mathcal{S}^{\sim}_{<_t A}$ s.t. $|\mathcal{T}| > |\mathcal{T}_{\bot}|$.

$$\frac{\Gamma^A \vdash Read(\phi^B) \qquad \Gamma^A; \phi^B \vdash \bot \qquad \Delta^{\mathcal{T}} \vdash \phi}{\Gamma'^A \vdash Trust(\phi^B)} \text{ weighted mistrust, for some } \Gamma^A \supset \Gamma'^A; \phi^B \vdash wf$$

with $\mathcal{T} \subset \mathcal{S}^{\sim}_{<_t A}$ s.t. $t(\mathcal{T}) > t(\mathcal{T}_{\bot})$.

$$\frac{\Gamma^A \vdash Read(\phi^B) \qquad \Gamma^A; \phi^B \vdash \bot \qquad \Delta^{\mathcal{S}^{\sim}_{<_t A}} \vdash \phi}{\Gamma'^A \vdash Trust(\phi^B)} \text{ complete mistrust, for some } \Gamma^A \supset \Gamma'^A; \phi^B \vdash wf$$

$$\frac{\Gamma^A \vdash Read(\phi^B) \qquad \Gamma^A \vdash Trust(\phi^B)}{\Gamma^A \vdash Write(\phi^B)} \text{ write}$$

Fig. 1. The system (un)SecureND: access rules.

anti vaccinations. While sources do not always identify themselves as part of one or the other, for many of them it is either clear what their stance is (e.g., when they explicitly 'attack' each other), or we can make safe assumptions based on our background knowledge (e.g., by assuming that authorities are pro vaccinations). We have at our disposal a set of assessments of these articles collected by means of user studies involving experts [6]. These assessments cover quality dimensions like accuracy and prediction, and present an overall quality score that is equivalent to the trustworthiness score defined here.

5.2   Data Preprocessing

We select a subset of 10 articles regarding this debate from a corpus of documents regarding the Disneyland measles outbreak[2]. The selection gives a small but diverse set of views on the topic in terms of stance (pro or anti vaccinations) and type of document (news article, official document, blog post, etc.). Provided

---

[2] The dataset is available online at https://goo.gl/aouDJH.

they all discuss the specific event selected, a clear network of references emerges. However, such a network is rather sparse since a large majority of these sources do not cite each other. As we are interested in capturing their polarity to compute the three trustworthiness dimensions, we reconstruct the network as follows: (1) a source criticizing another source is considered as a negative piece of evidence regarding the reputation of the source mentioned; and (2) a source citing data from another source, even in neutral terms, is considered a piece of evidence regarding the popularity of the source cited. The resulting network of references is represented in Fig. 2 and it illustrates only the relations emerging from the corpus considered, representing a partial view on the real scenario because we derive a source's trustworthiness using one or more documents published by it as a proxy; the more documents we observe from a source, the better we can assess its trustworthiness value. For example, we estimate the source knowledgeability from the number of citations of other sources. Some sources could be cited only in some articles by the source under consideration. Also, we derive a source's trustworthiness based on the references it receives from the other sources considered, but we know that the set of sources is limited, and the scenario might change when considering other sources (e.g., the number of citations of currently poorly cited sources could rise). Given these considerations, the smoothing factor added to Definitions 1, 2, and 3, helps to cope with the resulting uncertainty.

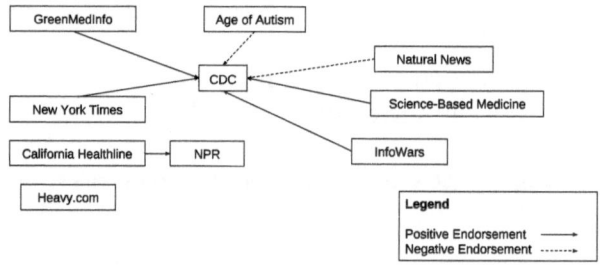

Fig. 2. Network of references resulting from the preprocessing of our corpus. Directed arrows indicate positive (continuous line) or negative (dotted line) references.

5.3   Sources Ordering

Based on the network depicted in Fig. 2, and using the formulas presented in Sect. 2, we compute the trustworthiness score for each of the sources in our sample. The trustworthiness score is computed by averaging the reputation, the knowledgeability, and the popularity of the sources, resulting in the scores reported in Table 1. Figure 3 shows a graphical representation of the resulting hierarchy of sources. Since the trustworthiness thus obtained shows a weak correlation (0.2) with the overall scores provided by the users in the user study, we explore alternative ways to aggregate the scores.

Weighted Trustworthiness. Applying weights to the trustworthiness parameters can yield a different hierarchy. Instead of applying an arbitrary weighing

Table 1. Trustworthiness scores of the sources considered for our use case. The score is computed by means of a simple average, where each component has the same weight.

Source	Reputation	Knowledgeability	Popularity	Trustworthiness
California Healthline	0.50	0.17	0.08	0.25
CDC	0.63	0.08	0.67	0.46
NYTimes	0.50	0.17	0.08	0.25
InfoWars	0.50	0.17	0.08	0.25
GreenMedInfo	0.50	0.25	0.08	0.28
Age of Autism	0.67	0.17	0.17	0.33
Science-Based Medicine	0.50	0.17	0.08	0.25
Heavy.com	0.50	0.08	0.08	0.22
Natural News	0.50	0.17	0.08	0.25
NPR	0.67	0.08	0.17	0.31

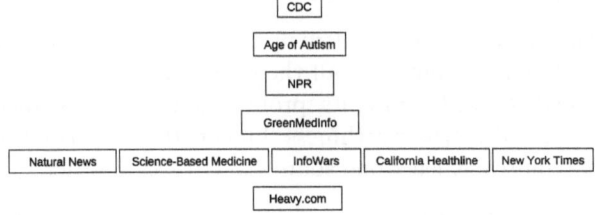

Fig. 3. Hierarchical ordering of the sources derived from the scores shown in Table 1

to the scores, we apply linear regression on the parameters, targeting the overall quality scores provided by the users in the study. Once we learn the weights for the parameters, we compute the trustworthiness scores. The resulting scores show a 0.6 correlation with those provided by the users. Moreover, we also run 3-fold cross-validation (split the dataset into 3 parts and, in round, use two parts as a training set for linear regression, and one for validation). For one item only, our model is unable to make a prediction. Excluding such item, the resulting average correlation between predicted and user-provided overall quality is −0.87 (Pearson) and −0.76 (Spearman). We consider these as promising results.

5.4   Applying Trustworthiness Selection Strategies

Here we illustrate how users could apply the selection strategies described in Sect. 3. Figure 4 shows the scenario where the trustworthiness selection strategies are applied. The sources analyzed in the previous step are now shown in white if they present a positive stance with respect to vaccinations, in grey otherwise. C is a new source with an unclear stance that joins the scenario. The stance of C (i.e., whether C *trusts* vaccines or not) will be determined by comparison with the other sources. Assume that the trustworthiness of C is higher than that of Heavy.com, but lower than the trustworthiness of all the other sources.

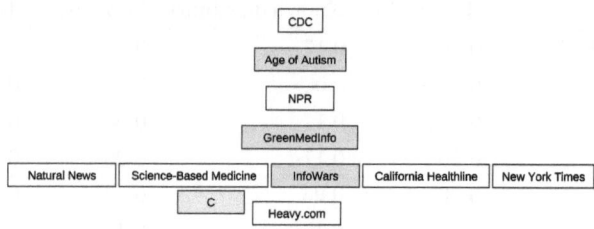

Fig. 4. Use case scenario. We adopt the same hierarchy as in Fig. 3. Sources in white trust vaccinations. Sources in grey do not. C denotes an additional source which takes part in the scenario and has not yet a clear stance.

Distrust. When C is confronted with Heavy.com and its lower trustworthiness score, following the distrust rule it will *distrust* vaccines.

Weak Trustworthiness. Let us follow up on the previous scenario. C now *distrusts* vaccines. When encountering all the other sources, if the `weak mistrust` strategy is applied, C will revise its profile: now C *trusts* vaccines because of several sources with trustworthiness higher than C *trust* ϕ. Note that `weak mistrust` requires at least one source to trust ϕ in order to follow suit.

Majority Trustworthiness. In an alternative scenario, when encountering the other sources, C can evaluate whether to trust ϕ or not based on whether the majority of the sources trusts vaccines. We partition the sources based on *vaccines* and *¬vaccines*. With any strategy for determining the majority (partition cardinality, average trustworthiness of the sources in the two partitions, sum of the cardinalities in the two partitions), *trust* in vaccines prevails.

Complete Trustworthiness. When complete trustworthiness is applied, C needs all the sources to agree on vaccines to add it to its profile. Since three sources disagree, by applying this rule, we obtain that C *distrusts* vaccines.

6   Discussion

The goal of our model is to provide means to mimic human thinking and provide a tool to systematically reason upon sources. The result of such reasoning is a relative reference system of sources. When oracles, fact-checkers, and other sources are available, such a reference system can be turned into an absolute one: if the user knows that a given set of statements is true or false, she can reason about the trustworthiness of the sources incorporating this additional information in the networks. When oracles are not available, the reference system can provide the user with a basis to coherently reason upon the sources she observes.

Frameworks like PageRank and its successors can be considered more evolved and successful alternatives to the present proposal. While PageRank can be applied to one or more networks to rank their sources, our system considers three distinct networks, aggregates them, and can be either extended with other networks or be used as reasoning support as it is. Hence we consider the present a viable complement to existing approaches.

While assessing the veracity of information is not the focal point of our system, the multidimensional approach we take shows promising robustness to possible attacks. Suppose that in an echo-chamber, sources cite each other positively in order to increase their own reputation and popularity. If their citations are limited to the sources in the echo chamber, their knowledgeability (and, thus, their trustworthiness) will necessarily be low. If to remedy this sources start citing others outside the echo chamber, their knowledgeability will rise, but they will also contribute to the popularity of these external sources. Still, vulnerability to the knowledgeability score is possible in sufficiently large echo chambers. Future developments will tackle this aspect more explicitly.

7   Related Work

Assessing the quality of information sources is a long-standing problem largely addressed in the fields of humanities, where specific guidelines and checklists have been proposed to address the issue of "source criticism" [3]. Such work has also been extended to Web sources in [6,7], where a combination of crowdsourcing and machine learning is adopted. Those works are complementary to the present contribution since they do not compare directly the references among sources. Counting links for a source as employed in this paper aims at mimicking the evaluation of the bibliography mentioned in the source criticism checklist. Another framework based on crowdsourcing is presented in [17].

Using fitness for purpose to assess information quality is a widely adopted strategy, see [12,13]. In the present work, we start from the assumption that where it is unclear or impossible for an agent to distinguish between contradictory data, source assessment based on trustworthiness is a valuable strategy. We show how such a protocol can be implemented through different selection strategies. A related topic is the one of fake news, tackled for instance in [4,25].

Research on trust in computational domains has been extensive in the last decades. Crucial aspects of the behavior of trust concern properties like propagation and blocking [8,10,14,16]. Solutions to these problems are various [2,9,11]. In the present work, we evaluate trust in information sources not on an absolute scale, but rather with varying degrees. A related approach is presented in [19], where a trust measure on agents is combined with the use of argumentation for reasoning about beliefs. Similarly, we propose a trust evaluation of sources to decide which information to maintain. The logic used in this work originates from a model designed to model trust in resource access control scenario, and to be able to block trust transitivity by design [21,23]. The logic has been applied to the Minimally Trusted Install Problem software management in [5], its negative counterpart [22], and tested to investigate optimal strategies to minimize false information diffusion [24]. For other accounts of negative trust, see [1, 18].

8   Conclusion

In this paper, we presented an extension of (un)SecureND, a logic modeling trust on information, with strategies for assessing the trustworthiness of sources as a function (average or otherwise) of their knowledgeability, popularity, and reputation, possibly weighted. We evaluated this extension on a real-life case study on the trustworthiness of Web sources and applied the selection strategies to the resulting source hierarchy. We showed that a linear combination of these parameters presents a decent correlation with user-provided assessments.

We plan to extend this work in two main directions. First, we will work on the automation of the preprocessing phase. We expect to use natural language processing for this and, in particular, author attribution to systematically identify references among the sources, and textual entailment to capture the perspectives taken by the different sources. Second, we will improve the parameters considered for assessing the trustworthiness. For instance, knowledgeability will have to be assessed based on the estimated level of the truthfulness of the statements made by the source. We plan to run an exhaustive user study to guide the design of source trustworthiness assessment and selection. Lastly, we will experiment with network centrality measures as alternative indicators for these parameters.

References

1. Abdul-Rahman, A.: A framework for decentralised trust reasoning. Ph.D. thesis, Department of Computer Science, University College London (2005)
2. Abdul-Rahman, A., Hailes, S.: A distributed trust model. In: NSPW, pp. 48–60 (1997)
3. American Library Association: Evaluating information: a basic checklist (1994)
4. Bessi, A., Coletto, M., Davidescu, G., Scala, A., Caldarelli, G., Quattrociocchi, W.: Science vs conspiracy: collective narratives in the age of misinformation. PLoS One **2**, e0118093 (2015)
5. Boender, J., Primiero, G., Raimondi, F.: Minimizing transitive trust threats in software management systems. In: PST, pp. 191–198. IEEE (2015)
6. Ceolin, D., Noordegraaf, J., Aroyo, L.: Capturing the ineffable: collecting, analysing, and automating web document quality assessments. In: Blomqvist, E., Ciancarini, P., Poggi, F., Vitali, F. (eds.) EKAW 2016. LNCS (LNAI), vol. 10024, pp. 83–97. Springer, Cham (2016). https://doi.org/10.1007/978-3-319-49004-5_6
7. Ceolin, D., Noordegraaf, J., Aroyo, L., van Son, C.: Towards web documents quality assessment for digital humanities scholars. WebSci **2016**, 315–317 (2016)
8. Chakraborty, P.S., Karform, S.: Designing trust propagation algorithms based on simple multiplicative strategy for social networks. Procedia Technol. **6**, 534–539 (2012). iCCCS-2012
9. Chapin, P.C., Skalka, C., Wang, X.S.: Authorization in trust management: features and foundations. ACM Comput. Surv. **40**(3), 9 (2008)

10. Christianson, B., Harbison, W.S.: Why isn't trust transitive? In: Lomas, M. (ed.) Security Protocols 1996. LNCS, vol. 1189, pp. 171–176. Springer, Heidelberg (1997). https://doi.org/10.1007/3-540-62494-5_16

11. Clarke, S., Christianson, B., Xiao, H.: Trust*: using local guarantees to extend the reach of trust. In: Christianson, B., Malcolm, J.A., Matyáš, V., Roe, M. (eds.) Security Protocols 2009. LNCS, vol. 7028, pp. 171–178. Springer, Heidelberg (2013). https://doi.org/10.1007/978-3-642-36213-2_21

12. Floridi, L., Illari, P. (eds.): The Philosophy of Information Quality. Springer, Cham (2014). https://doi.org/10.1007/978-3-319-07121-3

13. Illari, P.: IQ: purpose and dimensions. In: Floridi, L., Illari, P. (eds.) The Philosophy of Information Quality. SL, vol. 358, pp. 281–301. Springer, Cham (2014). https://doi.org/10.1007/978-3-319-07121-3_14

14. Jamali, M., Ester, M.: A matrix factorization technique with trust propagation for recommendation in social networks. In: RecSys, pp. 135–142. ACM (2010)

15. Jøsang, A.: Subjective Logic - A Formalism for Reasoning Under Uncertainty. Springer, Cham (2016). https://doi.org/10.1007/978-3-319-42337-1

16. Jøsang, A., Marsh, S., Pope, S.: Exploring different types of trust propagation. In: Stølen, K., Winsborough, W.H., Martinelli, F., Massacci, F. (eds.) iTrust 2006. LNCS, vol. 3986, pp. 179–192. Springer, Heidelberg (2006). https://doi.org/10.1007/11755593_14

17. Lee, Y.W., Strong, D.M., Kahn, B.K., Wang, R.Y.: AIMQ: a methodology for information quality assessment. Inf. Manag. **40**(2), 133–146 (2002)

18. Marsh, S., Dibben, M.R.: Trust, untrust, distrust and mistrust – an exploration of the dark(er) side. In: Herrmann, P., Issarny, V., Shiu, S. (eds.) iTrust 2005. LNCS, vol. 3477, pp. 17–33. Springer, Heidelberg (2005). https://doi.org/10.1007/11429760_2

19. Parsons, S., Tang, Y., Sklar, E., McBurney, P., Cai, K.: Argumentation-based reasoning in agents with varying degrees of trust. In: AAMAS, pp. 879–886 (2011)

20. Primiero, G.: A calculus for distrust and mistrust. In: Habib, S.M.M., Vassileva, J., Mauw, S., Mühlhäuser, M. (eds.) IFIPTM 2016. IAICT, vol. 473, pp. 183–190. Springer, Cham (2016). https://doi.org/10.1007/978-3-319-41354-9_15

21. Primiero, G., Boender, J.: Managing software uninstall with negative trust. In: Steghöfer, J.-P., Esfandiari, B. (eds.) IFIPTM 2017. IAICT, vol. 505, pp. 79–93. Springer, Cham (2017). https://doi.org/10.1007/978-3-319-59171-1_7

22. Primiero, G., Boender, J.: Negative trust for conflict resolution in software management. Web Intell. **16**(4), 251–271 (2018)

23. Primiero, G., Raimondi, F.: A typed natural deduction calculus to reason about secure trust. In: PST, pp. 379–382. IEEE (2014)

24. Primiero, G., Raimondi, F., Bottone, M., Tagliabue, J.: Trust and distrust in contradictory information transmission. Appl. Netw. Sci. **2**, 12 (2017)

25. Zhang, A.X., et al.: A structured response to misinformation: defining and annotating credibility indicators in news articles. In: WWW 18 Companion (2018)

A Fair (t, n)-Threshold Secret Sharing Scheme with Efficient Cheater Identifying

Hua Shen[1], Daijie Sun[1], Lan Zhao[1], and Mingwu Zhang[1,2]([✉])

[1] School of Computer Science, Hubei University of Technology, Wuhan, China
csmwzhang@gmail.com
[2] Hubei Key Laboratory of Intelligent Geo-Information Processing,
China University of Geosciences, Wuhan, China

Abstract. The fairness of secret sharing guarantees that, if either participant obtains the secret, other participants obtain too. The fairness can be threatened by cheaters who was hidden in the participants. To efficiently and accurately identify cheaters with guaranteeing fairness, this paper proposes a fair (t, n)-threshold secret sharing scheme with an efficient cheater identifying ability. The scheme consists of three protocols which correspond to the secret distribution phase, secret reconstruction phase, and cheater identification phase respectively. The scheme's secret distribution strategy enables the secret reconstruction protocol to detect the occurrence of cheating and trigger the execution of the cheater identification protocol to accurately locate cheaters. Moreover, we prove that the scheme is fair and secure, and show that the cheater identification algorithm has higher efficiency by comparing with other schemes.

Keywords: Secret sharing · Cheater identification · Fairness · Attack model

1 Introduction

In the reconstruction phase of a (t, n)-threshold secret sharing scheme, dishonest participants can reconstruct the real secret because of receiving the valid secret shares. It's unfair for honest participants that they gain the wrong secret because of accepting the invalid secret shares [1]. To address this issue, many researchers have come up with their solutions. Laih and Lee [2] proposed a v-fair (t, n)-threshold secret sharing scheme, in which all participants do not have to show their secret shares simultaneously to recover the secret with the same probability, even if there are $v(< t/2)$ dishonest participants. [3] and [4] further improved Laih scheme [2]. In 2003, Tian [5] utilized the consistency of secret

Supported by the National Natural Science Foundation of China (61702168, 61672010), Hubei Provincial Department of Education Key Project (D20181402), the open research project of Hubei Key Laboratory of Intelligent Geo-Information Processing (KLIGIP-2017A11).

W. Meng et al. (Eds.): IFIPTM 2019, IFIP AICT 563, pp. 122–132, 2019.
https://doi.org/10.1007/978-3-030-33716-2_10

shares to detect attackers, and constructed a fair (t, n)-threshold scheme with the help of the schemes of Tompa and Woll [6]. Harn and Lin [7] also used the consistency of secret share to design an algorithm to detect cheating behavior and identify cheaters. In 2014, Harn [8] pointed out that the research on asynchronous attack in scheme [5] was incorrect. In 2015, Harn [9] proposed a scheme that can resist asynchronous attacks of external attackers and internal attackers. In 2016, Liu [10] presented a Linear (t, n)-threshold secret sharing scheme in which there is only one honest participant can detect cheaters. Lin [11] constructed a secret sharing scheme which focuses on preventing cheating behavior rather than cheating detection. With the same purpose, in 2018 Liu [12] proposed a (t, n)-threshold secret image sharing scheme. In order to improve the efficiency of the verifiable secret sharing scheme, Mashhadi [13] and Cafaro [14] put forward their schemes respectively, but none of their schemes are unconditionally safe. In 2018, Liu and Yang [16] proposed a cheating identifiable secret sharing scheme by using the symmetric bivariate polynomial, but the scheme does not achieve fairness requirement of secret sharing.

In order to not only identify deception behavior but also efficiently and accurately locate cheaters, this paper propose a fair (t, n)-threshold secret sharing scheme which realizes the fairness through *Distribution protocol* and *Reconstruction protocol*, and achieves the efficiently cheaters identification through *Cheater identification protocol*. Moreover, the presented scheme is unconditional security because of not depending on any security assumptions, and is fair and secure based on four attack models.

The remainder of this paper is organized as follows. We introduce some preliminaries, in Sect. 2. In Sect. 3, we present a fair (t, n)-threshold secret sharing scheme with an efficient cheater identifying algorithm. In Sect. 4, we describe the fairness and security of the proposed scheme, followed by the performance analysis in Sect. 5. Finally, we conclude this paper.

2   Preliminaries

In this section, we briefly recall some fundamental backgrounds which are used in our scheme and then introduce the attack models of our scheme.

2.1   Shamir's (t, N)-Secret Sharing Scheme

Shamir's (t, n)-threshold secret sharing scheme [15] is based on Lagrange interpolating polynomial, in which there are n participants $\mathcal{P} = \{P_1, \cdots, P_n\}$, and a mutually trusted dealer $\mathcal{D}$. The scheme consist of two algorithms:

- *Distribution Algorithm*: The dealer $\mathcal{D}$ first randomly generates a polynomial: $f(x) = a_0 + a_1 x + a_2 x^2 + \cdots + a_{t-1} x^{t-1}$, in which the secret is $s = a_0$ and all the other coefficients $a_1, \cdots, a_{t-1}$ are chosen from a finite field $\mathbb{F}$, and then $\mathcal{D}$ computes the secret share $s_i = f(i)$ and sends it to the participant P_i, where $i = 1, 2, \cdots, n$.

- *Reconstruction Algorithm*: In the reconstruction phase, at least t participants submit their secret shares, the secret s can be reconstructed by calculating the Lagrangian interpolation polynomial through these secret shares.

2.2 Definitions of Consistency and Fairness

Definition 1. *(Consistency): In a (t, n)-threshold secret sharing scheme, suppose there are m $(m \geq t)$ participants reconstruct the secret. The m shares are consistent if any t shares in them can reconstruct the same secret.*

To check whether m shares are consistent or not, we only need to sequentially execute three steps as follows [5]. (i) Reconstruct a polynomial $g(x)$ using any t shares of the m secret shares. (ii) Check whether the degree of $g(x)$ is $t - 1$ or not. (iii) Check whether the remainder $m - t$ secret shares satisfy $g(x)$ or not. If (ii) and (iii) are satisfied, we can conclude that the m shares are consistent.

Definition 2. *(Fairness): A (t, n)-threshold secret sharing scheme is fair if it can guarantees that either each participant who takes part in reconstructing the secret obtains the same secret, or knows nothing about the mystery.*

Not difficult to find if the m secret shares are consistent, the corresponding scheme is fair.

2.3 Attack Models

The aim of our scheme is holding the fairness and secure under the following four attack models. :

- *Non-cooperative attack with synchronisation (NCAS)*: All participants submit the secret shares simultaneously, and that there are no cooperations between dishonest parties.
- *Non-cooperative attack with asynchronisation (NCAAS)*: All participants present secret shares successfully and that there are no cooperations between dishonest parties.
- *Collusion attack with synchronisation (CAS)*: The malicious parties modify their secret shares to deceive the honest parties. We assume that all participants submit their secret shares at the same time. Under this assumption, only when the number of malicious parties is more extensive than or equal to the threshold value t, can the malicious parties successfully deceive the honest parties.
- *Collusion attack with asynchronisation (CAAS)*: The dishonest parties collaboratively modify their secret shares to deceive the honest parties. The participants asynchronously release their secret shares. The best option for dishonest participants is to submit their accordingly modified secret shares after all honest participants have submitted their secret shares.

3   Our Schemes

In this section, we introduce our fair (t, n)-threshold secret sharing scheme which consists of three algorithms: distribution algorithm, reconstruction algorithm, and cheater identification algorithm.

3.1   Distribution

The dealer $\mathcal{D}$ wants to share a secret s among n participants $\mathcal{P} = \{P_1, \cdots, P_n\}$. $\mathcal{D}$ first randomly constructs an identifier sequence $\{a_1, a_2, \cdots, a_v\}$ from $\mathbb{Z}_q$, and q is big prime integer. The sequence must satisfy: $a_1 > a_2 > \cdots > a_{l-1} > a_{l+1} > \cdots > a_v > a_l$ where $l \in [1, v]$ is randomly determined by $\mathcal{D}$, and a_l is related to finally recover s. And then, based on the sequence, $\mathcal{D}$ generates v random polynomials through which $\mathcal{D}$ calculates the secret share $s_i = (s_{i_1}, \cdots, s_{i_v})$ for the ith participant. The distribution protocol is shown as:

Distribution protocol
INPUT: the secret s, the parameter v.
OUTPUT: the secret shares $s_1, s_2, \cdots, s_n$.

1. Randomly pick an integer $l \in [1, v]$;
2. Generate $a_1 > a_2 > \cdots > a_{l-1} > a_{l+1} > \cdots > a_v > a_l$;
3. Construct v polynomials of $(t-1)$-degree, like as follows:
   $f_k(x) = a_k + a_{k,1}x + a_{k,2}x^2 + \cdots + a_{k,t-1}x^{t-1} \bmod \mathbb{Z}_q$,
   where $k = 1, \cdots, v$, and $a_{k,1}, \cdots, a_{k,t-1}$ are randomly picked from $\mathbb{Z}_q$;
4. Calculate d to satisfy: $s = a_l \cdot d$;
5. Generate the secret share of ith $(i = 1, \cdots, n)$ participant by computing
   $s_i = (s_{i_1}, s_{i_2}, \cdots, s_{i_v}) = (f_1(i), f_2(i), \cdots, f_v(i))$.

3.2   Reconstruction

Suppose that $m(\geq t)$ participants $\mathcal{R} = \{P_1, \cdots, P_m\}$ cooperate to reconstruct s. Denoted by $\mathcal{P}_{-i} = \mathcal{R}/P_i$. The reconstruction protocol is shown below:

Reconstruction protocol
INPUT: $m(m \geq t)$ secret shares $\{s_1, s_2, \cdots, s_m\}$.
OUTPUT: the set of cheaters $\mathcal{A}$ and the secret s.

1. 1th round: P_i sends s_{i_1} to $\mathcal{P}_{-i}$, and then performs *Receive_share(k)*.
2. kth (k from 2 to v) round: If P_i receives all $(k-1)$th items of secret shares sent by $\mathcal{P}_{-i}$, then uses $\{s_{1_{k-1}}, s_{2_{k-1}}, \cdots, s_{m_{k-1}}\}$ to calculate a Lagrange interpolating polynomial $f_{k-1}(x)$. If $f_{k-1}(x)$ is $t-1$ degree,

then all participants send the kth items of their secret shares and then perform *Receive_share(k)*. Otherwise, all participants utilize the cheater identification protocol and obtain the set $\mathcal{A}$. If $|\mathcal{P}/\mathcal{A}| \geq t$, then all participants $\in \mathcal{P}/\mathcal{A}$ send the kth items of their secret shares and performs *Receive_share(k)*; otherwise, protocol is terminated.

Procedure *Receive_share(k)*: Receiving the kth item of secret share

1. When P_i has received all kth items of secret shares sent by $\mathcal{P}_{-i}$, he utilizes all these items $\{s_{1_k}, s_{2_k}, \cdots, s_{m_k}\}$ to compute the Lagrange interpolating polynomial $f_k(x)$. If the degree of $f_k(x)$ is $t-1$, then P_i performs step (b). Otherwise, all participants invoke the cheater identification protocol to identify the cheaters, and put them into the cheaters' set $\mathcal{A}$. If $|\mathcal{P}/\mathcal{A}| \geq t$, then the protocol turns to step b; otherwise, it is terminated.
2. Calculate the identifier by using the secret share sent by all participants in $\mathcal{P}/\mathcal{A}$, $a_k = f_k(0)$. If $a_k > a_{k-1}$, then $\mathcal{D}$ sends d to all participants in $\mathcal{P}/\mathcal{A}$, and these participants can calculate $s = a_{k-1} \cdot d$, and then the protocol is terminated; otherwise, all participants in $\mathcal{P}/\mathcal{A}$ send the $(k+1)$-th items of secret shares.

3.3   Cheater Identification

To identify the participants who input fake shares, We use a mark vector represents a kind of choice of selecting t participants from m participants, so there are $u = \binom{m}{t}$ mark vectors, denoted by $C_1, \cdots, C_u$. Each mark vector consists of m items, of which the value is 0 or 1, denoted by $C_j = (c_{j_1}, \cdots, c_{j_m}), j = 1, 2, \cdots, u$. Therefore, each mark vector includes t 1's and $m - t$ 0's.

Cheater identification protocol
INPUT: $m, t, k, \{s_{1_k}, s_{2_k}, \cdots, s_{m_k}\}$.
OUTPUT: the set of cheaters $\mathcal{A}$.
All the m reconstruction participants do:

1. Generate u mark vectors $C_1, C_2, \cdots, C_u$.
2. Based on the mark vector C_j ($j = 1, 2, \cdots, u$) (that is, based on $S'_k = \{s_{i'_k} | c_{j_{i'}} = 1\}$ ($i' = 1, 2, \cdots, m$)), each participant yields the Lagrange interpolating polynomial $f_k^j(x)$. Therefor, each participant can obtain $f_k^1(x), f_k^2(x), \cdots, f_k^u(x)$.

3. According to $f_k^1(x), f_k^2(x), \cdots, f_k^u(x)$, each participant can obtain u values of the identifier a_k, that is $a_k^1 = f_k^1(0), a_k^2 = f_k^2(0), \cdots, a_k^u = f_k^u(0)$. These values might different or the same. Find the most frequently occurring value in them, the value is the value of a_k.
4. And then extract the corresponding mark vectors from $\{C_1, \cdots, C_u\}$. Use $\mathcal{C}^{succ}$ denote the set of these corresponding mark vectors.
5. Perform Logic Or operation on $\mathcal{C}^{succ}$, the participants corresponding to the items whose values are 0 in the result mark vector are cheaters, and then add these participants to $\mathcal{A}$, finally return $\mathcal{A}$.

4   Security and Correctness Analysis

Theorem 1. *In our proposed scheme, the probability that each participant successfully guesses the secret s is $1/v$.*

Proof. The dealer $\mathcal{D}$ hides the secret s into the polynomial $f_l(x)$, where $l \in [1, v]$ is randomly chosen by $\mathcal{D}$, therefore, the participants successfully guess the value of l with the probability $1/v$.

$\mathcal{P} = \{P_1, \cdots, P_m\}$ ($t \le m \le n$) denotes all participants who take part in the secret reconstruction phase, $\mathcal{P}_I = \{P_{i_1}, \cdots, P_{i_\alpha}\} \subseteq \mathcal{P}$ denotes the set of cheaters in $\mathcal{P}$, $\mathcal{P}_{-I} = \mathcal{P}/\mathcal{P}_I$ denotes the set of honest participants in $\mathcal{P}$.

Theorem 2. *Under non-cooperative attack with synchronisation (NCAS), when $m > t$, our scheme is secure and fair.*

Proof. NCAS assumes that all participants present shares at the same time and that there is no cooperation between cheaters. Suppose that in the k-round reconstruction stage, the cheaters in $\mathcal{P}_I$ send invalid secret shares. Since there is no cooperation between the cheaters, their invalid secret shares can only be random numbers in $\mathbb{Z}_q$. When $m > t$, these secret shares could not pass the consistency test, and the attack is immediately detected. In order to restore s, the attackers in $\mathcal{P}_I$ need to guess in which polynomial s is hidden and which honest participants are involved. According to **Theorem 1**, the maximum successful probability is $1/v$. If v is large enough, the probability can be ignored. Therefore, under non-cooperative attack, when $m > t$, our scheme is secure and fair.

Theorem 3. *Under non-cooperative attack with asynchronisation (NCAAS), when $\{(m - \alpha < t - 1) \cap (m > t)\} \cup \{m - \alpha \ge t + 1\}$, our scheme is secure and fair.*

Proof. NCAAS assumes that all participants present shared shares successively without cooperation between attackers. A cheater' ideal attack is to show the secret share at the end, because he can obtain all the shares before others. When $m - \alpha \ge t + 1$, that is, there are no less than $t + 1$ honest participants, who show the secret shares firstly. Therefore, the attackers can reconstruct the correct polynomial $f_k(x)$ (suppose in k-round) based on t real secret shares, and then obtain the a_k. The attackers can show the real secret shares in the first l rounds and show a fake secret share in $(l+1)$th round. However, the fake secret share cannot pass the consistency test, and the attack behavior can be detected, which trigger the execution of cheater identification algorithm. The right identifier a_{l+1} can be reconstructed based on the $m-\alpha$ real secret shares, because $\binom{m-\alpha}{t} > 1$, the a_{l+1} is correct identifier which can be used to identify the attackers, therefore, the attackers could not gain d from the dealer to obtain s. When $m - \alpha < t + 1$, for an attacker, even if he finally shows his secret share, he can only obtain at most $t - 1$ real secret shares, so he can not reconstruct any $t - 1$-degree polynomial, as a result he can not recover s. In order to detect attacks, m should greater than t. In conclusion, when $\{(m - \alpha < t - 1) \cap (m > t)\} \cup \{m - \alpha \geq t + 1\}$, the proposed scheme is secure and fair.

Theorem 4. *Under collusion attack with synchronisation (CAS), when $\{(\alpha < t) \cap (m > t)\} \cup \{(\alpha \geq t) \cap (m - \alpha > \alpha + t - 1)\}$, our scheme is secure and fair.*

Proof. CAS assumes that all participants present secret shares simultaneously and that multiple attackers conspire to attack the scheme. Suppose there are α cheaters in k-round. (i) When $\alpha \geq t$, if the number of honest participants is less than t, that is, $m - \alpha < t$, then cheaters can cooperate to forge a set of invalid secret shares which can pass consistency detection. The specific process is as follows: Cheaters first use their secret shares to recover an interpolation polynomial, then utilize the polynomial to calculate the secret shares held by other honest participants, and then generate their false secret shares based on the secret shares of other honest participants. For example, $\alpha = t$, $m - \alpha = t - 1$, $m = 2t - 1$, use $\{P_1, \cdots, P_{t-1}\}$ denote honest participants, use $\{P_t, P_{t+1}, \cdots, P_{2t-1}\}$ denote cheaters. Cheaters can use their true secret share $\{s_{t_k}, s_{t+1_k}, \cdots, s_{2t-1_k}\}$ to calculate the interpolation polynomial $f_k(x)$, so they can show the true secret shares in the first l rounds, and in $(l+1)$th round, they can use $f_{l+1}(x)$ to obtain other honest participants' secret shares $\{s_{1_{l+1}}, \cdots, s_{t-1_{l+1}}\}$, and calculate another $(t-1)$-degree polynomial $f'_{l+1}(x)$ by using secret shares $\{s_{1_{l+1}}, s_{2_{l+1}}, \cdots, s_{t-1_{l+1}}\}$ and a random value $s'_{t_{l+1}}$. And then, cheaters use $f'_{l+1}(x)$ to calculate $t - 1$ invalid secret shares $\{s'_{t_{l+1}}, s'_{t+1_{l+1}}, \cdots, s'_{2t-1_{l+1}}\}$. Finally, the secret shares shown by all participants as follows: $\{s_{1_{l+1}}, s_{2_{l+1}}, \cdots, s_{t-1_{l+1}}, s'_{t_{l+1}}, s'_{t+1_{l+1}}, \cdots, s'_{2t-1_{l+1}}\}$. These m secret shares can pass consistency detection when $m - \alpha \geq t$. The secret shares forged by the above method in $(l+1)$th round cannot pass consistency detection. By executing the identification algorithm, m real secret shares can used to reconstruct the correct identifier a_{l+1} at $\binom{m-\alpha}{t}$ times, while $t-1$ real secret shares and an invalid secret share can be utilized to reconstruct a wrong identifier a'_{l+1} at $\binom{\alpha+t-1}{t}$ times. Therefore, we have $\binom{m-\alpha}{t} > \binom{\alpha+t-1}{t}$. That is, $m - \alpha > \alpha + t - 1$, under this condition, the invalid secret shares can be detected, and cheaters cannot obtain d from the dealer and recover s. But the honest participants can gain d and reconstruct s. (ii) If $\alpha < t$, these α cheaters can not use their real secret shares to forge the invalid secret shares that can pass the consistency detection. When $m > t$, this attack can not pass the consistency detection. If cheaters want to reconstruct s, they can only guess the value of l, the probability of successfully guessing is only $1/v$. From what has been discussed above, when $\{(\alpha < t) \cap (m > t)\} \cup \{(\alpha \geq t) \cap (m - \alpha > \alpha + t - 1)\}$, our scheme is secure and fair.

Theorem 5. *Under collusion attack with asynchronisation (CAAS), when* $m - \alpha > \alpha + t - 1$, *our scheme is secure and fair.*

Proof. CAAS assumes that all participants present secret shares successively and that multiple cheaters conspire to attack the scheme. For cheaters, the ideal mode of attack is to present the secret shares at the end, so that they can obtain the real secret shares presented by previous honest participants. When $m - \alpha \geq t$, there are not less than t honest participants, who first show the secret shares. Attackers use $t - 1$ real secret shares (according to the method of **Theorem** 4) to forge α invalid secret shares. Because $m - \alpha \geq t$, these invalid secret shares cannot pass consistency detection. By executing the identification algorithm, $m - \alpha$ real secret shares can be used to recover the correct identifier a_{l+1} $\binom{m - \alpha}{t}$ times, while $t - 1$ real secret shares and an invalid secret share can be utilized to reconstruct a wrong identifier a'_{l+1} $\binom{\alpha + t - 1}{t}$ times. Therefore, we have $\binom{m - \alpha}{t} > \binom{\alpha + t - 1}{t}$. Concretely, under $m - \alpha > \alpha + t - 1$, these invalid secret shares can be detected, and cheaters cannot gain d from the dealer and reconstruct s. But the honest participants can obtain d and recover s. Therefore, when $m - \alpha > \alpha + t - 1$, the proposed scheme is secure and fair.

Theorem 6. *Under the conditions mentioned above, our cheater identification algorithm is correct.*

Proof. The key to prove the correctness of the cheater identification protocol is to prove the most frequently occurring value in $\{a_k^1 = f_k^1(0), \cdots, a_k^u = f_k^u(0)\}$ is the correct value of a_k. In the cheater identification protocol, interpolating polynomials are reconstructed only based on t secret shares, therefore, only when the t secret shares are real can the correct value of a_k be recovered. To guarantee the most frequently occurring value in $\{a_k^1 = f_k^1(0), \cdots, a_k^u = f_k^u(0)\}$ is the correct value of a_k, the following condition must be satisfied:

$$\binom{m - \alpha}{t} > \frac{1}{2}\binom{m}{t}.$$

We have,

$$\frac{(m-\alpha)!}{(m-\alpha-t)!t!} > \frac{1}{2} \cdot \frac{m!}{(m-t)!t!} = \frac{1}{2} \cdot \frac{(m-\alpha)!\alpha!}{(m-t)!t!}$$

$$\Rightarrow \frac{(m-\alpha)!}{(m-\alpha-t)!} > \frac{1}{2} \cdot \frac{(m-\alpha)!\alpha!}{(m-t)!} = \frac{1}{2} \cdot \frac{(m-\alpha)!}{(m-\alpha-t)!}$$

Since the inequality is always true, our cheater identification algorithm is correct.

5 Performance

The following two examples are given to respectively calculate the maximum number of attackers α_{max} under the four types of attack models. Taking (7, n) threshold scheme as an example, assuming $m = 9$ and $m = 11$, where m is the number of participants who take part in the secret reconstruction phase. Under NCAS, according to **Theorem** 2, when $m > t$ our scheme is secure and fair, so $\alpha_{max} = 9$. Similarly, under NCAAS, according to **Theorem** 3, when $\{(m - \alpha < t - 1) \cap (m > t)\} \cup \{m - \alpha \geq t + 1\}$ our scheme is secure and fair, which means $\alpha_{max} = 9$. From the analysis of **Theorem** 4, Under CAS, when $\{(\alpha < t) \cap (m > t)\} \cup \{(\alpha \geq t) \cap (m - \alpha > \alpha + t - 1)\}$ the proposed scheme is safe and fair, so $\alpha_{max} = 6$. According to the analysis of **Theorem** 5, Under CAAS, our scheme can defend at most 1 cheaters, as shown Table 1. Based on a similar analysis process, when $m = 11$, the values of α_{max} are shown as in Table 1.

Table 1. (7,n)-threshold scheme, $m = 9$ or $m = 11$

Attack model	Conditions	$\alpha_{max}(m = 9)$	$\alpha_{max}(m = 11)$
NCAS	$m > t$	9	11
NCAAS	$\{(m - \alpha < t - 1) \cap (m > t)\} \cup \{m - \alpha \geq t + 1\}$	9	11
CAS	$\{(\alpha < t) \cap (m > t)\} \cup \{(\alpha \geq t) \cap (m - \alpha > \alpha + t - 1)\}$	6	6
CAAS	$m - \alpha > \alpha + t - 1$	1	2

Different from Tian and Peng's [17] scheme, our scheme does not depend on any security assumptions, it is a unconditional security scheme. Compared to Tian's [5], Harn's [8], Harn-Lin's [7] and Liu-Yang's [16] secret sharing schemes, our scheme achieves fairness but they do not have, as shown in Table 2.

Table 2. Security comparison

Scheme	Tian [5]	Harn-Lin [7]	Liu-Yang [16]	Tian-Peng [17]	ours
Security assumption	no	no	no	ECDLP	no
Fairness	no	no	no	no	yes

In [7], Harn and Lin proposed a secret sharing scheme that can identify cheaters. In their scheme, the correct secret needs to be confirmed and the secret share of each participant needs to be verified. In our scheme, we removed the process of validating each participant's secret share but achieves the same function of [7]. Therefore, our scheme has higher operating efficiency than [7].

6 Conclusion

In this paper, we study the cheater identification issue and the fairness problem in the reconstruction phase of secret sharing, and propose a fair (t, n) secret sharing scheme including a efficient cheater identification algorithm. By comparing with the existing verifiable secret sharing schemes, it can be found that our scheme achieves fairness. Compared with the fair secret sharing scheme, our cheater identification algorithm has a lower computational complexity. Moreover, we analyzed the security of our proposed scheme under four different attack models.

References

1. Zhang, M., Zhang, Y., Jiang, Y., Shen, J.: Obfuscating EVES algorithm and its application in fair electronic transactions in public cloud systems. IEEE Syst. J. **13**(2), 1478–1486 (2019)
2. Laih, C.S., Lee, Y.C.: V-fairness (t, n) secret sharing scheme. IEEE Proc.-Comput. Digital Tech. **144**(4), 245–248 (1997)
3. Lee, Y.-C.: A Simple (v, t, n)-fairness secret sharing scheme with one shadow for each participant. In: Gong, Z., Luo, X., Chen, J., Lei, J., Wang, F.L. (eds.) WISM 2011. LNCS, vol. 6987, pp. 384–389. Springer, Heidelberg (2011). https://doi.org/10.1007/978-3-642-23971-7_48
4. Yang J.H., Chang C.C., Wang C.H.: An efficient v-fairness (t, n) threshold secret sharing scheme. In: 2011 Fifth International Conference on Genetic and Evolutionary Computing, pp. 180–183. IEEE (2011)
5. Tian, Y., Ma, J., Peng, C., Jiang, Q.: Fair (t, n) threshold secret sharing scheme. IET Inf. Secur. **7**(2), 106–112 (2013)
6. Tompa, M., Woll, H.: How to share a secret with cheaters. J. Cryptol. **1**(3), 133–138 (1989)
7. Harn, L., Lin, C.: Detection and identification of cheaters in (t, n) secret sharing scheme. Des. Codes Crypt. **52**(1), 15–24 (2009)
8. Harn, L.: Comments on 'fair (t, n) threshold secret sharing scheme. IET Inf. Secur. **8**(6), 303–304 (2014)
9. Harn, L., Lin, C., Li, Y.: Fair secret reconstruction in (t, n) secret sharing. J. Inf. Secur. Appl. **23**, 1–7 (2015)
10. Liu, Y.: Linear (k, n) secret sharing scheme with cheating detection. Secur. Commun. Netw. **9**(13), 2115–2121 (2016)
11. Lin, P.: Distributed secret sharing approach with cheater prevention based on qr code. IEEE Trans. Ind. Inform. **12**(1), 384–392 (2016)
12. Liu, Y., Sun, Q., Yang, C.: (k, n) secret image sharing scheme capable of cheating detection. EURASIP J. Wireless Commun. Netw. **1**, 72 (2018)

13. Mashhadi, S., Dehkordi, M.H., Kiamari, N.: Provably secure verifiable multi-stage secret sharing scheme based on monotone span program. IET Inf. Secur. **11**(6), 326–331 (2017)
14. Cafaro, M., Pelle, P.: Space-efficient verifiable secret sharing using polynomial interpolation. IEEE Trans. Cloud Comput. **6**(2), 453–463 (2018)
15. Shamir, A.: How to share a secret. Commun. ACM **22**(11), 612–613 (1979)
16. Liu, Y., Yang, C., Wang, Y., Zhu, L., Ji, W.: Cheating identifiable secret sharing scheme using symmetric bivariate polynomial. Inf. Sci. **453**, 21–29 (2018)
17. Tian Y., Peng C., Zhang R., Chen Y.: A practical publicly verifiable secret sharing scheme based on bilinear pairing. In: International Conference on Anti-counterfeiting, pp. 71–75. IEEE (2008)

emmy – Trust-Enhancing Authentication Library

Miha Stopar[1]([⊠]), Manca Bizjak[1], Jolanda Modic[1], Jan Hartman[1], Anže Žitnik[1], and Tilen Marc[1,2]

[1] XLAB d.o.o., Ljubljana, Slovenia
{miha.stopar,manca.bizjak,jolanda.modic,jan.hartman,
anze.zitnik,tilen.marc}@xlab.si
[2] Institute of Mathematics, Physics and Mechanics, Ljubljana, Slovenia

Abstract. People, organizations, devices need to make many kinds of claims as part of their everyday activities. Digital credentials can enable to transmit instantly verifiable claims about their name, date of birth, gender, location, accomplishments. Some privacy-enhancing digital credentials enable revealing only part of your identity and thus hiding all information that is not necessarily needed for the online service. In the past two decades, several privacy- and trust-enhancing authentication techniques and approaches have been proposed to implement such verifiable digital credentials, mostly on the theoretical level. Some implementations exist, but either lack functionalities, rely on heavy computational machinery or are not available in open source. This paper presents emmy, a fully-fledged open source cryptographic library for secure, privacy-aware, and trust-enhancing authentication towards online services.

Keywords: Trust · Privacy · Zero-knowledge proofs · Identity management · Anonymity · Cloud services

1 Introduction

Service providers progressively form their strategies and base their business decisions on the data they can collect through their everyday operations. They have more data at their disposal than ever before, thanks to the increasing use of highly evolved ICT systems. While the opportunities to benefit from data collection rise, the data protection requirements are becoming more and more strict. With the GDPR and increasingly more privacy-aware individuals, organisations are seeking a compromise that will enable them to collect and analyse their users' data to innovate, optimize, and grow their businesses, while at the same time comply with data protection regulations and keep trust and confidence of their users. Trust in online services can really only be achieved if their users are given full control over their privacy, digital identities, and personal data. Privacy-concerned individuals and trust-seeking organisations thus require novel technologies that enable user-controlled privacy and, where possible, full anonymity.

© IFIP International Federation for Information Processing 2019
Published by Springer Nature Switzerland AG 2019
W. Meng et al. (Eds.): IFIPTM 2019, IFIP AICT 563, pp. 133–146, 2019.
https://doi.org/10.1007/978-3-030-33716-2_11

Credentials which consist of separate sets of individual claims which can be selectively revealed to the service provider and can be verified without contacting a centralized trust source are called verifiable credentials. There is a W3C Verifiable Claims Working Group [50] which aims to provide standards for expressing and exchanging the verifiable credentials. Verifiable credentials provide users with a fine-grained control about which parts of their personal information they want to reveal. For some online services revealing date of birth might suffice. Or users might need to reveal date of birth, gender, and nationality, but not name and address. In extreme cases, the user might only reveal the entitlement to the service and no claims.

By using verifiable credentials users get more control over their personal data and service providers get an assurance of the authenticity and accuracy of the data. It is well-known [35] that due to privacy concerns and unwanted marketing the users are often giving false information when registering online. Even if only a small percentage of database entries is corrupted, the accuracy of analyses can heavily decline.

In this paper, we present a cryptographic library *emmy* that encapsulates primitives and protocols used in *anonymous attribute-based credentials* (AABCs) which are the underlying cryptographic primitives for the verifiable credentials. We present its implementation and an example of a complete cloud system that uses AABCs for a privacy- and trust-enhancing service. Note that emmy is not the first implementation of an anonymous authentication scheme. It will soon be two decades since the first one has been designed and implemented, however, this emmy's predecessor never really made it to any real-world application as it is based on (too) heavy computational machinery and lacks functionalities. The goal of this paper is to show how our library can be easily integrated into cloud services to provide controlled privacy to finally support and facilitate the development of privacy-aware and trust-enhancing cloud services.

The library presented in this paper was partially implemented in European H2020 research projects FENTEC [20] (grant number 780108) and mF2C [36] (grant number 730929). The code with guidelines is available online [19].

Contributions. This paper addresses the lack of privacy-friendly and trust-enabling technologies by the following contributions:

1. *Overview of privacy-enhancing and trust-enabling technologies.* We provide an overview of currently known privacy- and anonymity-enabling cryptographic approaches and implementations in Sects. 2 and 3.
2. *Implementation of a library for AABCs.* In Sect. 4 we present a cryptographic library that enables trust-enhanced and anonymous authentication to cloud services. The library differs from others by incorporating an efficient communication layer which is crucial in systems that rely on complex interactions between clients and servers.
3. *Demonstration of a secure, privacy-aware, and trust-enhancing certificate authority system.* In Sect. 5 we present the emmy API and demonstrate how

it can be integrated into a self-sovereign identity system where users create, control, own, and maintain identities as data stored on a smartphone or computer.

2   Related Theoretical Work

The fundamental primitive for the AABCs is a so-called *Zero-Knowledge Proof* (ZKP). This is an interactive, two-party protocol between a *prover* and a *verifier*, where the prover claims to know something and needs to convince the verifier about this fact in a private manner. Namely, the prover will prove to the verifier that some statement is true, and the verifier will be fully convinced that the statement is true, but will not learn anything about the statement as a result of this process (the verifier will obtain zero knowledge).

Any proof system must be complete and sound. *Completeness* means that an honest prover can always convince an honest verifier of a true statement, and *soundness* means that a dishonest prover can almost never succeed in convincing an honest verifier of a false statement (there is a negligibly small probability of success). A ZKP must be complete, sound, and, additionally, it must satisfy the *zero-knowledge* property, which means that the proof does not reveal any information about the secret to the verifier, except for what is already revealed by the claim itself.

A typical ZKP is a proof of knowledge of a discrete logarithm. That is, given a publicly known number t, the prover wants to prove knowledge of a number x such that $g^x = t \,(mod \, p)$ where p is some prime number. This example of a ZKP was first proposed by Schnorr [43] in 1991. Schnorr-like protocols later became the basis for AABCs, introduced by Camenisch and Lysyanskaya in 2001 [11]. AABCs allow an identity provider (a trusted third party) to issue a credential to a user. This credential contains various claims, which describe different properties of the user, such as gender, age, address or date of birth, and also user's rights or roles, for example, access rights. Using the credential, the user can prove to some service provider the possession of a credential containing a given claim without revealing any other information stored in the credential.

A number of variants of the Camenisch-Lysyanskaya scheme have been proposed offering additional functionalities such as credential revocation [2, 10, 12, 37] and improvements such as efficiently encoding binary attributes [9] or verifiably encrypting attributes under some third party's encryption key [7, 13].

In 2012, a novel form of ZKPs was proposed [1], named *Zero-Knowledge Succinct Non-Interactive Argument of Knowledge* (zk-SNARK). A zk-SNARK is a non-interactive and succinct protocol where only one single message is sent from the prover to the verifier. It offers a very small proof that can be quickly verified even if a statement is very large. Contrary to the zk-SNARK protocol, a recently proposed new ZKP construct called *Bulletproofs* [5] requires no trusted setup. However, verifying a bulletproof is more time consuming than verifying a zk-SNARK proof.

Due to their efficiency, Bulletproofs and zk-SNARKs are highly suitable for blockchain-based applications and, in particular, cryptocurrencies. On the other hand, AABCs are specifically tailored for identity management and authentication processes. Emmy offers AABC primitives and currently does not contain any zk-SNARK or Bulletproof schemes. This does not mean it cannot be integrated with blockchains, the standards and recommendations of W3C Verifiable Claims Working Group [50] which is heavily focused on the scenarios with distributed ledgers fully rely on the AABCs.

The widely used techniques for transferring user attributes, like SAML [44], OpenID [38], and WS-Federation [51], present considerable privacy concerns. Namely, identity providers can track activities of their users or can even impersonate them. In contrast, with AABCs, issuers are not involved in the authentication process. Additionally, users disclose only those attributes that are required by services in a way that makes linking the transactions highly difficult.

3   Existing Implementations

While a significant amount of theory on Privacy-Enhancing Technologies (PETs) exist, there is a clear lack of implementations. The library most frequently used for demonstrating research innovations related to AABCs is Identity Mixer (idemix) [26] from IBM, which has also been integrated into the IBM cloud platform BlueMIX [25]. An older version of idemix is publicly available but lacks some core functionalities like an integrated communication channel for prover-verifier interactions. Moreover, this open-source idemix repository is no longer maintained.

A newer version of idemix is available [27] as part of the Hyperledger Fabric [24], a platform for distributed ledger solutions, but this version provides only a limited functionality and does not contain the ZKP machinery needed for fully-working AABCs (e.g., range proofs, proofs of partial knowledge). Besides Fabric, the Hyperledger consortium provides tools, libraries, and reusable software components for providing digital identities rooted on distributed ledgers so that they are interoperable across different administrative domains and applications. Hyperledger Indy is available as open-source [29] and also contains an implementation of the Camenisch-Lysyanskaya anonymous authentication scheme [11]. However, yet again, no machinery for ZKPs is provided. Microsoft released their version of a AABC system called U-Prove [49]. This library is complex and hardly usable for non-expert developers. It lacks functionalities such as range proofs and has not been maintained since 2014. U-Prove and idemix have been part of the ABC4Trust project [42] which addressed the federation and interchangeability of technologies that support ABCs.

IRMA [45] is another platform for privacy-friendly authentication, also based on the famous Camenisch-Lysyanskaya scheme [11]. IRMA provides attribute-based credentials integrated into the Android application and is thus not offered as a library which could be easily reused.

Recently, a group of researchers presented their implementation of an AABC system called CLARC [32]. The library implements a series of ZKP schemes but lacks a communication layer.

In 2003, the Trusted Computing Group [48] adopted and standardized the *Direct Anonymous Attestation* (DAA) scheme [4] as the method for remote authentication of a hardware module, called Trusted Platform Module (TPM), while preserving privacy of the user of the platform that contains the module. Over the years, DAA implementations improved [6,8], but they are still tightly bound to the TPM chip, which makes these constructions often too prohibitive for the use with low-resource devices (e.g., with smartcards). Additionally, the implementation is not offered as a library.

The Intel Enhanced Privacy ID (Intel EPID) technology [30] is being used in various applications that need a guarantee that involved devices are authentic, have not been hijacked or replicated into a non-genuine piece of hardware. The source code for Intel EPID is publicly available [46], but the library does not offer a modular architecture that could be used for combining cryptographic primitives into schemes other than Intel EPID. Also, the communication layer is not included.

As discussed above, several implementations of PETs that support the development of anonymous authentication solutions exist, however, there is no fully-fledged AABC library that could be easily integrated into cloud services to offer privacy-aware and trust-enhancing authentication. In the remainder of the paper, we address this problem by presenting our library that integrates the cryptographic primitives and protocols, the entire ZKP machinery, along with a robust communication layer required to enable anonymous authentication to cloud services.

4   Emmy Building Blocks

Emmy [19] is a cryptographic library written in the Go language. It offers various schemes enabling the development of privacy-aware and trust-enhancing authentication systems such as AABCs. It is a fully-fledged software library that contains low-level cryptographic primitives and protocols as well as high-level communication procedures to facilitate simple integration with existing cloud services. Emmy implements the following layers:

- **Utilities layer** provides various randomness related functions, like concurrent generation of *safe primes* (primes of the form $2p + 1$, where p is also a prime). It provides mathematical functions, for example, for the decomposition of positive integers into a sum of squares (Lipmaa decomposition [33]), which is needed for the implementation of range ZKPs (to prove, in zero-knowledge, that some secret value is an element of an interval). Furthermore, to turn interactive ZKPs into non-interactive ZKPs (three-move protocol into one-move protocol), the layer implements Fiat-Shamir heuristics [21].
- **Groups layer** provides various modular arithmetic and elliptic curve groups. A common API is provided to access functions for multiplying the elements, computing an inverse, retrieving the random element, and generating the group parameters for a given security parameter (for modular arithmetic groups). Four elliptic curves are offered (NIST recommended curves [18] over

prime fields: P-192, P-224, P-384, P-521) as wrappers around Go implementation of elliptic curves. Besides the basic modular arithmetic group of all integers smaller than n and coprime with n, denoted as $\mathbb{Z}_n^*$ (if n is a prime, we use notation $\mathbb{Z}_p^*$), emmy implements the *RSA group*, which is a group $\mathbb{Z}_n^*$, where n is a product of two distinct large primes. RSA group where only square elements are considered is named *QR RSA group*. Where n is a product of two safe primes, a QR RSA group $\mathbb{Z}_n^*$ is called a *QR special RSA group*. The final modular arithmetic group implemented by emmy is the *Schnorr group*, which is a cyclic subgroup of $\mathbb{Z}_p^*$, such that for its order q and some r it holds $p = qr + 1$ (p, q are primes). The order of a Schnorr group is smaller than the order of a group $\mathbb{Z}_p^*$, which means faster computations.

- **Commitments layer** provides several commitment schemes. Commitments enable one party of a protocol to choose some value and commit to it while keeping it hidden, with the ability to reveal the committed value later. Commitments are important to a variety of cryptographic protocols, including ZKPs. Emmy implements several commitment schemes. Pedersen commitment [40] is to be used in the *Schnorr group*, Damgard-Fujisaki [17] commitment in the *QR special RSA group*, and Q-One-Way-based commitment [15] in the *RSA group*.

- **ZKP layer** provides the core building blocks for anonymous authentication schemes. For historical reasons proofs for quadratic residuosity and nonresiduosity are implemented which were the first known ZKPs presented in a seminal paper [22]. For proving statements about discrete logarithms, emmy offers several different schemes. For proving knowledge of a discrete logarithm modulo prime, emmy implements Schnorr proof [43]. For proving a knowledge of equality of two discrete logarithms emmy offers proof introduced by Chaum and Pedersen [14]. A non-interactive version of proof of equality of discrete logarithms is also implemented by emmy, following the construction proposed by Lysyanskaya et al. [34]. For proving a partial knowledge of a discrete algorithm, emmy follows construction from [16]. Schnorr proof systems can be generalized to all one-way homomorphisms (one-way meaning that for a homomorphism f, one can easily compute $y = f(x)$ whereas computation of its preimage $x = f^{-1}(y)$ is practically infeasible; in Schnorr proof a homomorphism f is given by $f(x) = g^x$) [43]. Within emmy, proofs of homomorphism preimage knowledge and partial proofs of homomorphism preimage knowledge are implemented. Additionally, Schnorr can be generalized for proving the knowledge of multiple values $a_1, a_2, \ldots, a_k$ for a given number h such that $h = g_1^{a_1} \circ g_2^{a_2} \circ \cdots \circ g_k^{a_k}$. These are called representation proofs [3]. Emmy implements such proofs for Schnorr group and RSA groups.

- **Communication and portability layer** for client-server interaction via gRPC (for all messages exchanged between the prover and the verifier). It consists of a client, server, and communication layer supporting the execution of the client-server protocols. Communication between clients and the server is based on Google's Protocol Buffers [41] and gRPC [23]. Protocol buffers are a language- and platform-neutral flexible, efficient, and automated mechanism for serializing structured data. The developer needs to define the preferred structure of the data once, and then special generated source code is used to easily write and read the structured data to and from a variety of data streams, using different programming languages. In a client-server model, Remote Procedure Call (RPC) is a protocol that one program (client) can use to request a service from another program (server) located in a remote computer without having to understand network details. A gRPC is a high-performance, open-source communication system. Although emmy is written in Go, it comes with compatibility package providing client wrappers and types (based on gRPC) that can be used for quickly generating bindings for other languages.

The key ingredient of the Camenisch-Lysyanskaya scheme [11] is a representation proof in *QR special RSA group*. Heavily simplified, the scheme outputs a credential in the form of a triplet of large integers (A, e, v). The user proves to the verifier that he knows the attribute values $a_1, a_2, \ldots, a_k$ such that $A^e = g_1^{a_1} \circ g_2^{a_2} \circ \cdots \circ g_k^{a_k} \circ S^v$. If a user does not want to reveal a_1 (for example name, address or some other attribute which might reveal the user identity), he proves the knowledge of values $a_2, \ldots, a_k$ such that $A^e \circ g_1^{-a_1} = g_2^{a_2} \circ \cdots \circ g_k^{a_k} \circ S^v$

When the credential is issued, for some attribute values only commitments can be revealed to the issuer. The user can later still prove to the verifier that the committed value lies in some specific interval (for example age). This can be done by Damgard-Fujisaki scheme [17] which enables proving various properties of committed values: proofs that you can open a commitment, that two commitments hide the same value, that a commitment contains a multiplication of two committed values, that the committed value is positive, that the committed value is a square, that the committed value lies in some interval range. The latter is based on the Lipmaa scheme [33].

One might ask what is the value of such credentials. Why not simply use attributes in plaintext and signed by an issuer? Due to the randomization of a triplet and the usage of ZKPs, the verifier cannot determine whether any two credential proofs are coming from the same credential (if no unique attributes are revealed). This property is called unlinkability. Even the entity that issued a credential does not have any advantage in this sense.

5   Certificate Authority Based on the Photographed Personal Documents

In this section, we demonstrate the integration of the cryptographic library emmy into a real-world scenario where verifiable credentials are issued by Certificate Authority (CA) based on the photographed documents.

Whether the service provider is in fintech, sharing economy or cryptocurrency economy, before an account is opened, the user needs to provide an acceptable proof of identity and proof of address. This is often done by sending photographed personal documents which are then manually verified at the service provider. By having CA which would issue digital credentials based on the photographed documents, the user would need to go through the cumbersome process of photographing and uploading the documents only once. The service providers would need no manual verification as this would be done already by the CA.

The service providers which do not necessarily need the proof of identity can benefit from using verifiable credentials too as they get an assurance of the authenticity and accuracy of data.

The scenario comprises three different entities:

1. CA: a certificate authority where credentials are issued based on the photographed personal documents and new claims (e.g. driving license, education certificates) can be quickly added to the existing credential (again by sending photographed documents).
2. Service provider: any type of service provider which needs proof of identity or wants to get an assurance of the accuracy of users' data.
3. Users of the service provider from point 2.

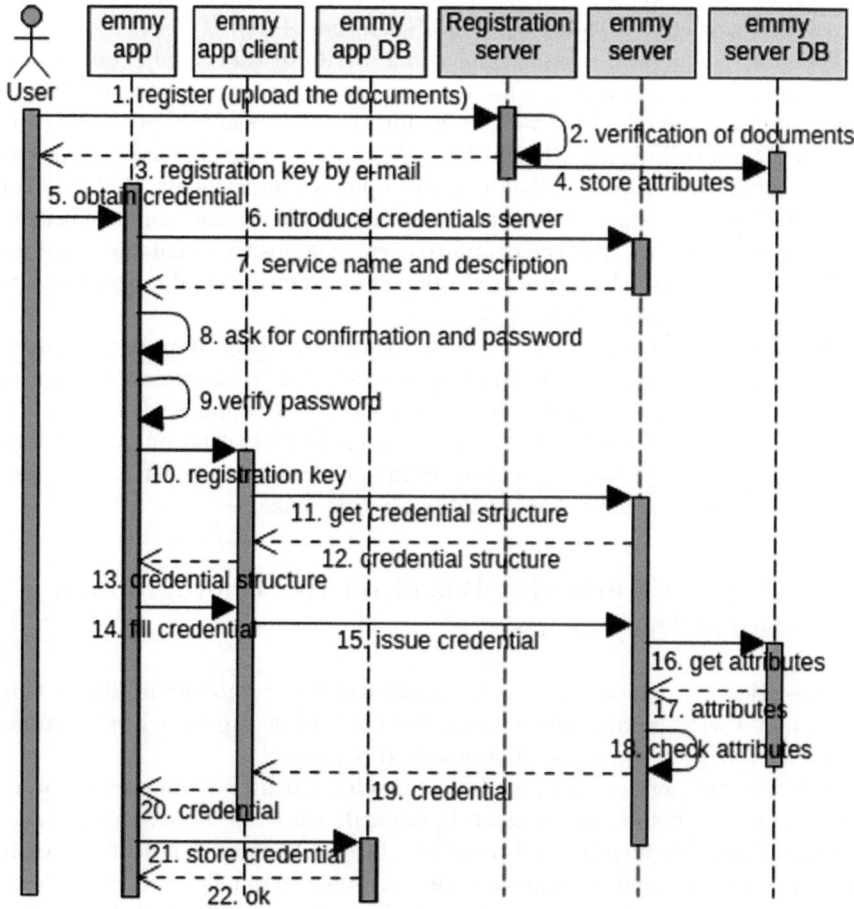

Fig. 1. Obtain credential.

The benefits of using such CA are multifold: service providers get credentials with verified personal data and are thus able to develop more accurate profiling and analysis models, users can selectively reveal data and get discounts from service providers in exchange for providing verified data. CA builds business model based on the fees users pay to obtain credentials.

By using emmy as an underlying library, such a system can be built quickly and efficiently as emmy provides all the required cryptographic primitives as well as the communication layer – all communication between the entities is already built-in.

5.1   Integration of Emmy into the Cloud Service

The user first needs to install the emmy app which is a smartphone app or browser extension (if emmy app is provided in a web browser, it has to be shipped as a browser extension which are installed in a secure way [28]). Emmy app offers a graphical user interface to the emmy client. The first time user uses emmy app a password needs to be set up. By using a password-based key derivation function PBKDF2 [39] emmy generates a key which is used to encrypt the secrets (credentials) that are stored internally in emmy app database.

The process to obtain a credential from the CA is depicted in Fig. 1. The user goes to the CA website and uploads the photographed documents. An authorized person verifies the documents and triggers registration key generation. The registration key is sent to the user by e-mail. The registration key is then passed to the emmy app and the CA emmy server is contacted to obtain a credential. CA comprises three components: registration server (website), emmy server, and emmy server database.

Obtaining a credential is a multi-step process. First, emmy app establishes gRPC connection and then executes a call to obtain a credential structure (*regKey* is the key returned from the Registration server):

```
client, err := NewCLClient(grpcClientConn)
rc, err := client.GetCredentialStructure(regKey)
```

Emmy server returns the structure of credentials it can issue. The structure can contain known and committed attributes. Respectively, these represent attributes with values known to the issuer and the attributes for which only the committment of a value is known to the issuer. For each attribute the type of the value (type: string/int/bool) is specified and whether the attribute value is known to the issuer or not (known: true/false). Note that in our case only known attributes are used and emmy server could fill the credential with values by itself as it has an access to the database where attributes corresponding to the registration key are stored. However, these values could be then changed by the user and have to be thus validated again when the credential is being issued.

Emmy API offers UpdateValue function to set the attribute values of the credential:

```
name, _ := rc.GetAttr("Name")
err = name.UpdateValue("Jack")
```

Before the client can call IssueCredential method, a user's master secret key needs to be generated and *CredManager* needs to be instantiated.

```
masterSecret := pubKey.GenerateUserMasterSecret()
```

Public key *pubKey* needs to be provided by an issuer. Among other parameters it provides information about the *QR special RSA group* which is used for attributes and *Schnorr group* which is used for a master secret key. Secret key *masterSecret* is encoded into every user's credential as a sharing prevention mechanism. User can only share a credential if he shares a master secret key. Thus, if he shares one credential, all his credentials are shared.

Whenever a session is established with an issuer, the client provides a pseudonym which is a Pedersen commitment [40] to a *masterSecret*.

```
cm, err := cl.NewCredManager(params, pubKey, masterSecret, rc)
```

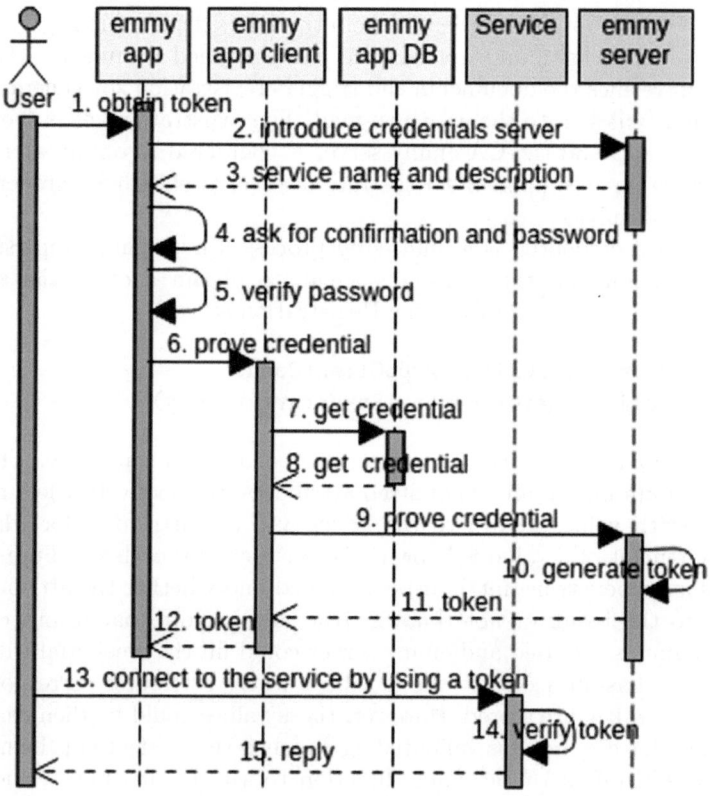

Fig. 2. Connect to the service.

CredManager manages all ZKP interactions between the emmy client and emmy server. The IssueCredential method can now be triggered:

```
cred, err := client.IssueCredential(cm, regKey)
```

CA (emmy server) retrieves the attributes from the database and checks whether they are the same as attributes sent from the user which are to be encoded in the credential. If everything is ok, the credential is returned to the emmy app. It stores it in the internal database which is encrypted by the key generated from the user's password. The credential comes in the form of a triplet of large numbers (A, e, v). Whenever the possession of a valid credential needs to be proved, properties of the triplet are being proved using ZKPs (see Sect. 4). To provide unlinkability, a triplet is randomized by *CredManager* before the possession of a credential is proved.

Verifiable credentials can provide (partial) anonymity: user can reveal only partial information which do not reveal the identity. However, service provider could still observe the IP address and could thus identify the user. To provide a fully anonymity, credentials need to be used together with the privacy tools that reroute Internet traffic via public nodes such as VPN services or TOR [47] software.

Once the service provider has integrated the emmy server and is thus able to verify its credentials, there are different ways to integrate the verification of the credentials into the authentication process. Emmy server might return a session key which is then used for the authentication to the actual service. If unlinkability is required, each time the user connects to the service a new session key needs to be provided as otherwise, the server can easily link the sessions which have the same session key. If unlinkability is not required, the session key can be set to be valid for some period of time. Alternatively, if some claims need to be associated with a session, JSON Web Tokens [31] can be used (see Fig. 2). They are self-contained and require only verification of the signature on the service side. Repeatedly using the same token breaks unlinkability but the service provider has an assurance of the authenticity and accuracy of the attributes which is in many cases the property of the verifiable credentials that service providers value the most. Thus, the attributes that are written to the token are verified and can be trusted.

When proving the possession of a valid credential, not all service providers might require all user's data. The user has control over which attributes are to be revealed to the service provider:

```
revealedAttrs = []string{"Gender", "BirthName"}
token, err := client.ProveCredential(cm, cred, revealedAttrs)
```

6   Conclusions and Future Work

Despite the internet reputation for anonymity, it is very difficult to perform any action online with true privacy. On the other hand, verifying identity is cumbersome and often relies on replicated versions of offline systems which are usually imperfect analogues to showing a physical credential to a human verifier. In this paper, we presented a cryptographic library which provides a complete analogue to reliable offline systems and at the same time provide many advantages due to its digital nature. Most notably, the user can reveal only selected claims to the service provider. In our future work, we plan to open source the emmy smartphone app and the registration server. Additionally, we plan to extend the registration server to support other verification processes, in particular, physical verification, QR code verification, and verification by using anonymous payment using cryptocurrencies.

Acknowledgement. The research was supported, in part, by grants H2020-DS-2017-780108 (FENTEC) and H2020-ICT-2016-730929 (mF2C).

References

1. Bitansky, N., Canetti, R., Chiesa, A., Tromer, E.: From extractable collision resistance to succinct non-interactive arguments of knowledge, and back again. In: Proceedings of the 3rd Innovations in Theoretical Computer Science Conference, ITCS 2012, pp. 326–349. ACM, New York (2012)
2. Brands, S., Demuynck, L., De Decker, B.: A practical system for globally revoking the unlinkable pseudonyms of unknown users. In: Pieprzyk, J., Ghodosi, H., Dawson, E. (eds.) ACISP 2007. LNCS, vol. 4586, pp. 400–415. Springer, Heidelberg (2007). https://doi.org/10.1007/978-3-540-73458-1_29
3. Brands, S.A.: An efficient off-line electronic cash system based on the representation problem. Technical report, CWI (Centre for Mathematics and Computer Science), Amsterdam, The Netherlands (1993)
4. Brickell, E., Camenisch, J., Chen, L.: Direct anonymous attestation. In: Proceedings of the 11th ACM Conference on Computer and Communications Security, CCS 2004, pp. 132–145. ACM, New York (2004)
5. Bünz, B., Bootle, J., Boneh, D., Poelstra, A., Wuille, P., Maxwell, G.: Bulletproofs: short proofs for confidential transactions and more. In: Proceedings of the 39th IEEE Symposium on Security and Privacy 2018, SP 2018, San Francisco, CA, US, pp. 315–334. IEEE (2018)
6. Camenisch, J., Chen, L., Drijvers, M., Lehmann, A., Novick, D., Urian, R.: One TPM to bind them all: fixing TPM 2.0 for provably secure anonymous attestation. In: Proceedings of the 38th IEEE Symposium on Security and Privacy, SP 2017, pp. 901–920. IEEE, NY (2017)
7. Camenisch, J., Damgård, I.: Verifiable encryption, group encryption, and their applications to separable group signatures and signature sharing schemes. In: Okamoto, T. (ed.) ASIACRYPT 2000. LNCS, vol. 1976, pp. 331–345. Springer, Heidelberg (2000). https://doi.org/10.1007/3-540-44448-3_25
8. Camenisch, J., Drijvers, M., Lehmann, A.: Universally composable direct anonymous attestation. In: Cheng, C.-M., Chung, K.-M., Persiano, G., Yang, B.-Y. (eds.) PKC 2016. LNCS, vol. 9615, pp. 234–264. Springer, Heidelberg (2016). https://doi.org/10.1007/978-3-662-49387-8_10
9. Camenisch, J., Groß, T.: Efficient attributes for anonymous credentials. In: Proceedings of the 15th ACM Conference on Computer and Communications Security, CCS 2008, pp. 345–356. ACM, New York (2008)

10. Camenisch, J., Kohlweiss, M., Soriente, C.: An accumulator based on bilinear maps and efficient revocation for anonymous credentials. In: Jarecki, S., Tsudik, G. (eds.) PKC 2009. LNCS, vol. 5443, pp. 481–500. Springer, Heidelberg (2009). https://doi.org/10.1007/978-3-642-00468-1_27

11. Camenisch, J., Lysyanskaya, A.: An efficient system for non-transferable anonymous credentials with optional anonymity revocation. In: Pfitzmann, B. (ed.) EUROCRYPT 2001. LNCS, vol. 2045, pp. 93–118. Springer, Heidelberg (2001). https://doi.org/10.1007/3-540-44987-6_7

12. Camenisch, J., Lysyanskaya, A.: Signature schemes and anonymous credentials from bilinear maps. In: Franklin, M. (ed.) CRYPTO 2004. LNCS, vol. 3152, pp. 56–72. Springer, Heidelberg (2004). https://doi.org/10.1007/978-3-540-28628-8_4

13. Camenisch, J., Shoup, V.: Practical verifiable encryption and decryption of discrete logarithms. In: Boneh, D. (ed.) CRYPTO 2003. LNCS, vol. 2729, pp. 126–144. Springer, Heidelberg (2003). https://doi.org/10.1007/978-3-540-45146-4_8

14. Chaum, D., Pedersen, T.P.: Wallet databases with observers. In: Brickell, E.F. (ed.) CRYPTO 1992. LNCS, vol. 740, pp. 89–105. Springer, Heidelberg (1993). https://doi.org/10.1007/3-540-48071-4_7

15. Cramer, R., Damgård, I.: Zero-knowledge proofs for finite field arithmetic, or: can zero-knowledge be for free? In: Krawczyk, H. (ed.) CRYPTO 1998. LNCS, vol. 1462, pp. 424–441. Springer, Heidelberg (1998). https://doi.org/10.1007/BFb0055745

16. Cramer, R., Damgård, I., Schoenmakers, B.: Proofs of partial knowledge and simplified design of witness hiding protocols. In: Desmedt, Y.G. (ed.) CRYPTO 1994. LNCS, vol. 839, pp. 174–187. Springer, Heidelberg (1994). https://doi.org/10.1007/3-540-48658-5_19

17. Damgård, I., Fujisaki, E.: A statistically-hiding integer commitment scheme based on groups with hidden order. In: Zheng, Y. (ed.) ASIACRYPT 2002. LNCS, vol. 2501, pp. 125–142. Springer, Heidelberg (2002). https://doi.org/10.1007/3-540-36178-2_8

18. Digital Signature Standard. https://csrc.nist.gov/csrc/media/publications/fips/186/3/archive/2009-06-25/documents/fips_186-3.pdf

19. emmy - Library for Zero-Knowledge Proofs. https://github.com/xlab-si/emmy

20. FENTEC Project Homepage. http://fentec.eu/

21. Fiat, A., Shamir, A.: How to prove yourself: practical solutions to identification and signature problems. In: Odlyzko, A.M. (ed.) CRYPTO 1986. LNCS, vol. 263, pp. 186–194. Springer, Heidelberg (1987). https://doi.org/10.1007/3-540-47721-7_12

22. Goldwasser, S., Micali, S., Rackoff, C.: The knowledge complexity of interactive proof-systems. In: Proceedings of the 17th Annual ACM Symposium on Theory of Computing, STOC 1985, pp. 291–304. ACM, New York (1985)

23. gRPC. https://grpc.io/

24. Hyperledger Fabric. https://wiki.hyperledger.org/projects/Fabric

25. IBM Bluemix. https://console.bluemix.net/catalog/

26. IBM Identity Mixer (idemix). https://www.zurich.ibm.com/identity_mixer/

27. Idemix. https://github.com/hyperledger/fabric/tree/release-1.2/idemix

28. In-browser Cryptography. https://tonyarcieri.com/whats-wrong-with-webcrypto

29. Indy Crypto. https://github.com/hyperledger/indy-crypto

30. Intel Enhanced Privacy ID (EPID) Security Technology. https://software.intel.com/en-us/articles/intel-enhanced-privacy-id-epid-security-technology

31. JSON Web Tokens. https://jwt.io/

32. Bemmann, K., et al.: Fully-featured anonymous credentials with reputation system. In: Proceedings of the 13th International Conference on Availability, Reliability and Security, ARES 1918, pp. 42:1–42:10. ACM, New York (2018)
33. Lipmaa, H.: On diophantine complexity and statistical zero-knowledge arguments. In: Laih, C.-S. (ed.) ASIACRYPT 2003. LNCS, vol. 2894, pp. 398–415. Springer, Heidelberg (2003). https://doi.org/10.1007/978-3-540-40061-5_26
34. Lysyanskaya, A., Rivest, R.L., Sahai, A., Wolf, S.: Pseudonym systems. In: Heys, H., Adams, C. (eds.) SAC 1999. LNCS, vol. 1758, pp. 184–199. Springer, Heidelberg (2000). https://doi.org/10.1007/3-540-46513-8_14
35. Marketing Week: Consumers are 'dirtying' databases with false details. https://www.marketingweek.com/2015/07/08/consumers-are-dirtying-databases-with-false-details/
36. mF2C Project Homepage. http://www.mf2c-project.eu/
37. Nakanishi, T., Fujii, H., Hira, Y., Funabiki, N.: Revocable group signature schemes with constant costs for signing and verifying. In: Jarecki, S., Tsudik, G. (eds.) PKC 2009. LNCS, vol. 5443, pp. 463–480. Springer, Heidelberg (2009). https://doi.org/10.1007/978-3-642-00468-1_26
38. OpenID Specifications. https://openid.net/developers/specs/
39. PBKDF2. https://en.wikipedia.org/wiki/PBKDF2
40. Pedersen, T.P.: Non-interactive and information-theoretic secure verifiable secret sharing. In: Feigenbaum, J. (ed.) CRYPTO 1991. LNCS, vol. 576, pp. 129–140. Springer, Heidelberg (1992). https://doi.org/10.1007/3-540-46766-1_9
41. Protocol Buffers. https://developers.google.com/protocol-buffers/
42. Sabouri, A., Krontiris, I., Rannenberg, K.: Attribute-based credentials for trust (ABC4Trust). In: Fischer-Hübner, S., Katsikas, S., Quirchmayr, G. (eds.) TrustBus 2012. LNCS, vol. 7449, pp. 218–219. Springer, Heidelberg (2012). https://doi.org/10.1007/978-3-642-32287-7_21
43. Schnorr, C.P.: Efficient identification and signatures for smart cards. In: Brassard, G. (ed.) CRYPTO 1989. LNCS, vol. 435, pp. 239–252. Springer, New York (1990). https://doi.org/10.1007/0-387-34805-0_22
44. Security Assertion Markup Language (SAML) V2.0 Technical Overview. https://wiki.oasis-open.org/security/Saml2TechOverview
45. Technical introduction to IRMA. https://credentials.github.io/
46. The Intel(R) Enhanced Privacy ID Software Development Kit. https://github.com/Intel-EPID-SDK/epid-sdk
47. TOR Project. https://www.torproject.org/
48. Trusted Computing Group. https://trustedcomputinggroup.org/
49. U-Prove. https://www.microsoft.com/en-us/research/project/u-prove/
50. Verifiable Claims Working Group. https://www.w3.org/2017/vc/WG/
51. WS-Federation. https://msdn.microsoft.com/en-us/library/bb498017.aspx

CrowdLED: Towards Crowd-Empowered and Privacy-Preserving Data Sharing Using Smart Contracts

Constantinos Pouyioukka[1], Thanassis Giannetsos[2(✉)], and Weizhi Meng[2]

[1] University of Surrey, Surrey, UK
cp00296@surrey.ac.uk
[2] Cyber Security, Department of Applied Mathematics and Computer Science,
Technical University of Denmark, Kongens Lyngby, Denmark
{atgi,weme}@dtu.dk

Abstract. In this research paper, we explore how Blockchain technologies and Smart Contracts can be used to fairly reward users for the data they share with advertising networks without compromising anonymity and user privacy. The novelty of using Blockchains alongside such systems is to understand and investigate how a proper and fair exchange of data can ensure that participating users can be kept secure and eliminate aggressive data collection by ad libraries; libraries that are embedded inside the code of smart-phones and web applications for monetization. There are a lot of privacy issues regarding mobile and online advertising: Advertising networks mostly rely on data collection, similar to a crowd-sensing system, but in most cases, neither consent has been granted by the user for the data collection nor a reward has been given to the user as compensation. Making a comparison between the problems identified in mobile and online advertising and the positives of the approach of using Blockchain, we propose "CrowdLED", a holistic system to address the security and privacy issues discussed throughout the paper.

Keywords: Blockchains · Online advertising · Smart Contracts · Security · Privacy · Fairness · Crowd-sourcing

1 Introduction

Internet of Things and subsequently its applications and systems are mostly based on a cloud-centric approach. To ensure proper security and smooth operation of processes that are involved in such paradigms, several authors explored the possibility of integrating Blockchain technologies in IoT operations [1].

Advertising Networks (ANs) work by relying on a mass scale data collection from participating users, leveraging smartphone applications, web applications,

---

C. Pouyioukka—*Research Fellow.*

© IFIP International Federation for Information Processing 2019
Published by Springer Nature Switzerland AG 2019
W. Meng et al. (Eds.): IFIPTM 2019, IFIP AICT 563, pp. 147–161, 2019.
https://doi.org/10.1007/978-3-030-33716-2_12

online services and internet browsing history. Data collection is achieved through advertising libraries that are embedded into the services and software. The collected data is then used to deliver specific ads, according to a user's online activity, ethnographic background and other information. In most cases, advertising networks aggressively collect user data without the necessary consent which in turn raises a number of questions regarding user anonymity and privacy [2].

ANs and subsequently their systems can be separated in *online* and *mobile* advertising. For setting the fundamentals of the research, we will explore online advertising as a whole; with mobile advertising as the core extend of that. Advertisers in general, rely on ANs to efficiently deliver ads to customers [3,4]. This is achieved through the use of smartphones, as such devices, contain rich information that are needed by the advertising network. Services and mobile applications that are offered free of charge, utilize such networks for monetization, via the equivalent advertising schemes in place.

When referring to ad delivery and targeted ad placement, we are not only referring to smartphones, smart homes or smart appliances but to the wider spectrum of IoT applications; e.g., Intelligent Transportation Systems [5,6]. Such smart vehicles and respectively their drivers, will be part of such aggressive data collection methods being utilized by advertising networks. As drivers and passengers consume a large portion of their daily lives commuting, these systems can be susceptible to location specific advertising [7]. This might be considered an alternative to static billboards. These systems require to communicate with the backend infrastructure and, thus, will also have to share data between them. Providing incentives in a transparent and fair way for users to participate, even in these services is of paramount importance.

Contributions: By taking all the information into consideration, this paper follows on to identify the main issues and share a brief insight on privacy-related solutions towards preventing aggressive data collection in the online and mobile advertising spectrum. Following, with an explanation of why blockchain technologies can be the solution and how they can be leveraged in such systems. Then we proceed with presenting the key challenges in designing and developing a viable solution coupled with the requirements that such systems need to fulfill as criteria, and an overview of the proposed architecture. This research paper finalizes with critiques of such an approach and how it can be enhanced further. Final thoughts and discussions are presented alongside our conclusions.

2   The Existing Problem in Web and Mobile Advertising

In websites, web applications and mobile applications, developers embed advertising libraries in their source code. This is a common way among companies to monetize their services, offering them for free instead of opting for a fee from their users. Those advertising libraries can then deliver targeted ads according to the specific online profile of a user. These libraries collect user data so that they can offer a more targeted approach when referring to ads.

This approach though comes with one major flaw; *the uncontrolled mass collection of user data risking privacy.* Technology giants in the likes of Google and Facebook offer their services for free, taking advantage of the advertising platforms they have developed over the years. In turn they act as brokers selling those advertising data to clients, to place targeted ads on their platforms. Clients/advertisers create campaigns on such platforms to promote their services or products. The advertisers can then request (through those platforms) where their ads will be placed, for how long and which specific groups of people will target, i.e.,: "People that make use of a smart-phone device, from the European Union aged between 25–40, who have an interest in football". This generic approach, mentioned as an example, can then be narrowed down even further with specific keywords provided by the advertising framework. Concluding that such techniques can be a major privacy issue, as developers implementing advertising libraries in their web or mobile applications, can collect personal data as an individual third party. Each platform and broker have their own payment systems in place, but the general approach is to pay according to the 'number of impressions' or 'how many times a link has been clicked' followed to the client's service. The more functional a platform is, the more revenue a broker can make from user data and in return their clients that use those platforms.

Although a straightforward process, data collection is happening aggressively without the user's consent especially in mobile applications. The most valuable asset of users, their data are given for free. When a service provider or an advertiser gets the revenue, a user doesn't get a share of that revenue.

Another important issue with advertising is the use of advertising libraries for malicious acts. Ads containing malicious code or misleading audiovisual content, with the sole purpose of extracting user sensitive information. Or forcibly through an ad, install ad-ware on a user's system to collect information in the background. This method is commonly referred to as "Malvertising" (Malicious Advertising). This practice is commonly used by perpetrators, as the advertising libraries provide a solid platform for malware to flourish and be distributed due to the intrusive nature of ads. Advertising libraries being intrusive by nature can ensure that a product or a service can gain traction by attracting loads of users. But at the same time can be a double-edged sword as it compromises user security and privacy. As advertising is now a normal process of selling products or services on legitimate websites and social networks, attackers can directly advertise malicious code websites or applications masked behind a valid ad without compromising those legitimate websites.

In this paper we aim to introduce an incentivized and privacy enforced solution towards mitigating the following issues: (i) *The uncontrolled and aggressive data collection of users,* (ii) *The non-incentivisation of user data to compensate users for participating in the advertising model,* and (iii) *The possible distribution of Malware or offensive ads using an advertising library.*

3   Privacy Preserving Solutions Towards Preventing Aggresive Data Collection

A lot of research has already been conducted towards ensuring that strict security and privacy mechanisms are clearly followed when collecting user data for ad placements [7]. Studies have mainly focused in measuring and identifying the security and privacy risks that are directly associated with the delivery of ads in web applications, websites and mobile applications. Results have identified that most advertising libraries abuse systematically the way they handle and gather data from host applications and their user base [2].

Pluto: ("Free for All! Assessing User Data Exposure to Advertising Libraries for Android") [2]. A framework notable for its usage in analyzing and detecting if an advertising library and by extension its host application is exposing targeted user data. Pluto is built in a novel way utilizing the power of language processing and machine learning and the equivalent data mining models. This is done to identify what type of user data is exposed and what information, advertising networks can extract from a list of installed applications in a device. Pluto can estimate the risks associated when developers choose to implement advertising libraries in their applications.

AdSplit: ("AdSplit: Separating smartphone advertising from applications") [8]. An application embedded to the Android Operating System that allows an application and the advertising library associated with it to run as separate processes on the system kernel. Each process is assigned a separate user-id, thus, eliminating the need for the main application to request permission to mine data on behalf of the advertising library. AdSplit, guarantees privacy of users but does not solve the problem of aggressive data collection.

PiCoDa: ("PiCoDa: Privacy preserving Smart Coupon Delivery Architecture") [9]. A privacy preserving smart coupon delivery system, with its main purpose of protecting user data on the client side rather than on the service side. This framework guarantees that when an ad is placed, a user is being verified if it is eligible for a coupon. It also offers protection to the service/vendor by not revealing any information about the targeting strategy.

Privad: ("Privad: Practical Privacy in Online Advertising") [10]. An advertising system that provides a balance between user privacy and placements of ads across the web. Privad makes use of keywords, demographics and user interests for prioritizing those data according to the needs of an AN via online auctions. Privad improves a user's browsing experience, while maintaining low costs when we are referring to costs of infrastructure for an advertising network.

RePriv: ("RePriv: Re-Imagining Content Personalization and In-Browser Privacy") [11]. A browser add-on system, that has as its main purpose to enable privacy for participating users. RePriv only discovers data after getting an explicit user permission. It then mines relevant user interests and shares this information with third party ANs. As the authors and developers claim, this data mining is happening in-browser and no drawbacks are being reported when we are referring to, a user's online browsing experience and the performance drawback of producing results.

From a brief description of the above solutions, we can conclude that while some of them are focusing in delivering privacy as their ultimatum, others, by compromising privacy, provide a sense of fairness. None of them, however, guarantees and solves the initial problem as a whole: *Providing the privacy, fairness and security as their core characteristics.* When referring to fairness, we imply the compensation of users for providing their data to advertising networks.

4   Using Blockchain Technologies, Smart Contracts and Incentives to Close the Gap

Blockchains work in such a way that can provide a 'shared governance', thus, ensuring trust and anonymity. And with the use of smart contracts, involved parties can benefit from shared agreements as well as the fair exchange of data without the need of a third-party intermediary being in charge. Blockchains for the IoT domain can be applicable in a plethora of applications and systems [12]. One field though that hasn't attracted much attention is the integration of blockchain technologies in advertising network applications.

The main challenge in such systems is **to fairly reward users while avoiding uncontrolled and aggressive data collection** of user's personal information and data. To overcome the issue of fair execution, an approach would be the use Smart Contracts. Using smart contracts, service providers can ensure that rewards provided by the service, and the data provided by users are exchanged simultaneously. This can be achieved because smart contract terms and conditions are strictly followed after they are agreed by the parties involved [13].

4.1   Advantages of Using Blockchains in Online/Mobile Advertising

Transparency: Users will have control over which data can be shared but also can opt out from the data collection process at any given time. Also, with Blockchains, advertisers and advertising libraries can verify that a user engagement on an ad is genuine. Users can be confident that an ad placement is not coming from a fraudulent entity as, through smart contracts, the ad of a service can be verified and validated on the network, i.e., if an ad is placed for an Amazon product the user will know that the advertiser has created an ad campaign that was placed directly by Amazon and not another fraudulent entity.

Incentives: Users can still support the advertising business model but can also be given the option of exclusion. ANs can be incentivized to collect only the necessary and minimum amount of data required for their services, as they will have to 'pay' for gaining further access to user data. Rewards can either be, monetary or non-monetary [14–16]. Systems with monetary incentives, reward their participants with real money or virtual redeemable credit which is equivalent to the actual price in currency. Non-monetary incentives do not include any real money rewards but can include a plethora of options such as entertainment, social and service incentives [3]. This can vary according to the advertisement library and the agreements set at the programming of smart contracts.

Fairness: Fairness can exist if the parties involved mutually agree on the terms of the Smart Contract. Those terms will be upheld and followed strictly as any node connected inside the network can validate the status of the contracts ensuring absolute trust between the parties involved.

Privacy and Anonymity: Using Blockchains, we can ensure user privacy and anonymity, as security mechanisms are implemented by default. Although, such mechanisms exist, we still need to take appropriate actions to identify any leakage of personal user information.

No Single Point of Failure: Data are distributed in such way where each node has an exact copy of the entire Blockchain since the genesis block. Even if nodes inside the network do fail, the network is still fully operational, and any workload is distributed to the other network nodes.

Open Source Software: Blockchain technologies are based on Open Source software, allowing a plethora of applications to be deployed. A huge community of developers is present that ensures the security and proper maintenance of the source code. Advertising libraries and providers of advertising libraries can benefit from the openness of this technology.

Direct Communication between Advertisers and Users: Based on the current mode of operation, current advertising libraries introduce a middleman between users and advertisers. Those middlemen can be in the likes of large corporations who act as brokers. With the use of Blockchains, these middlemen can be eliminated or become less powerful in terms of controlling user data. Thus, they will be deemed irrelevant to the final transaction of the smart contract. When advertisers leverage this direct contact to the end users, more robust and effective ads can be delivered.

Less Intrusive - More Effective Ad Placements: At their current state ads are very intrusive. Especially in mobile applications where the majority ads can take the form of video overlays that cannot be closed until a specific time interval has concluded. A good example of a privacy related application is the web browser Brave, which offers an approach of Blockchain related advertising. Brave allows users to opt – in or out for receiving ads. Following a similar approach, in our system, advertisers can benefit from receiving the data they need, without compromising user privacy.

Less Malicious Code Exploits and Elimination of Malware: One issue with intrusive ads is the possibility of distributing malicious code and fraudulent ads to the end-users. A big portion of advertising libraries have less checks in place to validate the authenticity of ad campaigns or do not have checks at all to ensure what ads are being served. Although already mentioned, with transparency in mind, assurance and quality of ads derives directly from Blockchains.

When a transaction is sent throughout the network, it is validated and then accessible to view by any valid user. If a malicious user tries to interact with the network, it can be traced back to the point it originated; thus, it can be deemed invalid and not safe for the entirety of a network.

Taking into consideration the benefits of Blockchain technologies, smart contracts and their characteristics, we aim to further expand on these technologies for finding the golden ration between advertisers, advertising networks and users. With the use of Blockchain technologies, the main problem of aggressive data collection can be remedied. As adopters of this system, can agree with their users, to receive specific data anonymously, in exchange of rewards. Users on their end can still support the advertising business model, by having the option to share (or not) their data. Advertising networks in turn can be incentivized to collect only the necessary data as they will have to 'pay' for the data they require. Thus, the problem of fairness can be solved as well. In the next section a more in-depth approach on the Blockchain underpinnings is conducted and we identify the key challenges in designing a system, like CrowdLED.

5   Key Challenges in Designing CrowdLED

As aforementioned, Blockchains can be used to enhance the advertising platform for better delivery of ads and a fair exchange of data for the appropriate user incentivization while ensuring verification and enhanced user privacy. All these objectives can be achieved by taking crucial measurements and identifying the key challenges that need answering before implementing CrowdLED.

From a "System Security" Perspective: *How can we ensure that users or mobile applications don't feed or spoof data to get a competitive advantage, or unfairly get compensated in a system? How can we ensure that the system proposed in its entirety is secure from user manipulation but also, how can we ensure users are secured from and by the system?* - This key challenge is very important in such systems to ensure their viability and properly compensate users according to their participation. By integrating Blockchain technologies and with the use of smart contracts, the security and privacy but also, the fairness aspects of the research questions can be solved.

From an "Economics Perspective": *How can a Smart Contract be implemented to accommodate the entities involved? What types of incentives can be offered as an acceptable form of compensation? What is the right amount of compensation for the right amount of data gathered?* – This key challenge is again important and needs to be addressed for properly incentivizing users according to the data they share. Compounding this issue, we need to implement metric mechanisms; using device metrics to quantify user privacy and data shared across parties.

From a "System Design" Perspective: *How is the data collected and shared, from user devices to advertising networks? Should there be a central system service that handles data requests, or an ad hoc mechanism handled by the device's* *operating system? Is the system secure by web-based attacks?* – Currently mobile and web applications offer ads, collect data and share them with an advertising network. Usually the data collection from such services is hidden from the host application, the operating system and the user itself. The decision on which app-roach needs to be taken into consideration for implementation, between a central system or an ad hoc mechanism, is solely based on examining the trade-offs of each approach. The solution should not be susceptible to tampering but also be efficient as not to impact the performance of a user's device or that of the system from delivering the ads.

From a "User Privacy" Perspective: *How can we ensure that proper user privacy practices are being followed? Is the system secure from social engineering attacks, with their main aim to identify users?* - As already mentioned, ANs rely on aggressive data collection to target specific ad placements to their users. This aggressive data collection extracts personal user information which users wouldn't share in the first place.

6   Closing the Gap Between ANs and Users

CrowdLED will be a fully operational system combining Blockchain technologies and Smart Contracts for enabling privacy and fairness when advertising networks collect user data. By using incentives and rewards, we can ensure a fair exchange of data and credits between a user and an advertiser. But also, enable correct security practices that ensure: **Privacy and Anonymity**, to the users involved and **Fairness and Security**, to the users and the system providers.

6.1   Data Collection

Data Collection Characteristics: The type of information that is to be col-lected from the users, but also the possible use of sensors in a smartphone so that data can be extracted. This data can take the form of raw application data, or statistical values such as maximum, average or minimum [14, 17–19].

The Frequency on Which Data is to be Transmitted and Time Dura-tion Characteristics: This includes the periodic submission interval that data is to be submitted to the advertising network. Time intervals can vary in time, length but also in frequency. Those time intervals might also have specific require-ments on the data that are to be submitted, i.e., every twenty (20) seconds for the time interval of two (2) minutes, submit the device's location where that location is above thirty (30) meters of sea level [17–19]. The duration of a task that users need to participate, and the time interval data sharing is live on the network, needs to be recorded [17].

Area of Interest and Incentive Characteristics: The area of interest that the system will be deployed for delivering ads on a specific area. The area can be defined as the population of a geographical area. Dense geographic areas are more of interest to ensure maximum ad placement and delivery [17]. *Incentives:*

The Incentive criteria, on which, the users will be rewarded according to the data they provide to the service.

Eligibility Criteria to Join: User devices must meet some pre-defined hardware or software specifications. Pre-defined eligibility criteria might fall in the category of specific user profiles or user groups. Examples might be software requirements like an Android or iOS operating system. Specific user profiling might include users who enjoy a specific outdoor activity to deliver ads based on environmental and user's activity data.

6.2   Security

Privacy Preserving and Fairness Mechanisms: Users participating, taking into consideration the time on a service and their contribution, should be rewarded *fairly* and *anonymously* [18,19]. Any external or internal observers shouldn't be able to identify any users. If there is the need for collecting sensitive personal information, users can either opt out or enable access with the equivalent reward [18,19].

Access Control and Authorization Mechanisms: Users participating, should only allowed to access areas of the system, according to the privileges provided to them by system administrators.

Confidentiality, Authentication and Integrity Mechanisms: The system must have specific mechanisms to ensure the proper authentication of participating users. Proper protection on their communications should be provided alongside strong confidentiality and integrity of the communication channels against unauthorized third parties with the purpose of causing harm to the system or its users [2,20].

Accountability Mechanisms: Any entity that might be deemed as offensive to the system, including participating users, administrators or components of the

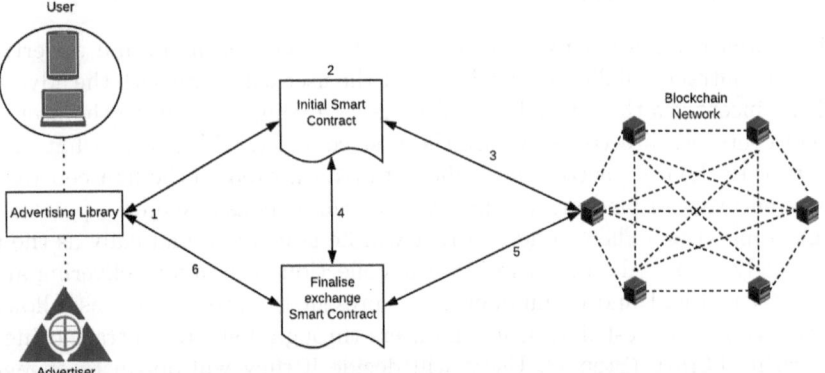

Fig. 1. User & advertiser interaction with the blockchain network - overview

system's infrastructure should be 'disciplined' based on a set of rules pre-defined by the system.

Trustworthiness and Validity of Data Mechanisms: The system must have the necessary mechanisms to ensure the validity of data and their trustworthiness as submitted by the participating users. Also, ads must be delivered in such a way to not affect performance and should be as accurate as possible [21].

6.3   Incentives/User Compensation

Well-laid out incentive schemes must cover basic requirements, which include:

- The maximization of profits for both users and the system [22];
- Avoid any risks, relating to users and system, having a 'damaging' cause. Incentives must be adequate to outweigh any drawbacks while transmitting data. Drawbacks might include: battery drainage, excessive usage of device resources, and the time the service is running on the background;
- The system should be aware of the exact population of participating users on demand at any given time. Also known as a stochastic population. This ensures that proper incentive allocation is fairly distributed across users.

7   An Architectural Blueprint of CrowdLED

Figure 1 depicts how users and advertisers could interact with each other when using smart contracts. The system is equipped with a direct communication scheme in place, between an advertiser and a user. Rather than relying on a broker to handle user data for specific ad campaigns on behalf of an advertiser, the advertiser is now responsible for placing ads; by having direct access to user data after consent has been granted. This approach can make data brokers irrelevant to the relationship between users and advertisers.

7.1   High-Level Overview

This approach follows a two-contract mandate between users and advertisers. The first contract will dictate the data that the user will share with the advertiser and the incentives the advertiser will issue as a compensation to the user. The second contract, directly issued by the first contract, will dictate what ad will be served to the user, according to the data transmitted on the first contract for a more effective ad placement. The first contract acts as a reference point of the initial transaction. The second contract will be issued automatically as the user has already approved and authorized the collection of data for delivering an ad. In respect to Fig. 1 and its numbering we present the process flow as follows:

Advertisers request data from the users through a smart contract using the advertising library (Step 1). Users will decide if they will opt-in to engage in the smart contract providing their data, with the option to select what data to distribute, i.e., Location and Interests. Advertisers then, according to the agreed amount of data that they will receive, they issue the amount of incentives that the user will receive (Step 2). As already discussed, incentives can be of monetary or non-monetary format. This can be settled on a universal mandate by the network and its participants. If the user is not happy with the incentives that will be issued after the transaction has been finalized, the user can choose to opt-out without further commitment and user data and incentives are omitted.

If all has been decided by the user and the advertiser, the contract is then encrypted and represented as a block to be broad casted and mined from the validating users (miners) of the network. Once the block has been mined, validated and the network approves the transaction, the block is permanently added to the chain. This is the initial block that will create a reference for the next block and the smart contract of delivering the ad (Step 3).

The second contract is issued automatically by the first contract, but its validity can still be rejected by the network. The advertiser issues the ad campaign according to the received data, and the contract is encrypted and represented as a block and follows the same journey of validation by the network. If the contract is validated according to the standards of the network, the user receives in an automatic approach the ad placement. If now the contract is deemed as containing an anomaly or any malicious code, or the ad doesn't meet the advertisement criteria, both the contracts are voided and reversed, and the advertiser is issued a penalty according to the severity of the anomaly (Steps 4, 5, 6).

This approach of a two-contract based system can have the benefit of identifying fraudulent users trying to circumvent the initial contract. With the issue of a penalty, advertisers can always make sure that they follow the network procedures without risking financial loss. Also, it gives the opportunity to users to select which advertisers to trust based on a feedback system.

7.2   CrowdLED Implementation Details and Execution Flow

As a first prototype, the system is being developed as an Android application. For future iterations, the system will leverage both web and mobile frameworks towards a universal deployment. Currently the Blockchain network used is Ethereum [10] Development branch with "CrowdLED token" being created as an incentive to compensate users. Geth [9] command line has been used to create a test bench for the development and for initializing a new Blockchain to test the communication between the Android application and the network. Open Source library Web3J [11] has been used to provide the necessary toolbox to enable the deployment of smart contracts from the Android application to the test Ethereum network. "CrowdLED token" has been created as part of the test network and has a fixed price. At the current stage of development, one token equals with sending one location packet to the service, for testing purposes. The location packet is making use of the sensing capabilities of the smartphone to send longitude and latitude in a string format.

Google Firebase acts as the equivalent of the advertising library (See Fig. 1) and is being used as a medium to exchange the data from the user to the advertiser. The back-end infrastructure communicates with two different versions of the application. One version is for the hypothetical user and another is for the hypothetical advertiser. Both the advertiser and user have unique wallet addresses bind to each application for simplicity. Once the user commits to send data to the service, the service asks for a consent to transmit the data. Moving on, from the Android Application, the back-end is responsible for transmitting the user's location to the advertiser only if the first contract has been validated. The user is then rewarded for the data and the back-end sends the information for the ad. The ad in this early development stage is just an image, again for testing purposes. Pre-loaded tokens from the Advertiser's account wallet are subtracted, according to the data a user is sending and are added to the user's account wallet. Smart contracts are written in Solidity; an object-oriented high-level language with syntax similar to JavaScript. Web3J library acts as a wrapper to deploy the smart contracts from the Android Applications to the Blockchain test network.

At this stage of development, the two contracts behave as they should, assuming the user always accepts the binding agreement of the first contract and the network has validated that the ad placement on the user's application is following the advertisement criteria of the network.

As already mentioned, CrowdLED is a work in progress. Everything discussed in this section and the current development stage is to give an overview of the system to the reader. The current development stage is to test the system in a scenario where everything works as intended.

8 Discussion and Critique

With respect to the benefits of using Blockchains, mentioned in Section IV, and the requirements set in section VI, there are still some open issues that need further investigation as they can have a negative impact on the system functionality.

The system needs to present a fair incentive model. What do we mean with fair incentives? Who is responsible for deciding what is a fair compensation to users that provide their data? Can the community of participating users decide what a fair compensation is? Or should the advertisers decide on what to compensate users according to the data they receive?

A simple approach is: 'a user sends an "X" amount of data to an advertiser for a fixed amount "Y" of compensating incentives.' Those compensating incentives can be unique for each advertiser, i.e., Amazon can offer discounts to its online marketplace or provide users with one month of premium shipping. There are a lot of approaches in the fairness model but also, algorithms that can be implemented to ensure that fairness can exist. Further research must be conducted to identify, design and implement a 'fair approach' algorithm.

The need for checking mechanisms to be implemented, to ensure that malicious ads or malware don't make their way to end users. Also, what other mechanisms can be implemented to ensure that any other form of attacks don't occur in such a system? As discussed in section VI, access control and accountability mechanisms need to be implemented in the final solution. Furthermore, research has been conducted towards ensuring security in the Blockchain. Security that it is not compromised by attacks. Such attacks can take many forms with most notable ones being Sybil and Eclipse attacks. These two attack vectors are the ones that need to be explored further as they can make the whole system and its validity of serving effective ads, ineffective. This danger is more prominent with Sybil attacks where in our case, a node in the network can act, as one with many identities, spamming the advertising libraries with repetitive data to 'win' more incentives.

When an advertiser has served a misleading or a 'fake' ad, with the purpose of extracting user sensitive information or misleading the end user, how is that advertiser penalized? Which entity inside the system is responsible for adjusting that penalty and what form of penalty is the most suitable one? Mechanisms need to be implemented to ensure that any type of mishap can be stopped and not occur again. A penalty system needs to be implemented in accordance to advertising policies.

When referring to ad validity, what types of ads can be deemed as misleading or fake? In order to address properly this issue, we need to follow Regulations, Policies and Laws set for Advertisers worldwide. Such examples include:

– The Advertising law from the Federal Trade Commission in the US;
– The Consumer Protection from Unfair Trading Regulations and the Business Protection from Misleading Marketing Regulations in the UK;
– EU's Audiovisual Media Services Directive for the EU.

One of the most notable open issues with such a system approach is the use of smart contracts and their security. How can we ensure security in smart contracts and in their entirety are not susceptible to attacks? When referring to the validity of the transactions in smart contract, it doesn't always mean that the security is not compromised. From further research it has been identified that, smart contracts can include bugs or critical security vulnerabilities, which in turn can make their way inside the Blockchain. The main reason such security vulnerabilities and bugs are present inside the smart contract code, is because of the way a smart contract is programmed. Common problems with smart contracts can be logical errors, the failure to use or implement cryptographic protocols during the binding of the contract, misaligned incentives and the details of the implementation approach of the contracts are error-prone. An attacker can then manipulate those errors inside the smart contract to its advantage if appropriate security mechanisms are not in place.

9   Conclusions

Throughout this research paper, we aim to identify current issues in Mobile and Online advertisement networks. By using Blockchains and smart contracts, we aim to introduce a feasible approach to close the gap between advertising networks and users. Also, the main aspect outlined in this paper is to ensure that Security, Anonymity, Privacy, Transparency and Fairness will be implemented as core characteristics in the proposed system. Making a brief comparison between the problems and the positives of such an approach, "CrowdLED" is being introduced: A system that when deployed to its full extend, will be evaluated to ensure its validity and effectiveness by comparing it against initial objectives and requirements set. A more in-depth paper following the algorithms involved and a thorough system architecture and how the two-contract based approach will work with adequate testing, will be released at a later stage.

Acknowledgments. This work was supported by the European Commission, under the ASTRID and FutureTPM projects; Grant Agreements no. 786922 and 779391, respectively.

Special thanks to Dr. Soteris Demetriou, Assistant Professor at Imperial College London, for his insights in privacy and security for mobile and online advertising, and the valuable feedback at the initial stages of drafting this paper.

References

1. Catalini, C., Gans, J.S.: Some simple economics of the blockchain. National Bureau of Economic Research Inc., NBER Working Papers 22952, December 2016
2. Meng, W., Ding, R., Chung, S.P., Han, S., Lee, W.: The price of free: privacy leakage in personalized mobile in-apps ads. In: NDSS. The Internet Society (2016)
3. Rastogi, V., Shao, R., Chen, Y., Pan, X., Zou, S., Riley, R.: Are these ads safe: detecting hidden attacks through the mobile app-web interfaces. In: 23rd Annual Network and Distributed System Security Symposium, NDSS 2016, San Diego, California, USA, 21–24 February 2016. The Internet Society (2016)
4. Shekhar, S., Dietz, M., Wallach, D.S.: AdSplit: separating smartphone advertising from applications. In: Proceedings of the 21st USENIX Conference on Security Symposium, Security 2012, p. 28 (2012)
5. Gisdakis, S., Lagana, M., Giannetsos, T., Papadimitratos, P.: SEROSA: service oriented security architecture for vehicular communications. In: VNC, pp. 111–118. IEEE (2013)
6. Whitefield, J., Chen, L., Giannetsos, T., Schneider, S., Treharne, H.: Privacy-enhanced capabilities for vanets using direct anonymous attestation. In: 2017 IEEE Vehicular Networking Conference (VNC), pp. 123–130, November 2017
7. Grace, M.C., Zhou, W., Jiang, X., Sadeghi, A.-R.: Unsafe exposure analysis of mobile in-app advertisements. In: 5th ACM Conference on Security and Privacy in Wireless and Mobile Networks, WISEC 2012, pp. 101–112 (2012)
8. Einziger, G., Chiasserini, C., Malandrino, F.: Scheduling advertisement delivery in vehicular networks, CoRR, vol. abs/1804.05183 (2018)
9. Geth: Official Go Implementation of the Ethereum Protocol. https://geth.ethereum.org/
10. Ethereum: A Decentralized Platform that runs Smart Contracts. https://www.ethereum.org/
11. Web3 Labs, Web3j: Where Jave meets the Blockchain. https://web3j.io/

12. Luu, L., Chu, D.-H., Olickel, H., Saxena, P., Hobor, A.: Making smart contracts smarter. In: Proceedings of the 2016 ACM SIGSAC Conference on Computer and Communications Security, CCS 2016, pp. 254–269 (2016)
13. Papadopoulos, P., Kourtellis, N., Rodriguez, P.R., Laoutaris, N.: If you are not paying for it, you are the product: how much do advertisers pay to reach you? In: Proceedings of the 2017 Internet Measurement Conference, IMC 2017, pp. 142–156 (2017)
14. Leontiadis, I., Efstratiou, C., Picone, M., Mascolo, C.: Don't kill my ads!: balancing privacy in an ad-supported mobile application market. In: Proceedings of the Twelfth Workshop on Mobile Computing Systems & Applications, HotMobile 2012, pp. 2:1–2:6 (2012)
15. Gisdakis, S., Giannetsos, T., Papadimitratos, P.: Shield: a data verification framework for participatory sensing systems. In: Proceedings of the 8th ACM Conference on Security and Privacy in Wireless and Mobile Networks, WiSec 2015, pp. 16:1–16:12 (2015)
16. Dimitriou, T., Giannetsos, T., Chen, L.: Rewards: privacy-preserving rewarding and incentive schemes for the smart electricity grid and other loyalty systems. Comput. Commun. **137**, 1–14 (2019)
17. Delmolino, K., Arnett, M., Kosba, A.E., Miller, A., Shi, E.: Step by step towards creating a safe smart contract: lessons and insights from a cryptocurrency lab. IACR Cryptology ePrint Archive, vol. 2015, p. 460 (2015). https://eprint.iacr.org/2015/460
18. Papadopoulos, P., Kourtellis, N., Markatos, E.P.: The cost of digital advertisement: comparing user and advertiser views. In: Proceedings of the 2018 World Wide Web Conference, WWW 2018, pp. 1479–1489 (2018)
19. Haddadi, H., Hui, P., Brown, I.: MobiAd: private and scalable mobile advertising. In: Proceedings of the Fifth ACM International Workshop on Mobility in the Evolving Internet Architecture, MobiArch 2010, pp. 33–38 (2010)
20. Gisdakis, S., Giannetsos, T., Papadimitratos, P.: SPPEAR: security & privacy-preserving architecture for participatory-sensing applications. In: Proceedings of the 2014 ACM Conference on Security and Privacy in Wireless and Mobile Networks, WiSec 2014, pp. 39–50 (2014)
21. Chiasserini, C.F., Malandrino, F., Sereno, M.: Advertisement delivery and display in vehicular networks: using V2V communications for targeted ads. IEEE Veh. Technol. Mag. **12**, 65–72 (2017)
22. Zyskind, G., Nathan, O., Pentland, A.: Enigma: decentralized computation platform with guaranteed privacy. CoRR, vol. abs/1506.03471 (2015)

SDKSE-KGA: A Secure Dynamic Keyword Searchable Encryption Scheme Against Keyword Guessing Attacks

Hongyuan Chen[1], Zhenfu Cao[1,2,3]($\boxtimes$), Xiaolei Dong[1],
and Jiachen Shen[1]($\boxtimes$)

[1] Shanghai Key Laboratory of Trustworthy Computing,
East China Normal University, Shanghai, China
51164500090@stu.ecnu.edu.cn, {zfcao,dongxiaolei,jcshen}@sei.ecnu.edu.cn
[2] Cyberspace Security Research Center, Peng Cheng Laboratory, Shenzhen, China
[3] Shanghai Institute of Intelligent Science and Technology, Tongji University,
Shanghai, China

Abstract. A number of searchable encryption schemes have been widely proposed to solve the search problem in ciphertext domain. However, most existing searchable encryption schemes are vulnerable to keyword guessing attacks. During keyword guessing attacks, with the help of the cloud, an adversary will learn what keyword a given trapdoor is searching for, which leads to the disclosure of users' privacy information. To address this issue, we propose SDKSE-KGA: a secure dynamic keyword searchable encryption scheme which resists keyword guessing attacks. SDKSE-KGA has constant-size indexes and trapdoors and supports functionalities such as dynamic updating of keywords and files. Formal proofs show that it is Trapdoor-IND-CKA and Index-IND-CKA secure in the standard model.

Keywords: Searchable encryption · Dynamic · Keyword guessing attack · Trapdoor-IND-CKA · Index-IND-CKA

1 Introduction

Searchable encryption is an effective way to solve the search problem in ciphertext domain. It not only protects users' privacy but also completes search task. During the process of searchable encryption, users need encrypt data before uploading it. Then, they use trapdoors of keywords to execute search task. So the cloud cannot get exact information about data and keywords.

Song et al. firstly proposed a searchable encryption scheme for mail system in [1]. Then, the concept of searchable encryption (SE) came into people's attention and aroused a series of researches [2–6]. According to the encryption methods, divide SE into searchable encryption scheme (SSE) and public-key encryption

W. Meng et al. (Eds.): IFIPTM 2019, IFIP AICT 563, pp. 162–177, 2019.
https://doi.org/10.1007/978-3-030-33716-2_13

with keyword search (PEKS). SSE has the advantages of high efficiency and practicability. So people tend to research the functionality of SSE. [7,8] realized the function of multi-keyword search. [9,10] realized the function of fuzzy search. [11] realized the ranking function of search results. PEKS has the advantage of strong security. So people tend to improve search expressions and security. [12,13] implement access control for users search privileges. [14] has the traceability for malicious users. [15] implements the revocation of malicious users privileges. [16] implements the verification of search results.

Consider one dynamic mail system: For user Alice, she has many friends and business partners in real life. So her inbox may received all kinds of mails everyday. The inbox will store these mails into cloud servers. Considering the cloud is not fully trusted, all information should be encrypted. When Alice checks mails, she will filter mails generally and search for parts of them. The search keywords are determined by Alice herself, and she is likely to change keywords according to the actual life. This application scenario requires our searchable encryption scheme to support dynamic keywords.

Kamara et al. firstly proposed a dynamic searchable symmetric encryption scheme in [17]. They gave the definition of dynamic CKA2 security and constructed algorithm by reverse indexes. But this scheme has the disadvantage of information leakage. They offered an improved scheme in [18]. It uses red black tree as index tree to protect information. But this advantage is at the cost of reducing search efficiency. Hahn et al. presented a new scheme in [19]. It leaks nothing except the access pattern and requires the scenario to have huge data and a few keywords. Xia et al proposed a multi-keyword ranked search scheme in [20], which supports dynamic environment, too. It uses balanced binary tree as index tree and sorts search results for users. But it lacks trapdoor indistinguishable security. Later, they presented a new scheme in [21]. For mail systems, it has significant reduction in IO cost. But the size of index is large. It will make pressure on communication overhead.

Meanwhile, Byun et al. first introduced the concept of keyword guessing attack in [25]. In keyword guessing attacks, adverseries take advantage of the fact that the keywords that one user are likely to use commonly are very limited. So they make guesses of the keyword corresponding to a trapdoor. With the help of the cloud, they are able to verify whether the guess is correct and shortly they will know which keyword this trapdoor is searching for. It is a crucial attack and violates the goal of searchable encryption.

The concept of offline keyword guessing attacks was proposed in [25]. Then Yau et al. presented the concept of online keyword guessing attacks in [26]. Tang et al. proposed a public-key encryption supporting registered keyword search in [27]. But it requires the sender and the receiver to negotiate registered keywords before the system was established. Compare with it, our scheme relaxes the restrictions on communication between senders and receivers. Chen et al. proposed a searchable encryption under dual systems in [28]. There are multiple interactions between front server and back server. It prevents independent servers from getting complete information to withstand attacks. Compare with it, the cloud server in our scheme has less computational and communication pressure.

For the above mail system, we construct a dynamic searchable encryption scheme which resists keyword guessing attacks. Our contribution is summarized as follows:

1. Our $SDKSE - KGA$ supports dynamic management of both keywords and files. In the mail system, senders may send messages anytime and receivers may delete messages too. The receiver may add or delete keywords by the binary tree. Compared with other papers, the cost of updating keywords and files is negligible. In addition, the update operation is completely executed by the receiver, so there is no risk of leaking private data.
2. Our $SDKSE - KGA$ has Index-IND-CKA(Index Indistinguishable against Chosen Keyword Attack) security and Trapdoor-IND-CKA(Trapdoor Indistinguishable against Chosen Keyword Attack) security. We will demonstrate security under the standard model. Moreover, the indexes and trapdoors are of constant size which helps to reduce transmission overhead significantly.
3. Our $SDKSE - KGA$ resists keyword guessing attacks. Therefore, our scheme has higher security level compared with other searchable encryption scenarios. In this scheme, the search task is assigned to the cloud server and the receiver, The cloud server performs fuzzy search while the receiver accurate search, The cloud server is not able to obtain specific information of keywords, so it cannot launch the keyword guessing attacks.

The rest of our paper is organized as follows. In Sect. 2, we will introduce the system model and security model, and describe some symbols used in our construction. In Sect. 3, we will introduce the keyword tree and fuzzy mapping function in detail. Section 4 depicts $SDKSE - KGA$ scheme in detail. Sections 5 and 6 will show security analysis and performance analysis of $SDKSE - KGA$. In the last section we will summarize this paper.

2   Definitions

2.1   System Model

There are three roles in our application scenario: mail senders, mail receivers and the cloud server. The sender is responsible for adding keywords to these files, encrypting files and generating exact indexes and fuzzy indexes for keywords, and uploading them to the cloud server. The receiver is responsible for managing all the keywords by constructing a binary tree, and generating fuzzy and exact trapdoors. After receiving a fuzzy trapdoor, the cloud server conducts fuzzy search upon fuzzy indexes and sends fuzzy results to the receiver. Then the receiver performs exact search on the fuzzy results based on the exact trapdoors to obtain final results. Figure 1 shows the system model.

Considering third-party cloud servers cannot be fully trusted, we hope the cloud server get as little information as possible. Moreover, with the help of the cloud, KGA will learn what keyword a given trapdoor is searching for, which leads to the disclosure of users privacy information. In our model, the cloud server is only allowed to perform fuzzy search. Even if it has access to all the fuzzy indexes of keywords and some of legal fuzzy trapdoors, it is still unable to get the exact information of the search. Moreover, this model not only protects the security of keywords, but also resists keyword guessing attacks.

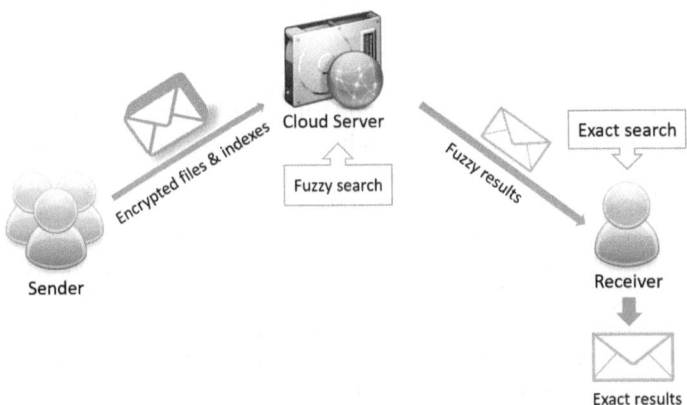

Fig. 1. System model

2.2   Security Model

In this part, we define $Index - IND - CKA$ security, $Trapdoor - IND - CKA$ security and adaptive KGA security. $Index-IND-CKA$ security means outside attackers cannot determine exact index $ExactIndex$ was generated by which keyword in case of they know nothing about the exact trapdoor of the given keywords. $Trapdoor - IND - CKA$ security means outside attackers cannot distinguish between the exact trapdoors of two challenge keywords [23]. The definitions of $Index - IND - CKA$ and $Trapdoor - IND - CKA$ are similar to these in [30]. We define the following security games to illustrate three kinds of security.

Game 1 : ($Index - IND - CKA$ security)
Setup. The challenger runs $Setup$ algorithm to obtain the public parameters and the master secret key. He retains the master secret key and gives the public parameters to the adversary $\mathcal{A}$.
Query phase 1. The adversary $\mathcal{A}$ adaptively selects keyword w to issue. The challenger generates ETd for w and sends it to $\mathcal{A}$.
Challenge. The adversary $\mathcal{A}$ selects target keywords w_0^* and w_1^*. Both of two target keywords has not queried before. Then, the challenger generates the exact index $ExactIndex$ for w_β^* and sends it to $\mathcal{A}$ where $\beta \in \{0,1\}$.
Query Phase 2. Repeat Query Phase 1. The adversary $\mathcal{A}$ continue to issue keywords except the target keywords w_0^* and w_1^*.

Guess. The adversary gives β' as the guess of β, if $\beta' = \beta$, then the adversary wins.

The advantage of $\mathcal{A}$ in this game is defined as follows:

$$Adv_{\mathcal{A}} = |Pr[\beta = \beta'] - \frac{1}{2}|$$

Definition 1. We say that SDKSE-KGA is Index-Indistinguishable security if $Adv_{\mathcal{A}}$ is negligible for any polynomial time attacker $\mathcal{A}$.

Game 2 : $(Trapdoor - IND - CKA$ security$)$
Setup. The challenger runs $Setup$ algorithm to obtain the public parameters and the master secret key. He retains the master secret key and gives the public parameters to the adversary $\mathcal{B}$.
Query phase 1. The adversary $\mathcal{B}$ adaptively selects keyword w to issue. The challenger generates ETd for w and sends it to $\mathcal{B}$.
Challenge. The adversary $\mathcal{B}$ selects target keywords w_0^* and w_1^*. Both of two target keywords has not queried before. Then, the challenger flips a coin $\beta \in \{0, 1\}$, generates the ETd for w_β^* and sends it to $\mathcal{B}$.
Query Phase 2. Repeat Query Phase 1. The adversary continue to issue keywords except the target keywords w_0^* and w_1^*.
Guess. The adversary gives β' as the guess of β, if $\beta' = \beta$, then the adversary wins.

The advantage of $\mathcal{B}$ in this game is defined as follows:

$$Adv_{\mathcal{B}} = |Pr[\beta = \beta'] - \frac{1}{2}|$$

Definition 2. We say that SDKSE-KGA is Trapdoor-Indistinguishable security if $Adv_{\mathcal{B}}$ is negligible for any polynomial time attacker $\mathcal{B}$.

Game 3 : $(Adaptive\ KGA$ security$)$
Setup. The challenger runs this algorithm to obtain the public parameters and the master secret key. Then he retains the master secret key and gives the public parameters to the adversary $\mathcal{C}$.
Query phase 1. The adversary $\mathcal{C}$ queries the fuzzy trapdoor and fuzzy index of any keyword.
Challenge. The adversary selects the keyword w_0^* and w_1^* as challenge keywords, and neither keyword has been quried before. Then the challenger randomly selects the keyword $w_\beta^*(\beta \in \{0, 1\})$, generates ciphertext $FTd_{w_\beta^*}$ for it, and sends the trapdoor to $\mathcal{C}$.
Query Phase 2. Repeat Query Phase 1. The adversary $\mathcal{C}$ continue to query the fuzzy trapdoor and fuzzy index of keywords except the target keywords w_0^* and w_1^*.
Guess. The adversary gives β' as the guess of β, if $\beta' = \beta$, then the adversary wins.

The advantage of $\mathcal{C}$ in this game is defined as follows:

$$Adv_{\mathcal{C}} = |Pr[\beta = \beta'] - \frac{1}{2}|$$

Definition 3. We say that SDKSE-KGA is Adaptive KGA security if $Adv_{\mathcal{C}}$ is negligible for any polynomial time attacker $\mathcal{C}$.

2.3   Notations

This part we will illustrate some symbols used in this scheme. To manage all the keywords, we build a binary tree denoted by $\mathcal{T}$, use L to indicate the height of $\mathcal{T}$. And the height L is related to N which means the number of keywords. The fuzzy keyword mapped by the keyword w is expressed as w_f. $[I_1, ..., I_h]$ represents the location of keyword in the tree. The exact index and fuzzy index of keywords are respectively represented by $ExactIndex$ and $FuzzyIndex$. The exact trapdoor and fuzzy trapdoor of keywords are respectively represented by ETd and FTd.

Definition 3 ($SDKSE - KGA$). A securely dynamic keyword searchable encryption scheme which resists keyword guessing attacks is a tuple of nine polynomial-time algorithms

$$SDKSE = (Setup, Encrypt, TDGen, FuzzySearch, ExactSearch, KWInsert,$$
$$IndexInsert, KWDelete, IndexDelete)$$

such that

- $Setup(\lambda, N) \rightarrow (params, MSK)$: In this algorithm, input the security parameter λ and the number of keywords N, generate keyword tree $\mathcal{T}$, output public parameters of the scheme $params$ and master secret key MSK.
- $Encrypt(params, w) \rightarrow (FuzzyIndex, ExactIndex)$: In this algorithm, input $params$ and keyword w. Generate fuzzy index $FuzzyIndex$ and exact index $ExactIndex$ for w.
- $TDGen(MSK, w) \rightarrow (FTd, ETd)$: In this algorithm, generate fuzzy trapdoor FTd and exact trapdoor ETd for keyword w by MSK.
- $FuzzySearch(FuzzyIndex, FTd) \rightarrow (FuzzyCipher \; or \; \perp)$: In this algorithm, input fuzzy index $FuzzyIndex$ and fuzzy trapdoor FTd to match. If the match operation is successful, add these files associated with $FuzzyIndex$ to the fuzzy ciphertext set $FuzzyCipher$. If the operation is failed, output $\perp$.
- $ExactSearch(ExactIndex, ETd) \rightarrow (C \; or \; \perp)$: In this algorithm, input exact index $ExactIndex$ and exact trapdoor ETd for operation. If the operation is successful, output file set which contain keyword w. If the operation is failed, output $\perp$.
- $KWInsert(w)$: Insert new keyword w to the tree $\mathcal{T}$.
- $IndexInsert(w)$: Notify related files to update keyword list and generate encrypted keyword C for new keyword w.
- $KWDelete(w)$: Disable node bound to keyword w from tree $\mathcal{T}$.
- $IndexDelete(w)$: Notify related files to update keyword list and delete existing index of w.

3   Preliminaries

3.1   Keyword Tree

The receiver is responsible for constructing the binary tree $\mathcal{T}$. The tree $\mathcal{T}$ has two tasks: managing keywords dynamically and running fuzzy mapping function.

Construct tree $\mathcal{T}$ based on the number of keywords N, height $L = \lceil log_2 N \rceil + 2$. Each leaf node may bind to one keyword. We call one leaf node that have not yet bound keyword as available node. The number of available nodes is denoted by $avlS$. In order to ensure the growth of the tree, we require $avlS \geq minS$, where $minS = 2^{L-2}$. Each leaf node has three states: disable, occupied, available. They are represented by $[0, 1, 2]$ respectively. Disable state means this leaf node is bound to one disable keyword. Occupied state means this leaf node is bound to one keyword. Available state means this leaf node has not been bound.

It is very easy to delete one keyword. We just need to set the state of the leaf node bound to this keyword to 0, and if this key is used again later, just change the state of the leaf node to 1. Adding keyword can be divided in two situations: If $avlS > minS$, select an appropriate available leaf node and bind it to the keyword. Then set its state value to 2. If $avlS = minS$, then generate child nodes of all available leaf nodes to double the number of available leaf nodes. The growth process is shown in Fig. 2. Now $avlS > minS$, so we continue to add keywords.

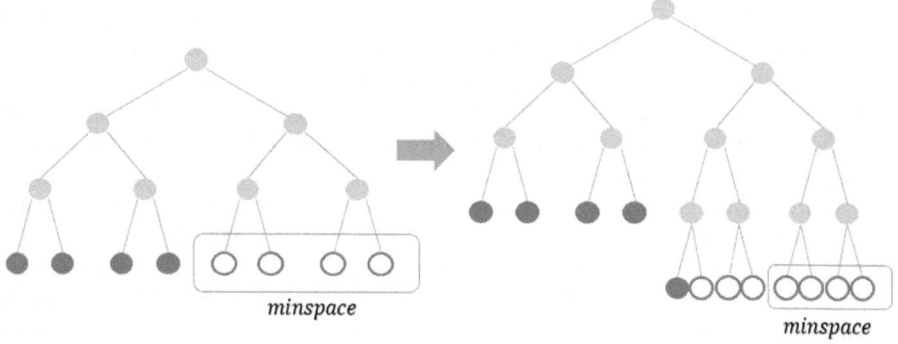

Fig. 2. Grow tree

Now we design fuzzy mapping function to map each keyword to a fuzzy keyword. The position of the fuzzy keyword in the tree will be used to generate the pair of fuzzy index and fuzzy trapdoor. The cloud server searches upon the fuzzy index-trapdoor pair while the receiver searches upon the exact index-trapdoor pair. Now we introduce the fuzzy mapping function. For one leaf node in the binary tree, trace it up to n levels where n is a parameter defined by users, the obtained node is the corresponding fuzzy node of it. If two leaf nodes have the same ancestor node after tracing the same layers, then these nodes share a fuzzy node.

3.2 Bilinear Map

In our scheme, we apply bilinear map to *FuzzySearch* and *ExactSearch* algorithm. The specific principle is as follows:

There is a composite group $\mathbb{G}$ with order $n = p_1p_2p_3p_4$ where p_1, p_2, p_3 and p_4 are distinct primes. Assume one of the generators of $\mathbb{G}$ is G, then the generators of $\mathbb{G}_{p_1}$, $\mathbb{G}_{p_2}$, $\mathbb{G}_{p_3}$ and $\mathbb{G}_{p_4}$ are G_1, G_2, G_3 and G_4 respectively. And $G_1 = G^{p_2p_3p_4}$, $G_2 = G^{p_1p_3p_4}$, $G_3 = G^{p_1p_2p_4}$, $G_4 = G^{p_1p_2p_3}$. We infer that for distinct i and j, $\forall R_i \in \mathbb{G}_{p_i}$, $R_j \in \mathbb{G}_{p_j}$, $e(R_i, R_j) = 1$ holds.

3.3   Complexity Assumptions

The security of our scheme is based on six complexity assumptions [22]. The hardness of these assumptions relies on the theorems proposed by [24].

In *Assumption* 1, given a group generator $\mathcal{G}$, input security parameter λ, then generate primes p_1, p_2, p_3, p_4, two groups $\mathbb{G}$, $\mathbb{G}_T$, and the bilinear map e. Set the integer $n = p_1p_2p_3p_4$. Select random element x from $\mathbb{G}_{p_1}$, similarly select G_3 from $\mathbb{G}_{p_3}$ and G_4 from $\mathbb{G}_{p_4}$. Set $D = \{\mathbb{G}, n, x, G_3, G_4\}$. $T_0 \in \mathbb{G}_{p_1p_2p_4}$, $T_1 \in \mathbb{G}_{p_1p_4}$ and $\beta \in \{0, 1\}$. Give (D, T_β) to the adversary $\mathcal{B}$, the adversary $\mathcal{B}$ outputs a guess β', if $\beta' = \beta$, then he succeeds. Define $Adv1_{\mathcal{G},\mathcal{B}}(\lambda)$ to denote the advantage of $\mathcal{B}$, $Adv1_{\mathcal{G},\mathcal{B}}(\lambda) = |Pr[\beta' = \beta] - \frac{1}{2}|$.

The following assumptions are very similar to *Assumption*1, so we only introduce their differences.

In *Assumption* 2,

$$D = \{\mathbb{G}, n, x, G_1G_2, G_3, H_2H_3, G_4\},$$
$$T_0 \in \mathbb{G}_{p_1p_2p_3}, T_1 \in \mathbb{G}_{p_1p_3}.$$

And $G_1 \xleftarrow{R} \mathbb{G}_{p_1}$, $G_2, H_2 \xleftarrow{R} \mathbb{G}_{p_2}$, $G_3, H_3 \xleftarrow{R} \mathbb{G}_{p_3}$, $G_4 \xleftarrow{R} \mathbb{G}_{p_4}$.

In *Assumption* 3,

$$D = \{\mathbb{G}, n, G_1, H_2H_3, G_3, G_4\},$$
$$T_0 = H_2H_3', T_1 \in \mathbb{G}_{p_1p_3}.$$

And $G_1 \xleftarrow{R} \mathbb{G}_{p_1}$, $H_2 \xleftarrow{R} \mathbb{G}_{p_2}$, $G_3, H_3, H_3' \xleftarrow{R} \mathbb{G}_{p_3}$, $G_4 \xleftarrow{R} \mathbb{G}_{p_4}$.

In *Assumption* 4,

$$D = \{\mathbb{G}, n, G_1, H_2H_4, G_3, G_4\},$$
$$T_0 \in \mathbb{G}_{p_2p_4}, T_1 \in \mathbb{G}_{p_4}.$$

And $G_1 \xleftarrow{R} \mathbb{G}_{p_1}$, $H_2 \xleftarrow{R} \mathbb{G}_{p_2}$, $G_3 \xleftarrow{R} \mathbb{G}_{p_3}$, $G_4, H_4 \xleftarrow{R} \mathbb{G}_{p_4}$.

In *Assumption* 5,

$$D = \{\mathbb{G}, n, x, G_1G_2, G_3, H_1H_2, I_2I_3, G_4\},$$
$$T_0 = e(G_1, H_1), T_1 \in \mathbb{G}_T.$$

And $x, G_1, H_1 \xleftarrow{R} \mathbb{G}_{p_1}$, $G_2, H_2, I_2 \xleftarrow{R} \mathbb{G}_{p_2}$, $G_3, I_3 \xleftarrow{R} \mathbb{G}_{p_3}$, $G_4 \xleftarrow{R} \mathbb{G}_{p_4}$.

In *Assumption* 6,

$$D = \{\mathbb{G}, n, G_1G_4, H_1H_2, I_2, I_3, I_4, J_1J_2J_4\},$$
$$T_0 \in J_1J_2'J_4', T_1 \in \mathbb{G}_{p_1p_2p_4}.$$

And $G_1, H_1, J_1 \xleftarrow{R} \mathbb{G}_{p_1}$, $H_2, I_2, J_2, J_2' \xleftarrow{R} \mathbb{G}_{p_2}$, $I_3 \xleftarrow{R} \mathbb{G}_{p_3}$, $G_4, I_4, J_4, J_4' \xleftarrow{R} \mathbb{G}_{p_4}$.

For *Assumption* 1–6, we have the following definition:

Definition 4: For any polynomial time, if $Adv - N_{\mathcal{G},\mathcal{B}}(\lambda)$ is a negligible function of λ, then we think the group generator $\mathcal{G}$ satisfies *Assumption N*, $N \in \{1, 2, 3, 4, 5, 6\}$.

4   Construction

In this section we will introduce *SDKSE-KGA* in detail.

Setup(λ, N) : First, the receiver builds the keyword tree $\mathcal{T}$ to manage initial keywords. For keyword w, encode it as $[I_1, \ldots, I_h]$ according to its position in the binary tree. Note $h = L - 1$. Next, runs group generator $\mathcal{G}$ and obtains $(p_1, p_2, p_3, p_4, \mathbb{G}, \mathbb{G}_T, e)$. Then, selects random elements $x, y, u_1, \ldots, u_h, \omega \leftarrow \mathbb{G}_{p_1}, G_3 \leftarrow \mathbb{G}_{p_3}, G_4 \leftarrow \mathbb{G}_{p_4}, R_4, R_{4,g}, R_{4,h}, R_{4,u_1}, \ldots, R_{4,u_h} \leftarrow \mathbb{G}_{p_4}$. G_3 is the generator of $\mathbb{G}_{p_3}$ and G_4 is the generator of $\mathbb{G}_{p_4}$ respectively. So a random element of $\mathbb{G}_{p_4}$ can be chosen by raising G_4 to random exponents from $\mathbb{Z}_n$. At last, set $n = p_1 p_2 p_3 p_4$, $X = x R_{4,g}$, $Y = y R_{4,h}$, $U_1 = u_1 R_{4,u_1}$, ..., $U_h = u_h R_{4,u_h}$, $E = e(g, \omega)$. The public parameters $params = [\mathbb{G}, n, X, Y, U_1, \ldots, U_h, R_3, R_4, E]$. The master private key $MSK = [x, y, u_1, \ldots, u_h, \omega]$. The receiver publishes the *params* and retains the MSK for generate trapdoors later.

Encrypt$(params, w)$: w represents the keyword to be encrypted, parse it to $[I_1, \ldots, I_h]$. The sender selects random integer $s \leftarrow \mathbb{Z}_n$ and random elements $\overline{R}_4, \overline{R}_4' \leftarrow \mathbb{G}_{p_4}$. Picks random message M. Next, set

$$CT_0 = ME^s,$$
$$CT_1 = (H\textstyle\prod_{i=1}^{h} U_i^{I_i})^s \overline{R}_4,$$
$$CT_2 = G^s \overline{R}_4'.$$

Set $CT \leftarrow [CT_0, CT_1, CT_2] \in \mathbb{G}_T \times \mathbb{G}^3$. Define $ExactIndex = [M, CT]$.

Then, according to the fuzzy mapping function, the keyword w is mapped to w_f, parse it to $[I_1, \ldots, I_{h_f}]$. The sender selects random integer $s_f \leftarrow \mathbb{Z}_n$ and random elements $\overline{R}_{f,4}, \overline{R}_{f,4}' \leftarrow \mathbb{G}_{p_4}$. Picks random message M_f. Next, set

$$CT_{f,0} = M_f E^{s_f},$$
$$CT_{f,1} = (H\textstyle\prod_{i=1}^{h_f} U_i^{I_i})^{s_f} \overline{R}_{f,4},$$
$$CT_{f,2} = G^{s_f} \overline{R}_{f,4}'.$$

Set $CT_f \leftarrow [CT_{f,0}, CT_{f,1}, CT_{f,2}] \in \mathbb{G}_T \times \mathbb{G}^3$. Define $FuzzyIndex = [M_f, CT_f]$.

TDGen(MSK, w) : w is the keyword to be retrieved. Parse w to $[I_1, \ldots, I_h]$. The receiver selects random integers $r_1, r_2 \leftarrow \mathbb{Z}_n$ and random elements

$$R_3^1, R_3^{2}, R_3^3, R_3^4, R_3^{5}, R_3^6 \leftarrow \mathbb{G}_{p_3}^4.$$

To obtain the exact trapdoor ETd of the keyword w. Set $Td_1 = x^{r_1} R_3^1$, $Td_2 = \omega(y\prod_{i=1}^h u_i^{I_i})^{r_1} R_3^2$, $Td_3 = u_h^{r_1} R_3^3$, $Td_4 = x^{r_2} R_3^4$, $Td_5 = \omega(y\prod_{i=1}^h u_i^{I_i})^{r_2} R_3^5$, $Td_6 = u_h^{r_2} R_3^6$. Set

$$ETd = [Td_1, Td_2, Td_3, Td_4, Td_5, Td_6].$$

Map the keyword w to w_f, parse it to $[I_1, ..., I_{h_f}]$. The receiver selects random integers $r_{f,1}, r_{f,2} \leftarrow \mathbb{Z}_n$ and random elements

$$R_{f,3}^1, R_{f,3}^2, R_{f,3}^3, R_{f,3}^4, R_{f,3}^5, R_{f,3}^6 \leftarrow \mathbb{G}_{p_3}^4.$$

To obtain the fuzzy trapdoor FTd of the keyword w. Set $Td_{f,1} = x^{r_{f,1}} R_{f,3}^1$, $Td_{f,2} = \omega(y\prod_{i=1}^{h_f} u_i^{I_i})^{r_{f,1}} R_{f,3}^2$, $Td_{f,3} = u_{h_f}^{r_{f,1}} R_{f,3}^3$, $Td_{f,4} = x^{r_{f,2}} R_{f,3}^4$, $Td_{f,5} = \omega(y\prod_{i=1}^{h_f} u_i^{I_i})^{r_{f,2}} R_{f,3}^5$, $Td_{f,6} = u_{h_f}^{r_{f,2}} R_{f,3}^6$. Set

$$FTd = [Td_{f,1}, Td_{f,2}, Td_{f,3}, Td_{f,4}, Td_{f,5}, Td_{f,6}].$$

FuzzySearch$(FuzzyIndex, FTd)$: Parse FTd to $[Td_{f,1}, Td_{f,2}, Td_{f,3}, Td_{f,4}, Td_{f,5}, Td_{f,6}]$. $FuzzyIndex = [M_f, CT_f]$, parse CT_f to $[CT_{f,0}, CT_{f,1}, CT_{f,2}]$. Compute

$$M_f' = CT_{f,0} \cdot \frac{e(Td_{f,1}, CT_{f,1})}{e(Td_{f,2}, CT_{f,2})}.$$

If $M_f = M_f'$, add all files containing exact keywords which mapping to w_f into the fuzzy result $FuzzyCipher$. Then $FuzzyCipher$ will be sent to the receiver.

ExactSearch$(ExactIndex, ETd)$: Parse ETd to $[Td_1, Td_2, Td_3, Td_4, Td_5, Td_6]$. $ExactIndex = [M, CT]$, parse CT to $[CT_0, CT_1, CT_2]$. Compute

$$M' = CT_0 \cdot \frac{e(Td_1, CT_1)}{e(Td_2, CT_2)}.$$

If $M = M'$, then output the file set C which contains the keyword w.

KWInsert(w) : Select an appropriate leaf node to bind the new keyword w in the binary tree.
IndexInsert(w) : Generate the index based on the location in the tree and add it into index list.
KWDelete(w) : Disable the keyword w in the binary tree.
IndexDelete(w) : Delete the index of w from the index list.

5   Security Proof

In this section, we will prove the security of $SDKSE-KGA$. Each keyword owns an exact trapdoor-index pair and a fuzzy trapdoor-index pair. The sender generates fuzzy indexes and exact indexes and sends them to the cloud. The receiver generates fuzzy trapdoors and exact trapdoors and sends fuzzy trapdoors to the cloud. Notice that in both *FuzzySearch* and *ExactSearch* algorithms, only if the location strings corresponding to the trapdoor and the index are identical, the match operation will succeed. Since the fuzzy trapdoors and fuzzy indexes are generated upon the position, which one-to-one mapped into the location string of the fuzzy node, the match operation will only succeed when the fuzzy trapdoor and fuzzy index are generated upon the same fuzzy node. On the other hand, fuzzy nodes and exact nodes are different from each other, so the match operation upon a fuzzy trapdoor and an exact index will always generates $\perp$. Therefore, even the cloud gets exact indexes, the privacy of users will not be destroyed.

Now we will prove our $SDKSE - KGA$ is $Index - IND - CKA$ and $Trapdoor - IND - CKA$ secure.

Theorem 1. *Our $SDKSE - KGA$ scheme is $Index - IND - CKA$ secure if a group generator $\mathcal{G}$ holds assumptions in [22].*

Proof. We will give the definitions of semi-functional indexes and semi-functional trapdoors for $ExactIndex$ and ETd , and show a series of games. Semi-functional indexes are composed by CT_0, CT_1, CT_2.

$$CT_0 = CT_0', CT_1 = CT_1' x_2^{rz_c}, CT_2 = CT_2' x_2^r.$$

where CT_0', CT_1' and CT_2' are components of CT generated in $Encrypt$ algorithm. And $x_2 \in \mathbb{G}_{p_2}$, $r, z_c \xleftarrow{R} \mathbb{Z}_N$. Semi-functional trapdoors are as follows:

$$Td_1 = Td'_1 x_2^{\gamma}, Td_2 = Td'_2 x_2^{\gamma z_1}, Td_3 = Td'_3 x_2^{\gamma z_2},$$
$$Td_4 = Td'_4 x_2^{\gamma'}, Td_5 = Td'_5 x_2^{\gamma' z_1'}, Td_6 = Td'_6 x_2^{\gamma' z_2'},$$

where Td'_1, Td'_2, Td'_3, Td'_4, Td'_5, Td'_6 are components of ETd generated in $TDGen$ algorithm, $x_2 \in \mathbb{G}_{p_2}$, and $\gamma, \gamma', z_1, z_1', z_2, z_2' \xleftarrow{R} \mathbb{Z}_N$.

In addition, we need to construct a series of games.

Game_Real: Game 1.
Game_Restricted: It is similar to **Game_Real** except that the adversary cannot query keywords which are prefixes of the challenge keyword modulus p_2.
Game_k: $0 \leq k \leq q$, and q is the number of queries made by the adversary. The difference between **Game_k** and **Game_Restricted** are query results. The challenge index is semi-functional index in two games and the first k results of trapdoor are semi-functional trapdoors in **Game_k**.
Game_Mhiding: It selects random elements from $\mathcal{G}$ and constructs CT_0 of the challenge index.
Game_Random: The second component and the third component of challenge indexes are independent random elements in $\mathbb{G}_{p_1 p_2 p_4}$ in this game.

In $Game_{Random}$, the adversary knows nothing about keyword from the challenge index. So we need prove $Game_{Real}$ and $Game_{Random}$ are distinguishable. First step, the adversary selects keywords w_0 and w_1, $w_0 \neq w_1 \ mod \ n$ and

$w_0 \equiv w_1 \bmod p_2$. The simulator $\int$ factor n by computing $gcd(w_0 - w_1, N)$. But the assumption 1,2,3 will prove that n cannot be decomposed. As a result, $Game_{Real}$ and $Game_{Restricted}$ are distinguishable. Second step, we will prove $Game_{Restricted}$ and $Game_k$ are distinguishable. According to assumption 1, construct a new game. In this game, if $T = T_0$, the index generated by challenger is semi-functional index. In this case, the game is equal to $Game_0$ eventually. If $T = T_1$, the index generated by challenger is normal index and the game is equal to $Game_{Restricted}$. T_0 and T_1 have the same distribution in statics, so $Game_{Restricted}$ and $Game_k$ are distinguishable. Third step, we will prove the series games $Game_k (0 \le k \le q)$ are distinguishable. Use the same way to construct a new game according to assumption 5. The trapdoors sent by challenger are semi-functional trapdoors. If $T = T_0$, the game is equal to $Game_q$. If $T = T_1$, the game is equal to $Game_{Mhiding}$. So $Game_q$ and $Game_{Mhiding}$ are indistinguishable. Continue to deduce, we will get the conclusion that $Game_{Mhiding}$ and $Game_{Random}$ are indistinguishable by constructing the new game according to assumption 6. Finally, $Game_{Real}$ and $Game_{Random}$ are distinguishable. The proof is completed.

Theorem 2. *Our $SDKSE-KGA$ scheme is $Trapdoor-IND-CKA$ secure.*

Proof. In $Game$ 2, the adversary selects target keywords w_0 and w_1, then receives $ETd_{w^*_\beta}$ from the challenger. As we all known, $ETd_w = [Td_1, Td_2, Td_3, Td_4, Td_5, Td_6]$ where $Td_1 = x^{r_1} R_3^1$, $Td_2 = \omega(y\prod_{i=1}^{h} u_i^{I_i})^{r_1} R_3^2$, $Td_3 = u_h^{r_1} R_3^3$, $Td_4 = x^{r_2} R_3^4$, $Td_5 = \omega(y\prod_{i=1}^{h} u_i^{I_i})^{r_2} R_3^5$, $Td_6 = u_h^{r_2} R_3^6$. $x, y, w, u_1, \ldots, u_h$ belong to public parameters, $R_3^1 \sim R_3^6$ are random elements selected from $\mathbb{G}_{p_3}^4$. So the adversary only infer the value of β from Td_2 or Td_5. According to the property of bilinear pairing, R_3^2 in Td_2 can be removed by elements of $\mathbb{G}_{p_i}$, $i \in [1, 2, 4]$. The location strings $[I_1, \ldots, I_h]$ of w_0 and w_1 are known to the adversary, he is able to compute $m_0 = y\prod_{i=1}^{h} u_i^{I_{i,0}}$ and $m_1 = y\prod_{i=1}^{h} u_i^{I_{i,1}}$. m_0 and m_1 are the elements in $\mathbb{G}_{p_1}$. In statistics, the distributions of m_0^r and m_1^r are exactly the same where r is a random element in $\mathbb{Z}_n$. So the adversary is not able to guess the value of β by m_0, m_1. In other words, the adversary should not be able to distinguish the trapdoors of w_0^* and w_1^*. The proof is completed.

Theorem 3. *Our $SDKSE-KGA$ scheme is Adaptive KGA secure.*

Proof. Case 1: If two challenge keywords will map to different fuzzy keywords, they will generate different fuzzy trapdoors. So the KGA security game is exactly the same as Trapdoor-IND security game. In this case, the advantage of adversary winning the game is negligible.

Case 2: If two challenge keywords will map to the same fuzzy keywords, they will generate the same fuzzy trapdoors. The challenge keywords w_0^* and w_1^* have the same distribution in statistics. The adversary cannot determine β based on the fuzzy trapdoor. In other words, he cannot distinguish between w_0^* and w_1^*.

In both cases, the advantage of the adversary winning the game is negligible.

6   Performance

This section mainly gives the performance analysis of SDKSE-KGA. The *Setup* algorithm requires $h + 2$ multiplications and one pairing, it takes $2(h + 3)$ multiplications and 6 modular exponentiations to generate one exact trapdoor where h denotes the height of keyword tree in the scheme. It takes $h + 2$ multiplications and 3 modular exponentiations to generate one index. For *Search* algorithm, it requires 2 pairings and 2 multiplications. The computational overhead of *KWInsert* and *KWDelete* are negligible.

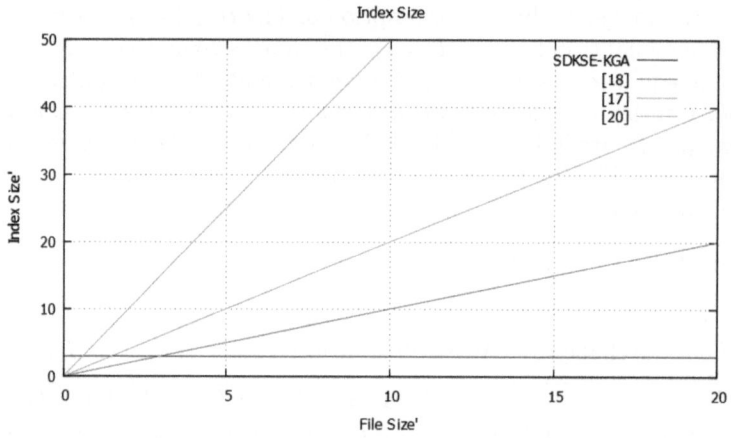

Fig. 3. Index size

Our $SDKSE - KGA$ scheme supports keyword and file updating at the same time. To add a document, [20] and [17] need to iterate through keyword arrays and [18] needs to traverse a KRB tree. So the updating cost is very high. In addition, the index and trapdoors of our scheme are of constant size which reduces transmission overhead significantly. Table 1 shows the efficiency comparison between [17, 18, 20] and SDKSE-KGA and Fig. 3 shows the comparison of the index sizes of different schemes.

Compared with other searchable encryption schemes which resist keyword guessing attacks, In terms of communication overhead, the size of index and trapdoor in SDKSE-KGA scheme is not affected by the number of files. Table 2 shows our advantages between this scheme and others. In this table, $\mathbb{G}$ represents a member of the group, *Pairing* means a bilinear pair operation, *Exp* means power operation while *Mul* means multiplication operation. n is the number of all files.

7   Conclusion

In this paper, we proposed a secure dynamic searchable encryption scheme $SDKSE - KGA$ which resists keyword guessing attacks for mail systems. The

Table 1. Comparisons with dynamic searchable schemes

Compare items	[20]	[17]	[18]	$SDKSE-KGA$
Dynamic file	✓	✓	✓	✓
Dynamic keyword	×	×	×	✓
Trapdoor-IND	✓	×	×	✓
Index size	$O(n^2)$	$O(n)$	$O(n)$	$O(1)$
Trapdoor size	$O(n^2)$	$O(1)$	$O(1)$	$O(1)$
Insert file	$O(n)$	$O(n)$	$O(n)$	$O(1)$
Insert keyword	N/A	N/A	N/A	$O(n)$

Table 2. Comparisons with schemes resisting KGA

Schemes	Index Size	Search Overhead	KGA	Dynamic
[27]	$2\,|\mathbb{G}|$	$Pairing$	✓	×
[28]	$3\,|\mathbb{G}|$	$(7Exp+3Mul)\,n$	✓	×
[29]	$2\,|\mathbb{G}|$	$Pairing$	✓	×
SDKSE-KGA	$3\,|\mathbb{G}|$	$2Pairing$	✓	✓

complexity of the index and the trapdoor of $SDKSE-KGA$ are both constant size. Therefore, $SDKSE-KGA$ is capable of supporting dynamic management of mails and keywords and resisting keyword guessing attacks. In addition, it is both $Index-IND-CKA$ and $Trapdoor-IND-CKA$ secure.

Acknowledgement. This work was supported in part by the National Natural Science Foundation of China (Grant No.61632012, 61672239, 61602180 and U1509219), in part by Natural Science Foundation of Shanghai (Grant No. 16ZR1409200), and in part by "the Fundamental Research Funds for the Central Universities".

References

1. Song, D., Wagner, D.A., Perrig, A., et al.: Practical techniques for searches on encrypted data. In: IEEE symposium on Security and Privacy, pp. 44–55 (2000)
2. Boneh, D., Crescenzo, G.D., Ostrovsky, R., et al.: Public key encryption with keyword search. In: Theory and Application of Cryptographic Techniques, pp. 506–522 (2004)
3. Waters, B., Balfanz, D., Durfee, G.E., et al.: Building an encrypted and searchable audit log. In: Network and Distributed System Security Symposium (2004)
4. Curtmola, R., Garay, J.A., Kamara, S., et al.: Searchable symmetric encryption: improved definitions and efficient constructions. In: Computer and Communications Security, pp. 79–88 (2006)
5. Wang, P., Wang, H., Pieprzyk, J.: Threshold privacy preserving keyword searches. In: Geffert, V., Karhumäki, J., Bertoni, A., Preneel, B., Návrat, P., Bieliková, M. (eds.) SOFSEM 2008. LNCS, vol. 4910, pp. 646–658. Springer, Heidelberg (2008). https://doi.org/10.1007/978-3-540-77566-9_56
6. Dong, J.P., Cha, J., Lee, P.J.: Searchable keyword-based encryption. IACR Cryptology Eprint Archive, 2005 (2005)

7. Moataz, T., Justus, B., Ray, I., Cuppens-Boulahia, N., Cuppens, F., Ray, I.: Privacy-preserving multiple keyword search on outsourced data in the clouds. In: Atluri, V., Pernul, G. (eds.) DBSec 2014. LNCS, vol. 8566, pp. 66–81. Springer, Heidelberg (2014). https://doi.org/10.1007/978-3-662-43936-4_5

8. Yang, Y., Liu, X., Deng, R.: Multi-user multi-keyword rank search over encrypted data in arbitrary language. IEEE Trans. Dependable Secur. Comput. **PP**(99), 1 (2017)

9. Fu, Z., Wu, X., Guan, C., et al.: Toward efficient multi-keyword fuzzy search over encrypted outsourced data with accuracy improvement. IEEE Trans. Inf. Forensics Secur. **11**(12), 2706–2716 (2017)

10. Wang, B., Yu, S., Lou, W., et al.: Privacy-preserving multi-keyword fuzzy search over encrypted data in the cloud. In: INFOCOM, 2014 Proceedings IEEE. IEEE, pp. 2112–2120 (2014)

11. Zhang, W., Xiao, S., Lin, Y., et al.: Secure ranked multi-keyword search for multiple data owners in cloud computing. In: IEEE/IFIP International Conference on Dependable Systems and Networks, pp. 276–286. IEEE (2014)

12. Ameri, M.H., Delavar, M., Mohajeri, J., et al.: A key-policy attribute-based temporary keyword search scheme for secure cloud storage. IEEE Trans. Cloud Comput. **PP**(99), 1 (2018)

13. Liang, X., Cao, Z., Lin, H., et al.: Attribute based proxy re-encryption with delegating capabilities. In: International Symposium on Information, Computer, and Communications Security, pp. 276–286. ACM (2009)

14. Cui, J., Zhou, H., Zhong, H., et al.: AKSER: attribute-based keyword search with efficient revocation in cloud computing. Inf. Sci. **423**, 343–352 (2017)

15. Hur, J., Dong, K.N.: Attribute-based access control with efficient revocation in data outsourcing systems. IEEE Trans. Parallel Distrib. Syst. **22**(7), 1214–1221 (2011)

16. Cui, H., Deng, R.H., Liu, J.K., Li, Y.: Attribute-based encryption with expressive and authorized keyword search. In: Pieprzyk, J., Suriadi, S. (eds.) ACISP 2017. LNCS, vol. 10342, pp. 106–126. Springer, Cham (2017). https://doi.org/10.1007/978-3-319-60055-0_6

17. Kamara, S., Papamanthou, C., Roeder, T., et al.: Dynamic searchable symmetric encryption. In: Computer and Communications Security, pp. 965–976 (2012)

18. Kamara, S., Papamanthou, C.: Parallel and dynamic searchable symmetric encryption. In: Financial Cryptography, pp. 258–274 (2013)

19. Hahn, F., Kerschbaum, F.: Searchable encryption with secure and efficient updates. In: Computer and Communications Security, pp. 310–320 (2014)

20. Xia, Z., Wang, X., Sun, X., et al.: A secure and dynamic multi-keyword ranked search scheme over encrypted cloud data. IEEE Trans. Parallel Distrib. Syst. **27**(2), 340–352 (2016)

21. Miers, I., Mohassel, P.: IO-DSSE: scaling dynamic searchable encryption to millions of indexes by improving locality. In: Network and Distributed System Security Symposium (2017)

22. Seo, J.H., Cheon, J.H.: Fully Secure Anonymous Hierarchical Identity-Based Encryption with Constant Size Ciphertexts. IACR Cryptology Eprint Archive 2011, 215–234 (2011)

23. Zhao, Y., Chen, X., Ma, H., et al.: A new trapdoor-indistinguishable public key encryption with keyword search. J. Wirel. Mob. Networks, Ubiquitous Comput. Dependable Appl. **3**(1/2), 72–81 (2012)

24. Katz, J., Sahai, A., Waters, B., et al.: Predicate encryption supporting disjunctions, polynomial equations, and inner products. In: Theory and Application of Cryptographic Techniques, pp. 146–162 (2008)
25. Byun, J.W., Rhee, H.S., Park. H.A., et al.: Off-line keyword guessing attacks on recent keyword search schemes over encrypted data. In: Very Large Data Bases, pp. 75–83 (2006)
26. Yau, W.-C., Phan, R.C.-W., Heng, S.-H., Goi, B.-M.: Keyword guessing attacks on secure searchable public key encryption schemes with a designated tester. Int. J. Comput. Math. **90**(12), 2581–2587 (2013)
27. Tang, Q., Chen, L.: Public-key encryption with registered keyword search. In: European Public Key Infrastructure Workshop, pp. 163–178 (2009)
28. Chen, R., Mu, Y., Yang, G., et al.: Dual-server public-key encryption with keyword search for secure cloud storage. IEEE Trans. Inf. Forensics Secur. **11**(4), 789–798 (2016)
29. Lu, Y., Li, J.: Efficient searchable public key encryption against keyword guessing attacks for cloud-based EMR systems. Cluster Comput. **22**(1), 285–299 (2019)
30. Chen, H., Cao, Z., Dong, Z., et al.: SDKSE: a secure dynamic keyword searchable encryption scheme for email systems. In: 2018 3rd International Conference on Security of Smart Cities, Industrial Control System and Communications (2018)

On Trust Confusional, Trust Ignorant, and Trust Transitions

Yoshinobu Kawabe[1]($\boxtimes$), Yuki Koizumi[2], Tetsushi Ohki[3], Masakatsu Nishigaki[3], Toru Hasegawa[2], and Tetsuhisa Oda[1]

[1] Graduate School of Business Administration and Computer Science, Aichi Institute of Technology, Yachigusa 1247, Yakusa-cho, Toyota, Aichi 470-0392, Japan
{kawabe,oda}@aitech.ac.jp
[2] Graduate School of Information Science and Technology, Osaka University, 1-5 Yamadaoka, Suita, Osaka 565-0871, Japan
{ykoizumi,t-hasegawa}@ist.osaka-u.ac.jp
[3] Graduate School of Science and Technology, Shizuoka University, 3-5-1 Johoku, Naka-ku, Hamamatsu, Shizuoka 432-8011, Japan
{ohki,nishigaki}@inf.shizuoka.ac.jp

Abstract. This paper introduces a two-dimensional representation for trust values that uses two metrics: "trust" and "distrust." With this representation, we can deal with such contradictory arguments as "The message is basically trustworthy but simultaneously not trustworthy." Such situations can be caused when a message is consistent with other messages, but the message is sent from an unknown sender. We also explore how to analyze the transitions of two-dimensional trust values with a theory of distributed algorithms and compare our trust representation with Jøsang's subjective logic.

Keywords: Two-dimensional trust representation · Fuzzy logic · I/O-automaton theory · Safety/liveness properties · Subjective logic

1 Introduction

During recent large-scale disasters, social media have been actively used to exchange various information about victims. Although such social media messages are helpful during disasters, some might be unreliable. For example, when a huge earthquake struck northern Osaka on the morning of June 18, 2018, many fake messages were distributed on Twitter and rapidly retweeted all over Japan, causing many problems.

Even if a message's content is true at one specific moment, the message may "become untrue" as time passes. For example, even if the following message, "A person is seriously injured but still alive," is true immediately at the beginning of a disaster, it might be false an hour later; the person might be dead. In this sense, some messages may not be reliable. If one receives a message from an

W. Meng et al. (Eds.): IFIPTM 2019, IFIP AICT 563, pp. 178–195, 2019.
https://doi.org/10.1007/978-3-030-33716-2_14

unknown sender, one might also suspect that it is unreliable. This might happen even if the message's content is relatively consistent.

To deal with such situations, we must properly evaluate the trust of messages and senders. Marsh and Dibben introduced a trust value, which ranges from -1 to 1, and classified trust notions into *trust, distrust, untrust,* and *mistrust* [13]. Their classification is one-dimensional; i.e., trust and distrust are at both extremities. However, for the notions of trust and distrust, Lewicki et al. [10] suggested that they are located at entirely separate dimensions. Cases exist where a one-dimensional expression is not sufficient for trust values.

Trust is a property that is closely related to human impressions. We believe that a technique for impression formation based on mathematical psychology should be applied for trust values. Oda [5,17–19] developed a Fuzzy-set Concurrent Rating (FCR) method with fuzzy logic that enables us to measure and analyze human impressions. Since the FCR method allows two or more dimensions for representing a truth value, trust and distrust notions can be described two-dimensionally by applying them to a trust representation. This enables us to describe situations in (i) confusional trust (e.g. "Although he can basically be trusted, in some cases he is not trustworthy") and (ii) ignorant trust (e.g. "Since I have never met him, I have no impression of him."). In this paper, we introduce a FCR-based, two-dimensional trust representation and show how it corresponds to the conventional trust representation of Marsh and Dibben.

We also deal with transitions of trust. If we regard a two-dimensional trust value as a state of an automaton, we can discuss properties defined with a series of state transitions. With results from the theory of distributed algorithms, we discuss safety-related trust properties (e.g. "A user never reaches a state of distrust" and "If a user exits the distrust region, she never returns to it") and liveness-related trust properties (e.g., "A user can finally reach the trust region."). We also discuss an efficient proof method for trust-related safety properties based on I/O-automaton theory.

This paper is organized as follows. After showing some notions and notations in Sect. 2, we introduce a two-dimensional trust representation in Sect. 3. In Sect. 4, we model and analyze trust transitions. Finally, in Sect. 5, we compare our trust representation with Jøsang's subjective logic.

2   Preliminaries

2.1   The FCR Method

A rating scale method (Fig. 1) is often used for questionnaires, where such adjectives as "poor," "fair," "average," "good," and "excellent" are given from which respondents choose. One problem with this method is that they tend to choose the middle item in the scale. This problem presents two cases. The first case is that the respondent has multiple answer candidates that are located at both extremities. The respondent usually chooses one of them, but if it is difficult for the respondent to choose one, a middle item may be chosen instead. The chosen middle item is not the true answer; the middle item is usually "average" or

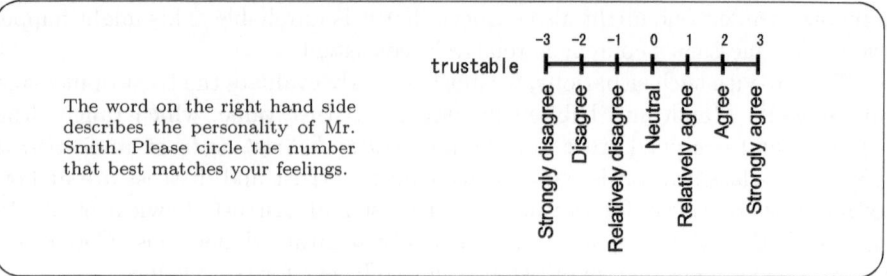

Fig. 1. Conventional questionnaire

"neutral," which complicates analysis. In the second case, since the respondent lacks sufficient knowledge/interest to answer, she chooses the middle value.

The word on the right hand side describes the character of Mr. Smith. Please check each of the seven scales. Each scale represents the ratio of your opinion. The left edge of the scale represents an opinion that never matches your feelings, and the right edge corresponds to a complete match with your feelings. The sum of the values need not equal 1.

"trustable"

Ratio how much you think so

0   1

Strongly disagree

Disagree

Relatively disagree

Neutral

Relatively agree

Agree

Strongly agree

Fig. 2. Rating with FCR method

To overcome this problem of choosing the middle item, in the FCR method, respondents are requested to describe their confidence in each item (Fig. 2); in other words, the respondents answer how much they believe the truthiness in each item. Then by applying fuzzy inference, we calculate the true answers of the respondents. From a theoretical viewpoint we have no restrictions on the dimensions (i.e., the number of items), but for simplicity we just employ two dimensions in the rest of this paper.

Hyper Logic Space Model. The FCR method employs the Hyper Logic Space model (HLS) as a logic space for multiple-dimensional multiple-valued logic. Figure 3 shows a two-dimensional space based on *true* and *false*. For any $t, f \in [0, 1]$, pair (t, f) is called an observation. t and f are independent; we do not assume such conditions as $t + f = 1$. We call $\{(t, f) \mid t, f \in [0, 1] \land t + f > 1\}$ the region of contradiction. $\{(t, f) \mid t, f \in [0, 1] \land t + f < 1\}$ is called the region of ignorance, or the region of irrelevance. Finally, $\{(t, f) \mid t, f \in [0, 1] \land t + f = 1\}$ is the consistent region.

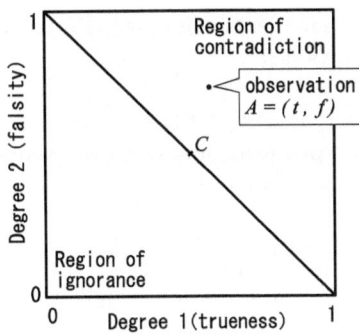
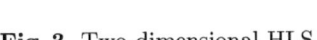

Fig. 3. Two-dimensional HLS

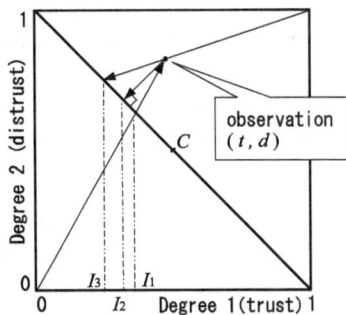

Fig. 4. Graphical calculation for integration values

Integration Value. Given observation (t, f), we need to calculate an actual truth value, which is called an integration value. Integration values can be calculated in several ways, and we employ the reverse-item averaging method, where integration value I_2 is defined with $I_2(t, f) = \dfrac{t + (1 - f)}{2}$. The integration value is the average of the degree of the positive elements and the complementary degree of the negative elements. $I_2(t, f)$ is calculated in a graphical manner (Fig. 4). The result of calculation is the value of "degree 1" after drawing a perpendicular line from (t, f) to Fig. 4's diagonal line.

Degree of Contradiction. Another important value in the FCR method is the degree of contradiction [5,17] or the contradiction-irrelevance degree. In the field of personality psychology, some situations are allowed, including "I like it, but I don't like it" or "I don't care for it at all." The degree of such confusion/irrelevance is formulated with the degree of contradiction.

For observation (t, f), degree of contradiction $C(t, f)$ should satisfy $C(t, f) = 1$ for complete confusion, $C(t, f) = -1$ for complete ignorance, and $C(t, f) = 0$ for a consistent situation. $C(t, f) = t + f - 1$ is usually employed where $C(t, f)$ represents the distance between (t, f) and the consistent region.

2.2 Trust Classification by Marsh and Dibben

A conventional trust value is a real number in $[-1, 1)$. Readers interested in the details of calculating trust values can find them here [13], but in this paper we omit them since they are beyond the scope of this paper and directly handle the calculated trust values. Marsh and Dibben introduced the following four notions of trust:

- *Trust*: This notion represents a case where a trust value is positive and exceeds a predefined value called a cooperation threshold. In this case, a trustee should be trusted, and the trust value is regarded as a measure of how much an agent believes the trustee.

- *Distrust*: Here the trust value is negative, and an agent believes that a trustee will actively work against her in a given situation.
- *Untrust*: Although the trust value is positive, it is not high enough to produce cooperation. An agent cannot determine if a trustee is actually trustworthy.
- *Mistrust*: Initial trust has been betrayed. More precicely, mistrust represents a situation either a former trust was destroyed or a former distrust was healed.

The mistrust notion is a time-related trust property discussed in Sect. 4. We address trust, distrust, and untrust notions in the following section. For these properties, see studies by Primiero [20] (on distrust and mistrust) and [21] (on trust and distrust).

3   FCR-Based Two-Dimensional Trust Representation

Suppose that you received a message, and you calculated its trust value. If the trust value is 0.9 and the cooperation threshold is 0.85, then from the definition of the trust notion, the message should be trusted. However, can you say that you have absolutely no distrust about this message? Since the maximum trust value is 1, a deficit of 0.1 exists. In this sense, the message might not be trusted enough.

We believe that this situation is caused by the limitations of the power of one-dimensional expressions. Hence, in this study we employ the degrees of trust *Trust* and distrust *DisTrust* defined with $Trust = DisTrust = \{v \mid 0 \le v \le 1\}$ and define a two-dimensional trust value as an element of $Trust \times DisTrust$. Following the FCR method, a two-dimensional trust value is also called an observation in this paper.

3.1   Understanding Two-Dimensional Trust Values

We semantically understand two-dimensional trust values by observing some of them.

Observation $(1,0) \in Trust \times DisTrust$ has a high degree of trust (1) and a low degree of distrust (0). $(1,0)$ represents a case where a trustee is completely trusted; this observation corresponds to (conventional) trust value 1. Observation $(0,1)$ represents a case of complete distrust and corresponds to trust value -1. Observation $(0.5, 0.5)$, which falls exactly between $(1,0)$ and $(0,1)$, corresponds to 0 in conventional trust values.

To define such trust notions as trust, distrust, and untrust in our two-dimensional trust model, we employ the following transformation:

$$\left[\begin{pmatrix} \cos\frac{\pi}{4} & -\sin\frac{\pi}{4} \\ \sin\frac{\pi}{4} & \cos\frac{\pi}{4} \end{pmatrix} \left\{ \begin{pmatrix} t \\ d \end{pmatrix} - \begin{pmatrix} 1 \\ 0 \end{pmatrix} \right\} + \begin{pmatrix} \frac{\sqrt{2}}{2} \\ 0 \end{pmatrix} \right] \times \frac{1}{\frac{\sqrt{2}}{2}} = \begin{pmatrix} t - d \\ t + d - 1 \end{pmatrix}.$$

Figure 5 shows the transformation and observations $(1,0)$, $(0,1)$, and $(0.5, 0.5)$ are respectively mapped to $(1,0)$, $(-1,0)$, and $(0,0)$. Below, the resulting point of the transformation is called (i, c). First element $i = t - d$ can be

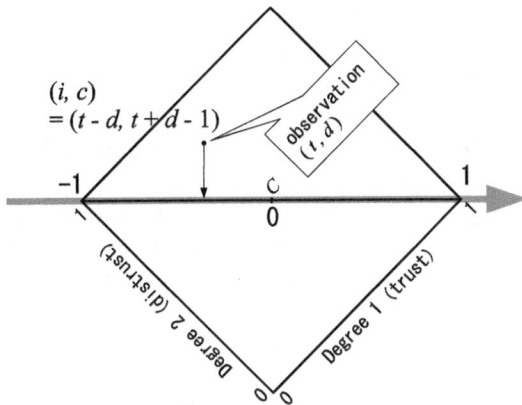

Fig. 5. Graphically understanding calculation of (i, c)

calculated with the reverse-item averaging method in Sect. 2.1. Actually, the value of i is calculated by normalizing $I_2(t, d)$ to be a value in region $[-1, 1]$; note that the range of integration value $I_2(t, d)$ was originally $[0, 1]$.

The value of i was regarded as a conventional trust value given by Marsh and Dibben. From the definition of $i = t - d$, a net trust value is calculated by subtracting the degree of trust from the degree of distrust, which matches our intuition. From Fig. 5, the consistent region, which is the line between $(1, 0)$ and $(0, 1)$ before the transformation, corresponds to the set of conventional trust values. Observation (t, d) in the consistent region satisfies $t + d = 1$ and is regarded as an assumption on the trust and distrust degrees. The theory of conventional trust values implicitly introduces this assumption.

Trust notions are defined with the value of i^1. Let CT be a cooperation threshold. If we have $i = t - d \geq CT$, then it is a case of trust; if i is negative then it is case of distrust; if we have $0 \leq i < CT$, then it is a case of untrust. Note that for the case of distrust, condition $i < 0$ is equivalent to $t < d$; i.e., a trustee is distrusted if the degree of distrust exceeds the degree of trust.

3.2 New Classification on Untrust

As shown in Fig. 4, integration values can be graphically calculated. Observing the graphical calculation, the two-dimensional trust values in the same perpendicular line have identical integration values. For example, observation $A = (t, d)$ and its nearest point on diagonal line $A' = (\dfrac{t + (1 - d)}{2}, 1 - \dfrac{t + (1 - d)}{2})$ have

---

[1] In this paper, we only define trust notions with the value of $i = t - d$ without the value of c. Our paper's trust notions are formalized with "linear" functions. For example, the trust and distrust notions are defined with restrictions $d \leq -t + CT$ and $d > t$. This is just for simplicity, and we believe it is possible to provide a finer definition for trust notions with both i and c; that is, we believe a "non-linear" definition is possible. This is future work.

the same integration value. However, for observations A and A', the distance from the diagonal line is different. The distance between observation (t, d) and the diagonal line in Fig. 4 is given by $|t + d - 1|$, which is the absolute value of second element $c = t + d - 1$ of point (i, c) defined in the previous section. The formula of c is equivalent to the degree of contradiction-irrelevance $C(t, d)$ of the FCR method.

If $C(t, d)$ is positive and high, then it is a state of confusion; both trust and distrust degrees are high. If $C(t, d)$ is negative and low (i.e., the absolute value of c is high), then it is regarded as a state of irrelevance; in this case, both the trust and distrust degrees are low. In the field of fuzzy logic, a state of confusion is caused by information overload, and a state of irrelevance is caused by a lack of information [5,17]. For information overload, there is too much evidence about a trustee, some of which may increase the trust value on the trustee, but others may increase the distrust value. This causes confusion, which leads to a situation where you cannot determine whether the trustee is trustworthy. If you lack sufficient evidence, i.e., if you ignore the trustee, you cannot discuss whether she is trustworthy.

This discussion demonstrates that two cases exist where one cannot determine whether the trustee is trustworthy. Therefore, we introduce two types of new untrust notions:

- *Untrust confusional*: the trustee is both trusted and distrusted. Formally, this is a case with $0 < i < CT$ and $c \geq 0$.
- *Untrust ignorant*: the trustee is ignored; in other words, the trustee is neither trusted nor distrusted. Formally, this is a case with $0 < i < CT$ and $c < 0$.

The original untrust notion [13] corresponds to the notion of untrust ignorant, and in this paper, we introduce a new kind of untrust notion from the viewpoint of confusion.

3.3   Example

In three countries, an opinion poll was conducted about the approval ratings of each country's governments. We used the following items to answer this question: "*Do you trust your government?*"

1. *I have no idea;*
2. *Yes, I do;*
3. *No, I do not;*
4. *Sometimes yes, sometimes no.*

For country c, the number of answers for each item is $a_1^c, \ldots, a_4^c$; also, we have $s^c = a_1^c + a_2^c + a_3^c + a_4^c$. In this example, we calculate the degrees of trust t_c and distrust d_c of the government with $t_c = \dfrac{a_2^c + a_4^c}{s^c}$ and $d_c = \dfrac{a_3^c + a_4^c}{s^c}$.

A survey was conducted with 100 residents each in the countries of X, Y, and Z, and the following are the results:

$$(a_1^X, a_2^X, a_3^X, a_4^X) = (10, 20, 30, 40),$$
$$(a_1^Y, a_2^Y, a_3^Y, a_4^Y) = (50, 30, 10, 10), \text{ and}$$
$$(a_1^Z, a_2^Z, a_3^Z, a_4^Z) = (20, 25, 5, 50).$$

For each country, the following are the degrees of trust t_c and distrust d_c:

$$(t_X, d_X) = (0.6, 0.7), (t_Y, d_Y) = (0.4, 0.2) \text{ and } (t_Z, d_Z) = (0.75, 0.55).$$

For each country we can also calculate the values of i and c:

$$(i_X, c_X) = (-0.1, 0.3), (i_Y, c_Y) = (0.2, -0.4) \text{ and } (i_Z, c_Z) = (0.2, 0.3).$$

From this result, the following analysis is possible. For country X, there is some degree of distrust of the government, and citizens in country X are somewhat confused since the degree of contradiction is positive. For country Y, the degree of trust exceeds the degree of distrust, but the degree of contradiction is negative, which suggests that the people have little interest in their government. For countries Y and Z, although their integration values are the same, the degree of contradiction is positive for country Z. Note that we can compare countries Y and Z, even though the conventional trust model cannot since the degree of contradiction is not addressed.

4   Transitions of Two-Dimensional Trust Values

Mistrust is a property with regard to misplaced trust. If the first estimation for an observation is in the region of trust (i.e. $i = t - d \geq CT$), but the next estimation is changed to the region of distrust (i.e. $i < 0$), then the first estimation was incorrect. With this understanding, mistrust can be modeled as a property for the changes or transitions of a trust value.

Transition-related trust properties must be analyzed, including mistrust or swift trust [14,23], especially during disasters [3,9,15]. In this section, we regard an observation as a state and analyze the transitions of trust values.

4.1   Dealing with Trust Values as States

I/O-automaton [11,12] is a formal system for distributed algorithms, where a distributed system is modeled as a state machine and its properties are formalized with observable actions. Some actions, such as keyboard input, display output, and open communication in the Internet are observable, and others are unobservable, such as internal processing and secret communication.

Formally, automaton X has set of actions $sig(X)$, set of states $states(X)$, set of initial states $start(X) \subset states(X)$, and set of transitions $trans(X) \subset states(X) \times sig(X) \times states(X)$. Transition $(s, a, s') \in trans(X)$ is written as

$s \xrightarrow{a}_X s'$. In this paper, a state is a tuple of values. Each element of the tuple has a corresponding distinct variable name. A variable's name is used as an access function to its value. Such modeling is standard in I/O-automaton theory and its extensions, such as [8]. In this paper, we use variables tr and dis for trust and distrust values. The trust and distrust degrees in state $s \in states(X)$ are called $s.tr$ and $s.dis$.

4.2   Formalizing Trace-Based Trust Properties

Let $\alpha \equiv s_0 \xrightarrow{a_1}_X s_1 \xrightarrow{a_2}_X \cdots \xrightarrow{a_n}_X s_n$ be a transition sequence of automaton X. We define $tr(\alpha)$ as a sequence of all the external (i.e., observable) actions in $a_1 a_2 \cdots a_n$, and write $s_0 \xRightarrow{tr(\alpha)}_X s_n$. If s_0 is an initial state, $tr(\alpha)$ is called a trace of α. A trace is a sequence of observable actions in an execution from an initial state.

In I/O-automaton theory, various properties of distributed systems are defined with traces (Section 8.5.3 of [12]). Well-known characteristics are safety and liveness properties. Informally, a safety property means that nothing bad ever happens in a system. For example, the following are safety properties: "no division by zero error occurs" and "after reaching special state s, the system never reaches an error state." A liveness property means that something good might happen. "A program can terminate" and "from any state, the system can reach an initial state" are typical liveness properties.

If we regard Sect. 3's observations as states, we can define safety/liveness properties related to trust transitions. "An observation never reaches the region of distrust" and "after reaching the regions of trust or untrust, an observation never reaches the region of distrust" are trust safety properties. "An observation can reach the region of trust" is a trust liveness property.

Formalizing Trust Safety Properties. Let CT be a cooperation threshold. We define the regions of trust $T(CT)$, distrust D, and untrust $U(CT)$:

$$\begin{cases} T(CT) = \{\, (t,d) \mid t \in Trust \wedge d \in DisTrust \wedge t - d \geq CT \,\} \\ D \quad\;\; = \{\, (t,d) \mid t \in Trust \wedge d \in DisTrust \wedge t < d \,\} \\ U(CT) = Trust \times DisTrust \setminus (T(CT) \cup D), \end{cases}$$

where $0 < CT \leq 1$ holds. Sets $T(CT)$, D, and $U(CT)$ correspond to Sect. 3.1's definitions for trust notions, where "linear" functions are employed; exploring a "non-linear" setting is a future work.

We introduce a predicate for the reachability from state s to state s':

$reachable(s, s')$
$\quad \Longleftrightarrow s = s' \vee \exists s'' \in states(X)\, \exists a \in sig(X)[\, s \xrightarrow{a}_X s'' \wedge reachable(s'', s')\,],$

and we define predicate $nonDistr(s)$:

$$nonDistr(s) \Longleftrightarrow \forall s' \in states(X)\,[\,reachable(s, s') \implies (s'.tr, s'.dis) \notin D\,].$$

With these predicates, we can formalize a trust safety property, "an observation never reaches the region of distrust," with $\forall s \in start(X) [\, nonDistr(s)\,]$. Another safety property, "after reaching the region of trust or the region of untrust, an observation never reaches the region of distrust," is formalized:

$$\forall s \in states(X)\, \forall s' \in states(X)$$
$$[\,(reachable(s, s') \wedge (s'.tr, s'.dis) \notin D) \implies nonDistr(s')\,].$$

Formalizing Trust Liveness Properties. We can also formalize trust liveness properties. Let $n \in \mathcal{N}$ be a natural number. We define $reach^n(s, s')$ to represent that state s' is reachable from state s with n-steps as follows:

$reach^0(s, s') \iff s = s'$, and
$reach^{k+1}(s, s') \iff \exists s'' \in states(X)\, \exists a \in sig(X)[\, reach^k(s, s'') \wedge s'' \xrightarrow{a}_X s'\,]$.

With $reach^n(s, s')$, "an observation can reach the region of trust" is defined:

$$\forall s \in states(X)\, \exists s' \in states(X)\, \exists n \in \mathcal{N}\,[\, reach^n(s, s') \wedge (s'.tr, s'.dis) \in T(CT)\,].$$

4.3   Efficient Proof Method for Trace-Based Trust Properties

Although we can directly prove the logic formulae in the previous section, this is inefficient. By employing a result in I/O-automaton theory, a more efficient proof is possible.

Figure 6 shows the specification of automaton `testerSafety`, which describes the transitions of a two-dimensional trust value. It is written in an I/O-automaton-based specification language called IOA [2]. This specification has three variables. Variables `tr` and `dis` are for the degrees of trust and distrust. Variable `stateOfAgent` is used for a trustee's internal state. Automaton `testerSafety` has three actions: `move`, `inDistr`, and `notInDistr`. Each action is described in a precondition-effect style, where the `pre`-part has a condition to fire the action and the `eff`-part has the action's body. Action `move` shows that an observation moves from (pt, pd) to $(pt + dt, pd + dd)$ when event `ev` occurs. Actions `inDistr` and `notInDistr` are special observable qualities that denote whether the current observation is in the region of distrust. Action `inDistr` is enabled if $(tr, dis) \in D$ holds, which is equivalent to `tr` < `dis`, and action `notInDistr` is enabled if $(tr, dis) \notin D$ holds.

To specify automaton `testerSafety`, we need a concrete definition for predicate `condition` in the `pre`-part of action `move`. If we define this predicate with

$$condition(stateOfAgent, ev, pt, pd, dt, dd)$$
$$\iff (pt, pd) \notin D \wedge (pt + dt, pd + dd) \notin D$$

then action `inDistr` cannot be enabled. None of `testerSafety`'s traces have occurrences of action `inDistr`. This creates a set of traces $traces(\texttt{testerSafety})$, where $traces(A)$ is used for the set of all the traces

```
automaton testerSafety
  signature
    internal move(ev:Event, pt: VL, pd: VL, dt: VL, dd: VL)
    output inDistr(t:VL, d:VL)
    output notInDistr(t:VL, d:VL)

  states
    tr: VL := 0,     % VL ranges over [-1, 1]
    dis: VL := 0,    % but we assume 0 <= tr, dis <= 1 at any state
    stateOfAgent: agtState := InitState

  transitions
    internal move(ev, pt, pd, dt, dd)
      pre     pt = tr
          /\ pd = dis
          /\ (0 <= (pt + dt) /\ (pt + dt) <= 1)
          /\ (0 <= (pd + dd) /\ (pd + dd) <= 1)
          /\ condition(stateOfAgent, ev, pt, pd, dt, dd)
      eff tr := tr + dt;
          dis := dis + dd;
          stateOfAgent := change(stateOfAgent, ev)

    output inDistr(t, d)
      pre tr < dis /\ t = tr /\ d = dis
      eff do nothing

    output notInDistr(t, d)
      pre ~(tr < dis) /\ t = tr /\ d = dis
      eff do nothing
```

Fig. 6. Automaton `testerSafety` written in IOA language

of automaton A and specifies the trust safety property "an observation never reaches the region of distrust in automaton `testerSafety`." Automaton `testerSafety` obviously satisfies $\forall s \in start(\text{testerSafety})\,[\,nonDistr(s)\,]$.

Automaton `traceSafety` is the specification automaton for a safety property, but we need to deal with a safety property of a concrete system. Let A be an automaton and let $traces(A)$ be a corresponding trace set. If trace inclusion $traces(A) \subseteq traces(\text{testerSafety})$ holds, then automaton A satisfies the safety property defined with automaton `testerSafety`'s traces. Therefore, to show $\forall s \in start(A)\,[\,nonDistr(s)\,]$, it suffices to show the trace inclusion.

I/O-automaton theory provides techniques that prove a trace inclusion of (possibly infinite-state) systems, which can be applied with a theorem-proving tool [2,22]. Finding a forward simulation between automata is one of the techniques. Forward simulation f from I/O-automaton $Conc$ to I/O-automaton $Abst$ is a binary relation over states satisfying the following conditions:

Initial state correspondence: For any initial state $a \in start(Conc)$, there is initial state $b \in start(Abst)$ and $f(a, b)$ holds.

Step correspondence: For any reachable states $a_1, a_2 \in states(Conc)$, $b_1 \in states(Abst)$ and any action $\pi_{Conc} \in sig(Conc)$, if $f(a_1, b_1)$ and $a_1 \xrightarrow{\pi}_{Conc} a_2$ hold, then there is a state $b_2 \in states(Abst)$ satisfying $f(a_2, b_2)$ and $b_1 \xRightarrow{\beta}_{Abst} b_2$ with $\beta = tr(a_1 \xrightarrow{\pi}_{Conc} a_2)$.

From Theorem 3.10 of [11], if there is a forward simulation from $Conc$ to $Abst$, then we have $traces(Conc) \subseteq traces(Abst)$. Therefore, to show trace inclusion $traces(A) \subseteq traces(\texttt{testerSafety})$, it suffices to find a forward simulation from A to $\texttt{testerSafety}$. This leads to a safety property: "an observation never reaches the distrust region in A."

4.4   Example

Figure 7 shows an I/O-automaton $\texttt{bbdSystem}$, which is a specification of a communication system that sends a user's message to an online bulletin board after evaluating an observation. Specifically, by action $\texttt{get\_mes}$, the system receives a message from a user, and an observation is evaluated with actions $\texttt{discard\_mes}$ and $\texttt{approve\_mes}$. If pair $(\texttt{tr+evalTr(i, m)}, \texttt{dis+evalDis(i, m)})$ of the next state's observation falls in the distrust region, the message is discarded by action $\texttt{discard\_mes}$; otherwise, it is sent by actions $\texttt{approve\_mes}$ and $\texttt{say}$.

If we hide observable actions $\texttt{get\_mes}$ and $\texttt{say}$ in $\texttt{bbdSystem}$, that is, if we deal with these observable actions as internal ones, we can find a forward simulation from automaton $\texttt{bbdSystem}\backslash\{\texttt{get\_mes}, \texttt{say}\}$ to automaton $\texttt{testerSafety}$. Consequently, we have $traces(\texttt{bbdSystem}\backslash\{\texttt{get\_mes}, \texttt{say}\}) \subseteq traces(\texttt{testerSafety})$ that provides the safety property defined with automaton $\texttt{testerSafety}$. A complete computer-assisted proof is found in [24].

5   Discussion

In this section we compare our two-dimensional trust representation with a similar approach found in Jøsang's subjective logic [7].

5.1   Two-Dimensional Representation in Subjective Logic

In probabilistic logic [16], the truth values of propositions are probabilities and are given based on the frequency of events. The confidence on a truth value is high if enough attempts can be made; for example, we can confirm the truthiness of proposition "the probability of heads when flipping a coin is 0.5" if we can toss the coin many times. In subjective logic, truth values are defined from an epistemic viewpoint. The confidence of a truth value is high if we know how a situation happens. For example, the confidence of the proposition, "the probability that Lee Harvey Oswald killed John F. Kennedy is 0.5" is high if the dynamics of the case are well-known; however, many aspects of this case remain unknown, so the confidence is not actually high.

```
automaton bbdSystem
  signature
    input get_mes(i:ID, m:MES)
    internal discard_mes(i:ID, m:MES)
    internal approve_mes(i:ID, m:MES)
    output say(i:ID, m:MES)
    output inDistr(t:VL, d:VL)
    output notInDistr(t:VL, d:VL)

  states
    tr: VL := 0,      % VL ranges over [-1, 1]
    dis: VL := 0,     % but we assume 0 <= tr, dis <= 1 at any state
    flg: Bool := false,
    mesQ: Seq[MES] := empty

  transitions              % Note: input actions does not have the
    input get_mes(i, m)    % "pre"-part since they are always enabled.
      eff mesQ := mesQ || (packet(i, m) -| empty)

    internal discard_mes(i, m)
      pre ~flg /\ mesQ ~= empty
          /\ packet(i, m) = head(mesQ)
          /\ ((tr + evalTr(tr, m))-(dis + evalDis(dis, m))) < 0
      eff mesQ := tail(mesQ)

    internal approve_mes(i, m)
      pre ~flg /\ mesQ ~= empty
          /\ packet(i, m) = head(mesQ)
          /\ ((tr + evalTr(tr, m))-(dis + evalDis(dis, m))) >= 0
      eff flg := true

    output say(i, m)
      pre flg /\ mesQ ~= empty
          /\ packet(i, m) = head(mesQ)
      eff tr := tr + evalTr(tr, m);
          dis := dis + evalDis(dis, m);
          mesQ := tail(mesQ);
          flg := false

Outputs "inDistr" and "notInDistr" are defined as in the case of
automaton "testerSafety."
```

Fig. 7. System never sends a message if a user might be distrusted

Subjective logic uses a domain, which is a set of distinct opinions. If a domain consists of opinions x and $\bar{x}$, it is called a binary domain. In this study, we deal with a binary domain where one opinion x corresponds to the trust notion and its contrary opinion $\bar{x}$ represents the distrust notion. A binomial opinion in subjective logic is defined with the following quadruple $\omega_x^A = (b_x^A, d_x^A, u_x^A, a_x^A)$:

- b_x^A: the amount of observer A's belief in x;
- d_x^A: the amount of observer A's disbelief in x;
- u_x^A: the amount of observer A's uncertainty about x;
- a_x^A: the prior probability in the absence of belief or disbelief.

We assume $0 \le b_x^A, d_x^A, u_x^A, a_x^A \le 1$ and $b_x^A + d_x^A + u_x^A = 1$ hold for any b_x^A, d_x^A, u_x^A and a_x^A. Values b_x^A, d_x^A, and u_x^A are depicted with a triangle in Fig. 8.

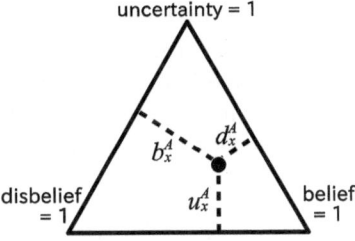

Fig. 8. Triangular representation of binomial opinion in subjective logic

The right bottom is the case where $b_x^A = 1$, the left bottom is where $d_x^A = 1$, and the top vertex is where $u_x^A = 1$.

A two-dimensional trust representation by b_x^A and d_x^A is possible in subjective logic, where b_x^A and d_x^A represent the degrees of trust and distrust.

5.2 Comparing Two Types of Trust Representations

Pair (b_x^A, d_x^A) in subjective logic corresponds to (t, d) of the FCR method in Sect. 3. We compare the two types of trust representations.

Considering Three Kinds of Opinions. We consider three kinds of opinions below. The first one is an opinion where $b_x^A = 1$ and is shown at the bottom right of the Fig. 8's triangle. This opinion's correspondence in the FCR-based model is in $\{(t, d) \mid t = 1 \wedge d \in DisTrust\}$ where the degree of trust is 1. However, as discussed later, since subjective logic does not deal with the region of confusion, thus the point where $b_x^A = 1$ exactly corresponds to $(1, 0)$ in the HLS model. Actually, in subjective logic the state where $b_x^A = 1$ is for an absolute opinion on x, and from a trust viewpoint trustee x is completely trusted by agent A.

The second type of opinion is where $u_x^A = 0$. In this case, we have $b_x^A + d_x^A = 1$; that is, the opinion is dogmatic and completely consistent. For this situation, the degree of contradiction is 0 in the FCR-based model. From a discussion in Sect. 3.1, such opinions are regarded as a conventional trust value by Marsh and Dibben.

Finally, we consider the case where $u_x^A = 1$. Here $b_x^A = d_x^A = 0$ holds since we have $0 \le b_x^A, d_x^A \le 1$ and $b_x^A + d_x^A + u_x^A = 1$. In subjective logic, this state is called vacuous or undefined. Observation $(0, 0)$ of the FCR-based model corresponds to this opinion.

Difference of Two Representations. Observation $(0, 0)$ represents the total uncertainty. However, in the FCR-based model, this is not the only observation of it. We have another observation, $(1, 1)$, where the trustee is highly trusted but simultaneously highly distrusted. In this situation, you cannot determine whether the trustee is trustworthy. From the following discussion, the subjective-logic-based approach cannot deal with such uncertainty.

From condition $b_x^A + d_x^A + u_x^A = 1$, we have $-u_x^A = b_x^A + d_x^A - 1$. The right hand side of this formula is equivalent to the degree of contradiction since pair (b_x^A, d_x^A) corresponds to (t, d) of the FCR method. $-u_x^A$ is the degree of contradiction. Moreover, we have $0 \leq u_x^A \leq 1$, which leads to $-1 \leq b_x^A + d_x^A - 1 \leq 0$. Hence, binomial opinions in subjective logic are either in the region of ignorance or in the consistent region. Therefore, we conclude that subjective logic does not deal with the region of contradiction. A similar logic space model without the region of contradiction is found in the A-IFS model [1].

As described in Sect. 3.2, a state of confusion is caused by information overload, and a state of irrelevance is caused by a lack of information. This observation suggests the following difference between subjective-logic- and FCR-based approaches:

- Let A be an observer and let x be a trustee. At the beginning of the computation, observer A is ignorant of trustee x, and no evidence exists upon which to judge whether x is trustworthy. Thus, we have $b_x^A = d_x^A = 0$ and $u_x^A = 1$ in subjective logic. In this study we assume that trust and/or distrust degrees increase if the observer collects evidence on x. If this is the case, as time passes, the values of b_x^A and d_x^A increase, and the value of u_x^A decreases. Finally, after collecting enough evidence, the value of u_x^A becomes 0. Since confusing situations are ignored in subjective logic, in the subjective-logic-based approach, there is an implicit assumption that an observer can finally calculate a trustee's trustworthiness.
- On the other hand, in the FCR-based trust representation, we have $t = d = 0$ at the beginning, as in the case of the subjective-logic-based approach. Thus, we have $C(0,0) = -1$ for the degree of contradiction. Note that the absolute value of $C(t, d)$ can be seen as the degree of uncertainty, which is maximum in the beginning. Hereafter, if the observer collects evidence about the trustee, the values of t and d increase and the value of $|C(t, d)|$ decreases. If the two-dimensional trust value (t, d) is near the consistent region, then $C(t, d)$ is almost 0, and in this situation the observer can calculate a trustee's trustworthiness. However, in the FCR-based model, we have the region of contradiction. If more evidence is collected, the values of t and d further increase, and the value of $|C(t, d)|$ also increases. Finally, the value of $C(t, d)$ becomes nearly 1, which is a contradiction. If an observer has too much evidence, she may not accurately evaluate the trustee. This is an assumption in the FCR-based approach.

The setting in the FCR-based approach is reasonable, but the assumption in the subjective-logic-based approach is considered too strong. Actually, in the example of Sect. 3.3, the cases for countries X and Z cannot be dealt with in the subjective-logic-based approach since the degree of contradiction is positive. If we modify t_c and d_c with $t_c = \dfrac{a_2^c + 0.5 \times a_4^c}{s^c}$ and $d_c = \dfrac{a_3^c + 0.5 \times a_4^c}{s^c}$ in the example of Sect. 3.3, then $t_c + d_c - 1 \leq 0$ is always satisfied. The weight of 0.5 is introduced for variable a_4^c, and this enables us to handle the cases for countries X and Z in the subjective-logic-based approach. We can see that, in the modified example, the trust and distrust values of a respondent are 0.5 if the respondent chooses the fourth item:

4. *Sometimes yes, sometimes no.*

Note that the sum of the values equals 1. Hence, when we employ the weight of 0.5 in estimating t_c and d_c, we implicitly assume that a respondent choosing the fourth item can consistently evaluate the trustworthiness to her government. However, we do not use such an assumption in the example of Sect. 3.3, since we address the suggestion [10] that trust and distrust notions should be located at completely separate dimensions. Hence, in order to deal with trust and distrust degrees independently, we need to handle not only the case of $t_c + d_c \leq 1$ but also the case of $t_c + d_c > 1$. Therefore, the region of contradiction $\{(t, d) \mid t + d > 1\}$ is required. Actually, in the modeling of Sect. 3.3's example, the trust and distrust degrees of the fourth item's respondent are 1, which means that the sum of the trust and distrust degrees equals 2. Some readers may consider this modeling is coarse, but we believe that a more accurate evaluation is possible if we define $t_c = \dfrac{a_2^c + a_{4pos}^c}{s^c}$ and $d_c = \dfrac{a_3^c + a_{4neg}^c}{s^c}$ with:

$$a_{4pos}^c = \sum_{i \in S_{4th}} \text{trust degree of respondent } i, \text{ and}$$

$$a_{4neg}^c = \sum_{i \in S_{4th}} \text{distrust degree of respondent } i,$$

where S_{4th} is the set of respondents choosing the fourth item.

6   Conclusion

This paper proposed a two-dimensional trust representation based on fuzzy logic. An observation was given as a pair of trust and distrust degrees, and we discussed the validity of its representation by showing a mapping to conventional one-dimensional trust representation. We also introduced a new classification of untrust. Additionally, this paper discussed such trace-based trust properties as safety properties and liveness properties. We showed how a simulation-based proof method for trace inclusion can be applied for trust safety properties. Finally, we compared our two-dimensional trust representation with a trust representation based on subjective logic.

It is important to ensure the applicability of this paper's modeling of trust properties and the proof technique to actual systems. This study is a part of a research project on disaster communication systems, and future work will prove the trust properties of a real communication system with social media, such as a communication system for disaster management [4,6]. In real systems, an analyst may receive conflicting evidence from different sources, which means that some source of information provides wrong evidence. We believe that the degree of contradiction is applicable to handle this situation. If there are many wrong information sources, then the degree of contradiction becomes high. Hence, the analyst can use the degree of contradiction to judge whether she should discard and re-collect evidence.

Although this paper has discussed safety properties such as "If a user exits the distrust region, she never returns to it," this sort of assertion is considered too strong in the real world. To use this paper's techniques for real systems, we need proper sufficient conditions. Finding such conditions is an important future work.

Finally, we must introduce a "non-linear" definition for trust notions (see the footnote in Sect. 3.1), which employ both i and c.

Acknowledgments. This work was supported by the National Institute of Information and Communications Technology in Japan (Contract No. 193).

References

1. Atanassov, K.T.: Intuitionistic Fuzzy Sets: Theory and Applications, 1st edn. Physica-Verlag GmbH, Heidelberg (2010)
2. Bogdanov, A.: Formal verification of simulations between I/O-automata. Master's thesis, Massachusetts Institute of Technology (2000)
3. Busa, M. G., Musacchio, M.T., Finan, S., Fennell, C.: Trust-building through social media communications in disaster management. In: Proceedings of the 24th International Conference on World Wide Web, pp. 1179–1184. WWW 2015 Companion. ACM, New York (2015). https://doi.org/10.1145/2740908.2741724
4. Chen, J., Arumaithurai, M., Fu, X., Ramakrishnan, K. K.: CNS: content-oriented notification service for managing disasters. In: Proceedings of ACM Conference on Information-Centric Networking, pp. 122–131. ACM (2016)
5. Deng, J., Oda, T., Umano, M.: Fuzzy logical operations in the two-dimensional hyper logic space concerning the fuzzy-set concurrent rating method. J. Jpn. Assoc. Manage. Syst. **17**(2), 33–42 (2001)
6. Jahanian, M., Xing, Y., Chen, J., Ramakrishnan, K.K., Seferoglu, H., Yuksel, M.: The evolving nature of disaster management in the internet and social media era. In: 2018 IEEE International Symposium on Local and Metropolitan Area Networks, LANMAN 2018, Washington, DC, USA, June 25–27, 2018, pp. 79–84 (2018). https://doi.org/10.1109/LANMAN.2018.8475116
7. Jøsang, A.: Subjective Logic: A Formalism for Reasoning Under Uncertainty, 1st edn. Springer, Cham (2016). https://doi.org/10.1007/978-3-319-42337-1
8. Kaynar, D., Lynch, N., Segala, R., Vaandrager, F.: The Theory of Timed I/O Automata. Morgan & Claypool Publishers, San Francisco (2010)
9. Lemieux, F.: The impact of a natural disaster on altruistic behaviour and crime. Disasters **38**(3), 483–499 (2014)
10. Lewicki, R.J., McAllister, D.J.B., Bies, R.J.: Trust and distrust: new relationships and realities. Acad. Manag. Rev. **23**, 438–458 (1998)
11. Lynch, N., Vaandrager, F.: Forward and backward simulations – part I: untimed systems. Inf. Comput. **121**(2), 214–233 (1995). https://doi.org/10.1006/inco.1995.1134
12. Lynch, N.A.: Distributed Algorithms. Morgan Kaufmann Publishers, San Francisco (1996)

13. Marsh, S., Dibben, M.R.: Trust, untrust, distrust and mistrust – an exploration of the Dark(er) side. In: Herrmann, P., Issarny, V., Shiu, S. (eds.) iTrust 2005. LNCS, vol. 3477, pp. 17–33. Springer, Heidelberg (2005). https://doi.org/10.1007/11429760_2

14. Meyerson, D., Weick, K.E., Kramer, R.M.: Swift Trust and Temporary Groups in Trust in Organizations: Frontiers of Theory and Research. SAGE, Thousand Oaks (1995)

15. Murayama, Y.: Issues in disaster communications. J. Inf. Process. **22**(4), 558–565 (2014). https://doi.org/10.2197/ipsjjip.22.558

16. Nilsson, N.J.: Probabilistic logic. Artif. Intell. **28**(1), 71–88 (1986). https://doi.org/10.1016/0004-3702(86)90031-7

17. Oda, T.: Fundamental characterestics of fuzzy-set concurrent rating method. J. Jpn. Assoc. Manage. Syst. **12**(1), 23–32 (1995). In Japanese

18. Oda, T.: Fuzzy set theoretical approach for improving the rating scale method: proposing and introducing the FCR-method and the IR-method as novel rating methods. Jpn. Psychol. Rev. **56**(1), 67–83 (2013). In Japanese

19. Oda, T.: Measurement technique for ergonomics, section 3: psychological measurements and analyses (3) measurements and analyses by kansei evaluation. Jpn. J. Ergon. **51**(5), 293–303 (2015). In Japanese

20. Primiero, G.: A calculus for distrust and mistrust. In: Habib, S.M.M., Vassileva, J., Mauw, S., Mühlhäuser, M. (eds.) IFIPTM 2016. IAICT, vol. 473, pp. 183–190. Springer, Cham (2016). https://doi.org/10.1007/978-3-319-41354-9_15

21. Primiero, G., Raimondi, F., Bottone, M., Tagliabue, J.: Trust and distrust in contradictory information transmission. Appl. Network Sci. **2**, 12 (2017). https://doi.org/10.1007/s41109-017-0029-0

22. Søgaard-Andersen, J.F., Garland, S.J., Guttag, J.V., Lynch, N.A., Pogosyants, A.: Computer-assisted simulation proofs. In: Courcoubetis, C. (ed.) CAV 1993. LNCS, vol. 697, pp. 305–319. Springer, Heidelberg (1993). https://doi.org/10.1007/3-540-56922-7_25

23. Wildman, J., Shuffler, M., Lazzara, E., Fiore, S., Burke, S.: Trust development in swift starting action teams: a multilevel framework. Group Organ. Manage. **37**(2), 137–170 (2012)

24. https://aitech.ac.jp/kwb/proof4testerSafety/

A Framework for Blockchain-Based Verification of Integrity and Authenticity

Anirban Basu[1(✉)], Theo Dimitrakos[2,3], Yuto Nakano[1],
and Shinsaku Kiyomoto[1]

[1] KDDI Research, Inc., Fujimino, Japan
{basu,yuto,kiyomoto}@kddi-research.jp
[2] CSPL, Huawei Technologies Dusseldorf GmbH, Dusseldorf, Germany
theo.dimitrakos@huawei.com
[3] University of Kent, Canterbury, UK
t.dimitrakos@kent.ac.uk

Abstract. In many application scenarios, such as cloud computing and network function virtualisation, entities from different domains or their interactions are short-lived. Yet, it is often necessary to ensure accountability of events recorded by such entities about their application-specific interactions. The distributed and multi-domain nature of this problem makes a decentralised architecture imperative, particularly in the context of key management and trust. This architecture also needs to address challenges in terms of cross-domain privacy and confidentiality of shared data. For concreteness and without loss of generality, we consider the use case of firewalls as virtual network functions (VNFs) across multiple domains where short-lived firewall VNF instances spin up and down, logging events (e.g., security incidents) during their life spans. Such event logs need to exist, for purposes of accountability, beyond the life-cycles of their generating entities. In this position paper, we present a dual blockchain framework that facilitates the verification of integrity as well as authenticity of events while supporting privacy and confidentiality of data shared across multiple domains.

Keywords: Integrity · Authenticity · Confidentiality · Decentralised verification · Trust

1 Introduction

The emergence of the cloud, network functional virtualisation (NFV), edge computing and IoT paradigms has necessitated the accountable collection of

A. Basu—This work was done while Anirban was with KDDI Research. He currently works for Hitachi R&D within Hitachi Ltd. He is also a Visiting Research Fellow with the University of Sussex and is reachable at a.basu@sussex.ac.uk.

T. Dimitrakos—This work was partly done while Theo was visiting KDDI Research as a NICT-supported invited researcher.

W. Meng et al. (Eds.): IFIPTM 2019, IFIP AICT 563, pp. 196–208, 2019.
https://doi.org/10.1007/978-3-030-33716-2_15

distributed logs and audit information over multiple administrative domains or trust realms and across service provision paths in complex ICT supply networks. There is an ever increasing need to develop scalable technologies that ensure the integrity of such critical information (log, audit data, etc.) to enforce accountability and non-repudiation while taking into account the scope of use of the corresponding services, network functions or devices.

Blockchains and other forms of distributed ledgers (the underlying technologies of the Bitcoin [1] cryptocurrency, Ethereum [2] and other applications including cryptocurrencies [3–11]) offer cryptographic irreversibility of recorded data agreed upon by consensus amongst a set of decentralised entities. This property is useful for reliably logging event information generated by virtualised functions with short-lived, stateless and on-demand instances that reside on cloud infrastructures. Industry verticals, such as financial services, telecommunications, energy and smart vehicles – to name a few – are looking into distributed ledger technologies (including but not restricted to blockchains) for improving the integrity and availability of their services, their cross-service data flow and secure information sharing.

1.1 Objectives

In this paper, we consider the application scenario of a firewall as a virtual network function (VNF) and demonstrate how blockchains can be utilised to design and implement the distributed event log architecture. Our main objectives in this context are:

(1) to protect the integrity and confidentiality of important information of VNFs and IoT gateways such as events, configurations, policies, credentials, and so on;
(2) to strengthen the authenticity, accountability and integrity of security policies, security capabilities and VNF and IoT gateways;
(3) to reduce the risks of impersonation and privileged access abuse;
(4) to reduce the difficulties of cryptographic key management, revocation and trust management complexities; and
(5) to assess suitability and potential benefit of leveraging emerging technologies for multi-ledger and smart-contracts.

In this work-in-progress short paper, we consider the application scenario of a firewall as a VNF and demonstrate how a dual blockchain framework can be utilised to design and implement the distributed event log architecture. In general terms, we develop a multi-ledger model that protects the integrity of key information in a large-scale distributed computing systems and assures authenticity and accountability of modifications.

2   Proposed Dual Blockchain Framework

Use-Case Scenario Overview. A virtualised network function (VNF) is a software code, an instance of which can run inside a virtual machine, on top of actual physical hardware. A distributed stateless firewall abstracted as a firewall VNF can have multiple, possibly geographically dispersed, instances that can be spun up on demand. Each such instance logs events and incidents that it "sees". These logs need to be cryptographically signed to preserve their integrity. However, due to the short-lived and volatile lifespans of such VNF instances, maintaining and sharing signing keys between all instances of the same VNF is challenging even when there are separate keys per domain.

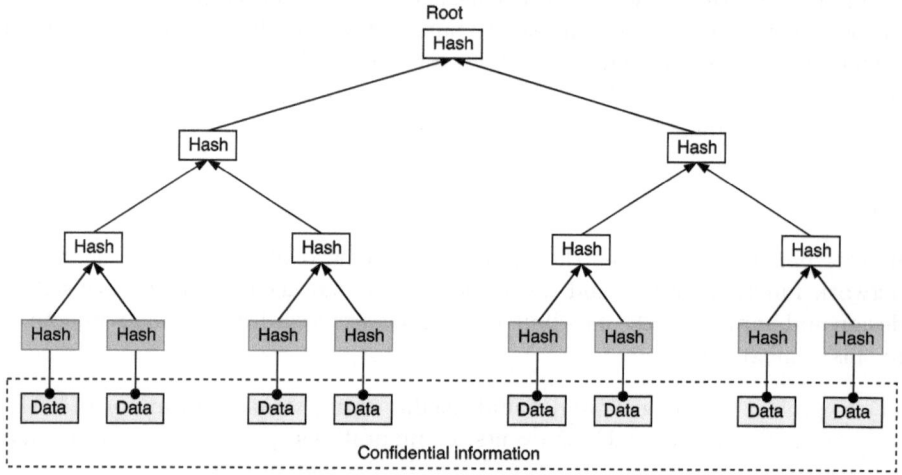

Fig. 1. Event log report structure.

In [12], we proposed a preliminary direction for accountability and integrity of data management making use of blockchains. In this paper, we describe an architecture for VNF logs that are verifiable in terms of integrity and authenticity. We propose the use of two blockchains for two separate purposes. The first blockchain is a permissioned blockchain used to verify the integrity of the data logged by individual firewall instances (called the **i-Ledger** from now on) while the second public blockchain helps with the verification of the authenticity of the logged data (called the **a-Ledger** hereafter). Due to the public nature of the second blockchain, the actual event log data is either not stored in it or stored with some confidentiality-preserving transformation (e.g., keyed hash, encryption). These two blockchains are not necessarily linked in terms of actual connectivity between nodes, but are semantically 'linked' during the data verification process since data on one blockchain needs to be cross-checked with the information recorded in the other to help verify consistency.

2.1   Event Log Reports

Central to the idea of the blockchain for integrity is the way a VNF instance generates an event log report. The events considered in this log are typically security incidents, but we use the general terminology – events – throughout this paper. The individual events are added as leaf nodes to a hash tree, e.g., a Merkle Tree [13]. The level of granularity of the events is configurable, i.e., a VNF may wish to combine multiple events together instead of writing one event as one leaf of the Merkle Tree. While for the rest of the paper we stick to Merkle Trees for the property of independent verification of sub-trees, any generalised hash tree satisfying the same property will suffice. The root of the Merkle Tree along with the entire tree structure is what constitutes a complete event log report, as illustrated in Fig. 1. The actual event data on the leaf nodes can be privacy sensitive. Information from hash trees can be trimmed, similar to the delete operation in our existing work – VIGraph [14], which uses generalised hash trees for selective disclosure of information.

2.2   System Overview

Figure 2 describes the overall system using a multi-domain scenario for the two blockchains involving three domains as well as an external notary. The blue lines indicate the topology of the i-Ledger whereas the red lines represent that of the a-Ledger. The domain on the left illustrates some of the actors in one organisational domain, such as the **entities** (VNFs in this case) that generate events and event log reports; the **Life-cycle Event Manager (LEM)** which generates events related to the life-cycle of entities; the **log manager** in charge of maintaining the **i-Ledger** and the **notary** in charge of maintaining the **a-Ledger**. The *Domain security manager* is responsible for controlling confidential data sharing policies and agreements, which we discuss later. The *Auditor* is responsible for cross-verifying the integrity and authenticity of events across the two blockchains.

2.3   Blockchain for Integrity – the i-Ledger

The purpose of verifying the integrity of a data log is to ensure the signature on the log is valid, and that the signing entity is an authorised entity, i.e., an authorised firewall instance, in our running use-case. With the traditional certificate authority (CA) based keys, a CA signs the public key of an entity. However, the traditional CA style architecture requires the presence of a centralised and trusted certificate authority. It also assumes the existence of long-lived public-private key pairs. Neither of these hold true in our architecture of the distributed VNFs spanning across organisations.

A VNF instance generates an ephemeral private key (could remain stored only in volatile memory), which is removed when the VNF instance spins down gracefully or crashes. The corresponding public key, however, lives on. In our architecture, each separate administrative domain has its own **key manager**

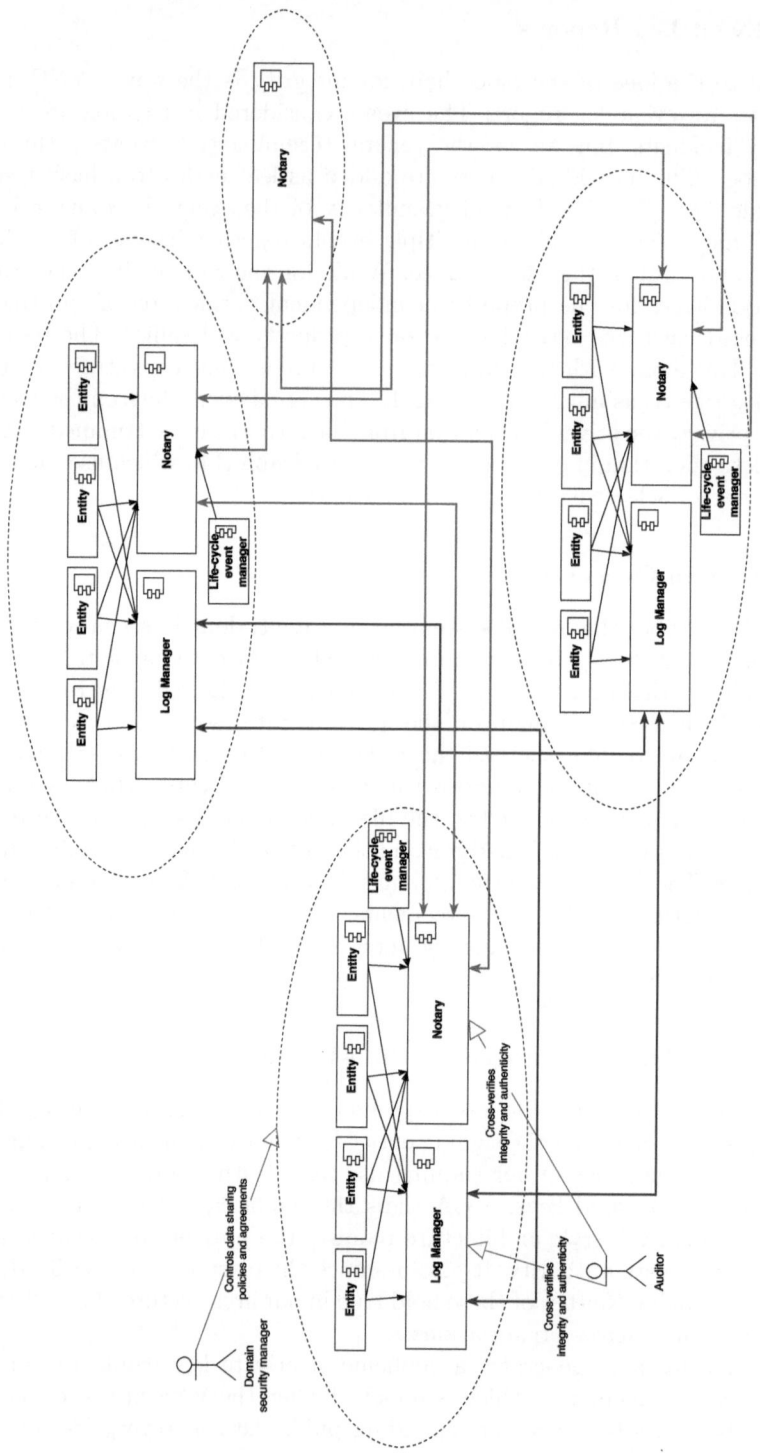

Fig. 2. A multi-domain system overview. (Color figure online)

and **log manager.** Either the log manager or the life-cycle event manager may provide the key management functionality, and thus we do not specify a key manager separately. This key-pair can be generated based on a Hardware Security Module or a Trusted Platform Module (HSM/TPM) backed seed, and the public key is registered with the key manager. A VNF instance collates its logs in a report (Fig. 1), adds a monotonically increasing numeric identifier and signs the Merkle Tree root and the numeric ID. This constitutes the main information for the block of varying size in this blockchain, illustrated in Fig. 3, with the event data in green signifying privacy sensitive information.

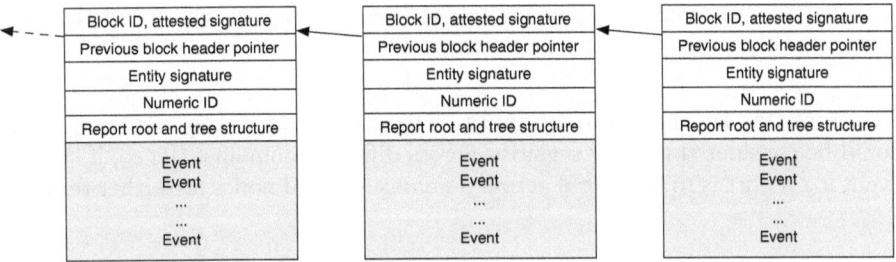

Fig. 3. Block structure for event log reports in i-Ledger. (Color figure online)

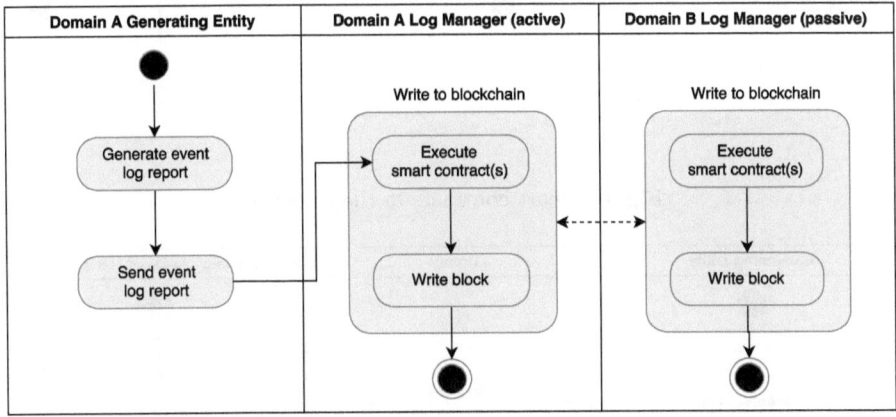

Fig. 4. Operation of the i-Ledger.

Due to the short-lived and resource-constrained nature of the VNF, it does not participate directly in reading from or writing to the blockchain. That task is delegated to the log manager of the domain. The pointer to the previous block and the block ID are, in turn, signed by the log manager that acts as a domain attester. The log managers across all the domains maintain the i-Ledger. The entire operation of the i-Ledger is shown in Fig. 4, involving three actors:

(a) generating entity in the active domain (Domain A);
(b) the active domain log manager; and
(c) any other domain (Domain B) log manager.

A log manager runs a smart contract on the event log report before it accepts the block. Each log manager in each domain knows the identity (i.e., public key) of every other participating log manager from every other domain. Thus, the smart contract running on the log managers conceptually looks like the one illustrated in Fig. 5, encapsulated as the "Execute smart contracts" state in Fig. 4. The active domain contains the entity (i.e., VNF instance) that is attempting to write the report to the blockchain while the passive domain contains the log manager that accepts the event log report based on the acceptance of the valid identity of the active domain log manager.

Confidential Information Sharing. The event data in the event log report could be considered privacy sensitive across different domains. Hence, if such an event log report is to be shared across domains, the leaf nodes are either removed

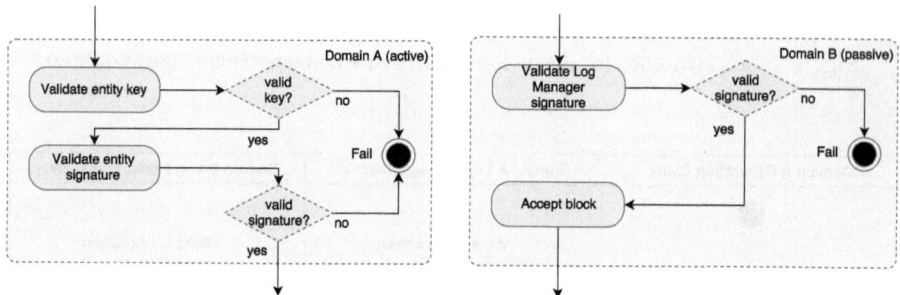

Fig. 5. Smart contracts in the i-Ledger.

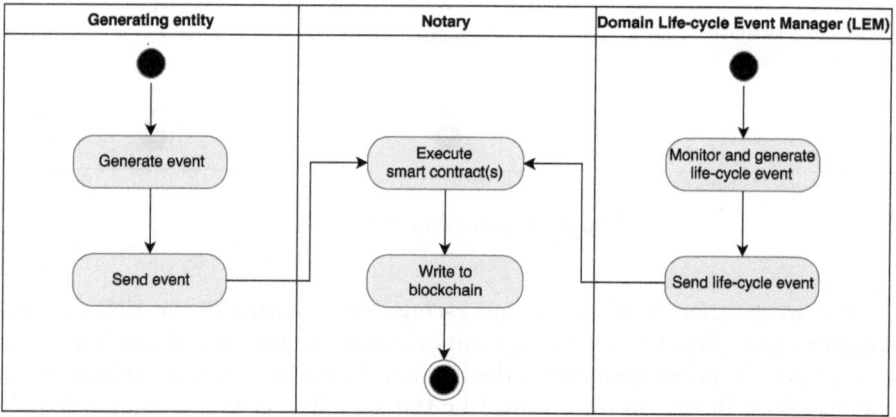

Fig. 6. Operation of the a-Ledger.

from the tree structure while keeping their hashed parents intact; or the leaf nodes go through some confidentiality preserving transformation, e.g., symmetric key encryption where the relevant key is shared with authorised entities; or it could be attribute based encryption (ABE) where relevant entities have their access control policies defined in the ABE structure, in the keys (KP-APE) or in the ciphertexts (CP-ABE). This type of confidential information sharing policy is controlled the domain security manager as illustrated in Fig. 2.

2.4 Blockchain for Authenticity – the a-Ledger

The purpose of verifying the authenticity of the data log is to ensure that the publicly recorded log of the data (without details of the actual data to preserve confidentiality) corresponds to an actually recorded log in the i-Ledger that verifies it integrity. It also ensures that logs made by the same entity can be linked and their partial orders validated. Furthermore, with the records of life-cycle events, the a-Ledger allows a verifier to check that a specific log made by a specific VNF instance happened while it was active.

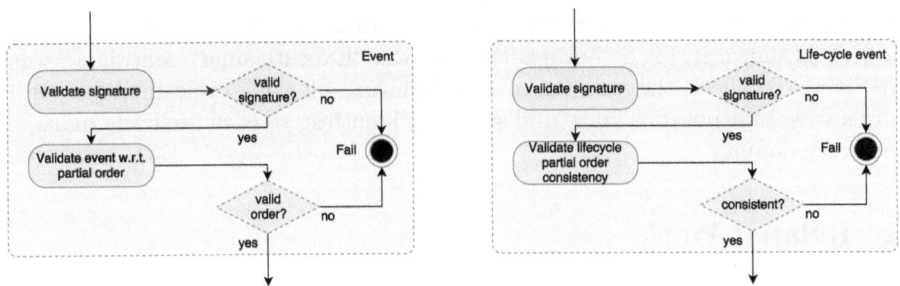

Fig. 7. Smart contracts in the a-Ledger.

The entities maintaining this public a-Ledger are **notaries** that can exist in the aforementioned domains, but also in other unrelated domains, as shown in Fig. 2. For instance, the VNF use-case could exist in domains such as telecommunications carriers while notaries could exist in other external domains such as financial and legal institutions. Unlike the permissioned i-Ledger, the block in this a-Ledger is not equivalent to a single event log report. Instead, blocks in this blockchain contain single events from the event log report as well as entity life-cycle events. Any such event is recorded as a *transaction* and many such transactions form a block in this blockchain. In order to facilitate life-cycle event reporting, we have the **life-cycle manager** per domain, which is typically a virtual machine monitor that knows when a VNF instance is up or down.

The transaction for an event (i.e.., VNF generated event) is a tuple consisting of:

(a) a specific event, E;
(b) the monotonically increasing numeric identifier for the event specific to the generating entity, n_t at time t; and
(c) the signature from the generating entity, sig_{entity}.

The transaction for a life-cycle log is a tuple consisting of:

(a) the life-cycle event (LE) to be recorded, e.g., LE_{start}, LE_{end} and so on;
(b) the public key of the entity whose life-cycle event is being recorded, i.e., $pubK_{entity}$; and
(c) the signature from the life-cycle manager, i.e., sig_{LEM}.

The entire operation of the a-Ledger is shown in Fig. 6, involving three actors:

(a) generating entity;
(b) a notary in any domain; and
(c) the life-cycle manager in the same domain as the generating entity.

The notaries run two smart contracts depending on the type of event being added, as shown in Fig. 7, encapsulated as the "Execute smart contracts" state in Fig. 6. To check the validity of the signature of a life-cycle manager, it is imperative that notaries know and store the identities of each life-cycle manager for every domain.

3   Related Work

Bozic et al. [15] present an on-going work on a blockchain-based mechanism to protect cloud and NFV orchestration operations, specifically the authentication of orchestration commands in the lifecycles of cloud services. The scheme proposed in [16] helps ensure the necessary integrity and confidentiality properties application provenance in a cloud environment. Rübsamen et al. presented, in [17], a system that uses distributed software agents for secure evidence collection to enable automated evaluation during cloud accountability audits. In [18], Redfield and Date proposed a system where data is signed on the device that generates it, transmitted from multiple sources to a server using a signature scheme, and stored with its signature on a database running a protocol for long-term archival systems that maintains the data integrity of the signature even over the course of changing cryptographic practices. Sanz et al. [19] proposed a framework for automatic performance evaluation of service function chaining in network function virtualisation. The paper in [20] described the idea of securing drone data collection and communication with a public blockchain for provisioning data integrity and cloud auditing. In [21], authors proposed an architecture to secure federated cloud networks by enforcing a global security policy on all network segments of a federation, and local security policies on each network of the federation. In the context of the IEC 61499 standard [22] for distributed control systems, the work in [23] proposed an ongoing research on the implementation of function blocks as smart contracts executed by a blockchain as well as the integration with the edge nodes that are responsible for process control. The work in [24] adopted blockchains to address the lack-of-trust problem by mapping a business process onto a peer-to-peer execution infrastructure that stores transactions in a blockchain. Amongst the various benefits of their approach, an audit trail for the complete collaborative business processes, for which payments, escrow, and conflict resolution can be enforced automatically. The authors presented the idea of using blockchain as a service for IoT and evaluates the performance of a cloud and edge hosted blockchain implementation in [25]. In [26], the authors proposed a blockchain-based architecture for the secure configuration management of virtualised network functions (VNFs), which provides immutability, non-repudiation, and auditability of the configuration update history as well as integrity and consistency of stored information; and the anonymity of VNFs, tenants, and configuration information. Authors in [27] presented an architecture of a collaborative mechanism using smart contracts to investigate the possibility of mitigating a DDoS attack in a fully decentralized manner whereby the service providers can not only signal the occurrence of attacks but also share detection and mitigation mechanisms. Xu et al. [28] proposed a blockchain-based solution for trust in virtual machine images to reduce the risk of DoS attacks and at the same time provide a signature verification service for Docker images. Kouzinopoulos et al. discussed, in [29], the benefits of using blockchains to strengthen the security of IoT networks through a resilient, decentralized mechanism for connected home use-case that enhances the network self-defense by safeguarding critical security-related data. Kataoka et al. presented [30] a 'trust list', which describes the distribution of trust among IoT-related stakeholders and provides autonomous enforcement of IoT traffic management at the edge networks by integrating blockchains and Software-Defined Networking (SDN). This, according to the authors, helps automating the process of doubting, verifying, and trusting IoT services and devices to effectively prevent attacks and abuses.

4   Conclusions and Future Work

The work-in-progress short paper presented a preliminary concept regarding the use of blockchains to provide accountability of events. Our running example use-case has been virtual firewalls instances as VNFs, but this architecture can be extended to other use cases with similar short-lived entities, e.g., various IoT and connect car scenarios. A number of avenues for future work exist, which include but are not limited to:

(i) validating the proposed architecture with a proof-of-concept on blockchains with an abstraction for the virtual network functions;

(ii) fully adopting a thorough security controls architecture utilising controls from the CSA Cloud Controls Matrix (e.g., CCM v3.0)[1] in order to build an actual working example of cloud-based virtual network functions with the proposed event logging architecture implemented on the two blockchains; and

(iii) investigating the use of post-quantum signature schemes, e.g., Lamport or Merkle in the event log reports because their hash-tree like structures lend themselves well to such signatures.

Acknowledgement. This work was partially done during Theo's visit to KDDI Research, Inc., Japan under the Japan Trust International Cooperation programme funded by the National Institute of Information and Communication Technology (NICT) in Japan.

References

1. Nakamoto, S.: Bitcoin: a peer-to-peer electronic cash system (2008)
2. Wood, G., et al.: Ethereum: a secure decentralised generalised transaction ledger. Ethereum project yellow paper, vol. 151, pp. 1–32(2014)
3. Wilkinson, S., Boshevski, T., Brandoff, J., Buterin, V.: Storj: a peer-to-peer cloud storage network (2014)
4. Vorick, D., Champine, L.: Sia: Simple decentralized storage. White paper (2014). https://sia.tech/sia.pdf
5. Danezis, G., Meiklejohn, S.: Centrally banked cryptocurrencies. arXiv preprint arXiv:1505.06895 (2015)
6. Koning, J.P.: Fedcoin: a central bank-issued cryptocurrency. R3 report 15 (2016)
7. Hopwood, D., Bowe, S., Hornby, T., Wilcox, N.: Zcash protocol specification. Technical report, Zerocoin Electric Coin Company (2016)
8. Gilad, Y., Hemo, R., Micali, S., Vlachos, G., Zeldovich, N.: Algorand: scaling byzantine agreements for cryptocurrencies. In: Proceedings of the 26th Symposium on Operating Systems Principles, pp. 51–68. ACM (2017)
9. Al-Bassam, M., Sonnino, A., Bano, S., Hrycyszyn, D., Danezis, G.: Chainspace: a sharded smart contracts platform. arXiv preprint arXiv:1708.03778 (2017)
10. Kokoris-Kogias, E., Jovanovic, P., Gasser, L., Gailly, N., Ford, B.: Omniledger: a secure, scale-out, decentralized ledger. IACR Cryptology ePrint Archive, vol. 2017, p. 406 (2017)
11. Zamani, M., Movahedi, M., Raykova, M.: RapidChain: scaling blockchain via full sharding. In: Proceedings of the ACM SIGSAC Conference on Computer and Communications Security, pp. 931–948. ACM (2018)
12. Basu, A., Daniel, J.J., Ruj, S., Rahman, M.S., Dimitrakos, T., Kiyomoto, S.: Accountability and integrity for data management using blockchains. In: Poster at the 21st International Conference on Financial Cryptography and Data Security (FC), Malta (2017)
13. Merkle, R.C.: Method of providing digital signatures (1979). https://www.google.com/patents/US4309569

---

[1]   https://cloudsecurityalliance.org/working-groups/cloud-controls-matrix/.

14. Basu, A., Rahman, M.S., Xu, R., Fukushima, K., Kiyomoto, S.: VIGraph - a Framework for verifiable information. In: Proceedings of the IFIP WG 11.11 International Conference on Trust Management (IFIPTM), Göteborg, Sweden, pp. 12–20 (2017)

15. Bozic, N., Pujolle, G., Secci, S.: Securing virtual machine orchestration with blockchains. In: Cyber Security in Networking Conference (CSNet), pp. 1–8. IEEE (2017)

16. Zawoad, S., Hasan, R.: Secap: Towards securing application provenance in the cloud. In: 9th International Conference on Cloud Computing (CLOUD), pp. 900–903. IEEE (2016)

17. Rübsamen, T., Pulls, T., Reich, C.: Security and privacy preservation of evidence in cloud accountability audits. In: Helfert, M., Méndez Muñoz, V., Ferguson, D. (eds.) CLOSER 2015. CCIS, vol. 581, pp. 95–114. Springer, Cham (2016). https://doi.org/10.1007/978-3-319-29582-4_6

18. Redfield, C.M., Date, H.: Gringotts: securing data for digital evidence. In: IEEE Security and Privacy Workshops, pp. 10–17. IEEE (2014)

19. Sanz, I.J., Mattos, D.M.F., Duarte, O.C.M.B.: Sfcperf: an automatic performance evaluation framework for service function chaining. In: IEEE/IFIP Network Operations and Management Symposium (NOMS), pp. 1–9. IEEE (2018)

20. Liang, X., Zhao, J., Shetty, S., Li, D.: Towards data assurance and resilience in IoT using blockchain. In: IEEE Military Communications Conference (MILCOM), pp. 261–266. IEEE (2017)

21. Massonet, P., Dupont, S., Michot, A., Levin, A., Villari, M.: An architecture for securing federated cloud networks with service function chaining. In: IEEE Symposium on Computers and Communication (ISCC), pp. 38–43. IEEE (2016)

22. Vyatkin, V.: The IEC 61499 standard and its semantics. IEEE Ind. Electron. Mag. **3**(4), 40–48 (2009)

23. Stanciu, A.: Blockchain based distributed control system for edge computing. In: 21st International Conference on Control Systems and Computer Science (CSCS), pp. 667–671. IEEE (2017)

24. Weber, I., Xu, X., Riveret, R., Governatori, G., Ponomarev, A., Mendling, J.: Untrusted business process monitoring and execution using blockchain. In: La Rosa, M., Loos, P., Pastor, O. (eds.) BPM 2016. LNCS, vol. 9850, pp. 329–347. Springer, Cham (2016). https://doi.org/10.1007/978-3-319-45348-4_19

25. Samaniego, M., Deters, R.: Blockchain as a service for IoT. In: IEEE International Conference on Internet of Things (iThings) and IEEE Green Computing and Communications (GreenCom) and IEEE Cyber, Physical and Social Computing (CPSCom) and IEEE Smart Data (SmartData), pp. 433–436. IEEE (2016)

26. Alvarenga, I.D., Rebello, G.A., Duarte, O.C.M.: Securing configuration management and migration of virtual network functions using blockchain. In: IEEE/IFIP Network Operations and Management Symposium (NOMS). IEEE (2018)

27. Rodrigues, B., Bocek, T., Lareida, A., Hausheer, D., Rafati, S., Stiller, B.: A blockchain-based architecture for collaborative DDoS mitigation with smart contracts. In: Tuncer, D., Koch, R., Badonnel, R., Stiller, B. (eds.) AIMS 2017. LNCS, vol. 10356, pp. 16–29. Springer, Cham (2017). https://doi.org/10.1007/978-3-319-60774-0_2

28. Xu, Q., Jin, C., Rasid, M.F.B.M., Veeravalli, B., Aung, K.M.M.: Blockchain-based decentralized content trust for Docker images. Multimedia Tools Appl. **77**(14), 18223–18248 (2018)

29. Kouzinopoulos, C.S., et al.: Using blockchains to strengthen the security of Internet of Things. In: Gelenbe, E., et al. (eds.) Euro-CYBERSEC 2018. CCIS, vol. 821, pp. 90–100. Springer, Cham (2018). https://doi.org/10.1007/978-3-319-95189-8_9
30. Kataoka, K., Gangwar, S., Podili, P.: Trust list: Internet-wide and distributed IoT traffic management using blockchain and SDN. In: 4th World Forum on Internet of Things (WF-IoT), pp. 296–301. IEEE (2018)

TPL: A Trust Policy Language

Sebastian Mödersheim[1]($\boxtimes$), Anders Schlichtkrull[1], Georg Wagner[2],
Stefan More[2], and Lukas Alber[2]

[1] DTU Compute, Formal Methods, Technical University of Denmark,
2800 Kongens Lyngby, Denmark
{samo,andschl}@dtu.dk
[2] Institute for Applied Information Processing and Communications (IAIK),
Graz University of Technology, Inffeldgasse 16a, 8010 Graz, Austria
{gwagner,smore,lalber}@iaik.tugraz.at

Abstract. We present TPL, a Trust Policy Language and Trust Management System. It is built around the qualities of modularity, declarativity, expressive power, formal precision, and accountability. The modularity means that TPL is built in a way that makes it easily adaptable to different types of transactions and signatures. From the aspect of declarativity and expressive power, the language is built such that policies are always formulated in a positive form and the language is Turing complete. The formal precision and accountability of the language eliminates ambiguity and allows us to achieve verified evaluations. The idea is that for any decision, the system can generate a proof that can then be checked by a prover that is formally verified, in Isabelle/HOL, to be sound with respect to a first-order logic semantics.

1 Introduction

We introduce **TPL** – not only a **T**rust **P**olicy **L**anguage but also a trust management system geared to support and integrate today's existing trust schemes to create a trust infrastructure. A trust management system is a system that helps companies and organizations to automatically process trust decisions about electronic transactions they receive. TPL helps to specify and automatically implement a company's business policy for trust decisions.

TPL is designed in the context of the LIGHT^{est} project that aims to create a *Lightweight Infrastructure for Global Heterogeneous Trust management in support of an open Ecosystem of Stakeholders and Trust schemes.* The idea is that there are a number of trust schemes like the European eIDAS, but no scheme on which the whole world agrees on. To achieve this TPL supports different formats of electronic documents and transactions. It also allows authorities behind a trust scheme to define translations from other schemes. Translations can be

This work was supported by the LIGHT^{est} project, which is partially funded by the European Commission as an Innovation Act as part of the Horizon2020 program under grant agreement number 700321.

automatically processed, but are only "recommendations": a policy designer can decide whether to accept trust translations. TPL also supports trust delegations.

TPL has simple, clear and precise semantics as first-order clauses interpreted with respect to an environment representing TPL's interaction with the outside world. Despite the simplicity, the ATV's implementation – the Automated Trust Verifier connecting parsers and server lookups with logical evaluation – is complex. A concern is the reliability of trust decisions, i.e., that bugs in a component cannot lead to false positives. Thus TPL's architecture allows for boiling down this problem to the correctness of isolated components. For the logical decision of whether a decision follows from a policy, we offer a reliable logical *verification*: we feed the decision and policy, together with a logical representation of all documents and which signatures have been verified with respect to which keys, into the automatic theorem prover RP_X [16–19] to check that the given decision logically follows from the policy and the given documents. This is a double check by a very special "extra pair of eyes": the correctness of RP_X was formally proven using the theorem prover Isabelle. When a positive policy decision of the ATV is verified by RP_X, we believe, it is virtually impossible that it could be due to a flawed implementation of TPL's semantics.

In TPL's design we focused on three key qualities. The first is *modularity* in order to support arbitrary attribute-value based data formats. To connect a new data format to the ATV infrastructure, one only needs to write a parser from the concrete format to an abstract syntax representation. Thus there is no need to "adjust the world" – our system easily fits with existing schemes.

The second quality is *declarativity and expressive power*. TPL is inspired by Prolog (without the cut operator and negation) and thus policies are always formulated *positively*, i.e., under which conditions the policy is fulfilled. Nonetheless, TPL is Turing complete, i.e., every computable policy can be expressed; this programming aspect, in particular, allows generating templates for the most common kinds of policies. LIGHT^{est} has also produced graphical interfaces to TPL for users with different degrees of experience with policy specification [13,22].

The third quality is *formal precision and accountability*. Since we expect to deal with transactions of substantial value, it is crucial that there are no undefined corner cases or bugs in the implementation. It should be possible for an independent third party to easily review a decision. An example of such a review is the mentioned verification with RP_X. Another example could be the review in case of a legal dispute.

Parts of this paper are adapted from our technical report [12].

2   TPL by Example

We present TPL using the example of an online platform for auction houses. We do not consider peer-to-peer auction houses like eBay, but focus on platforms connecting traditional auction houses to the digital world. The auctions in question may easily range up to thousands of Euros for a single item, leading to the problem of ensuring that the successful bidder indeed pays the sum they have bid. The auction house wants no entrance barrier for new customers who just "stumbled" upon an item by an Internet search. On the other hand, they want to avoid manipulations such as shill bidding (somebody anonymously bids on an item to push the price) and payment defaults.

In the analog world, the solution is that one has to bring references from other auction houses or a bank statement or be present at the auction, proving one's identity. We show how to transfer these aspects to the digital world using LIGHT^{est} in a way where one can benefit from the digital world's potential without losing the security and trust guarantees of analog auction houses.

The first step of digitalization is the creation of online catalogs, where a user can click on items they want to bid on and enter a maximum amount. This is basically an electronic version of the classical paper bidding form. After filling out this form, the user sends it as an HTTPS transaction to the auction house.

This paper introduces a number of example policies defining which forms the auction house accepts. One example policy in natural-language is the following:

Example Policy Rule 1. *The auction house accepts any form which is of the "Auction house 2019" format and contains a bid up to* 100 *Euro.*

As the first example of a TPL policy, let us consider how to write the above mentioned Example Policy Rule 1 in TPL:

Policy Rule Specification 1

```
accept(Form) :−
   extract(Form, format, theAuctionHouse2019Format),
   extract(Form, bid, Bid),
   Bid <= 100.
```

In this example, the variable Form is the transaction, here a bidding form in question in some concrete data format. extract is a predicate that can extract the attributes from the form: this is the interface to the parser for the respective data format. The first extraction generally is the check for the expected type of format, here the format used by the concrete auction house, identified by the constant theAuctionHouse2019Format. Next, we extract the bid field, which is bound to the variable Bid, and finally, we check that the value is below 100.

Semantically, the policy can be seen in two ways: (1) As a formal specification in first-order logic of Example Policy Rule 1. (2) As a program that can check if a form lives up to Example Policy Rule 1. In the following section, we will go in to detail with forms, formats and these semantics.

3   Syntax and Semantics

3.1   Formal Definition

The language of TPL mainly consists of *definite horn clauses*. Its syntax is based on that of first-order logic and Prolog.

We define four disjoint sets of symbols: (1) Variable symbols – starting with upper-case letters. (2) Function symbols – starting with lower-case letters and having fixed arity. (3) Constant symbols – starting with lower-case letters. (4) Predicate symbols – starting with lower-case letters and having fixed arity.

With this in place, we use a grammar to define the syntax of TPL specifications, as shown in Fig. 1.

TPLPolicy ::= Clause*

Query ::= (Predication,)* Predication.

Clause ::= Predication.
        | Predication :− (Predication,)* Predication.

Predication ::= PredicateSymbol
             | PredicateSymbol((Term,)* Term)

Term ::= VariableSymbol
      | ConstantSymbol
      | FunctionSymbol((Term,)* Term).

Fig. 1. Syntax in TPL specified by a grammar.

3.2 Semantics

We here briefly sketch two ways to formally define the semantics of TPL.

Logical Semantics. A logical view of the semantics can be obtained if we consider the Horn clauses as logical formulas of first-order logic, where :− is ← (logical implication from right to left), the comma is logical conjunction and all variables of every Horn clause are universally quantified, e.g., $p(X, Y) :− q(X), r(Y, X)$ becomes $\forall X, Y.\ p(X, Y) \leftarrow q(X) \wedge r(Y, X)$.

Special care must be taken for built-in predicates, i.e. the interface to the environment, in particular, such as extract that is the interface to the concrete formats and their parsers, as well as lookup that is the interface for looking up information on a server. For the semantics, we fix the meaning of these built-in predicates to an (arbitrary) snapshot of the world; in particular, we assume that during the checking of the policy, the state of the world does not change.[1] One may also evaluate logically a historical policy decision by specifying the environment as it was at some point in the past in order to answer the question of whether a given document was within the policy at a previous point in time.

More formally, given a set of Horn clauses H and a query $q_1, \ldots, q_n$, the solutions are those substitutions σ of the variables in the q_i such that it holds that $H \models \sigma(q_1) \wedge \ldots \wedge \sigma(q_n)$ where $\models$ is the semantics of first-order logic as defined in any standard textbook. A policy might use built-in predicates which go beyond logical reasoning such as lookup which performs a call to a server. To define the semantics of the solutions in this case we, for a specific policy, allow the inclusion of a formula f that partially specifies this external environment. Such an f could be a trace of the interactions that happened in an execution of the policy. This f simply consists of a number of clauses. As such the semantics is defined as $H \wedge f \models \sigma(q_1) \wedge \ldots \wedge \sigma(q_n)$.

Executable Semantics. TPL is similar to Prolog, but does not include the ! operator or negation as failure. Such "counter-logical" elements would forbid interpretation as logical formulas and the resulting clear and simple semantics. Policies are lists of definite Horn clauses and TPL also shares most of Prolog's syntax.

TPL's executable semantics is the same as that of Prolog except that in TPL our unification always includes the occurs check. The semantics of Prolog can be described as an interpreter – see e.g. Deransart, Ed-Dbali and Cervoni's textbook [5], in particular, in Sect. 4.2. TPL's built-in predicates (such as extract, lookup, <=) are not part of TPL's core language but are defined outside it.

3.3 Forms and Formats

Policies work on forms represented by a variety of concrete data formats, from X.509 certificates and DNS resource records to custom data formats for electronic forms. TPL supports all of these in a flexible way without cluttering the policies with low-level details like parsing. We consider an abstract notion of *formats*, similar to abstract syntax, namely like a *paper form* with fields to fill in and

---

[1] With respect to the assumption that the world does not change during policy evaluation, consider the following example. A policy could ask that a transaction is only accepted if approved by officials in two distinct sections, A and B, of a company, where the policy designer (unspokenly) relied on the fact that by company policy, no employee works in both sections. Then it is conceivable that an employee approved the transaction, who happens to *move* from section A to section B – with the corresponding trust list entries being updated just while some transaction is checked against the policy. It could thus happen that the policy is "accidentally" fulfilled by the single employee's approval, even though the trust list never actually showed any employee as members of two sections at the same time. Indeed if such "race conditions" are relevant, this must be solved by a kind of locking of databases for the duration of the policy checking. We believe this kind of scenario is extremely atypical for trust policies and not practically relevant.

each field having a unique identifier. This abstracts from concrete measures (like XML) to structure this information, and any concrete format can be connected to TPL by providing a parser and pretty-printer for it, i.e. the transformation between actual byte strings and abstract syntax. Let us consider a form for the auction house example. Abstractly, it is a set of attribute-value pairs:

```
{(format, the_auction_house_2019), (bidder_name, "John Doe"),
 (street, "Dartmouth St"'), (city, "Midfarthington"),
 (country, "England"), (lot_number, 54678), (bid, 60),
 (signature, ...), (certificate, ...)}
```

The actual transaction on the string level could be an XML representation:

```
<?xml version="1.0" encoding="UTF-8"?>
<format name="the_auction_house_2019" />
<person>
  <name>John Doe</name>
  <street>Dartmouth St.</street>
  <city>Midfarthington</city>
  <country>England</country>
</person>
<lot_number>54678</lot_number>
<bid>60</bid>
<signature> ... </signature>
<certificate> ... </certificate>
```

The idea is that abstract symbols like `bidder_name` should be a sound abstraction of their concrete byte-level format [11]. Notice that the XML representation's tree structure and the attribute value pair set representation are not the same: it is often nice to have a layer on top of an XML format, so one does not have to browse the XML parse tree but has an immediate representation of the data suitable for one's purposes. TPL provides a built-in predicate extract connecting the interpreter with the appropriate parser so that attributes can be extracted from the format as specified by the attribute value pair representation.

3.4   Implementation

For the LIGHT^{est} project, we implemented the Automated Trust Verifier (ATV), at the core of which is a TPL interpreter. The ATV is implemented in Java, using the ANTLR parser generator to implement the grammar from Fig. 1.

Besides the interpreter core, the ATV implements the built-in predicates like extract whose truth value depends on extra-logical facts and actions. These predicates are implemented as external functions that are invoked by the native Java code. For this, it is necessary to partition the parameters of built-in predicates into *inputs* and *outputs*; e.g. for extract, the first two arguments (the form and the attribute) are inputs, and the resulting value is the output. It is required that all the input arguments must be ground terms (containing no variables) when the interpreter reaches them. After finishing an external call like a server lookup, the control is given back to the interpreter.

3.5   Built-In Predicates

This section describes the built-in predicates of TPL in more detail, as they are currently found in our reference implementation ATV.

Built-in Predicate 1 (extract). *The* extract *predicate is used to extract information from a document (e.g. a transaction, certificate, or trust list entry). This predicate gives a uniform interface to all kinds of data formats; the interpreter is designed modular so that new data formats can easily be integrated by providing a parser for the respective data structure. For a call*

extract(From, What, Out)

we have that Form *is an input document,* What *is a field of the document, and* Out *is the output, i.e., the value of that field.*

The set of fields that are available depends on the format. Thus, when trying to extract a field that does not exist in the present format, the predicate fails. For every format at least one field is defined, namely format which returns the unique identifier for the document's format.

Built-in Predicate 2 (lookup and trustlist). *The* lookup *predicate allows to perform lookups at DNS name servers and HTTP queries authenticated using DANE. The input parameter* Domain *defines the DNS domain to query, while the output parameter* Entry *contains the desired document. In a similar manner, the* trustlist *predicate is a more specific case, which is used to retrieve a single entry, identified by the parameter* Certificate, *from a trust list.*

lookup(Domain, Entry)
trustlist(Domain, Certificate, TrustListEntry)

Built-in Predicate 3 (trustscheme). *The* trustscheme *predicate checks if a trust scheme claim (a domain name) represents a trusted scheme. Both parameters are input parameters. A call*

trustscheme(TrustSchemeClaim, eIDAS_qualified)

is true if and only if the trust scheme claim is a claim for an eIDAS membership.

Built-in Predicate 4 (verify_signature). *The* verify_signature *predicate has two input parameters. For a call*

verify_signature(Form, PubK)

the TPL interpreter will use the appropriate signature verification function for the format of FORM *and succeeds if and only if the signature on the form can be verified using the given public key.*

Built-in Predicate 5 (verify_hash). *The* verify_hash *predicate checks if an object evaluates to the correct hash value. So for a call* verify_hash(Form, Hash)

the TPL interpreter will use the appropriate hash function for the format of FORM *and succeed if and only if the parameter* Form *has the same hash as passed by the parameter* Hash.

In addition, our implementation comes with additional built-in predicates to support encoding of domains and concatenation of strings.

4   Using TPL

So far, our example auction house only accepts bids up to a certain number but puts no constraints on who may place a bid. For large bids the auction house needs to know who they are and that they can be trusted. This is achieved by issuing certificates to users, and publishing a list of trusted authorities who may issue certificates. Such a list is a trust list and is for example published by the European Union in the eIDAS framework. Therefore, we extend our example:

Example Policy Rule 2. *The auction house accepts any bid up to 1500 Euro, if it is signed by an eIDAS qualified signature.*

Thus, we need to perform the following checks: (1) Is the bid amount smaller than 1500 Euro? (2) Has the bidder's certificate been issued by an eIDAS qualified authority? (3) Did the bidder actually sign the bid?

Signatures and Signable Formats. To verify signatures we use the built-in predicate verify_signature and signable formats: A signable format is a format for which a signature verification function is specified. For a form of the specified format and a public key, we can verify if the form is properly signed.

Trust Scheme Lookups. We need to verify the trust scheme membership of the bidder's issuer and thus have to obtain the associated trust list. Trust lists are discovered using a trust scheme claim which is inside the bidder's or issuer's certificate. In LIGHT^{est} this claim is represented by a domain name [21], e.g. the (fictional) URL qualified.trust.ec.eu for the trust scheme of qualified eIDAS authorities.

The trustlist built-in predicate (see Sect. 3.5) triggers a server lookup. It will succeed if a certain trust scheme exists, the trust list is available, and the desired certificate is on that list. It fails otherwise. It, therefore, acts as a requirement in a policy that the given certificate is on the claimed trust list.

To claim a trust scheme membership, a certificate includes a field trustScheme that states the trust scheme (represented as a domain) it claims to be in. In order to ensure that the domain actually belongs to our desired trust scheme, we use the built-in predicate trustscheme (see Sect. 3.5).

Specifying the Policy. We translate Example Policy Rule 2 into a TPL rule:

Policy Rule Specification 2

```
accept(Form) :−
  extract(Form, format, theAuctionHouse2019format),
  extract(Form, bid, Bid), Bid <= 1500,
  extract(Form, certificate, Certificate),
  extract(Certificate, pubKey, PK),
  verify_signature(Form, PK),
  check_eIDAS_qualified(Certificate).

check_eIDAS_qualified(Certificate) :−
  extract(Certificate, format, eIDAS_qualified_certificate),
  extract(Certificate, issuer, IssuerCertificate),
  extract(IssuerCertificate, trustScheme, TrustSchemeClaim),

  trustscheme(TrustSchemeClaim, eIDAS_qualified),
  trustlist(TrustSchemeClaim, IssuerCertificate, TrustListEntry),

  extract(TrustListEntry, pubKey, PkIss),
  verify_signature(Certificate, PkIss).
```

When this is added to a TPL specification containing Policy Rule Specification 1, then any form that lives up to the requirements of either rule is accepted. Policy Rule Specification 2 requires that the format of the form is the auction house format, and extracts the bid to check that it is at most 1500. After that it extracts the bidder's certificate. This a form, and the policy extracts the public key of the bearer, given in the pubKey field. Then the verification of the signature of the form is done with respect to the public key using the verify_signature predicate. Afterward, the policy checks that the certificate is eIDAS qualified. This is done in a separate predicate. From the bidder's certificate, it extracts the issuer's certificate, given in IssuerCertificate. From the IssuerCertificate it then extracts the TrustSchemeClaim, which is a domain name used to address the trust scheme and to verify the issuer's trust scheme claim. The policy checks that the trust membership claim is really eIDAS qualified. This is done using the trustscheme predicate. A lookup is then done using the trustlist predicate, which discovers and retrieves the trust list and verifies that the IssuerCertificate is on the list. Lastly, the issuer's public key is extracted from the trust list entry and then used with verify_signature to verify the signature on the bidder's certificate. The TrustListEntry must contain at least the public key of the issuer, such that it can be verified to be the same as the issuer key recorded in the certificate.

This shows that policies can be specified on an abstract level avoiding specifying the whole interaction with the Internet and the checks that need to be performed on the response to authenticate it.

4.1   Allowing Trust Translation

Trust schemes can define translations, i.e. they might consider other schemes equivalent to them. We extend our example policy accordingly:

Example Policy Rule 3. *The auction house accepts any bid of at most 1000 Euro with a signature from a scheme outside eIDAS if the scheme is deemed equivalent to eIDAS via a translation scheme of eIDAS.*

We introduce the notation of equivalence modulo a translation relying on the trust translation schemes provided by the authority of the target scheme. The used example policy is similar to Policy 2, but the trustscheme predicate is changed to trustschemeX which allows trust translation and is defined explicitly in TPL: trustschemeX checks that a trust scheme membership claim belongs either directly to the scheme we are trusting, or belongs to an equivalent scheme:

```
trustschemeX(Claim, TrustedScheme) :-
  trustscheme(Claim, TrustedScheme).


trustschemeX(Claim, TrustedScheme) :-
  encodeX(Claim, TrustedScheme, Domain),
  lookup(Domain, Entry),
  extract(Entry, translation, equivalent).
```

For a claim for a foreign scheme and the name of a trusted scheme, the built-in predicate encodeX generates a domain for the trust translation scheme. Suppose Claim is a (hypothetical) Swiss scheme located at example.admin.ch and the TrustedScheme is eIDAS_qualified. Then the URL should point to e.g. admin.ch._translation.qualified.trust.ec.eu (i.e. it should escape the domain of the original scheme, and select the corresponding Translation scheme of eIDAS qualified). This domain should refer to the entry about the Swiss scheme at eIDAS. The entry is then used to discover information which can be used to verify equivalence. In the example case, we check if the translation field is set to equivalent.

4.2   Delegation

An important concept is *delegation*: A *mandator* can *delegate* rights to a *proxy*, who then acts on behalf of the mandator. This allows us to extend the auction house service even further:

Example Policy Rule 4. *The auction house accepts any bid of at most 1000 with a signature from a proxy. The proxy must be within the eIDAS trust scheme.*

Within the delegation we have several fields where the mandator can define what the proxy is allowed to do [20]. In this case, the mandator must allow the proxy to place bids. Put in practice, the mandator could also set a maximum amount up to which the proxy is allowed to place bids. Thus the fields must be verified in order to place bids. Further, for the public key, it is checked that it is within the eIDAS trust scheme. Lastly, the policy checks at the delegation provider that the delegation is still valid and that nobody tampered with the delegation. This leads us to the specification of the delegation in Policy Rule Specification 3.

Policy Rule Specification 3

```
checkQualifiedDelegation(Document, Mandate) :-
        checkMandate(Document, Mandate),
        checkMandatorKey(Document, Mandate),
        checkValidDelegation(Document, Mandate),
        extract(Document, bid, Bid), Bid <= 1000.

checkMandate(Document, Mandate) :-
        extract(Mandate, format, delegation),
        extract(Mandate, proxyKey, PkSig),
        verify_signature(Document, PkSig),
        extract(Mandate, purpose, place_bid).

checkMandatorKey(Document, Mandate) :-
        extract(Mandate, issuer, MandatorCert),
        extract(MandatorCert, trustScheme, TrustSchemeClaim),
        trustscheme(TrustSchemeClaim, eIDAS_qualified),
        trustlist(TrustSchemeClaim, MandatorCert, TrustListEntry),
        extract(TrustListEntry, pubKey, PkIss),
        verify_signature(Mandate, PkIss).

checkValidDelegation(Document, Mandate) :-
        extract(Mandate, delegationProvider, DP),
        lookup(DP, DPEntry),
        extract(DPEntry, fingerprint, HMandate),
        verify_hash(Mandate, HMandate).
```

5   Verification

Jim [9] introduced the trust management system SD3 with certified evaluation. When SD3's evaluator decides whether a transaction lives up to a policy, it provides a proof of this. A separate proof checker can then check the proof's correctness. The proof checker is a very simple program, and thus it is easy to inspect and understand its code – making it highly trustworthy.

TPL also allows certified evaluation, with the crucial difference that the trustworthiness of the proof checker does not come from a claim that its code is simple. Instead, we base our proof checker on the prover RP_x [16–19] which is, with exception of its parser, verified in Isabelle/HOL [14]. Isabelle is a proof assistant i.e. a computer program that allows its user to prove theorems in e.g. computer science. The idea is that Isabelle ensures the proofs' correctness because RP_x is proved in Isabelle/HOL to be sound and complete for first-order clausal logic.

For successful queries the interpreter can construct a proof certificate as a triple $(p, (q_1, \ldots, q_n), b)$ where p is the policy, $q_1, \ldots, q_n$ is the query and b is a record of the results from all calls to the built-in predicates that happened during execution including server-lookups, extractions from forms, signature verification and comparisons of e.g. numbers. The proof checker works as follows:

1. Let c be $p \wedge (\neg q_q \vee \cdots \vee \neg q_n) \wedge b$ encoded in the input format of RP_x.
2. Run RP_x on c.
3. If RP_x is successful in proving the formula unsatisfiable, then the proof check was successful.

The idea is that we want prove $p \wedge b \models q_1 \wedge \ldots \wedge q_n$. This is equivalent to proving that $p \wedge (\neg q_q \vee \cdots \vee \neg q_n) \wedge b$ is unsatisfiable, and RP_x can do that for any correct positive decision thanks to its soundness and completeness.

Our integration of RP_x in TPL is currently in the state of an early prototype. We have written a program that can encode a triple $(p, (q_1, \ldots, q_n), b)$ in RP_x's input format. Using this program, we have run RP_x on a number of such triples and seen that it gives the correct result. One could argue that this is not necessary since RP_x is formally verified, however, one should, as e.g. Paulson [15] recently pointed out, not see formal verification as a replacement for testing. Indeed we have run RP_x on a number of encoded triples but more systematic testing would be needed to ensure a production quality certifier. Notice also that while the core of RP_x is verified, the encoding of the formula $p \wedge (\neg q_q \vee \cdots \vee \neg q_n) \wedge b$ in $RP_x's$ input format is still left unverified and so is the parser of RP_x. Notice also that the verification of RP_x's soundness and completeness is only with respect to unsatisfiability in Herbrand models. This is not a problem though since it implies its soundness and completeness with respect to arbitrary models, but this has yet to be formally proven for RP_x.

6   Discussion and Related Work

Blaze et al. [4] coined the term trust management system and introduced Policy Maker, one of the first such systems. PolicyMaker was refined to create KeyNote [2, 3]. The relation between access control policies and trust policies was early recognized. Herzberg et al. [8] sees trust policy languages as an extension of access control mechanisms, thereby, as Li et al. [10] point out, generalizing authorization. Due to the similarity, a popular idea used in access control languages is often used for trust policy languages, namely logic programming.

For a large number of works, including ours, policies are always formulated positively: every policy rule describes under which conditions one is trusted and the decision is negative when no policy rule is fulfilled. This makes it a lot simpler than languages including negative rules such as Dong and Dulay's [6] Shinren: While it is convenient to also formulate negative constraints, the integration into the reasoning process results in a rather complicated semantics with a nine-valued logic and requires policy rules to be annotated with priorities. We believe that it is enough to limit the use of negation to black listing, i.e. checking that an entity is not on a black list which can be part of a server lookup with a built-in predicate. Note also that pure Horn clauses are Turing complete, i.e. every computable trust policy decision can be expressed in TPL.

Several of these languages borrow from logics of knowledge and belief such as Li et al.'s DL [10], Becker et al.'s SecPAL [1] as well as Gurevich and Neeman's DKAL [7]. In particular, they contain a modal operator, *says*, so that the fact that an agent stated a formula is itself a formula. This allows for easily relating the reasoning of participants but leaves the area of classical logic due to modal interpretation in different worlds. Basing a policy language on logic also allows us to achieve proof certification, i.e. checking that a policy decision indeed follows logically from a policy, reducing the chance of a false policy decision due to an implementation error. Jim [9] used this idea to allow for a simple proof checker to check the policy decisions made by a more complicated program. Jim's unverified proof checker's trustworthiness came from simplicity rather than being verified.

7 Conclusion

We have presented TPL, a trust policy language and trust management system. We have shown the language's syntax and semantics as well as the idea of using formats to represent transactions abstractly. We also showed how the language supports signatures, translation and delegation. By basing the semantics on first-order logic, we have also achieved a way to verify policy decisions, by way of a prover that is formalized sound and complete in the Isabelle proof assistant.

We argued that TPL has the qualities of "modularity", "declarativity and expressive power" and "formal precision and accountability". By being modular TPL allows for heterogeneity. By providing declarativity and expressive power, TPL ensures that it has the expressibility needed to write the policies needed by users. By providing formal precision and accountability, TPL ensures that businesses and organizations can feel safe about the correctness of the automatic trust decisions. TPL is a central component of LIGHT^{est} and with the above qualities we believe that TPL can help LIGHT^{est} achieve its goal of providing a lightweight infrastructure for global heterogeneous trust management in support of an open ecosystem of stakeholders and trust schemes. We hope that this will provide a step towards wider adoption of TPL and trust management systems.

Acknowledgement. Andreas Viktor Hess suggested many improvements.

References

1. Becker, M.Y., Fournet, C., Gordon, A.D.: SecPAL: design and semantics of a decentralized authorization language. J. Comput. Secur. **18**(4), 619–665 (2010)
2. Blaze, M., Feigenbaum, J., Ioannidis, J., Keromytis, A.D.: The keynote trust-management system version 2 (1999)

3. Blaze, M., Feigenbaum, J., Keromytis, A.D.: Keynote: trust management for public-key infrastructures (position paper). In: Proceedings of the 6th International Workshop Security Protocols, Cambridge, UK, 15–17 April 1998, pp. 59–63 (1998)

4. Blaze, M., Feigenbaum, J., Lacy, J.: Decentralized trust management. In: 1996 IEEE Symposium on Security and Privacy, Oakland, CA, USA, 6–8 May 1996, pp. 164–173 (1996)

5. Deransart, P., Ed-Dbali, A., Cervoni, L.: Prolog - The Standard: Reference Manual. Springer, Heidelberg (1996). https://doi.org/10.1007/978-3-642-61411-8

6. Dong, C., Dulay, N.: Shinren: Non-monotonic trust management for distributed systems. In: Proceedings of the 4th IFIP WG 11.11 International Conference on Trust Management IV, IFIPTM 2010, Morioka, Japan, 16–18 June 2010, pp. 125–140 (2010)

7. Gurevich, Y., Neeman, I.: DKAL: distributed-knowledge authorization language. In: Proceedings of the 21st IEEE Computer Security Foundations Symposium, CSF 2008, Pittsburgh, Pennsylvania, USA, 23–25 June 2008, pp. 149–162 (2008)

8. Herzberg, A., Mass, Y., Mihaeli, J., Naor, D., Ravid, Y.: Access control meets public key infrastructure, or: assigning roles to strangers. In: 2000 IEEE Symposium on Security and Privacy, Berkeley, California, USA, 14–17 May 2000, pp. 2–14 (2000)

9. Jim, T.: SD3: a trust management system with certified evaluation. In: 2001 IEEE Symposium on Security and Privacy, Oakland, California, USA, 14–16 May 2001, pp. 106–115 (2001)

10. Li, N., Feigenbaum, J., Grosof, B.N.: A logic-based knowledge representation for authorization with delegation. In: Proceedings of the 12th IEEE Computer Security Foundations Workshop, CSFW 1999, Mordano, Italy, 28–30 June 1999, pp. 162–174 (1999)

11. Mödersheim, S., Katsoris, G.: A sound abstraction of the parsing problem. In: IEEE 27th Computer Security Foundations Symposium, CSF 2014, Vienna, Austria, 19–22 July 2014, pp. 259–273 (2014)

12. Mödersheim, S., Schlichtkrull, A.: The LIGHTest foundation. Technical report, Technical University of Denmark (2018)

13. Mödersheim, S.A., Ni, B.: GTPL: a graphical trust policy language. In: Open Identity Summit 2019 (2019)

14. Nipkow, T., Wenzel, M., Paulson, L.C. (eds.): Isabelle/HOL - A Proof Assistant for Higher-Order Logic. LNCS, vol. 2283. Springer, Heidelberg (2002). https://doi.org/10.1007/3-540-45949-9

15. Paulson, L.C.: Computational logic: its origins and applications. Proc. R. Soc. A: Math. Phys. Eng. Sci. **474**(2210), 20170872 (2018)

16. Schlichtkrull, A., Blanchette, J.C., Traytel, D.: A verified functional implementation of Bachmair and Ganzinger's ordered resolution prover. Arch. Formal Proofs (2018). Formal proof development. http://isa-afp.org/entries/Functional_Ordered_Resolution_Prover.html

17. Schlichtkrull, A., Blanchette, J.C., Traytel, D.: A verified prover based on ordered resolution. In: Proceedings of the 8th ACM SIGPLAN International Conference on Certified Programs and Proofs, CPP 2019, Cascais, Portugal, 14–15 January 2019, pp. 152–165 (2019)

18. Schlichtkrull, A., Blanchette, J.C., Traytel, D., Waldmann, U.: Formalization of Bachmair and Ganzinger's ordered resolution prover. Arch. Formal Proofs (2018). https://www.isa-afp.org/entries/Ordered_Resolution_Prover.html

19. Schlichtkrull, A., Blanchette, J.C., Traytel, D., Waldmann, U.: Formalization of Bachmair and Ganzinger's ordered resolution prover. Arch. Formal Proofs (2018). Formal proof development. http://isa-afp.org/entries/Ordered_ Resolution_Prover.html

20. Wagner, G., Omolola, O., More, S.: Harmonizing delegation data formats. In: Open Identity Summit 2017, Gesellschaft für Informatik, Bonn, pp. 25–34 (2017)

21. Wagner, G., Wagner, S., More, S., Hoffmann, M.: DNS-based trust scheme publication and discovery. In: Open Identity Summit 2019, Gesellschaft für Informatik, Bonnd, pp. 49–58 (2019)

22. Weinhardt, S., Omolola, O.: Usability of policy authoring tools: a layered approach. In: International Conference on Information Systems Security and Privacy (2019)

Author Index